ROUTLEDGE LIBRARY EDITIONS: REVOLUTION IN VIETNAM

Volume 6

WAR AND AFTERMATH IN VIETNAM

WAR AND AFTERMATH IN VIETNAM

T. LOUISE BROWN

LONDON AND NEW YORK

First published in 1991 by Routledge

This edition first published in 2022
by Routledge
2 Park Square, Milton Park, Abingdon, Oxon OX14 4RN

and by Routledge
605 Third Avenue, New York, NY 10158

Routledge is an imprint of the Taylor & Francis Group, an informa business

© 1991 T. Louise Brown

All rights reserved. No part of this book may be reprinted or reproduced or utilised in any form or by any electronic, mechanical, or other means, now known or hereafter invented, including photocopying and recording, or in any information storage or retrieval system, without permission in writing from the publishers.

Trademark notice: Product or corporate names may be trademarks or registered trademarks, and are used only for identification and explanation without intent to infringe.

British Library Cataloguing in Publication Data
A catalogue record for this book is available from the British Library

ISBN: 978-1-03-214885-4 (Set)
ISBN: 978-1-00-324163-8 (Set) (ebk)
ISBN: 978-1-03-215462-6 (Volume 6) (hbk)
ISBN: 978-1-03-215463-3 (Volume 6) (pbk)
ISBN: 978-1-00-324425-7 (Volume 6) (ebk)

DOI: 10.4324/9781003244257

Publisher's Note
The publisher has gone to great lengths to ensure the quality of this reprint but points out that some imperfections in the original copies may be apparent.

Disclaimer
The publisher has made every effort to trace copyright holders and would welcome correspondence from those they have been unable to trace.

War and Aftermath in Vietnam

T. Louise Brown

London and New York

First published 1991
by Routledge
11 New Fetter Lane, London EC4P 4EE

This edition published in the Taylor & Francis e-Library, 2002.

Simultaneously published in the USA and Canada
by Routledge
a division of Routledge, Chapman and Hall Inc.
29 West 35th Street, New York, NY 10001

© 1991 T.Louise Brown

All rights reserved. No part of this book may be reprinted or reproduced or utilized in any form or by any electronic, mechanical, or other means, now known or hereafter invented, including photocopying and recording, or in any information storage or retrieval system, without permission in writing from the publishers.

British Library Cataloguing in Publication Data
Brown, T.Louise *1963–*
   War and Aftermath in Vietnam.
   1.Vietnamese wars, 1954–1975
   I. Title
   959.7042

ISBN 0-203-08300-8 Master e-book ISBN

ISBN 0-203-22116-8 (Adobe eReader Format)
ISBN 0-415-01403-4 (Print Edition)

Library of Congress Cataloging-in-Publication Data
Brown, T.Louise, 1963–
   War and aftermath in Vietnam/T.Louise Brown.
     p. cm.
   Includes bibliographical references.
   Includes index.
   ISBN 0-415-01403-4
   1. Vietnamese Conflict, 1961–1975. I. Title.
   DS557.7.B76 1991   90–47899
   959.704′3–dc20   CIP

Contents

	List of abbreviations	iv
	Chronology	vi
1	Vietnam: the background to war	1
2	The first Indochina conflict and the United States' drift to war	24
3	Lyndon B.Johnson and the tragedy of Vietnam	52
4	Negotiations 1964–73	76
5	The war at home	103
6	Politics, economics and religion: a revolution in Vietnamese society	131
7	People's revolutionary war	155
8	America's war: the strategy and tactics of the United States' military in Vietnam	183
9	Pacification and the attempt to build a viable South Vietnamese state	212
10	The war in five capitals—the international context of the Vietnam War	237
11	The end of the war and its aftermath	255
	Bibliography	277
	Index	287

List of abbreviations

AID	Agency for International Development
ARVN	Army of the Republic of Vietnam (South Vietnam)
AWOL	Absent Without Leave
CAP	Combined Action Platoon
CIA	Central Intelligence Agency
CIDG	Civilian Irregular Defense Groups
CIP	Commercial Import Program
COMUSMACV	Commander, United States Military Assistance Command, Vietnam
CORDS	Civil Operations and Revolutionary Development Support
COSVN	Central Office for South Vietnam
DEROS	Dated Expected Return Overseas
DMZ	Demilitarized Zone
DRV	Democratic Republic of Vietnam (North Vietnam)
GVN	Government of Vietnam (South Vietnam)
HES	Hamlet Evaluation System
ICP	Indochinese Communist Party
JCS	Joint Chiefs of Staff
KIA	Killed In Action
MAAG	Military Assistance Advisory Group
MACV	Military Assistance Command, Vietnam
MAT	Mobile Action Teams
MRP	Mouvement Republicain Populaire
NLF	National Liberation Front
NSAM	National Security Action Memorandum
OSS	Office of Strategic Services
PAVN	People's Army of Vietnam
PF	Popular Forces

PLAF	People's Liberation Armed Forces
POW	Prisoner of War
PRC	People's Republic of China
PRG	Provisional Revolutionary Government
PRP	People's Revolutionary Party
RCA	Riot Control Agents
RF	Regional Forces
ROE	Rules of Engagement
RVNAF	Republic of Vietnam Armed Forces
SDS	Students for a Democratic Society
SEAC	South East Asia Command
SEATO	South East Asian Treaty Organization
USAF	United States Air Force
USIA	United States Intelligence Agency
VC	Viet Cong
VCI	Viet Cong Infrastructure
VCP	Vietnamese Communist Party
VNQDD	Vietnamese Nationalist Party

Chronology

111 BC China incorporates Vietnam into its empire.
AD 939 Vietnam wins independence from China.
1861 French forces take control over Saigon.
1883 Tonkin and Annam become French protectorates.
1930 Indochinese Communist Party established by Ho Chi Minh
1939 Second World War begins.
1940 France surrenders to Germany and begins collaboration with Japan in South East Asia.
September Japan occupies Indochina but preserves facade of French rule.
1941 Viet Minh formed.
1945 **9 March** Japanese stages a *coup d'état* which formally ends French rule.
August Japan surrenders. The August Revolution brings the Viet Minh to power. **2 September** Ho Chi Minh declares Vietnamese independence and the founding of the DRV (Democratic Republic of Vietnam).
1946 **November-December** After months of negotiations, hostilities break out between the French and the Viet Minh. The First Indochina War begins.
1949 Establishment of the People's Republic of China. 1950 Korean War begins.
1954 **7 May** French are defeated at the battle of Dien Bien Phu.
8 May-21 July Geneva Conference on Indochina. Vietnam is divided at the seventeenth parallel. The communists under Ho Chi Minh are to rule the North and the non-communists under Emperor Bao Dai and prime minister Ngo Dinh Diem are to rule the South.

Chronology vii

1960   **20 December** National Liberation Front established.
1963   **1 November** Diem is overthrown in a military coup.
22 November Kennedy assassinated. Vice president Lyndon Johnson becomes president.
December North Vietnam decides to step up intensity of the conflict in the South.
1964   **2–4 August** Gulf of Tonkin incidents.
7 August Gulf of Tonkin Resolution approved by US Congress.
August-September North Vietnam decides to send combat troops to South Vietnam.
3 November Lyndon Johnson elected as president.
1965   **7 February** NLF attacks US base at Pleiku.
24 February Operation *Rolling Thunder*, the sustained bombing of North Vietnam begins.
8 March First US combat troops arrive in South Vietnam.
1968   **30–31 January** Tet Offensive begins.
31 March President Johnson announces partial bombing halt and withdraws from the presidential race.
3 April DRV responds to peace overture and agrees to begin talks.
5 November Richard Nixon elected as US president.
1969   **18 March** US begins secret bombing of Cambodia.
10 June Provisional Revolutionary Government (PRG) established by NLF.
1970   **20 February** Henry Kissinger begins secret talks with Le Duc Tho in Paris.
30 April US troops stage Cambodian 'incursion'.
1971   **8 February** In Operation *Lam Son* 719 the South Vietnamese Army attacks the Ho Chi Minh Trail in Southern Laos.
1972   **30 March** The North Vietnamese begin their Easter Offensive.
15 April President Nixon authorizes bombing of areas near Hanoi and Haiphong.
8 May Nixon announces mining of North Vietnam's ports.
8 October DRV presents the US with a draft agreement to end the war.
7 November Nixon reelected.
18 December US begins intensive bombing of Hanoi and Haiphong, otherwise known as the Christmas Bombing.
1973   **27 January** Peace Agreement signed by US and DRV.
1974   **9 August** Nixon resigns over Watergate scandal.
1975   **10 March** North Vietnam begins offensive against the South.
30 April Saigon is defeated.

1 Vietnam: the background to war

Land, water and rice are the building blocks of Vietnamese society. In what is modern day northern Vietnam, the ancestors of the Vietnamese built a culture upon wet rice cultivation. Archeological evidence indicates that Late Neolithic and Bronze Age cultures were flourishing in the Red River Delta in the third millenium BC (Taylor 1983:4).

Over time, native Vietnamese development came to be greatly influenced by the Chinese. Attracted to Vietnam principally as a source of tropical goods (Taylor 1983:126), China started to meddle tentatively in the region and then, in 111 BC, exercised its power by drawing what is now northern Vietnam within its empire. For the first 150 years Chinese authority was loose and informal and the native leadership was allowed to retain significant powers. This relaxed control, however, changed radically in response to a revolt of the local chiefs.

Anxious to preserve their privileges from usurption by the Chinese, the indigenous leadership rebelled in AD 40 (Buttinger 1969:31). When the unrest was quelled and the Chinese reimposed their authority two years later, the Vietnamese found the new form of Chinese rule to be far harsher and more authoritarian. To forestall any further challenges to its control, the native elite was stripped of power and a new hierarchy was imported from the north. Pre-modern Vietnam had lost its independence and had become a colonized nation under Chinese occupation.

Although the degree of Chinese control varied according to the fortunes of its dynasties, Vietnam remained a satellite of its powerful neighbour for nine more centuries and, in the process, became imbued with many of its social and political values. A new hybrid ruling class developed as Chinese officials intermarried with the local elite (Taylor 1983:48–57) and all aspects of life for this thoroughly sinicized group were infused with pervasive Chinese overtones. Notwithstanding their cultural affinity, the Sino-Vietnamese elite increasingly saw its interests as distinct from those of the Chinese and they eventually emerged as the focus of opposition to colonial rule.

Given that Vietnam was occupied for so long and was effectively a part of south China for almost a millenium, it is surprising that its people did not become Chinese. Yet far from being assimilated like many of their social superiors, the peasantry preserved a distinctly Vietnamese way of life in their tightly knit rural communities. They accomplished this partly because contact with other races living in the region left an imprint upon their culture that made it distinct from that of China, and partly, and crucially, because they did not want to be Chinese (Taylor 1983:229).

Apart from a brief but ruthlessly exploitative period under Ming rule (1407–27), direct Chinese control over Vietnam ended in AD 939, when an alliance between the disgruntled elite and an even more disgruntled peasantry coincided with a downturn in China's domestic fortunes. However, once independent, the new rulers of tenth-century Vietnam assumed the same form and style of leadership as their erstwhile masters. In practice this meant a centralized, monarchical state working in tandem with a bureaucracy of mandarins. The adoption of this system was motivated by four factors. Firstly, the Vietnamese had few alternative governmental structures from which to choose. Secondly, Chinese methods had proved efficient in controlling the people. Thirdly, it offered a satisfactory means of preserving national independence, and finally the system was necessary to build and maintain the network of dykes which were vital to irrigation and the control of floods (Nguyen Khac Vien 1974:19).

Confucianism was central to the structure and functioning of this independent state. Originally inherited from China, Confucianism continued to provide a sophisticated framework of thought for the higher echelons of Vietnamese society once the controlling hand of the Chinese was removed. In the process, it became a code of behaviour and a prop to the ruling elite. Its doctrine stressed the fundamental importance of filial piety and deference—both designed to solidify and strengthen existing familial, social and political structures. Hence, Confucianism became the ideology of the elite, its teaching a method of indoctrination and its emphasis upon orthodoxy a means of control.

In pre-colonial Vietnam the village commune or *xa* was the basic administrative unit. In the long-established communities of the north a solid social organization had been fostered by the combined efforts of many people who struggled every year to irrigate their paddy fields and to build dykes and channels in order to save their land and themselves from the sporadic yet violent floods of the Red River. Technically, each village was an autonomous unit but, in reality, its independence was subject to infringements by the mandarinate and the ruling dynastic house.

Egalitarianism and the need to ensure each family an adequate level of subsistence were vitally important principles of life in the rural communities. They were important because they smoothed the functioning of the corporate village in which each family had to cooperate in the irrigation and farming processes. Even so, economic and social stratification existed within the village and appears to have increased over the centuries. From the early 1600s, serious food shortages became a fact of life in the north of Vietnam (Popkin 1979:87). Undoubtedly, this population pressure worked against the corporate ideal as families vied over smaller and smaller pieces of land and, hence, almost inevitably, sought to better their own position and level of subsistence at the expense of that of their neighbours. Overpopulation gave rise to an agrarian crisis and problems of law and order because it ultimately generated a landless poor. These people were cut adrift from, and unable to re-enter the villages because existing inhabitants feared a further subdivision of the community's rice lands.

Real power in the village was exercised by those who had positions on the village governing body, the Council of Notables. At one time the ranking system in the villages had been based on age (Popkin 1979:110), but in the centuries preceding French colonial penetration, the notables were drawn almost exclusively from the community's wealthiest families. Only the wealthy could realistically become leading figures. This was because all those who held high office were obliged to make material contributions to the religious and social life of the village. Significant financial outlays were therefore necessary in order to ascend in the political hierarchy. Despite this, many aspired to a position on the Council because the initial sacrifices could be recouped several-fold as political influence granted the notables the right to manipulate land distribution and the taxation system to their own advantage (Murray 1980:413, Popkin 1979:99).

Theoretically all the land belonged to the emperor and his subjects paid him taxes in return for the right of usufruct. Taxes were assessed on the basis of the number of people who appeared on the official village registers and it was the community rather than the individual which was responsible for payment. The compilation of these vital registers was the responsibility of the notables and they had vested interests in keeping it as restricted as possible. Firstly, the amount of tax to be paid was not based upon the real number of people in the village, but upon the number appearing on the register. As the tax bill was divided equally amongst all villagers, with the exception of those granted exemptions by the notables, a small register naturally meant that each individual had to pay less. Secondly, the inclusion of more people on the register would be tantamount to increasing the charmed circle to which the notables belonged. This arose because inclusion on the register granted people official status. It allowed them, for instance, to travel safely outside the village and to call upon a mandarin to adjudicate in disputes. The notables' right to grant tax exemptions and to decide who was eligible for inclusion in the register consequently gave them great power within the community and facilitated the consolidation of their economic and political position.

Land was the key to political and social status in traditional Vietnam and, inevitably, it was managed by the elite for its own benefit. In the aftermath of the Ming interregnum (1407–27) the new Le emperors strenuously endeavoured to tackle the problem of land ownership which had tended to become concentrated during the occupation. Accordingly, a variation of the Chinese 'equal field' system was adopted (Ngo Vinh Long 1973:5–6) and, henceforth, the system made provision for each individual to receive a share of land commensurate with his social rank and equal to that of his peers. Coupled with periodic land redistributions, it mitigated at least some of the socially harmful effects of the long-term accumulation of land in the hands of a few.

In addition to the village land allotted to individual members under the 'equal field' system, communal land was a feature of well established Vietnamese settlements and was used for a variety of administrative and internal welfare purposes which protected the poorest. In principle, communal land was distributed to the most needy but, as with all village lands, it came to be allotted on the base of rank and social status, hence ensuring that those least in need received the most fertile land (Popkin 1979:101). The result of this manipulation of village resources and obligations meant that, rather than being a levelling force working for the benefit of an egalitarian xa, the Council of Notables was a self perpetuating elite whose powers and procedures, in effect, preserved and increased social and economic stratification (Popkin 1979:106).

Despite this degree of inequality, a number of historians who were critical of French colonial policy developed a romanticized view of the pre-colonial village. In accordance with a view that saw the *xa* as a corporate body acting for the common good, the disintegration of Vietnamese society under French rule was interpreted as a new phenomenon produced by the undermining of the traditional village hierarchy (Mus and McAlister 1970, Fitzgerald 1972). Nevertheless, it would be more accurate to see increased rural stratification under colonial rule as an acceleration of an existing process by which egalitarianism was already being subverted by struggles for power at the village level. The French presence acted as a stimulant to an already apparent trend by increasing the opportunities for those seeking to replace egalitarianism with individualism (Popkin 1979:139–40).

Abuse of privilege was common amongst the mandarins who administered the nation for the emperor. Frequently the justice that they dispensed was dictated by the size of the petitioner's purse, while patronage systems ensured that those well connected to the mandarin consistently strengthened their economic and social positions. This applied, in particular, to those locally influential individuals on the Council of Notables.

Many avenues were open to mandarins who wanted to become wealthy and powerful but their success was conditioned by the degree of restraint which the emperor managed to impose upon them. As a result of the power which tended to accrue to the mandarins, Vietnam's pre-colonial history is primarily the history of a struggle between the centrifugal forces of powerful individuals and the centralizing forces of the monarchy (Buttinger 1969:42). This struggle centred upon the level of control which regional powers exerted over the peasantry. In many respects, the mandarin's ability to exploit the local population was an accurate indicator of the monarchy's general condition. When the influence of the ruling dynasty waned, local powers increased their control *vis-à-vis* the population and, hence, had the means to make social and economic divisions more acute. This led to the stripping away of communal lands which, in turn, led to popular unrest and to the overthrow of the dynasty and its replacement by one strong enough to prune regional power (Wiegersma 1988:50). By limiting the influence of the mandarinate and attempting, if not always succeeding, in enforcing periodic land redistributions, the emperor reallocated to the poor some of the land appropriated by wealthy individuals. Far from being examples of the social concern of the court, these acts were designed to ensure its self preservation, firstly by quelling peasant unrest and secondly by weakening the power and influence of aspiring individuals whose cumulative strength could threaten the imperial dynasty.

The emperor stood at the apex of the Vietnamese social hierarchy. Although not of divine status, he was the mediator between man and God and all his subjects owed him allegiance. But, despite the idealization of loyalty to the emperor, the weakness of central authority and the inevitable dynastic cycle resulted in long periods of endemic civil strife. Thus, in the sixteenth century, Vietnam was wracked by internecine conflict which culminated in the division of the country, initially for fifty years and then, after an interlude of three decades, for a period of 150 years. During the second period of political division, dating from 1620, each half of Vietnam was headed by a regionally based dynasty which formed a *chua* or overlordship in a style similar to that of the *shoguns* of Japan. As a result, while the Trinh family ruled the north and the Nguyen the south of Vietnam, the emperor was reduced to the status of a puppet under the control of the Trinh.

The Nguyen state encouraged an ongoing southward migration of the Vietnamese people. Population pressure in the Vietnamese homeland of the Red River Delta had become so serious by the fifteenth century that a 'March to the South' began. It took hundreds of years for this human frontier to move down the length of modern day Vietnam but by the eighteenth century it was gradually spilling out into the vast, untamed Mekong Delta.

The importance of this migration lies in the nature of the new settlements that were established. Unlike their forefathers in the north, the frontier people settling the fertile lands of the south did not build tightly knit communities. Without the restrictions imposed by overpopulation they created dispersed villages which spread out, linear fashion, along waterways and newly built canals. The more even flow of the Mekong River rendered elaborate flood prevention methods unnecessary and, therefore, the degree of corporate activity within the community was reduced (Cotter 1968:20–1). Consequently, the fewer demands placed upon collective action resulted in a diminution of the ideal of the *xa*. Individualism became a far more common feature of the south and contrasted with the constantly strived for, if not always achieved, egalitarian ideal of northern and central Vietnam.

The further the frontier people moved from the heartland of Vietnamese culture, the more tenuous a grip it had upon them. They were liberated progressively from the mental parameters set by traditional Vietnamese society and felt free to dispense with some of its restricting dogma. In doing so they produced a phenomenon that has been aptly described as 'cultural washout' (Hickey 1964:82). However, although social and attitudinal differences had begun to emerge in the recently settled areas by the mid-nineteenth century, the peasants of both north and south Vietnam still shared aspects of a common culture and together shouldered a growing burden of exploitation.

The Tay Son rebellion (1773–86), or revolution as it is sometimes termed, was a reflection of the Vietnamese people's dissatisfaction with the established order. A whole host of problems appeared to be besetting Vietnam. Administrative corruption was rife, malnutrition and epidemics were common and the agrarian crisis had worsened. Under these conditions the initial rebellion in 1773 proved to be a catalyst and springboard from which deep peasant discontent erupted throughout both halves of divided Vietnam. First the Nguyen state of the south fell to the rebels and by 1786 the northern-based Trinh had also succumbed, thus uniting all of Vietnam under a Tay Son emperor.

The new leadership embarked on some radical programmes but they proved unable to carry them through to fruition. Divided by their own internal conflicts, the triumph of the Tay Son was to be short-lived and in 1802 they were crushed by Nguyen Anh, one of the remaining scions of the Nguyen family which had ruled southern Vietnam and which had been almost wiped out by the Tay Son.

Nguyen Anh established a dynasty which survived until 1955 and which was to preside over Vietnam's conquest by a European power. Under the rule of this new imperial house, Vietnam would later collapse in the face of French aggression. The superior military capability of the Europeans and fundamental, long-term problems of Vietnamese society, lay at the root of this collapse.

In response to the upheavals of the Tay Son period, the Nguyen resolved to control the people and subdue dissent by enforcing an exaggerated conservatism within the villages (Woodside 1971:111). Based on the Chinese system, the remodelled Confucianism of the Nguyen proved itself to be even more doctrinaire and inflexible than the Chinese original (Woodside 1971:231). This rigid system worked well only when circumstances rendered society unchanging and it was already exhibiting signs of strain long before the arrival of the French. Its slowness to react to and accommodate even limited social change left it prey to the internal pressure of social discord and the external threat of French colonialism. Contact with the West highlighted the system's impermeability, for rather than learning from outside, and therefore, at some later date being in a position to take stock of the realities of power and combat European penetration, the Vietnamese hierarchy, like that of the Chinese, retreated and hid from the world behind its brittle Confucian orthodoxy. Many committees were established and modernization programmes suggested, but none was ever put into practice (Marr 1971:28). Thus, ironically, although the Nguyen adopted its ultraconservatism in order to protect and sustain itself, it may actually have made the dynasty the 'grave-digger of Vietnamese independence' (Hodgkin 1981:129).

Under the Nguyen, the endemic problem of maintaining law and order, especially in the peripheral provinces of the newly united Vietnam, remained unaddressed and regional power bases were not removed. The dynasty battled with financial problems, a plague of natural disasters was visited upon the country, the mandarins continued to be an acute source of instability and the peasantry were little better off despite a land re-distribution of 1839. In practice, the strict observance of Confucian orthodoxy had been turned into a weapon to be used to repress the people (Marr 1971:20) and, hard as it tried, the Nguyen were never able to establish the legitimacy of their authority within the villages (Marr 1971:24–5). Into the midst of this social disquiet came the French who, while ostensibly usurping imperial authority, might, in reality, have saved the beleagured Nguyen, even if only as a symbol, from the threat of possible deposition at the hands of their own subjects (Duncanson 1968:64).

THE ARRIVAL OF THE EUROPEANS

The eighteenth century was a watershed in the history of mainland South East Asia, for it witnessed the twilight of the traditional world. The impact of the West was to strike most forcibly in the late nineteenth and early twentieth centuries, irretrievably destroying established patterns of life, catapulting the region into a new era and making the hope of a return to the ways of pre-colonial society little more than a millennial dream.

Colonialism came rather late to Vietnam. European trading missions were established in the seventeenth century but, with the exception of a Portuguese trading office, all were abandoned by the end of the century once a peace between the warring Nguyen and Trinh dried up the demand for armaments. As such, the first inauspicious contact between Vietnam and Europe ended quietly.

It was left to missionaries to form the vanguard of colonialism in Vietnam. Initial contacts between the Vietnamese people and the Jesuits were made in the sixteenth century and Christianity soon made astonishing progress. In fact, proselytizing in Vietnam proved to be amongst the most successful in Asia. To a great extent its success was rooted in the peasantry's dissatisfaction with the established order. The missionaries responded to their discontent and, in many cases, became social and community leaders. Consequently, Christianity always proved most popular in the strained, overcrowded villages of the north. In the south, on the other hand, it fared less well (Osborne 1969:25–6).

It increasingly fell to France to spearhead the religious crusade in Vietnam but the hyperbole of the missionaries did not entice Paris into conducting a colonial crusade as well. This attitude began to change when French interests began to coalesce around the prospect of gaining an empire. In the East, these newly awakened imperial ambitions focused upon Vietnam primarily because the great Mekong River was believed to provide a direct route into the interior of China with its rich spoils and vast unexploited markets which the British had laid bare through their victory in the Opium Wars.

When French colonial rule did come to Vietnam it was established in two distinct phases. During the initial phase (1858–67), control was gained over the south, and in the second phase (1882–3). French authority was extended to encompass northern and central Vietnam. The pretext for French involvement was the persecution of Catholics and certainly the Vietnamese elite did interpret the spread of Catholicism as a challenge to their authority and as a threat to the fabric and homogeneity of society. However, despite an imperial edict of 1833 which aimed to suppress Catholicism and despite the martyrdom of a number of missionaries, religious persecution was little more than a convenient rationale for French action.

Fifteen years separated the two phases of colonial expansion. France's preoccupation with the Franco-Prussian War and Napoleon III's Mexican adventure contributed to the lull in activity, but as the 1880s approached, the tide began to turn and imperialism was hailed as a solution to France's ills. The industrializing economy needed raw materials and markets for its products and the nation clamoured to recoup lost prestige through the creation of a glorious empire. Thus, in 1880, when Jules Ferry swept to power on a wave of nationalist fervour, France was set to embark on an re-energized, expansionist foreign policy.

French control over Vietnam was achieved with remarkable ease. Vietnam's government in Hue appeared weak and vascillating during the whole period of colonial conquest, and under its studious, melancholy ruler, Tu Duc, the Vietnamese government adopted a defeatist policy (Truong Buu Lam 1967:7). In 1862 the emperor signed an agreement effectively rescinding all authority which he exercised over the three provinces surrounding Saigon. But given the inherent weaknesses of the imperial throne, seemingly inadequate resistance to the French was hardly surprising. The dynasty was having difficulty maintaining tenuous control over its own subjects. It could not simultaneously contain domestic upheaval and combat foreign penetration (Marr 1971:29). Thus when faced with the alternative of quelling a rebellion in northern Vietnam or combatting the French who had occupied parts of the south, Emperor Tu Duc chose the former (Buttinger 1969:88–9, Hodgkin 1981:132).

His decision was also influenced by other pressures. First, *de facto*

French control over the Mekong Delta had resulted in an interruption of rice exports to the food deficient areas of the north. Given the volatile state of the countryside this seriously threatened a precariously balanced rural equilibrium and it also limited the regime's ability to raise and maintain an army to fight the French (Buttinger 1969:87–8). Moreover, Tu Duc probably thought that the French would be appeased by his surrender of a portion of Vietnamese territory and that their imperialist drive would slacken (Truong Buu Lam 1967:33). For a time it did, but when aggression was renewed in 1882, the monarchy was not able to put up anything more than token resistance. The death of Tu Duc on the eve of the extension of colonial rule had plunged Hue into an enfeebling succession crisis. What strength the Vietnamese elite could muster for the defence of the nation was dissipated as war and peace factions vied for power (Truong Buu Lam 1967:23).

VIETNAM UNDER FRENCH COLONIALISM

French rule in Vietnam was one of the worst examples of nineteenth- or twentieth-century European colonialism. In the age of imperialism the French were swept along by their implicit faith in *La Mission Civilisatrice*. They possessed an unquestioned belief that their nation in particular had an obligation to share the benefits of their own brand of culture, civilization and religion with 'simple' and 'childlike' peoples such as the Vietnamese. It was an aggressively conceited and racist ideology that wrought misery upon the people whom it supposedly raised from ignorance, sloth and backwardness.

This cultural offensive was predicated on the assumption that the Vietnamese could be assimilated. They would become Frenchmen and women in all but physical appearance. However, the concept was increasingly modified by the policy of association. Association was supposed to imply a definite distinction between French and Vietnamese cultures and institutions, both of which would work in harmony for the benefit of the Empire and Vietnam. Neither would become a junior partner in this alliance. In practice both assimilation and association were applied superficially and the French judiciously extracted and utilized those elements of each approach which buttressed their own authority to the detriment of that of the Vietnamese.

Under the French, Vietnam never existed in the form of a single administrative unit. It was only a part of the Indochinese Union established by the French in 1887. The Union also included Cambodia, annexed in 1867 as a buffer against suspected British influence in Siam (modern day Thailand), and later Laos, which was added to the Union in 1893. It was expected that the three countries would lose much of their identity and that their inhabitants would become members of the Union rather than of separate states. Yet, despite efforts to the contrary, French Indochina remained, from the outset, a totally artificial creation held together solely by the force of foreign domination.

While maintaining Vietnam's general borders, the French dissected the country into three units, each with differing administrative structures. The southern portion of Vietnam, named Cochinchina, had been colonized first and, in fact, formed the only true colony in constitutional terms. Here, colonial penetration was much more thorough, especially as the traditional administrative hierarchy of mandarins had withdrawn to Vietnamese controlled territory following the French annexation of Cochinchina. In effect, this forced France to substitute them with a group of pro-French Vietnamese (Osborne 1969:59). It was an action which had long-term implications for Vietnam's future political development.

Northern and central Vietnam, termed Tonkin and Annam respectively, were accorded the status of protectorates and there the governmental framework was very different in appearance although less so in substance from that in Cochinchina. In Annam, the emperor remained as the nominal head of the administrative structure but this maintenance of the apparatus of indigenous rule was a mere facade for French control. Tonkin was also ruled through this same dual system until 1897, when it was severed from Annam by the appointment of a representative of the emperor in Hanoi in the unlikely guise of a French *resident superior* who took orders directly from the colonial Governor General.

The arbitrary dissection of Vietnam into three units was compounded by the application of separate policies for each. Through this strategy the French attempted to thwart unity by encouraging regional tendencies and, hence, to diminish the likelihood of a united opposition to their rule (McAlister 1969:40–1). By increasing the number of local administrative districts, from thirty prior to conquest, to over sixty, the French multiplied the divisions and barriers in Vietnamese society in an effort to foster allegiance to the locality rather than to the concept of a nation (Steinberg 1971:181). Complementing this policy, the colonial authorities aimed to divide and rule still further by promoting ethnic antagonism between the lowland Vietnamese and the primitive tribes who lived in the mountains of Vietnam. In this aim they were largely successful.

One direct consequence of French rule was the emasculation of the traditional elite. Stripped of power the emperor was no longer the mediator between man and God, and the imperial court ceased to exercise real power. Although they preserved the symbolic accoutrements of imperial authority, the French did not even allow the Vietnamese a voice in the running of their own country, and the bulk of legislation directly affecting Indochina was enacted in Paris.

However, a section of Vietnamese society welcomed French rule. A large proportion of these *collaborateurs* were Catholics who indentified with the French because of their religion. Naturally, many Vietnamese allied themselves with the colonialists in the hope of gaining wealth and power. However, others, far from seeking personal gain from collaboration, sincerely believed that the advent of the colonial age boded well and that France would help modernize and resurrect an ailing Vietnam.

In every respect, the social and economic impact of colonial rule was immense. Vietnam provided raw materials and markets upon which French industry and French dominated agriculture could generate profit. Industrial development within the colony was firmly discouraged as manufacturers in the mother country feared competition and the disappearance of colonial markets over which they had a stranglehold. As a rule, French policy was designed to cut Indochina off from its immediate economic environment and to tie its trade exclusively to the French Empire through rigid protectionism. Thanks to this policy Indochina became a source of immense profit for a few French businessmen although, ironically, it proved to be a financial drain upon the treasury in Paris.

Three main arms of colonial policy facilitated the opening up of Vietnam to French exploitation (Murray 1980:48–9). Firstly, private property rights were substituted for customary landholding arrangements. Land thus became a marketable commodity which could be traded and acquired with ease. Secondly, taxation was increased, and thirdly, compulsory labour was demanded of the peasantry. Although this had also been a feature of pre-colonial society, the new requirements were more arbitrary and far more onerous because it was through the unpaid labour of the Vietnamese peasant that the authorities hoped to produce an infrastructure conducive to French investment.

Such policies worked well in bringing about rapid changes in traditional ways of life. Two themes swiftly came to characterize the social and economic processes underway in Vietnam. First was the commercialization of agriculture and the second was what has been described as the 'progressive pauperization of the countryside' (Lancaster 1961:65).

Rapid growth rates were, indeed, achieved in certain areas of the Vietnamese economy. Rubber and tea plantations in Cochinchina and parts of Annam flourished and in the process brought huge profits to their owners. Extractive industries, particularly coal mining in Tonkin, also expanded under colonial rule. However, it was the production and export of rice which dominated the economy.

Vast land concessions, perhaps involving as much as half the cultivated area in Vietnam (Ngo Vinh Long 1973:115) were granted to the French and their Vietnamese collaborators. The alienation of land was most pronounced in Cochinchina where the government rapidly sold or granted away large blocks of reclaimed marsh and swamp. This was especially the case during the 1890s and 1900s when there was a dramatic expansion in the area under cultivation as vast tracts were opened up through ambitious hydraulic engineering projects inaugurated by the colonial authorities.

Prior to conquest, the monarchy's weakness had forced it to curtail the power of elites at the local level and, as a by-product, to lessen the exploitation of the peasantry. When the French replaced the Nguyen they did not replicate their weakness and therefore did not feel it necessary to place a check upon the accumulation of wealth and power. The monarchy had traditionally restrained the more rapacious mandarins and members of the elite, but once emasculated by the French, it could no longer act as a check upon the abuse of privilege (Popkin 1979:166). The security which power gave to the French, moreover, allowed them to ignore the needs of the peasantry and, unlike the imperial court before them, they did not display sensitivity to rural conditions by tempering their financial demands in lean years (Popkin 1979:149).

Under French rule the peasantry's established pattern of life came under attack and their meagre subsistence levels were eroded by taxation, land expropriation, usury and indebtedness. Pre-colonial Vietnam had possessed a predominantly subsistence rural economy. Trade was limited and turnover in the local markets was small. Peasants obtained most of their needs through bartering and although they did use money, they did so on a very restricted scale, primarily to pay village fines and a proportion of their taxes (Wiegersma 1988:64). French rule changed this. Taxation rose in absolute terms and a higher percentage of it was demanded in cash rather than in kind. In Cochinchina, for example, total tax receipts increased from half a million gold francs in the 1860s to 35 million in 1887 (Buttinger 1969:124). Furthermore, while the old system had placed the onus for the payment of taxes upon the community as a whole, under the French the burden fell upon the individual. Assessments were no longer based on the fictional size of the community as represented in the village registers. Because payment of the customary assessment had been divided between official and unofficial taxpayers alike, the impact of this change was to raise the number of people officially liable to taxation and to increase the sum each paid (Mus and McAlister 1970:57).

To meet their heavy tax obligations many peasants were forced to seek work in French-owned enterprises. Interestingly, the colonial authorities insisted that heavy taxation of the French in Indochina reduced their incentives to invest, while harsh taxation of the local population was lauded because it encouraged the otherwise backward peasant to integrate himself into the money economy and to undertake economically productive activities (Murray 1980:68-9). More pointedly, it meant that the peasant became a cheap source of labour.

Even so, payment often proved impossible and for those families unable to meet their obligations, ruin was averted by making some unenviable decisions. Those who owned land could mortgage their property and risk losing control of it to a large landowner. Others resorted to loans at usurous rates and, for those who were really desperate, there was always the option of selling their children into debt slavery.

Direct taxation was compounded by odious government monopolies which, from 1902, always contributed at least half of the colonial budget (Murray 1980:74). The production and sale of alcohol, which was essential in religious rites, came under government control. Each village was assigned a statutory quota and the community was penalized if it failed to consume the stipulated amount. Salt, a basic necessity of life, was also controlled by the colonial authorities, as was opium. Previously only legal in the final years of the Nguyen as they scraped the barrel for much-needed finance, the use of the drug was encouraged by the French in order to swell their revenue at the expense of those unfortunate addicts wealthy enough to afford it.

Increasing rural poverty was accompanied by the growth of indebtedness. In Tonkin, especially, the population continued to expand and stretch resources, and agricultural involution, or the extreme intensification of land utilization, became increasingly apparent in the densely settled areas of the delta. In this environment, as in the south, usury was rife and peasants weighed down with extortionate interest rates, often of between 100 and 200 per cent per annum (Ngo Vinh Long 1973), entered a vicious circle of debt-loan dependency simply in order to stay alive.

While the old order had at least exercised some degree of compassion towards the plight of the peasantry, the new order did not. Customary land rights were ignored (Murray 1980:56). Instead, formal property rights based on land as a marketable commodity were established and those peasants who could not stake an adequate claim to their land were disentitled. Not understanding the complexities of the French bureaucratic and legal systems, many were cheated out of their land by unscrupulous colonialists and the comprador Vietnamese elite. Taking advantage of the liberty which French rule gave them to abuse their privilege, local level leadership began to strip villages of their communal lands (Murray 1980:67) and to strengthen their positions within the community. What this did, in effect, was to remove the vital welfare safety net that had existed in the pre-colonial period.

A dramatic reorganization of landholding was produced by the land concessions granted in Cochinchina and by the stimulus that colonial rule gave to the consolidation of the native elite's control over land and their fellow Vietnamese. Absentee landlordism and tenancy were extremely common in Cochinchina and a strong, agrarian based, native bourgeoisie emerged. Here in the south, the process of socio-economic differentiation was more pronounced than in the north (Murray 1980:376, 436). In Tonkin and Annam, overcrowding and poverty meant that there simply was not the scope for a similar degree of rapid cleavage to develop between rich and poor.

The rich indigenous class that had established itself in Cochinchina during the early part of the twentieth century comprised individuals whose ancestors were not major figures in Vietnamese society prior to the arrival of the French. Rather, they were descendants of lesser figures from the local elites who had seized the opportunity to take advantage of French land policies (Osborne 1969:143). It was a class, therefore, which had come to see its interests as synonymous with those of the colonial power that had facilitated its aquisition of undreamed-of wealth. This creation of a land-based bourgeoisie in Cochinchina was extremely significant for the development of social revolution in modern Vietnam.

Although the penetration of capitalism was not uniform, a large proportion of the agricultural sector became commercialized under colonial rule. Commercialization was facilitated by the accumulation of land by the few, while, in turn, it encouraged its concentration. Rice export was promoted and in Cochinchina rose from 57,000 tons in 1860, to 229,000 tons ten years later and to an enormous 1,223,000 tons in 1929 (Murray 1980:58–60). Significantly, though, this expansion was accompanied by a drop in the per capita consumption of rice (Hodgkin 1981:179).

Plantations represented the highest level of commercialization in the agricultural sector and, apart from the crisis years of the 1930s, guaranteed almost certain prosperity for their owners and a life of misery for those labourers who worked on them. The conditions on plantations producing tropical and semi-tropical crops were atrocious. Employers' attitudes towards the Vietnamese were deplorable and in both private and public enterprises indentured labour was frequently used. Peasants from overcrowded Tonkin had to be coerced into working in the plantations of central and southern Vietnam. Despite the people's poverty, the reputation of the 'Slaughterhouses', as they were called, was such that market forces alone could not guarantee an adequate workforce (Murray 1980:84–5, 377). Rubber plantations, in particular, had a most unenviable record, with mortality rates far exceeding the national average. It was not uncommon, for example, for a quarter of the workforce to die each year (Ngo Vinh Long 1973:112–13). Yet, even so, few measures aimed at curtailing the worst aspects of plantation agriculture were undertaken by the French authorities. A 1927 Labour Code did little to improve conditions and it was only in the late 1930s when a more progressive Popular Front government came to power in Paris that any significant changes were temporarily felt.

The commercialization of large sectors of production ensured that the destabilizing influence of the market economy was felt throughout Vietnam. By exploiting Vietnam and incorporating it within the framework of global imperialism, France drew it into the Western mercantile system and, hence, made a hitherto closed economy subject to the vagaries of the cyclical depressions of world trade. The implications of this dependency on an unreliable foreign market for the export of a restricted number of primary products was made tragically clear in the slump years of the Great Depression which dislocated the Vietnamese economy and considerably worsened social conditions.

Small urban and rural proletariats were formed in the process of developing extractive industries and large-scale plantations in a country where major commercial enterprises were previously unknown. In the towns and cities a tiny urban proletariat emerged during the late nineteenth and early twentieth centuries. The labour force that worked upon the plantations was also relatively small but because there was a high turnover of personnel, a larger number of people came to experience a new way of working and a new set of class relations. However, because their exposure proved to be of short duration, the development of class consciousness was also retarded (McAlister 1969:68–9).

The decade after the First World War was a period of accelerating economic and social change in Vietnam. A working class, comprising no more than 2 per cent of the population, was established (Marr 1971:264–5) and a small, native bourgeoisie and petite bourgeoisie developed in northern and central Vietnam owing to the emergence of native industries that had grown up when the war had interrupted the flow of imports to the colonies (Marr 1971:262). In the south, the wealthy, native agrarian bourgeoisie was consolidating itself. By 1930, 2 per cent of French and Vietnamese landowners controlled 45 per cent of the cultivated land in the Mekong Delta (McAlister 1969:70–1)

In the years prior to the Second World War, a distinct landholding and socio-economic pattern had developed in Vietnam. In Tonkin and Annam there was an impoverished peasantry and a small middle class, while in Cochinchina the major part of the peasantry worked as tenants on the land of the colonialists and the strong native elite which had a vested interest in supporting the colonial regime (Woodside 1976:121–2).

Throughout Vietnam, French rule had removed traditional controls on the accumulation of land and wealth. Local elites within the villages were therefore keen to preserve foreign rule because it helped them to improve and preserve their social and economic advantages. Accordingly, in the decade prior to the outbreak of the Second World War there developed an 'unspoken power sharing agreement' between the conservative village hierarchies and the colonial authorities (Woodside 1976:147).

Enrichment for the native elite and for the French was consistently won at the expense of living standards for the peasantry. The government frequently attempted to justify its draconian policies and, in particular, the high levels of direct and indirect taxation by extolling the achievements of colonial rule. It pointed to hydraulic engineering projects, to the provision of education, to the construction of a communications infrastructure and also to the provision of basic medical services. However, the Vietnamese people paid an extremely heavy and unfair price for the limited benefits which they received.

RESISTANCE TO FRENCH RULE

The French faced spirited opposition to their rule from the outset. Because their policies brought hardships to so many people and because they severely restricted the role of the Vietnamese in the running of their own country, the French increasingly came to sit upon a powder keg of resentment and frustration.

Vietnamese nationalism was very much a product of the colonial experience. The sharing of a common culture had produced a loose, ill-defined proto-nationalism in pre-colonial Vietnam. The vicissitudes of

French rule served to bring that common bond into perspective, to unite the people against an alien force and to place their struggle within a framework which saw Vietnam as a coherent, national entity, which had fought first Chinese and then French domination.

Unlike other colonial nations, France never really contemplated home rule and an eventual relinquishment of control to a native elite groomed in Western-style democracy. This failure to pave the way for self-rule and a smooth hand-over of power to a strong, politically mature, nationalist bourgeoisie had dramatic implications for the nation's political future, especially as the traditional rulers were unlikely to resume the mantle of authority. Without the authority to command respect, and encumbered with the disgrace of weakness in the face of French aggression, the monarchy had ceased to be a symbol of social and national unity. Its puppet status reflected the subjugation of orthodox Vietnamese values to radically different European ideas. Confucian society as represented by the court was paralysed and discredited and the emperor, its symbol of strength, had fallen into foreign hands.

Salvaging some honour for Confucianism in Vietnam were elements of the scholar-gentry class. These were Confucian-educated scholars who were not part of the official mandarinal hierarchy and who had maintained their intellectual and political integrity (Nguyen Khac Vien 1974:40–1). It was around this group of patriotic men that the *Can Vuong* or 'Royalist Movement' of the 1880s coalesced. Although this first threat to French rule was doomed from the outset and was primarily backward-looking because it promised a return to known or imagined days of abundance and harmony under a revitalized imperial court, the movement was of great relevance to later struggles for independence because it sustained a long-running tradition of resistance to foreign rule. Their resistance, although fruitless, was a statement of Vietnamese will to secure independence. This determination and the symbolic acts that preserved it and allowed it to be passed on from one generation to the next was, as David Marr argues, one of the keys to an understanding of the anticolonial movements in Vietnam (Marr 1971:274–6).

Other disturbances punctuated France's first decades in Vietnam. Riots in the rural areas were frequent but the majority had little political impact. Often sparked off by hunger and understandable fear as the advance of capitalism impinged upon the already strained rural community, the disturbances were designed to improve local conditions rather than to force radical social change. Moreover, in many respects such disturbances had their counterparts in the pre-colonial era.

Basically, in the early period of colonial rule, the peasantry posed little real threat to the French as resistance to imperialism was not articulated in a manner likely to attract the support of the masses, to whom 'liberation' and 'freedom' were rather meaningless concepts when the prime struggle was to win a sufficient livelihood to avoid starvation. Rural disturbances, therefore, tended to have localized roots which ensured that what opposition there was to the colonial authorities was not welded together into a national movement but remained characterized by fragmentation and inspired by disparate regional conditions.

Modern Vietnamese nationalism developed in three separate stages (Duiker 1976:290). The first stage was dominated by the 'traditionalists' of the patriotic scholar-gentry class. Scholars also led the second stage. This apparently more constructive phase belonged to the 'transitionalists' who envisaged an independent or semi-independent modernized Vietnam that was either a democratic republic or was ruled by an enlightened monarch. By the end of the First World War the best-known transitionalist leaders had passed the pinnacle of their influence and were soon to lose their grip upon the independence movement. Their greatest failing was that, along with other early exponents of liberation, they promoted an elitist form of nationalism which failed to grasp the significance of attracting the peasantry to its cause.

Between 1900 and 1920 the independence movement underwent a metamorphosis from which it emerged into its third, modern stage. Several events were important in this process. Firstly, the Japanese victory over Russia in 1905 shattered the myth of Asian inferiority. Secondly, the Chinese Revolution of 1911 encouraged Vietnam's own nationalist cause, and thirdly, the First World War did much to discredit the European powers, especially as 100,000 Vietnamese labourers were sent to Europe where they witnessed the carnage and the astonishing fact that not all white men could, by right, stand on the top rung of the social ladder. Most significantly, in 1917, the Russian Revolution gave heart to all those who searched for a new kind of society.

In the process of metamorphosis, the national resistance movement acquired a political framework which, paradoxically, was nurtured and made increasingly sophisticated by the intensity of repression. Despite French regulation of political groups, censorship of the press, prohibition of trade unionism and blatant infringement of human rights, it proved impossible to halt the growth of clandestine and semi-clandestine political and politico-religious groups as the twentieth century progressed. The Mekong Delta, in particular, became the scene of vigorous activity as thousands of peasants joined two new religious groups, the *Hoa Hao* and the *Cao Dai,* which had strong social and political undertones.

Ironically, Western-style education, which was directly attributable to French rule, was to help nurture the seeds of its destruction. By exposing even the small number of Vietnamese who received more than a rudimentary education to the philosophy of the West, the French opened up the possibility of their rule being undermined by the West's own political concepts. 'Liberty', 'freedom' and 'nationalism' were added to the ideological armoury of the Vietnamese and, in time, Marxism-Leninism added its own contribution.

A vast number of minuscule, often hostile and internally factionalized radical groups made up the nationalist opposition to French rule during the 1920s and 1930s. This was especially true in Cochinchina where French political control was slightly more relaxed. Two parties, in particular, were to play central roles in the process of Vietnamese independence. These were the Vietnamese Nationalist Party (VNQDD) and the Indochinese Communist Party (ICP). The VNQDD was established in 1927 as a replica of the Chinese Kuomintang and, although more radical than previous organizations, it was primarily a moderate, middle-ground, nationalist party. Sensing its very existence threatened by a French crackdown, the VNQDD attempted to orchestrate a rebellion amongst Vietnamese-staffed garrisons in 1930. The result was a disaster. Poor planning and a misreading of the political climate meant that only one garrison, that of Yen Bay, mutinied and was subsequently crushed. The rebellion was an ignominious failure and, as a consequence of concerted repression, the higher levels of the VNQDD network were wiped out. 1930 thus witnessed the nadir of the VNQDD as an effective organization and a blow from which it never really recovered.

On orders from Comintern, the Indochinese Communist Party was established in February 1930. It was organized by a leading Vietnamese revolutionary, Ho Chi Minh, and incorporated a number of radical nationalist groups. Its establishment coincided with the revolutionary upsurge of the early 1930s which was brought about by the global economic crisis. Communist led and inspired insurrections proved to be the first real threat to French authority, and their scale, for a short time, rocked the very foundations of colonial rule.

The Nghe-Tinh Soviets are worthy of specific note. In 1930, in Nghe An and Ha Tinh, two provinces of northern central Vietnam, the ICP stimulated the overthrow of French authority and the establishment of Vietnamese-governed Soviets. It was a genuinely popular movement and illustrated the immense possibilities to be gained from combining nationalist aspirations with a Marxist social programme (Osborne 1974:53). For nearly a year the Soviets successfully resisted subjugation but when repression finally succeeded, its brutality was intense and, as a result, the ICP was almost annihilated and as much as 90 per cent of its leadership was executed or imprisoned (Duiker 1981:41). However, despite ruthlessly pursuing a goal of total political control, the French were unable to stem the rising tide of popular discontent. Although 1931 was the bleakest, most desperate year that the nationalist groups had endured, with their sources estimating the victims at 10,000 killed and over 50,000 deported (Buttinger 1969:180), the Vietnamese independence movement did not collapse. Instead, as government repression increased, the nation became locked into an escalating cycle of repression and resistance.

After the devastating shocks of 1930–1, the mid and late 1930s were years of regeneration for sections of the Vietnamese nationalist movement. Although often seen as dark years for progressive forces in Vietnam, and especially for the ICP, the 1930s were, in fact, a decade in which the left emerged as the leading element in Vietnamese politics (Osborne 1974:53). It had not yet gained control over political life but it increasingly influenced the political agenda.

Throughout the 1930s Comintern and the requirements of Stalinism moulded the policies of the ICP (Duiker 1975:40–2). Moscow-trained communists assumed control of the ICP following the decimation of the Party leadership and, in keeping with the Kremlin's revolutionary dogma, sought to incite revolution amongst the small urban proletariat. Appeals to nationalism did not figure prominently in this strategy. Given that nationalism was emerging as a powerful force amongst the middle classes and that the peasantry comprised the major part of the population, this emphasis upon the proletariat did not appear to be a promising strategy. Events in Europe, nevertheless, gradually forced this approach to be modified.

In 1935 Moscow ordered that a worldwide popular front should be constructed against the threat of fascism. In order to comply, the ICP had to decrease its militancy so that it could successfully form a Democratic United Front. This proved to be beneficial to the fortunes of the party in Vietnam because it widened the appeal of its policies (Duiker 1975:34).

In 1936 a Popular Front government was elected in France and this led to a relaxation of political control in the colony. But when Stalin signed the Nazi-Soviet pact in 1939 there was an immediate crackdown on the ICP. The communists had no choice but to abandon their work in the cities and instead to retreat to the countryside which then became their new locus of activity. This transfer of revolutionary work to the rural areas would have immense consequences, as it set in train a movement towards the peasantry as the focus of the revolutionary struggle (Duiker 1975:39–40).

The start of a reorientation in ICP strategy was one of several factors that was pushing Vietnam towards revolution. In particular, the petite bourgeoisie of Tonkin and Annam had begun to mature politically and to move to the political forefront. As such it provided important leadership for the nationalist movement (Marr 1971:263). The middle classes in Vietnam came to assume this role because of their growing frustration at the limits that French rule placed upon their social, political and economic advancement (McAlister 1969:7, 322–4). Armed with an education and with enough money to have tasted success, they wanted and expected more. Anger at finding avenues blocked to them led elements of this group to seek revolutionary alternatives.

It was against this background of the slow but steady build-up of nationalist opposition to French rule that the Second World War took place. The cataclysmic scale of the conflict reorientated the struggle for independence and destroyed the existing balance of forces within Vietnam. The French would emerge from the war as no match for a nationalist opposition which was at last united within one organization. That organization was the Viet Minh, a creation of the ICP. The war was the catalyst and the Viet Minh the vehicle by which a partial independence was to be achieved.

That this task fell to the communist-led Viet Minh owed much to the fact that most other nationalist opposition was factionalized or defunct, thanks to French repression, and also to the fact that Comintern no longer had an iron grip on the Party. This allowed the leader of the Vietnamese communists, Ho Chi Minh, to use his political skills to rapidly move the ICP towards an alliance with all progressive, anti-French elements in Vietnamese society. Thereafter the ICP concentrated upon the appeal of nationalism and looked to the peasantry as the leading revolutionary force.

When he returned to Vietnam in 1941 to undertake this momentous task it was the first time that Ho had visited his homeland for thirty years. He had left Vietnam in 1911 at the age of twenty-two and had roamed the world as an itinerant worker and spokesman for the cause of Vietnamese independence. Although much of this part of his life is obscure, it is known that he lived for many years in France and studied and trained in the Soviet Union and China, in the process serving an apprenticeship that was later to pay handsome dividends for the Vietnamese Revolution.

Ho assumed control of the nationalist movement in 1941 and then proceeded to transform it. Vietnamese independence was his priority and communism a secondary goal. However, by combining the prospect of freedom from colonial rule with the promise of a better life, Ho was to accomplish a feat that had eluded his predecessors who had offered independence and yet a preservation of social inequality. He became the symbol of a national unity which had been missing since the emasculation of the imperial throne and consequently, for a short time, attracted the support of a large section of the nationalist middle class. On the other hand he also incorporated the aspirations of millions of impoverished peasants within the social programme of the Viet Minh. Notwithstanding the inherent contradiction that this implied, Ho Chi Minh's political acumen was to make him and his policies seem, for a fleeting but vital moment, the answer to Vietnam's political crisis and to centuries of social and economic bitterness.

2 The first Indochina conflict and the United States' drift to war

The Second World War gave birth to an era in which the global balance of power had been irretrievably shifted. European imperial powers had been eclipsed and they could no longer maintain their hold over vast continents. The war was a catalyst, accelerating the process of social and political change so that independence from colonialism became urgent and inevitable in many developing nations. Overarching this inexorable process was the emergence of two superpowers which polarized the world into ideologically opposed camps and threatened it with total destruction. This new global configuration and ideological cleavage superimposed itself upon the struggles for independence, so that, in the minds of Cold War ideologues, they became linked with the advance of world communism. Perhaps understandable, given the historical context, this was, nevertheless, a naive belief which was to carry war and destruction in its wake.

The Second World War profoundly affected Vietnam. As in other Asian nations, nationalist sentiment was given a new impetus and the post-1945 colonial authorities were faced with the challenge of ruling a country in which a new and far-reaching political agenda demanded urgent attention. The French, perhaps more than any other European power, were unable to perceive the extent of these changes and the political processes that had come to fruition during the Pacific War. Their inability to appreciate that there could be no recreation of the prewar days of unquestioned colonial supremacy led to seven years of bloody and bitter conflict.

When the French government collapsed in the face of Hitler in 1939, its South East Asian colonies became exceedingly attractive targets for Japanese expansionism. Japan was further encouraged by the comparative weakness of the French colonial forces which could muster only some 70,000 men and a paltry assortment of obsolete equipment (Fall 1963:22). It was hardly surprising, therefore, that Japanese control of Indochina was won with relative ease. Some isolated resistance did occur but, in general, the series of ultimatums which Japan presented to the Vichyite regime and which granted Tokyo greater and greater power and authority in the colony were complied with and accepted as the unavoidable price for maintaining the facade of French control. Consequently, although the French collaborated with them until the final stages of the war, when the Vichyite administration was overthrown by a coup, the Japanese ruled Indochina.

Japanese control shattered a vital myth and performed a psychologically liberating function for the Vietnamese people. It was concrete proof that the white man could be defeated by orientals and that his superiority and natural right to rule over the poorer, non-Caucasian races of the world was not preordained. It was this discrediting of the French in Indochina, and of the other colonial powers in South East Asia—all of which were roundly defeated by the Japanese within the space of six months—that was one of the lasting and most far-reaching consequences of the Pacific War in Asia.

However, the Vietnamese did not hail their new rulers as liberators and they were not content to substitute one imperial authority for another. Although the Japanese encouraged nationalist movements which were sympathetic to their own interests, they were concerned, first and foremost, with extending and consolidating their own control and with exploiting Indochina for their own ends. Local agriculture, for example, was manipulated and rice lands were turned over to the production of cotton and jute. It was a policy which, in the rice-deficient areas of northern Vietnam, was to have terrible consequences.

Inevitably the war entailed significant military, economic and political dislocation in Vietnam. Political attitudes became sharpened and the partial interruption in French control presented the Vietnamese nationalists with an ideal opportunity. Accordingly, in 1941 Ho Chi Minh and a group of followers established the *Viet Nam Doc Lap Dong Minh Hoi* (the Viet Minh). It was an organization intended to promote limited social change and to weld together the various disparate strands of Vietnamese nationalism into one powerful body to fight both the Japanese and the French.

The Viet Minh was not the only nationalist group to gain prominence during the war. Other organizations sponsored by the Japanese and Chinese flourished, but none could command the depth and breadth of support that the Viet Minh did. Rapidly winning the allegiance of the middle classes who were gripped by nationalist fervour and the peasants who were attracted by its social programme, the Viet Minh became the unchallenged leader of the nationalist movement in Vietnam. By early

1943, it had consolidated its control over a portion of the Highland provinces in north-eastern Vietnam and this area increasingly became a testing ground for future Viet Minh social and administrative policy.

Elsewhere, however, the organization's success was not as dramatic. In the autumn of 1940 the Communist Party apparatus in Cochinchina had authorized a local uprising in the belief that the time was then ripe for the revolutionary movement to capitalize upon the weakening French position. The action, however, contravened a decision taken by the Party's national leadership to avoid precipitate action in the south where the revolutionary base was considered too underdeveloped to sustain a direct attack upon the colonial authorities (Duiker 1981:63). The outcome of the rebellion in Nam Ky was a disaster for the Communist Party in Cochinchina. The insurrection was precipitately quelled, the Party infrastructure decimated by repression, and the revolutionary movement, which had hitherto been strongest and best developed in the south, was left as a pale shadow of its former self (Thayer 1975:30–3, Duiker 1981:63, Kolko 1986:31). Naturally the premature action of the southern branch of the Party had a debilitating influence on radical politics in Cochinchina and contributed, in no small part, to the laggardly advance of the revolution in the south during the post-war decades.

The Viet Minh developed a military wing. Initially its forces were extremely poorly equipped and they sought arms from whatever quarter possible. The Chinese supplied them with a limited amount of arms and, paradoxically, so did the United States. This early relationship between the Viet Minh and the US was developed through the auspices of the OSS (Office of Strategic Services), the forerunner of the CIA. The two organizations worked together in a very loose and unofficial manner, the Viet Minh volunteering information, sabotaging a few Japanese installations and rescuing Allied pilots shot down by the Japanese over the jungles of Vietnam. In exchange they hoped to receive arms, ammunition and recognition for their cause. In reality the support offered to them was token in nature and amounted to little more than a few small arms (Shaplen 1965:33). But it was clear that OSS members were sympathetic to the Viet Minh and acknowledged that it had popular support (Porter 1979:76–7). This had the effect of giving the Viet Minh a great morale boost which was out of all proportion to the scale of the aid provided.

As the war drew to a close, OSS personnel were sent on a mission to Indochina to work with and train anti-Japanese forces. Finding no other coherent resistance groups, the OSS team, known as the 'Deer Team', in an ironic twist of fate, came to train as many as 200 Viet Minh guerrillas who were the forerunners of the very forces against which the United States would fight in subsequent years (Patti 1980:125–9).

THE INTERNATIONAL BACKGROUND TO THE RETURN OF FRENCH COLONIALISM

The Viet Minh's belief that the United States would support their struggle for independence was not without foundation. The US was the first true colony to win its independence and it had consistently denounced the evils of colonialism, even if periodic lapses into a neo-imperialist mentality had served to sully its lofty rhetoric. F.D.Roosevelt, the US president during the war, had made plain his opposition to colonialism. Together with many others in the US administration he did evince genuine concern for the plight of subjected peoples. But it could hardly escape notice that the US opposition to imperialism married suspiciously well with US self-interest and especially with the desire to find freer access to markets in a post-war world in which it was apparent that America would reign economically supreme.

Roosevelt was extremely interested in Indochina, even though he had no intimate knowledge or direct experience of it. He was adamant, furthermore, that the region should not be returned to French rule after the war. In 1944 he decried France's record in Indochina, claiming that Paris had 'milked it for one hundred years,' and that the 'people of Indochina [were] entitled to something better than that' (United States-Vietnam Relations Vol. 7 1971:30).

Roosevelt's plan for the region was to create an international trusteeship which would oversee the transfer of power and culminate in the granting of independence in approximately twenty to thirty years. But although Roosevelt discussed the idea with Stalin, Chiang Kai-shek and Churchill, the trusteeship plan was not officially developed. Instead it remained a matter of personal interest to the president and was not pursued by his State Department as a policy objective (Hess 1972:356).

Roosevelt's attitude towards Indochina naturally created friction with the British. Churchill saw the concept of trusteeship as a threat to British colonialism and believed that it would set a dangerous precedent. Differing national perspectives over the long-term political future of South East Asia inevitably led to disputes between Allied commanders conducting the war in the region (Dunn 1985:105–23). Under pressure from the British, SEAC (South East Asia Command) was created to oversee operations in the region and was headed by Lord Louis Mountbatten. That the Americans uncharitably nicknamed SEAC 'Save England's Asian Colonies' was indicative of the degree of ill-feeling generated by the colonial issue.

Control over military operations in the Indochina region became contentious as the war drew to a close. Initially Indochina came within

SEAC's orbit, but when the boundaries for future Allied military operations were defined, the US unilaterally decided to place Indochina within the Chinese military theatre, which was effectively under American control. Although a section of it was later transferred back to the British, during the final throes of the Pacific War Indochina was ostensibly the responsibility of the United States and the Chinese. However, contrary to US wishes, the British persisted in aiding the French by allowing them to attach a military mission to SEAC headquarters. This mission, although very small and limited in scale, existed specifically to orchestrate the French reoccupation of Indochina (Hess 1972).

Despite the limited practical help offered by the British, the French had a difficult task to accomplish. In March 1945 the Japanese had overthrown the Vichyite Indochinese regime in a *coup de force*. Fearful of the stab in the back that the French might inflict when Allied forces arrived in the region, the Japanese removed the facade of French control and dismantled the French security apparatus that had been essential to the maintenance of colonial rule. In a few isolated cases, the French put up fierce resistance to the coup, and sections of the colonial forces began to retreat and fight their way through the jungles of Tonkin and into China. By and large, however, the removal of the tricolour was achieved without a great deal of opposition from the French.

Roosevelt's death on 12 April 1945, some months before the war in the Pacific finally ended, led to a revised US attitude towards Indochina and to a diminution of Francophobia in the White House under his successor, President Truman. However, the seeds of the reorientation in US policy were sown during Roosevelt's own lifetime. As victory in the war seemed increasingly secure, Roosevelt began to retreat from his original position on an international trusteeship for Indochina (Lafeber 1975). His vision of a stable Asia presided over by a friendly China malleable to US pressure was appearing distinctly questionable as the Kuomintang seemed likely to be permanently divided by reactionary elements, hostile to the United States. To complicate matters, the Chinese communists appeared threateningly strong. In this context, the return of French colonial rule, whilst undesirable, did have the advantage of providing some short-term political stability.

The softening of the US administration's attitude towards a French role in Indochina was reflected a few days after the end of the war when part of Indochina was moved back under the control of SEAC. The British were given the responsibility for coordinating and overseeing the surrender and disarming of Japanese forces in Indochina, south of the sixteenth parallel. North of this line, the task fell to the Chinese. This was a vitally important decision which was to have dramatic consequences for the establishment of a free and independent Vietnamese nation.

THE AUGUST REVOLUTION

The surrender of the Japanese, following closely upon the collapse of French power in Indochina, left a vacuum into which the Vietnamese nationalists quickly moved. Economically and politically, the country was in turmoil. Japanese conversion of rice lands, their disruption of the transport system which carried supplies to the rice-deficient areas of the north, together with Allied bombing of the communications infrastructure gave rise to a tragic food crisis in northern Vietnam. Estimates vary, but it is thought that between one and two million people died of starvation in Tonkin during the famine of 1944–5 (Kolko 1986:36).

In northern Vietnam it was the food crisis, perhaps more than any other single factor, which enabled the Viet Minh to muster support from the peasantry, and to organize and radicalize the masses with ease (Truong Chinh 1963:26). By seizing grain stored by the Japanese and distributing it to the needy, they helped, in some measure, to answer the immediate demands of hunger. On a more long-term basis, their social programme offered the peasantry the hope of an end to the most flagrant economic injustices that had become even more apparent during the famine. In this sense, the food crisis has been termed the 'engine upon which the Revolution rode to power' (Beresford 1988:19). Moreover, the unrest which the famine unleashed catapulted the Viet Minh to power without them having to draw up an extremely radical programme that carried with it the possibility of arousing the hostility of moderate, nationalist elements in the cities (Duiker 1981:103).

Support for the Viet Minh snowballed following the Japanese surrender and the hand-over of power to a caretaker government composed of pro-Japanese Vietnamese. This support was greatest in the rural areas of the north where the Viet Minh had, for many years, nurtured its revolutionary movement and established its wartime liberated zone. In the south, where there was no famine and where the Communist Party's organization had not recovered from the abortive Nam Ky rebellion, the scale of support for the Viet Minh was correspondingly reduced.

On 19 August 1945 the Viet Minh seized power in Hanoi and Ho Chi Minh became the head of the provisional Republic of Vietnam. Bao Dai, the pre-war puppet emperor and, more latterly, a collaborator with the Japanese, prudently abdicated his throne and became a councillor in the new government. Spontaneous popular demonstrations pledging support for the Viet Minh and for independence broke out in Hanoi and the momentum of revolution swiftly gained ground and spread southwards down the length of Vietnam. On 2 September Ho Chi Minh then declared Vietnamese independence before tumultuous crowds in Hanoi. At least in the north, therefore, the August Revolution had placed the Viet Minh in power.

By contrast, in Saigon the quest for independence and, more importantly, who was to lead it, was not so clear-cut. Traditionally, the political spectrum in south Vietnam was much broader and the Viet Minh had to compete for support with a wide variety of political and politico-religious organizations. Its assumption of power was consequently not inevitable. A United National Front government, which included the Viet Minh, had taken control in Saigon following the Japanese surrender but, after popular demonstrations in favour of the Viet Minh, the Front collapsed and the Viet Minh were able to establish a Provisional Executive Committee for the south on 25 August. Although the Committee recognized the authority of the Republic of Vietnam based in Hanoi, in practice it functioned independently of Ho Chi Minh's administration.

The regional government of Cochinchina was less stable than that of the north. Different groups vied for power and although none could muster sufficient strength to overthrow the Provisional Executive Committee, they nevertheless made the task of consolidating power all the more difficult. Tension was generated in the uncertain political environment and fears began to grow that the British would encourage the reinstatement of French rule when they arrived to disarm the Japanese. This tension was ignited on 2 September, the day Ho Chi Minh declared independence. There was disorder in the streets of Saigon, and houses belonging to French colonialists were ransacked.

Within a very short time of coming to office Truman had abandoned what remained of Roosevelt's anticolonial crusade. Indeed it is doubtful that he even knew of his predecessor's desire for an Indochinese trusteeship when he became president (Fifield 1973:49). Viewed from the White House, the world was suddenly a dangerous and chaotic place which needed order stamped upon it even if this meant compromising high ideals. The fundamental problem with Roosevelt's trusteeship concept was that it had failed to anticipate the gathering momentum of Asian nationalism to which independence at some unspecified time in the distant future would be anathema. Moreover, in the hard light of day, the US administration, prompted by its military leadership, the Joint Chiefs of Staff, saw the advantages that a new kind of loose, unofficial colonialism could offer them in terms of military bases and politically 'safe' areas in a potentially hostile world (Fifield 1973:50, Thorne 1976:92–3).

Not that all concern for colonial peoples was conveniently brushed aside. The Far Eastern Division of the State Department, whilst not advocating immediate independence for Indochina, did suggest that the French give assurances as to when Indochina would become independent. However, these considerations were put to one side as the European Division insisted that forcing the French out of Indochina would dangerously threaten France's domestic equilibrium and would weaken its international status. This would thereby jeopardize US interests in Europe (La Feber 1975, Hess 1972). In this context, America reluctantly relinquished its support for Vietnamese independence as it did not accord with US global objectives. Consequently, the United States lost a vital opportunity to ally itself with the powerful movement for social change and independence in Vietnam (Shaplen 1965:xx). Even Dean Rusk, who was to play a significant role in the formulation of America's Vietnam policy, conceded that if there had been a time to set Vietnam along a different path, it would have been at the crucial juncture at the end of the Second World War (Charlton and Moncrieff 1978:18). In failing to seize the opportunity, the US abandoned what influence it had to mould the very force it would later come to fight.

THE RETURN OF THE FRENCH

Reclaiming their prized Indochinese colonies was considered vital by all French political parties in the aftermath of the war. Despite being on the eventual winning side, the French had been humiliated at Hitler's hands and few in France questioned the necessity of restoring the nation's prestige and world status by re-establishing the glories of its empire.

In southern Vietnam the return of the colonial authorities was facilitated by the role of the British. It is probable that the British commander, General Gracy, went beyond his purely military role and exceeded the orders given to him by becoming closely involved in the political process (Dunn 1985:167–83). With the knowledge and participation of the British, French prisoners of war, who had recently been released from internment, mounted a *coup* in Saigon on 23 September. Seizing control of public buildings they deposed the Provisional Executive Committee. Panic swept the city and the air was rife with lurid tales of massacres. On the night of 24–25 September, the crisis deepened when a mob massacred around 300 Europeans in the Cite Heyraud district of Saigon. In an attempt to restore order, Gracy turned to the Japanese troops to help keep the peace and, as a result, they participated in the founding up of suspected Viet Minh, in manning road blocks and in general policing activities (Dunn 1985:266). Consequently, the Japanese, under Gracy's command, were instrumental in excluding the Viet Minh from government in the south of Vietnam.

From a British perspective, smoothing the way for a return to French rule and the use of Japanese troops to help in the maintenance of law and order were entirely logical. The war was over and the British forces wanted to return home without undue delay. Becoming entwined in the labyrinth of Vietnamese politics was the last thing that they wanted. The priority, therefore, was to achieve their objective of overseeing the surrender as quickly as possible and to divest themselves of responsibility for a chaotic situation by an expedient hand-over of power to the French, at the earliest possible date. The practical application of this strategy meant that during the nine months that the British were in Vietnam, they effectively oversaw the gradual reintroduction of French rule in Cochinchina. It also gave rise to their involvement, alongside the newly arrived colonial forces, in military operations which undercut Viet Minh power in all key areas of the south.

In the north of Vietnam the situation was markedly different. The Chinese, who were responsible for disarming the Japanese above the sixteenth parallel, were sidetracked from overt manipulation of politics by the opportunity that their position gave them to garner enormous riches. Pressure was placed upon the Viet Minh government in order to force it to incorporate pro-Chinese elements within its ranks, and this it obligingly did. But the occupation forces did not attempt to usurp the power of the new Republic because the Viet Minh had taken a conscious decision to appease the Chinese and not to antagonize them by protesting against their economic rape of Tonkin. The Chinese exacted a heavy price for this favour. Perhaps as much as the equivalent of half the total annual pre-war economic output of the whole of Indochina was extracted from the impoverished north, which was already reeling under the effects of war and famine (McAlister 1969:243–4). What the Viet Minh purchased, thanks to this costly transaction, was a breathing space and some time to consolidate its authority and extend its administrative structure throughout the north.

It was apparent that the breathing space was certain to be short when, in February 1946, the Chinese signed an agreement with the French. In return for wide-ranging economic concessions, the Chinese agreed to withdraw their forces and to allow the reintroduction of the French. By the early summer of 1946 most of the Chinese had left and contingents of colonial forces had arrived in the north. An uneasy peace then ensued between the government of Ho Chi Minh and the French who waited restlessly to re-establish their authority.

NEGOTIATING A SOLUTION

Efforts to resolve the crisis in Vietnam through negotiations were undertaken during 1946. All proved failures and, by the end of the year, hostilities had broken out. This failure stemmed from the simple fact that the French were unwilling to compromise and give Vietnam any degree of real independence even though the Viet Minh would have been willing to accept a diluted form of independence in the short term.

On 6 March 1946, a temporary agreement was signed between the French and Ho Chi Minh. Acknowledging that they could not oppose the return of French troops, the Viet Minh gave formal recognition to the French presence in Vietnam. In return for this recognition, the French agreed to grant a vague and imprecise form of independence to Vietnam. The agreement was wholly inadequate but it did offer some hope in that it superficially stabilized the situation and was ill-defined enough to be widely interpreted by both sides.

However, further talks exposed the great gulf that existed between the French and the Viet Minh and revealed the very restricted interpretation that the French gave to the March Agreement. Vietnam was to be part of an Indochinese federation ruled over by a French High Commissioner. This scenario, coming only months after the Vietnamese had unilaterally declared their independence, appeared preposterous to Ho Chi Minh and his government. Worse, however, was to follow when a conference at Fontainebleau in France, which was supposed to decide the future of Indochina, broke down because the conditions that the French proposed were hazy and offered no prospect of an independent Vietnam.

The major stumbling block to Vietnamese independence was the political situation in France and, as 1946 progressed, this situation appeared increasingly less favourable to the Viet Minh cause. No political party, apart from the socialists, was willing to listen to Ho Chi Minh (Irving 1975:24). In a shameful example of the way in which the principle of international solidarity was sacrificed for short-term political gain, this even applied to the French Communist Party.

In the immediate post-war period the axis of the French Assembly gradually drifted to the right and it was the Christian Democratic MRP *(Mouvement Republicain Populaire)* which came to be the guiding hand upon foreign policy. The MRP was influenced by the staunchly colonialist stance of the Gaullists, who became increasingly popular during 1946 and 1947. Both the Gaullists and the MRP were competing over the same constituency and it was the fear of losing support to de Gaulle's party that encouraged MRP leaders to assume an inflexible position and resist concessions to Vietnamese nationalism (Irving 1975:24–52, 140). Ultimately no party wished to preside over the dismemberment of a French Union that was to help restore national pride.

THE FIRST INDOCHINA WAR

The uneasy peace came to a dramatic end in November 1946. The fighting was triggered off by a relatively minor incident over customs control in Haiphong Harbour but it soon escalated into major hostilities which allowed the French to utilize their military superiority in order to oust the Viet Minh from power. As they did so, they embarked upon harsh and indiscriminate repression. The Viet Minh realized the vulnerability of their position and, in order to preserve their patiently accumulated strength, they did not remain in Hanoi to fight the French in the face of unfavourable odds. Instead, they chose to stage a strategic retreat into the mountains of Tonkin where they operated as an alternative government and developed their ability to resume the military struggle against the French.

The early optimism of the French was soon dispelled. Events proved that the subjugation of the Viet Minh would not be accomplished as easily and as quickly as anticipated. The French were faced with a fundamental dilemma. Either they could fight the Viet Minh in the mountains or they could garrison the populous Tonkin Delta. They could not, however, do both. Although attempts were made to achieve the two objectives there were simply too few troops to accomplish either to any satisfactory degree. Thus the Viet Minh were left to run rings around the confused French troops who, once away from the safety of their base camps, were forced to assume defensive and static positions. From 1951, French commando groups fought in Viet Minh-held territory (Fall 1963:262–74) but, despite achieving some notable successes, these groups were only a limited part of the French military strategy which relied far more on large, set-piece battles where they could use their considerable firepower.

In Cochinchina the French did not face such a strong enemy. The Viet Minh failed to mobilize the south to the same degree as they did the north for three main reasons. Firstly because of the unique development of the revolutionary movement in the south. Secondly because Cochinchina was far from the Viet Minh's base area in Tonkin, consequently rendering supply and communication lines long and frequently unreliable. And thirdly because the flat open plains of the Delta offered few secure areas for guerrilla activity. Despite these significant handicaps for the revolutionary movement, the French were unable to consolidate their control over the area and were able to manage the Mekong Delta only by permitting the proliferation of a variety of independent groups which operated their own small fiefdoms and which opposed the extension of Viet Minh power (Duncanson 1968:186–9). Consequently, the French were forced by their own weakness to parcel out control to an odd assortment of dubious organizations. Even this policy, however, did not prevent the Viet Minh from establishing particularly strong revolutionary bases in remote rural areas.

The appeal of the Viet Minh was simple. They demanded that their country should be free and independent from external influence and they combined this with a social programme designed to mitigate some of the harsher apects of life in Vietnam. As the Viet Minh expanded their control they carved out large liberated zones in the north Vietnamese countryside and, to a lesser extent, in the south. An effective military strategy and genuine support from a large proportion of the population therefore allowed the Viet Minh to extend and consolidate their power at the expense of the colonial regime. As a result, the French never managed to achieve a really firm grip upon Vietnam and when, after 1947, they abandoned their half-hearted attempts to negotiate with Ho Chi Minh, their untenable position and the hollowness of their strategy forced them to begin the search for an alternative solution.

THE BAO DAI SOLUTION

Because the Viet Minh would not give up and lay down their arms, and because the French military strategy was patently failing to destroy them, Paris concluded that its aims would be better served by political and diplomatic means. This meant finding a figurehead around whom the nationalist aspirations of the Vietnamese would coalesce but who, at the same time, would prove amenable to French control. By acquiring a pro-French 'nationalist', Paris hoped, in effect, to divide and disorientate the opposition to its rule and to turn the anticolonial war into a civil war (Hess 1987:313).

The individual upon whom this difficult task fell was the former emperor, Bao Dai, a man who was notable chiefly for his ability to bend with the wind and to come to an accommodation with whichever group was in power. In 1947 he could be found languishing in Hong Kong and living up to his image as the playboy emperor after having been sent there two years previously on a diplomatic mission for the Viet Minh.

Bao Dai was first approached by the French in early 1947. Despite his dilettante reputation, he appeared to be the only figure who stood any likelihood of satisfying the nationalists whilst still being susceptible to French influence (Irving 1975:56). In order to persuade him to return to Vietnam, ostensibly as Head of State, but in fact to rule the country for them, Paris conceded a limited form of independence to Vietnam. The Elysee Agreement of March 1949, which formalized this semi-independence, ensured, nevertheless, that the French retained significant powers within the country. When Bao Dai then returned to Vietnam he was not welcomed by Vietnamese nationalists. His authority and the independence that he had supposedly wrested from the French was nothing but a charade. What is more, no one, except for the French, imagined that it could be considered as anything else.

A fundamental problem flawed the Bao Dai solution and made it untenable from the outset. The emperor could not rally the nationalists because he was so closely associated with the colonial power and yet he could not survive politically if he dispensed with support from Paris. He was courted by the French because he did not demand as much as Ho Chi Minh and yet the only way he could acquire popular legitimacy was to become a genuine nationalist (Hammer 1966:217). His French-sponsored governments were dismal failures and the vaguest sign of their independence was firmly stamped upon. Political confusion and instability thus marked the years of Bao Dai.

In an attempt to prove Vietnam's independence, the emperor undertook two important initiatives. Firstly, he began to build up a national army and secondly, he scheduled municipal elections for January 1953. Unfortunately for Bao Dai, the results of the vote underlined the superficial extent of his popularity. Rather than supporting the emperor through the election of his candidates, the unimpressed electorate, small and restricted though it was, clearly expressed their dissatisfaction with the political impasse. In Hanoi this was illustrated by the election of an old revolutionary comrade of Ho Chi Minh. By 1953, militarily and politically, French policy was teetering on the brink of disaster.

FRENCH MILITARY FAILURE AND THE INTERNATIONALIZATION OF THE WAR

It was of some comfort to France that, by 1953, it did not stand alone and that its policy was no longer condemned in Washington. This was thanks to the Internationalization of the conflict. In the late 1940s and early 1950s the US and the Soviet Union were embroiled in the Cold

War. This conflict inevitably superimposed itself upon the process of US foreign policy formulation in respect to many areas of the world. In post-war Washington, 'rollback' and 'containment of communism' were enshrined as political necessities and successive presidents acted upon them as if they were gospel. It was the Cold War which, therefore, gave shape to the development of the war in Indochina.

Prompted by its Cold War perspective and by its fears of a Soviet-dominated Europe, the US abandoned its support for total Vietnamese independence. Washington wanted France to play a significant role in Western Europe in order to help it contain the Soviet threat and consequently the US ceased to make suggestions that might weaken France domestically. The battle between the Europe-centred strategy advocated by the European Division of the State Department, and the Asian-centred strategy advocated by the Far Eastern Division, which had been fought since the end of the war, was thus settled in the summer of 1949 (Hess 1972). It was considered more important to maintain the political stability of France than to risk encouraging political change in South East Asia.

It was in 1947 that the famed 'domino theory' made its debut in relation to the Truman Doctrine on Greece. But it was during the presidency of Eisenhower that it assumed the status of a dogma to be applied to a specific situation. That situation was Vietnam. Eisenhower's Secretary for Defense was the legendary John Foster Dulles, a man known for his virulent anticommunism and for his belief in the righteousness of crusading against the 'red menace'. He and the president believed that once a nation had become communist then all other nations bordering upon it would succumb, in succession, to communism. As applied to Indochina, this meant that once Vietnam had been taken over, then the future for all of South East Asia looked bleak indeed. To avert this threat to the region's stability, great efforts had to be made in order to ensure that communism did not gain a foothold in Vietnam.

This belief had been strengthened by the 'fall' of China. The victory of the Chinese communists in 1949 confirmed all of Washington's worst fears. They were beset by a vast conspiracy and communists in Moscow were plotting to take over the world. The movement of China into the opposing superpower camp triggered a wave of anticommunist panic in the United States which led to officially-sanctioned witch hunts against those failing to express unbounded hatred towards communism. On an international level, the establishment of communist rule in China led to a swift drawing up of battle lines over the war in Indochina.

By December 1949 Chinese communists arrived at the frontier with Vietnam. It was a fact which, in the eyes of the US, would radically alter the complexion of the anticolonial war against the French.

Henceforth the French were seen as fighting a war on behalf of the Free World. In January 1950, Ho Chi Minh's government was recognized by the new People's Republic of China and by the Soviet Union, and in February, Bao Dai's government was recognized by the US and Britain. To highlight the international polarization, the Korean War began in June of the same year.

United States aid for the French began to arrive in significant quantities in 1951. The US thereby assumed the role of a supporter of colonialism rather than a promoter of independence. Through this process, the war shifted, piecemeal, from a war fought by the Vietnamese against a foreign colonial power to one fought by the Vietnamese against the West.

France's ability to continue fighting the war was due in large part to US military aid which, by 1954, contributed 78 per cent of the French war budget (Pentagon Papers Vol. 11971:77). America was drawn into providing support on this scale partly because of its plans to remilitarize Germany. The French would not accept this while they were being drained financially and militarily by the conflict in South East Asia. Washington's answer, therefore, was to underwrite France's war in Indochina (Hess 1987:352).

Despite US largesse, by 1953 the French military position was very weak and, while they held on to control of the cities, much of the countryside was in Viet Minh hands. Hoping to turn the tide, the French commissioned General Henri Navarre to become military commander in Indochina. His scheme, the Navarre plan, sanctioned and encouraged by the US, was thought to offer the hope of military success. It was bold and optimistic yet, in hindsight, totally unsuited to the situation in Vietnam where the colonial forces had consistently failed to develop appropriate strategy and tactics to deal with the challenge of guerrilla warfare. Navarre's concept was to increase dramatically the number of native Vietnamese troops fighting on behalf of the French, to consolidate south of the eighteenth parallel by the end of the 1953–4 campaigning season and then to switch to offensive action in the north. At the same time he would seek to draw the Viet Minh into large-scale battles where their lines could be decimated by superior French firepower. However, before the policy could have a chance to prove its questionable effectiveness, political changes began to render it obsolete.

THE GENEVA CONFERENCE AND DIEN BIEN PHU

At the Geneva Conference of 1954, talks were to be held in order to reach a peace in Indochina. In theory the French were in favour of a negotiated agreement. French public opinion was weary of the unsuccessful conflict, but Paris was still mindful of the blow to national prestige that an ignominious retreat from Indochina would cause. They therefore tended to waver, secretly holding on to the prospect of US military intervention as an honourable way out. The United States, for their part, were eager to avoid a communist victory but were also keenly aware of the opprobium linked to involving the US in another Asian land war so soon after Korea.

Meanwhile, on the military battlefield events were moving to a climax. Navarre's scheme to engage the Viet Minh in a major, set-piece battle was coming to fruition and the Vietnamese were gradually building up their forces around the French-held garrison of Dien Bien Phu in the mountains of Tonkin. While initial French pronouncements on the probable outcome of the battle were optimistic and they declared the garrision impregnable, an element of caution soon crept in and Navarre conceded that Dien Bien Phu could be lost. Situated in a large valley surrounded by jungle-covered mountains, the garrison was a strategic nightmare and it was not long before Viet Minh forces began to close in. Dien Bien Phu looked as if it might well fall. In response to the rapidly developing crisis in Indochina, the French started to demand US intervention.

Washington stalled. The military emergency forced decisions upon the US which it would rather have avoided. At the very highest level, consideration was given to the possibility of military involvement. Although ultimately redundant, plans were drawn up for an operation, code-named *Vulture,* in which American bombers, flying from bases in the Philippines, would launch a night-time attack on Viet Minh lines surrounding the fortress. The use of tactical nuclear weapons was also debated but discarded.

Caught in a dilemma, the Eisenhower administration did not want to intervene for fear of arousing hostile public opinion. Conversely, Washington did not want to incur the political costs of being seen to abandon an ally to the mercy of the communists. Eisenhower therefore developed an expedient, face-saving tactic. He would demand co-operation and joint action from allied governments as a condition of US intervention whilst knowing that they would be reluctant to comply (Ambrose 1984:177). The scheme meant that the onus for failing to respond to French pleas would not be shouldered by the United States alone and Washington could then make loud and threatening noises in the safety of the knowledge that it would not be required to act.

The Geneva Conference opened against the background of fierce fighting at Dien Bien Phu and the battle overshadowed the entire proceedings. The prospect of a French defeat seemed almost certain. This was important, not because it would have crushed the French and rendered them militarily unable to continue the war, but, instead, because it would have been so psychologically damaging that it would have sapped their very will to fight.

On 7 May, one day before talks on Indochina began at Geneva, Dien Bien Phu surrendered. Two thousand French soldiers were killed in the battle and untold numbers of Viet Minh died in the human wave attacks that had overwhelmed the fortress. At a great cost in terms of lives, the Viet Minh had won a politically momentous victory.

To a significant degree, this victory was not translated into a diplomatic triumph for the Viet Minh at Geneva and the terms of the Accords were significantly less favourable to Ho Chi Minh and his government than might have been expected. This occurred primarily because of Soviet and Chinese pressure. Molotov and Chou en-Lai were genuinely concerned about Washington's sabre-rattling. Here, at least, Dulles' brinkmanship was well calculated and resulted in the two great allies of the Viet Minh persuading the Vietnamese to accept unsatisfactory provisions.

According to the terms of the Geneva Accords, the French were to withdraw from Indochina. Vietnam was to be temporarily divided at the sixteenth parallel and was to be ruled in the north by Ho Chi Minh's Democratic Republic of Vietnam (DRV) and in the south by Bao Dai, pending national elections which were to be held in 1956 and which would unify the country. In the meantime, provision was made for an exchange of prisoners and for those wishing to move from the north to the south, or *vice versa,* to do so. Limits were placed on the extent of foreign military aid to North and South Vietnam and the number of foreign military personnel was frozen at existing levels.

The Accords also made provisions for Laos and Cambodia, where fighting had also led to instability. In Laos, a coalition government was supposed to be formed and the communist forces were assigned a regroupment area. In Cambodia, on the other hand, the revolutionary forces were not recognized nor given an official role in the political future of the country which was to be ruled over by its monarch, Prince Sihanouk.

Significantly, however, no independent body with any meaningful power was established in order to arbitrate disputes arising from Geneva. Although an International Control Commission was set up to monitor the implementation of the Accords, it could not enforce adherence because it lacked the requisite political muscle. Moreover, the United States and the South Vietnamese government even refused to sign the final settlement. In a legal sense the Accords were filled with loopholes—none larger than that created when two of the principal actors in the drama refused to ratify them in total. The Geneva Accords were a failure even before they were implemented.

NGO DINH DIEM AND THE UNITED STATES

The 1954 Geneva Conference was a watershed in the history of Vietnam. It brought the First Indochina War to a close and inaugurated a period in which the US steadily augmented its commitment to the non-communist regime in the South. Until 1963 Washington gave almost unconditional support to the man who came to rule South Vietnam. The recipient of this favour was Ngo Dinh Diem.

Bao Dai had offered Diem the premiership of the soon-to-be-created South Vietnamese government in June 1954 and, consequently, Diem was the head of government when the Accords were concluded at Geneva. Diem remained as prime minister for a little over a year until he decided to free himself of the restricting influence of Bao Dai. In October 1955, in a referendum to decide whether South Vietnam should be a monarchy or a republic, Diem unseated Bao Dai as Chief of State. There was nothing surprising about his victory, although perhaps the scale of his triumph was rather startling. Diem polled some six million votes and Bao Dai a mere 60,000, while in the Saigon-Cholon district a miraculous turn-out afforded Diem the support of 140 per cent of the registered electors. The Republic of Vietnam was thus born and Diem became its president.

The man who had risen to power in Saigon was a long-standing, non-communist, Vietnamese nationalist who had refused to work with either the French or the Viet Minh and who had bided his time until the moment was opportune for him to exercise what he considered to be his destiny to rule. Diem was a Catholic from Hue in central Vietnam. A devout, dignified and scholarly man of considerable intellect, Diem was singularly unable to communicate either with his own people or with his allies. He embodied all the foibles of the traditional mandarin classes. Perhaps seeing himself as a twentieth-century emperor, he evinced a haughty disdain for those beneath him. To make matters considerably worse the president was afflicted with a pronounced persecution complex. He therefore cocooned himself from the outside world, and became unwilling to delegate authority for fear that it might lead to a diminution of his personal power. For a time, this even extended to the point of signing all exit visas himself and personally deciding on the siting of trees in the palace gardens (Fitzgerald 1972:97). The only people he really trusted were his own family and, ultimately, the South

Vietnamese political structure became dominated by an oligarchy increasingly divorced from, and unpopular with, the people it ruled.

Admittedly Diem had significant problems to face upon his accession to power. Many Cochinchinese distrusted his Annamese origin and his Catholic background. He had few men on whom to call to fill his cabinet; those who had experience in government were tarnished with the record of working with the French and those whose political credentials were impeccable had no experience. From North Vietnam, upwards of one million refugees had taken advantage of the provision in the Geneva Accords allowing the transfer of people from one half of the country to the other and their absorption posed a difficult but successfully resolved organizational task for the South Vietnamese Government (GVN).

From Bao Dai and the French, Diem had inherited the problem of strong sects and autonomous organizations whose writ ran throughout large sections of South Vietnam. Indeed, just prior to Diem's take-over of power in 1955, Bao Dai had sold the post of Saigon's Chief of Police to the Binh Xuyen, a band of gangsters, for $1 million. Diem tackled the power of the sects and the vestiges of pro-French factions and his ability to achieve a degree of control over them gave the new ruler credibility and set the seal upon US support for his regime (Smith 1983:46–51).

The Geneva Accords prohibited the South Vietnamese Government from joining a formal military alliance but military aid and the provision of advisers was acceptable providing that they did not exceed the limits set at Geneva. In order to furnish Saigon with the security of belonging to an alliance while still remaining true to the spirit of Geneva, and in order to regain credibility after failing to act over Dien Bien Phu, the US established SEATO (South East Asian Treaty Organization) in 1954. This was a collection of nations which pledged to act in the event of a communist attack in the region. Without being party to SEATO, the GVN was thereby covered by its provisions and the US was safeguarded politically by the acquisition of allies.

Backed by the US, Diem set about consolidating his power. He drafted a new constitution in 1956 which granted him far more powers than the pre-colonial emperors or the French Governor Generals had ever wielded. With this authority he then refused to abide by the Geneva Accords and hold national elections to decide who was to rule the united Vietnam. Diem's refusal to comply owed less to his avowed reason that the North Vietnamese Government (DRV) would rig the election and that the numerical superiority of the North Vietnamese would produce a biased result, than to his realization that any free, nationwide election would have resulted in a sweeping victory for Ho Chi Minh. The US also appreciated this fact and, hence, was at pains to support Diem's decision to repudiate this particular provision of the Accords.

Washington supported Diem primarily because there were few other candidates. Despite Diem's increasingly dictatorial rule the US continued this support. Both presidents Eisenhower and Kennedy steadily increased the US's commitment to the maintenance of the South Vietnamese regime through an expansion in military and economic aid. This aid reached vast proportions and yet it did little to create a viable state in the South since it was used primarily to hold the line against communism rather than to help create better lives for the people.

Diem used US aid to create a vast army and civilian bureaucracy. It did little to endear him to his subjects, but this did not worry him unduly. He did not court public opinion precisely because he did not need to. US money guaranteed him a support base independent of his own people. He even proved insensitive to the importance that the Vietnamese public ascribed to symbolism. Consequently, the flag and the anthem of the new Republic of Vietnam were the same as those of the former, discredited Bao Dai government (Fitzgerald 1972:92).

In a nation in which political control had to be handled with consummate skill, Diem proved to be a disaster. Concerned lest any individual or group should challenge his authority, Diem systematically destroyed virtually all the non-communist political opposition to his rule. Rather than strengthening his position, the tactic merely served to deprive him of allies and to create numerous enemies. Even such unlikely revolutionaries as former French collaborators did not escape his wrath. When in November 1960, eighteen of them, known as the Caravelle group, produced a manifesto denouncing his style of politics and calling for reforms, most were summarily thrown into prison. These were just the sort of people with whom Diem should have been able to construct a powerful anticommunist alliance.

It was the Communist Party and the vestiges of the Viet Minh who had not travelled to North Vietnam under the provisions of the Geneva Accords that suffered most under Diem's repression. But rather than subduing the organization, the GVN's reliance upon force served only to galvanize it into activity. In 1959, under pressure from the southern branch of the Communist Party, the North Vietnamese authorized a resumption of the armed struggle in order to forestall the complete decimation of the revolutionary apparatus. Militant opposition to Diem's rule, which had been growing steadily since 1954, thereafter became an increasingly serious threat to the Saigon regime and, in acknowlegement of the strength of the movement, the National Liberation Front (NLF) was established in 1961 to coordinate and direct the war for the liberation of the South. The revolutionary war had officially begun.

The United States continued to back the GVN in the face of profound and often self-inflicted difficulties. In 1961, Vice President Johnson eulogized Diem, referring to him as 'the Winston Churchill of Asia' (Halberstam 1972:135). Perhaps the level of ignorance concerning Vietnam in the US helped to forestall pertinent questions about Diem's fitness to govern and certainly it was not until 1962 or 1963 that the US public took a great deal of interest in Vietnam. Even so, it would have needed a very blinkered view not to realize, as the 1960s began, that Diem's policies were pushing South Vietnam to the verge of a precipice.

With the exception of his programme to resettle refugees who had fled from the North, Diem's agricultural and pacification programmes were marked by a woeful lack of achievement. Significantly, unlike the Viet Minh who were an outgrowth of, and provided a response to, Vietnam's social crisis, Diem offered no suitable answers to the country's deep-rooted social and economic problems. Land reform should have been high on the list of priorities to be undertaken by any Saigon regime, especially after the success the Viet Minh had achieved as a result of their redistribution of land. The GVN did pass land reform legislation but it was insufficient to the task and few peasants benefited from it.

Diem and his advisers, particularly his infamous brother Ngo Dinh Nhu, realized the importance of separating the South Vietnamese people from communist influence. They therefore chose to embark on a series of militarily-inspired programmes designed to isolate the villages from the outside world. In 1959 this policy found expression in the development of 'agrovilles' and was to reach its apogee with the introduction of the Strategic Hamlet concept. The logic behind these programmes was that the people had to be separated from the National Liberation Front by herding them into concentrated settlements which had fortified perimeters and were defended by local militia. Not only were the programmes inefficiently run and inappropriate in the light of existing settlement patterns, but they were also a great affront to the peasantry. Perhaps it was a blessing in disguise then when it was discovered, in 1963, that the majority of the strategic hamlets existed only on paper and that US aid supplied to build them had been siphoned off by lax and corrupt officials.

Diem inherited a poorly trained and led army which he then proceeded to expand whilst retaining all of its earlier faults. Its weaknesses were compounded by Diem's eagerness to fashion the armed forces and civilian bureaucracies into bodies which would protect him as opposed to ones which could successfully prosecute a war. All the top posts were filled with men whom he believed he could trust, irrespective of whether or not they were the most suitable candidate for the job. This clearly had the effect of improving Diem's personal security at the expense of military and administrative efficiency. Moreover, the entire structure of the armed forces was an administrative nightmare. It was compartmentalized and communication between regional commanders was all but impossible through official channels. All lines of communication ran directly to Diem because, in this manner, he hoped to keep tabs on his officer corps and to forestall any united effort which might threaten his rule.

In its pursuit of political control, the regime consistently abused human rights. Political prisoners filled the jails and an unspecified number were tortured and killed. Press censorship was practised and a wide-ranging political clampdown restricted opposition to the government. Special military tribunals with the power to pass the death sentence were established to judge crimes against the state—for example, sabotage and assassination (Duncanson 1968:234–5)—but these tribunals were allegedly manipulated for questionable political ends.

Under Diem, South Vietnam acquired its own brand of ideology. This was the Personalist philosophy developed by Diem and his brother Nhu from a bewildering variety of sources. They never really gave a definitive interpretation of this vague and muddled philosphy and refused to commit the confused thoughts to paper. In as much as it is possible to define Personalism, it was an ideology based around the primacy of the nation and the community to which individuals, concentrating on inner, spiritual growth, should harness their energies. In 1956, Nhu created the *Can Lao,* the Personalist Labour Party, as the vanguard to spearhead the development of Personalism. In practice, however, it functioned as an avenue for pro-Diem and pro-Nhu officals to gain career advancement and, more significantly, as Nhu's own surveillance body which sought out, monitored and informed upon all those deemed suspicious by the regime.

As the years progressed Nhu showed signs of mental instability and he increasingly emerged as one of Diem's greatest liabilities. Yet the president contined to work closely with his brother, accepting his advice when at times he would listen to no one else. Nhu's wife, the beautiful and viperous Madam Nhu, also played a part on the centre stage of political life in South Vietnam and her caustic tongue gained her a high profile.

When President Kennedy came to office in 1961 it was not Vietnam but Laos that was the focus of interest in Washington. Attention, however, soon switched to Vietnam where opposition to the Diem regime was mounting. Although Kennedy's refreshing and dynamic image created an almost revolutionary break with the staid Eisenhower administration, his policies and the ideas of the young, intellectual 'New Frontiersmen' who advised him, differed more in style than in substance from the old well-worn policies of the Cold War era (Paterson 1978). He held just as firmly to the policy of containment and to strong-arm tactics against the communist threat as his predecessors had done. To add to the imperative of keeping Vietnam and, by inference, the rest of the region free from communism was Kennedy's long-term vision of South East Asia. Specifically, he wanted to maintain enough stability in the area to allow Indonesia and Malaysia, in particular, to develop economically and politically and thereby buttress the region against destabilizing communist subversion (Smith 1985:142-3). Consequently, as the Diem regime came under greater threat, the US expanded its military presence in South Vietnam, especially between 1961 and 1963. Covert operations were initiated against North Vietnam and more American personnel were sent to the South. In the process, the number of advisers outstripped the ceiling placed upon the extent of permissable military aid to South Vietnam laid down in the Geneva Accords. While the American military contingent did not comprise combat troops but only advisers and maintenance experts, in reality US personnel took part in more fighting than their advisory role officially warranted. While in 1960 there were around 875 US advisers in Vietnam, by the time of Kennedy's assassination this figure had soared to over 16,000 (Lewy 1978:24).

The deepening of the US commitment to the GVN was gradual. In October 1961 the president sent his most trusted general, Maxwell D. Taylor, together with a presidential adviser, Walt Rostow, on a mission to investigate the situation in South Vietnam. Their report emphasized that the GVN's confidence had to be boosted by the knowledge of a firm US commitment and that the regime, though weak, could be saved if America was willing to lead the way. The optimism of the main body of the report was contradicted, to an extent, by appendices written by other members of the mission. But rather than heeding their more pessimistic advice, Kennedy gave greater credence to Taylor's upbeat assessment and, while the administration did not provide Saigon with the scale of aid suggested by the report, the US commitment to Diem deepened considerably after the Taylor-Rostow mission. Henceforth, 'limited partnership' were to be the watchwords of the US/GVN relationship.

Washington wanted some significant concessions in exchange for its new level of commitment. In particular, it wanted Diem to undertake some long-overdue reforms, and the aid was made conditional upon real change. Diem characteristically refused to comply. In effect, he called Washington's bluff and won. US aid continued to flow. In practice Washington could exert little pressure over a president who was confident that the only thing that it could threaten him with—the withdrawal of aid—would, in the absence of any alternative to his rule, place serious constraints upon its efforts to 'hold back' communism in Vietnam. Diem could consequently continue his practice of being deaf to the suggestions of American ambassadors and diplomats. His usual response to their entreaties was one of his near-legendary, four or five hour monologues which caused frustrated supplicants to give up with sheer fatigue. Virtually no headway was ever made.

Inevitably the Kennedy administration became exasperated by Diem's unwillingness to comply with their requests. Increasingly, they could see that his popularity was extremely limited and that his policies were alienating the people and providing a welcome fillip to the National Liberation Front which consistently capitalized upon his mistakes. Not all official US reports emanating from South Vietnam were optimistic. A number were extremely pessimistic. Yet, significantly, none questioned the fundamentals of the US role and objectives. They concentrated instead on the feasibility of strategies to achieve them. The two, of course, were entirely different matters.

From the perspective of US policymakers there was no option but to support Diem. If there had been a likely alternative government waiting in the wings they probably would have backed it. In 1960 Washington became aware of a coup to overthrow the president and they did nothing to inform him. The coup failed and the knowledge that the US had had prior warning of the attempt to unseat him did little to lessen Diem's persecution complex and a great deal to magnify the hostility that he felt towards certain Americans, chiefly the press.

Ironically, it was not a political but a religious crisis that initiated the slide that culminated in Diem's downfall. Although Buddhism, in its purer forms, was the religion of a minority in Vietnam, a majority adhered to elements of the Buddhist faith and were its sympathetic supporters. When a crisis therefore ensued between the government and the Buddhists in 1963, many South Vietnamese, despairing of the regime's poor record, began to give support to its new adversary.

The crisis emerged as a result of a relatively minor issue in April 1963, when a dispute arose over the flying of Buddhist flags during a religious holiday. Behind the dispute was the discontent fostered by

Diem's very real discrimination in favour of Catholics and Catholicism. Demonstrations took place and, in Hue, the Civil Guard fired on a group of protestors, killing eight. Notwithstanding the government's efforts to calm the rising tension, the crisis released a flood of anti-Diem feeling throughout the country. On 11 June the first in a series of ritual immolations occurred when a senior Buddhist, Thich Quang Duc, drenched himself in gasoline and set himself alight in a Saigon street in order to protest against the GVN's religious discrimination. Pictures of his self-sacrifice were on the front pages of newspapers all around the world and did much to turn international opinion against the GVN. Madame Nhu did not help matters either when, with characteristic insensitivity, she referred to the suicides as 'barbecues'.

Nhu managed the crisis, not with finesse, but with an iron fist. On 22 August he authorized raids upon pagodas in South Vietnam's major cities during which Buddhist priests were molested. The raids were a catastrophic misjudgement for they galvanized thousands into action. Vast demonstrations filled the streets and the Diem regime came face to face with a hitherto unseen expression of popular outrage.

The Buddhist crisis caught the attention of the United States in a way that no other series of events in Vietnam had done for many years. In Washington, it gave, as one observer stated, a 'peg on which to hang long standing exasperation with Diem and Nhu' (Duncanson 1968:335). Muted but powerful calls also began to be heard for a change in the GVN leadership.

In the White House the crisis prompted a serious debate over the political future of South Vietnam and, in particular, over the US role in encouraging or discouraging a potential coup. By the early autumn, Washington received indications that preparations for a coup were underway within the armed forces, and US representatives were given instructions to encourage the plotters. Their task was aborted, however, because the plans to overthrow Diem were abandoned When, in September, another group of army officers then approached the US for support, the Kennedy administration was more cautious. Firstly, it was mindful of the difficult position that it would find itself in with Diem should it encourage a coup that failed. Secondly, Washington was hesitant because of the dissent within its own ranks. Men such as Frederick Nolting, who had been US ambassador to South Vietnam until August 1963, and General Harkins, the top military man in Saigon, were enthusiastic about Diem and rejected the advisability of a change of government. They warned that there was no alternative to Diem, that the military situation was more positive and should not be destabilized, and that the GVN president, given suitable entreaties, would prove amenable to American wishes. Bearing these points in mind, the US decided that rather than 'encourage' a coup it would 'not thwart' one. The distinction to enthusiastic coup plotters may not have appeared so profound.

Army officers planning to overthrow Diem were informed by a CIA operative that the US would back a successful coup. This promise was vital because it was essential for any prospective government to be assured of American financial support. The GVN was otherwise completely untenable. To reverse the argument, it would have been unlikely, if not impossible, for any group to initiate a coup without securing the promise of future US aid. It is therefore logical to assume that concerted American opposition could have averted Diem's downfall.

The extent to which the US was dirctly responsible for the coup is debatable. Certainly, they did not initiate it. A member of the CIA, Lucian Conein, was present at the headquarters of the armed forces, during the execution of the coup and it is probable that he provided advice to the conspirators (Rust 1985:164). More contentious is the claim made by one of the participants that Conein proffered material support to the coup plotters on a number of occasions (Tran Van Don 1978:98). While it remains arguable whether there was overt US participation in Diem's ousting, few would claim that there was not a degree of complicity. Moreover, when Washington's reluctance to dissuade prospective coup organizers was combined with significant new economic measures in the autumn of 1963, a powerful incentive was given to those hoping to seize an opportunity to overthrow Diem. In order to pressurize the regime to undertake long-postponed reforms, the US put a selective suspension of aid into effect. This decision came at a crucial juncture in South Vietnamese politics and it conveyed an important message to Diem's opponents. The government could no longer count on the unconditional backing of the Americans. Washington may not have considered the suspension of aid to be a green light to a *coup d'état,* but if it did not, it seriously underestimated the degree to which its involvement in South Vietnam conditioned the political process there (Rust 1985:148).

Ngo Dinh Diem was deposed by a coup on 1 November 1963 in which both he and his brother Nhu were murdered. The US did not wish Diem to be killed but, on the other hand, they made no provision for his safety. There was, for example, no plane waiting to fly him out of South Vietnam. This amounted to a 'chilling indifference' to the fate of a man who had been America's ally for almost a decade (Hammer 1987:297). Ironically, Kennedy's assassination took place only three weeks later and it was his successor, Lyndon B.Johnson, who inherited the fast-developing political and military crisis in Vietnam. The coup had done nothing to improve the GVN's capacity to fight a war against the NLF because it opened a Pandora's box of military rivalries which led to a succession of weak and inept juntas. It was not until 1965 that some degree of stability was at last achieved under Generals Ky and Thieu.

One direct consequence of Diem's fall was that it tied Washington even more closely to the fate of the GVN, and many observers and participants in America's Vietnam tragedy claim that it was a crucial decision and one which was ultimately disastrous for the US and its goals in Vietnam (Taylor 1972:302, Kattenburg 1980:119). Having acquiesced in the coup, the US felt a moral obligation to stand by its decision (Taylor 1972:407). Conceivably, Washington could have used the overthrow of Diem to lessen its commitment to the untried regimes that followed. They were, after all, not long-standing US allies in the sense that Diem had been. Once this transitory opportunity had been lost, however, the Americans found themselves 'sucked into the vacuum' following from Diem's overthrow (Hammer 1987:315) and encumbered with an obligation to support a series of disastrous governments.

In the aftermath of Diem's fall the military position of the GVN deteriorated further. The momentum of the NLF's campaign increased and the instability of the post-Diem regimes gave it an added boost. It was in order to forestall an impending military collapse of the GVN that President Johnson then took the decision to escalate the war during 1964 and 1965.

A futile debate later developed over what would have been Kennedy's action, in respect to Vietnam, had he not been assassinated. Specifically, would he have involved the United States in a combat role as his successor did? It has been claimed that Kennedy, on the eve of his murder, was preparing to pull the US out of Vietnam (O'Donnel and Powers 1972:229). A number of Kennedy's admirers, chiefly men who had served him, doubt that he would have committed the US to escalation. On the other hand, a good case can be made for the supposition that Kennedy would have gone down the same path as Johnson, but that he would have done so with more of a flourish and with a good deal more style. Given that his record on foreign policy indicated that he was not averse to confronting communist aggression whenever he perceived it, it has been suggested that he might have sought a means to dramatize the conflict, thus making it a major East-West issue in the manner of the Cuban Missile Crisis (Smith 1985:15–16). This would have given him the opportunity to exercise his brinkmanship in a short but intense emergency situation. Whether this would have proved successful and whether the revolutionary movement in South Vietnam would have heeded the pleas of nervous Soviet,

Chinese and North Vietnamese leaderships remains exceedingly questionable.

There is very little profit to be gained by theorizing over what might have been, and if Kennedy's Vietnam policy is to be judged, it should not be on the basis of supposition over whether he might have pulled the US back from the abyss, but on the basis of his administration's gradual but consistent build-up of US military and political commitment to South Vietnam. It has even been argued that Kennedy bears a large share of the responsibility for America's Vietnam nightmare because he increased the nation's investment in the GVN without taking full measure of the conflict and the potential costs of that investment, and because he failed to take the requisite steps to halt the insurgency before it grew to become an almost insuperable challenge (Podhoretz 1982:63). In Vietnam, he inherited a largely political problem from Eisenhower but he bequeathed a military one to Johnson (Kahin 1986:129). Less controversially, there is room to question Kennedy's judgement over his acquiescence in the removal of Diem. This was particularly questionable as Washington had only scanty knowledge of those who were going to replace him.

Kennedy built upon the commitment of the Elsenhower years and deepened an already intractable problem by allying future US policy with an unknown quantity. Diem may have had his idiosyncracies and he may have made more than his fair share of political blunders, but at least his mistakes were predictable. The new South Vietnamese regimes were not so obliging and the US was left groping in the dark and searching for a native political leadership which could provide the GVN with a modicum of stability. Failing to find any such leadership, the US then substituted its own force of arms.

3 Lyndon B. Johnson and the tragedy of Vietnam

Lyndon Baines Johnson had a burning ambition. He wanted to be remembered as a great president and for his name to rank alongside those of Lincoln and Roosevelt. He hoped to achieve this by legislating into existence a far more caring and liberal society. This aim was of fundamental importance to the way in which his administration conducted the Vietnam War. Tragically, both for LBJ and the American and Vietnamese peoples, the conflict simply overwhelmed his 'Great Society'. The crumbling of his vision of a new America, the failure of the US military to win in South East Asia and the domestic furore that the war caused left Johnson an embittered man. For Vietnam and for thousands of US servicemen, the costs were incalculable.

Sworn in as president of the United States on 22 November 1963, just hours after J.F. Kennedy had been killed by an assassin's bullet in Dallas, Texas, LBJ was conscious that he had achieved office by default. For a year after the assassination, therefore, Johnson presided over a caretaker administration until the 1964 election gave him, in his opinion, the opportunity to become president through his own merit.

Although the manner of his elevation to the presidency was sudden and shocking, Vice President Johnson was particularly well prepared to meet the challenge. As Senate Majority Leader he had transformed a position of little consequence into an office of great influence and prestige. The ease with which he came to handle the Senate was an impressive testimony to his skill as a political intriguer who had a sophisticated understanding of the domestic political scene and of the individuals who moved within it.

The contrast between LBJ and his predecessor could not have been more profound. Kennedy was young, urbane and handsome—a member of cultured circles who was happy in the company of intellectuals and artists. Johnson, relatively uncultured, unattractive and possessing flair for often astonishingly vulgar language, was hewn out of a far rougher stone. Moreover he knew that he lacked many of Kennedy's personal charms and his feeling of inferiority haunted him constantly. Yet, paradoxically, it was Johnson who turned Kennedy's ideas into more than just rhetoric because he enacted policies which went far beyond those that the dead president had envisaged. LBJ embarked on this course because he was a true social reformer—a politician who was committed to building a better kind of society in the USA. This was partly because he felt that he had an obligation to improve the lives of the poor and partly because such good works would enshrine his name in the history books. Consequently, on coming to office he proceeded to push an extensive legislative programme through Congress.

While Johnson was a master of domestic politics, he was neither particularly knowledgeable about, nor interested in, foreign affairs. Diplomacy and the subtleties of international relations were not his forte. Foreign policy did not give him the opportunity to employ the legendary 'Johnson Treatment' and there was none of the eyeball-to-eyeball contact for which Johnson was famous. So instead of managing world affairs through an analytical appraisal of the issues involved, he tended to reduce complex problems to readily understandable formulae and often to view situations as struggles between personalities involved in tests of power (Kearns 1976:195). Basically, Johnson's political experience and perspective left him ill-suited to deal with other nations and many of their leaders remained, in Johnson's opinion, infuriatingly and incomprehensibly immune to either his charm or his blandishments.

Owing to his comparative lack of interest in reordering US foreign affairs, Johnson's Vietnam policy followed the path set by the Kennedy administration. Inheriting the conflict at a time of particular crisis in South Vietnam, LBJ's first foreign policy decision underscored the United States' continued commitment to the GVN. Accordingly in NSAM 273 (National Security Action Memorandum) of 26 November 1963, the new president requested plans for increased covert operations against North Vietnam (Porter 1979:221–3).

Intelligence reports reaching the White House in late 1963 stressed the fragility of South Vietnam. In December, Secretary of Defense Robert McNamara painted a gloomy picture after reviewing the situation at first hand. The prospects appeared bleak indeed and time was fast running out for the GVN. Its support was rapidly evaporating whilst that for the NLF was on the increase. The coup that had overthrown Diem in October 1963 had ushered in a period of great instability and chaos which made seasoned observers look back upon Diem's dictatorship as a era of relative calm and order. The military junta which replaced Diem never managed to establish itself and after a mere four months in power it was overthrown. The power struggles, political manoeuvering and the transitional nature of the governments which followed were confusing even to the well informed

Two themes can be unravelled from this turbulent period. First was the dominance of the military. For the most part, military juntas ruled South Vietnam and even when a civilian government was technically in authority, real power rested with a number of leading generals. Second was the overt involvement of the US in the civilian/military politics of South Vietnam. Concern over the rapidly deteriorating political and military situation led the US to intervene directly in order to maintain or alternatively encourage the accession to power of a suitable regime. As none of the short-lived governments was amenable to American plans, Washington deemed that they could be dispensed with without undue ceremony. When, in 1965, the White House believed that it had a 'cooperative instrument' in the government of Generals Ky and Thieu, great efforts were made to ensure its political stability. Thereafter new coups were unwelcome (Kahin 1979:672–3).

Disorder within the very highest echelons of the GVN gave the NLF further opportunity to extend its influence through South Vietnam. The US-backed regimes lacked the continuity of leadership essential to maintain a much-needed degree of stability and order. With each change of government, new factions came to prominence even at provincial and local levels. The old guard of experienced men was pushed aside in favour of new, more politically acceptable individuals who took time to establish themselves and to become effective leaders. Indicative of the scale of the disruption is the fact that in the few months succeeding the Diem coup, some thirty-five of forty-one incumbent province chiefs were replaced at least once and that all major military command posts had changed hands at least twice (Pentagon Papers Vol. III 1971:52–3).

In March 1964, on a visit to South Vietnam, McNamara estimated that the NLF controlled or partly controlled a massive 40 per cent of the nation's territory, that NLF pressure had been stepped up in the rural areas and that although the conflict was managed by the North Vietnamese, the movement against the US and the GVN remained largely indigenous (Pentagon Papers Vol. III 1971:501). Faced with this deteriorating situation, the administration produced NSAM 288 on 17 March. It was the most comprehensive statement of US objectives in Vietnam produced to that date. Whereas NSAM 273 had confined its aims to the aiding of the GVN, NSAM 288 elevated the importance of the US role in Vietnam. It was now official: Vietnam was crucial to the defence of freedom not only in South East Asia but in the West Pacific as well (Pentagon Papers Vol. III 1971:50).

As his pessimism grew, Johnson began to believe that some form of direct US military action might become necessary in order to prop up the crumbling South Vietnamese regime. The difficulty inherent in such action lay in reconciling Congress and the American public with active participation in the war. In June 1964, the White House began to discuss the possibility of obtaining a congressional resolution supporting US policy in South East Asia. The administration hoped that the resolution, which was subsequently drawn up in draft form, would give it the flexibility to take whatever action it deemed necessary. In particular, it would mobilize Congress and public opinion and pave the way for an expanded US military role in Vietnam. By accomplishing this, the administration would thereby increase the credibility of US power on the international scene and would also send threatening messages warning Hanoi to desist from its support for the insurgents in the South.

In August 1964, a series of events occurred which gave Washington the opportunity to enact its resolution. On 2 August the USS *Maddox*, a destroyer on patrol in the Gulf of Tonkin off North Vietnam, reported being harassed by North Vietnamese patrol boats and that a torpedo had been launched against it. It is highly probable that the North Vietnamese believed that the US ship was involved in amphibious raids by South Vietnamese commandos which had taken place at the end of July. Two days later the *Maddox*, together with another ship, the USS *Turner Joy*, then reported a night time attack by North Vietnamese vessels. Owing to the paucity of evidence, it seems unlikely that these second attacks ever took place. While the reports were not deliberately falsified, bad weather and unusual atmospheric conditions gave rise to an interpretation of natural phenomena, such as thunder and interference on electronic devices, as consistent with an attack. In response to the DRV's aggression, Washington authorized retaliatory air strikes against an oil depot and naval installations in North Vietnam. Labelling the incidents in the Gulf a deliberate provocation, it resolved to use them to ensure that Congress would accept an action-legitimizing resolution. Probably more important than the legitimization of action at this juncture, however, was the thought that the resolution would provide the administration with a means to strengthen support for its Vietnam policy in preparation for the upcoming presidential elections (Pentagon Papers Vol. III 1971:109). Accordingly, three days after the second 'attack' took place, the administration submitted a Joint Resolution to Congress which, in effect, approved in advance 'all necessary steps, including the use of armed force', to assist South Vietnam or any other member or protocol state of SEATO 'in defense of its freedom' (Porter 1979:307). Support for the Resolution was such that it was passed unanimously in the House and by a majority of eighty-two to two in the Senate.

Significantly, however, Johnson took no other action in response to the events in the Gulf of Tonkin. This has led to questioning of the extent to which his controlled reaction may have helped to foster the impression that the US was not eager to use force in Vietnam. In other words, if the first, confirmed incident was Hanoi's way of testing American resolve, Washington's unwillingness to respond with more than a token military showing meant that the US had, in effect, 'lost' the Gulf of Tonkin crisis (Smith 1985:302).

Also on this question of the failure to respond adequately to perceived aggression, another writer has questioned whether US passivity led to the loss of an opportunity to alter the course of the war (Davidson 1988:322). During the first half of 1964 the NLF had launched a series of fairly minor attacks on US personnel and installations. No retaliation was taken for these assaults and even the bombing raids in August were 'surgical'. It was with the knowledge, firstly that the US had been restrained in its military action and secondly that Johnson's presidential campaign speeches indicated no desire to go to war in Vietnam, that the DRV made the momentous decision, some time in August or September 1964, to send North Vietnamese combat troops to fight in the South (Davidson 1988:326–7). Believing that the GVN would be swiftly toppled and also that the US would not intervene in force, Hanoi seized the opportunity to bring the war for the liberation of the South to a speedy and successful conclusion. It was a miscalculation of epic proportions.

The great speed with which the Gulf of Tonkin Resolution was rushed through Congress gives credence to the view that it was inspired, to a great extent, by the immediate demands of electoral politics. This seems especially true as the administration did not act on the Resolution until 1965. In August 1964, Johnson was only three months away from a presidential election in which his rival, the republican candidate, Barry Goldwater, was an ultraconservative, keen to maintain a monopoly on militant anticommunism. By demonstrating his ability and willingness to act positively through the Gulf of Tonkin Resolution, LBJ scored two political points. He illustrated that, like Goldwater, he was prepared to act to preserve American interests in the world and he also showed that he could respond firmly but in a measured way that would not incur the significant dangers associated with Goldwater's sabre-rattling.

In later years Johnson was attacked for allegedly duping the American public into believing that he was a peace candidate in the 1964 elections and that he convinced them, despite his own knowledge to the contrary, that he would not involve the US in a war in Vietnam. It is true that, on occasions, Johnson spoke out against direct US military involvement in South East Asia. But, by and large, the failure of Vietnam to figure prominently in his presidential campaign owed less to Johnson's desire to avoid a sensitive subject than to the fact that Vietnam had not yet assumed the proportions of a major, divisive issue. Moreover, compared to Goldwater, Johnson really was a peace candidate and given that the options open to those wishing to vote for a pro-peace candidate were grossly limited, it is not surprising that their aspirations should have fallen upon Johnson. He was, after all, the best alternative that they had.

The election was a foregone conclusion. Despite his highly variable public image, Johnson had impressed the nation with his handling of the presidency in the transitional period following Kennedy's death. Goldwater, on the other hand, was clearly identified as a right-wing extremist and a totally unsuitable candidate for the Republican party. Consequently, the only question that remained in November 1964 was the margin by which Johnson would win. As expected, his victory was sweeping. After months of nagging doubts, Johnson won the highest proportion of the popular vote ever scored by a presidential candidate and at last he felt that his holding of office was endorsed by the American people.

Following the election, the rapidly deteriorating position of the GVN began to cause alarm in Washington. To many, it appeared that 1965 would witness the demise of the government in the South. But for a time President Johnson delayed taking any firm decision upon Vietnam. In late 1964 and early 1965 his major concern remained the implementation of a wide range of social programmes designed to build the 'Great Society'. Action in Vietnam, he concluded, would merely distract from important developments at home. But as the situation in Saigon worsened, Johnson had no option but to make important decisions about the future role of the US in South East Asia.

On 7 February NLF forces attacked a US helibase at Pleiku, killing eight Americans. The US responded immediately, carrying out air strikes against North Vietnamese barracks and staging areas just north of the Demilitarized Zone (DMZ) which formed the dividing line between North and South Vietnam. The operation, code-named *Flaming Dart*, was a reprisal specifically for the Pleiku attack but it soon paved the way for a more regular bombing campaign. This new programme, named *Rolling Thunder*, was described as a response, not to an isolated incident, but to an entire programme of aggression conducted by the revolutionary movement. In this way the whole reprisal strategy was broadened so that, by mid-March, *Rolling Thunder* was transformed into a regular and sustained operation.

The decision to begin the bombing of North Vietnam was motivated by a number of interrelated factors. It was not simply a response to the Pleiku incident. The NLF had attacked an airbase at Bien Hoa and had killed several Americans four months earlier but this action had elicited no response, probably as it came only days before the US presidential elections. The bombing of North Vietnam had been advocated very forcefully on a number of occasions in Washington and McGeorge Bundy had even suggested 'sustained reprisal' along the lines of *Rolling Thunder* prior to the attack at Pleiku (Porter 1979:349–357). But what motivated the administration to implement the suggestions at that moment was the near collapse of the GVN. By bombing, the US believed that it could hinder the North Vietnamese war effort, and, just as importantly, could buoy up the sagging morale of the GVN.

America's military leaders, the Joint Chiefs of Staff (JCS), argued for intensive and extensive air strikes which would totally disable the DRV and stop it from sponsoring the war in the South. Civilian policymakers, in contrast, tended to agree with the president that a slow and steady escalation of bombing was inherently safer. Firstly, it would not arouse a war fever in the US. The president wanted to avoid this at all costs because he believed that it would lead to public pressure to conduct an all-out war which would then necessitate economic stringency measures and thus endanger his beloved 'Great Society'. Secondly, the policy would not carry such a high risk of drawing China or the Soviet Union into the conflict. Indeed, such was Johnson's concern to avoid a wider war that he kept a tight control over the scope and intensity of the bombing, personally authorizing the selection of targets in weekly and later bi-weekly packages. As he once half joked, the JCS were not allowed to bomb an out-house in Vietnam without his express permission (Westmorland 1980:153).

Johnson later claimed that by fighting in Vietnam the US was preventing a third world war (Johnson 1972:147–8). The disastrous consequences of the policy of appeasement in the 1930s certainly played an important role in defining LBJ's perspective on this issue and in early 1965 he acted according to his beliefs. In his memoirs, he outlined what he believed would have been the consequences of an American failure to act in Vietnam. South East Asia would, following the logic of the domino theory, have fallen to communism. A divisive debate, far more damaging than that of the McCarthy era, would then have ensued in the US, in time creating isolationist pressure and causing the US to pull back from its commitments in Europe and the Middle East. Finally, US prestige would have been irreparably damaged and her allies would have believed her word to be worth nothing (Johnson 1972:151-2).

It was with these ideas in mind that Johnson authorized the deployment of the first American ground forces in Vietnam. *Rolling Thunder* had not forced Hanoi to stop supporting the war and the GVN seemed poised to disintegrate both politically and militarily. On 8 March 1965, two marine battalions arrived at Danang, charged with the task of protecting the US installation there. They were not in Vietnam ostensibly to fight. Johnson's decision to send the troops has, in retrospect, been seen as an action of great magnitude—a watershed in the history of American participation in the Vietnam War. At the time, however, it was not perceived as such by the Johnson administration. They did not view it as a significant departure and the decision was taken without very much discussion and planning (Pentagon Papers Vol. III 1971:433). The GVN, despite official US pronouncements that American troops had been invited into South Vietnam, was not even consulted and the deployment created little more than a ripple at home.

Under great pressure from the military, the role of US troops began to alter within a matter of weeks. On 6 April, NSAM 328 authorized a 'change of mission for all marine battalions deployed in Vietnam to permit their more active use...'. This approval of action which would involve US troops directly in the fighting, albeit in defence of and within a short radius of US bases, deepened the American commitment to Vietnam and made NSAM 328, in the words of the Pentagon Papers, a 'pivotal document' (Pentagon Papers Vol. III 1971:447). The move towards greater involvement was further accelerated in June when General Westmoreland, the commander of US forces in Vietnam, was given presidential approval to use American troops in support of South Vietnamese forces if and when the situation should warrant it (Pentagon Papers Vol. III 1971:472).

Despite the increased commitment to the war, Johnson was convinced that South Vietnam would collapse without a greater input of US military assistance. He thought that to withdraw would be political suicide and yet to stay in Vietnam would require the United States to escalate the war. Complicating the decision for the president was the current state of his Great Society. Important legislation was locked in crucial debates in Congress and LBJ was loathe to declare a war and risk derailing the proposals (Berman 1982:128). He therefore wanted to find a compromise policy which would meet the immediate challenge by doing the minimum necessary to forestall an NLF victory but which would, at the same time, avoid upsetting the political apple cart at home.

The key to the success of the plan would be Johnson's ability to keep the war low-key in the public mind and to build a consensus for his Vietnam policy within the adminstration and within society at large.

Johnson set about moulding the consensus within the adminstration very cleverly. Secretary of Defense McNamara was sent to Vietnam in July in order to review the options open to the US. His report outlined what he considered to be America's three alternatives. One was to 'cut our losses and withdraw'—an option which he described as 'humiliating' to the US. The second was to 'continue at about the present level', with the prospect that the US would have to choose between withdrawal and escalation at some later date. The third and final option, and the one which McNamara recommended, called for the US to expand its military commitment 'promptly and substantially' as this alternative offered 'a good chance of producing a favourable settlement in the long run' (Porter 1979:385–91). McNamara recommended that the troop level should rise from 75,000 to 175,000 and that the bombing of North Vietnam should be increased.

This was exactly what the president wanted. In the debate that followed, Johnson did not mislead his advisers or browbeat them into submission in order that they accept McNamara's recommendations. He did not have to do this. Instead he manipulated the debate so well, increasingly restricting the parameters of the discussion so that individuals were channelled into accepting a single course of action. Those who opposed escalation were given opportunity to speak. However, there was no adequate analysis of their views and this constricted the options available and made it easier to forge a consensus which gave the president's policies a degree of legitimacy not only within the adminstration but also outside it (Berman 1982:152). Johnson knew what his actions would be before the debate and even before McNamara went on his mission and so he used the discussions, not for advice and help in the formulation of policy, but instead for political ends. Consequently, the advisory process was only 'incidental' to the making of real decisions on Vietnam (Berman 1984:21).

Challenging this interpretation is a view which sees Johnson as a kind of administration dove whose advisers did not give him adequate alternatives to escalation, as they failed to distinguish between their personal prestige and careers and what was good policy for the United States (Kahin 1986:245). However, given LBJ's renowned ability to control his advisers, his passion for the Great Society and the belief that it could be damaged by a backlash if he failed to act in Vietnam, this interpretation, although persuasive, does not appear as convincing.

Whilst Johnson was pursuing a war in South East Asia, he was trying to fulfil his plans for a Great Society at home. 'I was determined to be a leader of war and a leader of peace', he said later (Kearns 1976:283) and the war was always conducted with the domestic situation in mind. It was this emphasis upon 'guns and butter' that has been cited as one of the principal factors contributing to America's lack of success in Vietnam. Critics, particularly within the military, have claimed that the US would have stood a better chance of winning if Johnson had been prepared to make political sacrifices, declare war and so commit Americans psychologically and emotionally to the war in Vietnam (Summers 1982:11–33, Davidson 1988:810, Palmer 1984:189–90).

Instead, Johnson thought that a prosperous US could afford to wage war and to finance an ambitious domestic social programme simultaneously. On the one hand he was convinced that the war had to be fought but on the other hand he did not want it to threaten what he hoped would be his key to the pantheon of history. He feared that if the nation was put on a war footing, all hope of creating the Great Society would founder upon a 'right wing stampede' (Kearns 1976:280). Consequently, he refused to declare a state of emergency, to request higher taxes to fund the fighting or even to announce that the United States was officially at war. Moreover, Johnson consistently ignored the requests of the military to authorize a full-scale call-up of the reserves. As a result, the total number of men that the Joint Chiefs of Staff could commit to Vietnam was limited. By mobilizing the reserves Johnson would have given tacit recognition to the Vietnam conflict as a real war. Therefore the point at which mobilization would become necessary was of great significance in setting the parameters which defined the extent of the US role in South East Asia. As one analyst has argued, the issue of mobilization dictated the entire formulation of America's Vietnam policy (Schandler 1977:56).

Johnson trod this middle path not because he was unsure or hesitant and unable to decide between the pursuit of the war or the creation of the 'Great Society'; he '*chose* not to choose' between the two. It was, perhaps, LBJ's 'greatest fault as a political leader' (Berman 1982:150).

The desire to conduct what was, in all essence, a full-scale war by covert means led the Johnson administration to tell Congress and the public no more than was absolutely necessary and, quite frequently, to embellish reports of success. LBJ had a keenly felt need to maintain a consensus of opinion because he believed that an appeal to all constituencies was the best way to sustain his political support. So, in an endeavour to maintain equilibrium at home, he sought to satisfy, at least partially, both the pro-war and antiwar lobbies. This even applied to the policy of gradually escalating the bombing of North Vietnam. Supporters of the war would be placated by the prospect of continually increasing US action, while those opposed to the war would be consoled, in some measure, by seeing that the administration was exercising a degree of restraint. The strategy was Johnson's idea of consensus politics applied to the fighting of a war. Concerned in case war fever gripped the popular imagination, he made only a half-hearted attempt to rally the people around the cause of the war. Despite his undoubted political acumen he failed to appreciate that wars are rarely won without an attempt to arouse a nation's emotions and its will to fight.

At intermittent intervals between 1965 and 1967, Johnson authorized pauses in the bombing programme. These pauses must be seen in the light of this search for consensus. The two longest pauses lasted from 12–17 May 1965 and the second for a longer period lasting from 25 December 1965 to 31 January 1966. Ostensibly these pauses were authorized in the hope of encouraging the DRV to agree to negotiations to end the war. They would illustrate the White House's good faith and would push Hanoi into discussions because it feared a resumption of the bombing. In reality, however, the US administration expected no real move to be made towards negotiations. Indeed, Washington was actually opposed to negotiations on the grounds that the US was in fact winning militarily and that it would only be a matter of time before the NLF and North Vietnam were defeated.

Until 1968, bombing pauses were simply a matter of posturing. World opinion was a consideration and Washington was concerned not to be cast in the role of a vicious, superpower bully hammering a defenceless little North Vietnam into oblivion. More important, however, was US domestic opinion. By interrupting the bombing and proposing negotiations, the administration pandered to those critics, generally called 'doves', who wanted to see an end to the war and who objected, to varying degrees, to US action in Vietnam. On the other hand, when Hanoi refused to respond to American pleas for negotiation, the US was given an admirable justification for resuming the bombing on an even greater and more intensive scale. It could thus appeal to the demands of the pro-war constituency, who were generally known as Hawks'.

Washington concluded, correctly, that it would have to substitute its own forces for those of the GVN if the regime was to be saved from certain defeat. The South Vietnamese government and armed forces were too weak to stand on their own so America had to fight their war for them. That it would have been preferable for the GVN to fight its own battles was obvious. Having a vast American presence in the country did little to enhance the GVN's credibility as an independent, sovereign government. What Washington intended was to subdue the military threat to the GVN, whereupon Saigon could then set about solving its own political problems. In the words of the Pentagon Papers it would mean 'a massive US effort in the short-run leading to and enabling a GVN effort in the long-run' (Pentagon Papers Vol. II 1971:284). But what the administration had not bargained on was the size of the military commitment needed to achieve this objective.

A vast number of US troops were sent to Vietnam. At its height, in spring 1969, the US military presence totalled almost 550,000 men. During the 1960s many who sympathized with the NLF claimed that North Vietnamese troops were first sent into South Vietnam as a reaction to this American troop build-up. This was not true. The decision was made to deploy North Vietnamese soldiers in autumn 1964 and the first complete unit, a regiment of the 325th Division, left for the South soon after (Karnow 1984:401). When US combat units arrived in Vietnam in March 1965 there were already around 5,800 North Vietnamese regulars in the South (Lewy 1978:38–40). What the arrival of the US troops prompted, however, was a further escalation. The DRV matched each expansion of US forces by expanding the number of its own units.

American military leaders never had any doubt that they could defeat the North Vietnamese and their southern compatriots. Their faith in technology was unbounded. Morally and technically they were superior. Affluent, advanced America could not lose its first war (Baritz 1985:44–51). But this war was annoyingly different to those in military textbooks. There were no front lines and so how could anyone tell who was winning? There were thus few concrete ways of determining how the war was developing and a good deal of room for vastly differing interpretations.

Reports from the military in the field were generally upbeat. They told of the number of enemy soldiers killed and how many tons of bombs had been dropped. According to military logic these statistics meant that the US *had* to be winning. Others were not so sure. Critics argued that an understanding of Vietnamese culture and politics and not an ability to count dead bodies was the only way to comprehend what was going on in Vietnam. Once this was understood, it then became clear that the US military, contrary to what it might like to tell the people back at home, had not got the NLF on the run. Indeed, the NLF appeared to be doing alarmingly well.

Some reports that emanated from Vietnam and from analysts in Washington were pessimistic. The overwhelming number were written by civilians who increasingly gave an interpretation of events that was out of line with what the military was saying and, in some cases, flatly contradicted it. The CIA, in particular, produced some pertinent analyses (Cooper 1972:223–36). The administration, nevertheless, tended to overlook pessimistic reports in its search for reassurance.

There were always a few individuals within the administation who doubted America's policy in Vietnam. Under-Secretary of State, George Ball, was an early dissenter. In 1965, during the debate over escalation, Ball had made plain his disquiet. 'Politically, South Viet-Nam is a lost cause,' he stated in a memorandum. The US, he declared, would be making a 'catastrophic error' in pursuing its interventionist policy because 'Hanoi has a Government and a purpose and a discipline. The "government" in South Viet-Nam is a travesty' (Pentagon Papers Vol. IV 1971:22–3). His remarks were prescient—and ignored.

As the war dragged on, more people within the government began to move into the camp of the dissenters. In February 1966, Robert McNamara, the Secretary of Defense, began to display the first obvious signs of disquiet (Karnow 1984:498) and by early 1967 a division over strategy had emerged within the Johnson administration. On the one hand there were the hard-liners, mainly military men together with a few civilians like Walt Rostow, special adviser to the president, who supported a tougher line. On the other hand there were a number of sceptics including McNamara, some of his civilian aides at the Pentagon, some State Department officials and analysts within the CIA who were increasingly unhappy with pursuing the familiar strategy.

In particular, controversy centred on the bombing of North Vietnam. The sceptics insisted that this was having little impact upon the DRV's capacity to wage war in the South and that it should be curtailed. Counterposing their argument were the military who maintained that bombing was productive and that it was providing essential support to US troops in the South. Johnson, the key figure, sided with the JCS in the controversy but the coalition of doubters grew ever larger with each new escalation in the intensity of the air war and the consequent realization that it had not achieved the desired effect (Thompson 1980:52–65).

Johnson's style of leadership, however, did not facilitate the articulation of dissent. Whilst many of the president's advisers and assistants admired him, others deplored his tendency to browbeat his staff into submission and complained that he rarely allowed them to voice opinions which were opposed to his own fiercely-held ideas. By the sheer force of his personality, Johnson could compel his assistants to agree with him, and the handful of dissenters who emerged to raise doubts about the conflict were jettisoned from discussions on the formulation of policy. The fundamental strategy employed by the US was not seriously questioned and debate was restricted to the best way to pursue current strategy. Johnson was dismissive of alternative interpretations of US progress in the war and gradually he limited his circle of advisers on Vietnam to a select few who met each Tuesday lunchtime to discuss current operations.

The president's personal style led to a 'closed' as opposed to an 'open' system of decision making (Cooper 1971:416). He thought he could maintain some freedom of action by limiting information to a privileged number. Even the debates of the Tuesday Lunch Group were so secret that there was no agenda and no minutes were taken (Cooper 1971:414–15). The president exerted tight control over the conflict and no Vietnam 'high command' was created to oversee and coordinate the war. It has been claimed that this failure to reorganize the bureaucratic structure arose because most people thought that the war would be over quickly and that the disruption was therefore not justified (Cooper 1971:423–5). Perhaps it was also due to the fact that Johnson wanted to feel in complete control. If the war was serious enough to threaten his Great Society, then only he was sufficiently capable of handling it.

McNamara's disenchantment was a blow to the president. He took it especially hard as his Secretary of Defense had been one of the principal architects of United States' policy in Vietnam. By 1967 McNamara's dissatisfaction with the conduct of the war was becoming a source of increasing friction with the JCS, who were confident that the war was being won. It is unclear whether pressure from the military hierarchy forced Johnson to fire McNamara or whether McNamara tendered his resignation. Whatever the case, in November 1967 it was announced that McNamara was leaving to become president of the World Bank.

By 1967 the drain on the US economy caused by three years of war was all too apparent. The steady build-up of troops in Vietnam and the vast expenditure on a war budget which amounted to a colossal $20.6 billion dollars in FY 1967 was too much of a strain for a peace-time economy to withstand. The budgetary crisis which revealed itself stemmed directly from Johnson's decision to conduct the war whilst making no sacrifices at home. Taxes were not raised and public spending controls were not introduced To exacerbate the problem, expenditure on the war had been vastly underestimated. The result was a rise in inflation. Johnson's critics claimed that he knew of the potential costs of the war but that he misrepresented and even lied about the costs to Congress and to his own advisers in order to avoid taking harsh financial measures (Halberstam 1972:603–10). It is more likely, however, that the economic mess in which the administration found itself was the result of a misjudgement of the vast outlays that the war would demand and, most importantly, of a misreading of the way in which the economy was functioning and would respond to the war (Kettl 1987:67–72). In a move that came far too late to mitigate the harmful effects of his earlier inaction, Johnson announced a 6 per cent (later raised to 10 per cent) surcharge on personal and corporate taxes in his State of the Union message in 1967. It took a full eighteen months, however, before the tax increases could be pushed through a highly intransigent Congress. To many observers it appeared that Johnson was losing his war both at home and abroad.

LBJ's poor relations with the media made a significant contribution to the erosion of domestic support for the war. Although the 'credibility gap', as a phrase, began to come into common parlance in 1965, Johnson set about creating it almost as soon as he came to office. A dichotomy existed between what the administration said about Vietnam and what was actually happening. Washington's reports on progress in the war were consistently more optimistic than the situation warranted and whilst this strategy worked for some time in muting significant discontent, it was inevitable that the strategy, resting as it did on precarious foundations, would one day prove to be a liability.

A large minority of the American public began to doubt official pronouncements when it appeared that the war was not only proving to be a vast drain upon resources but also that the anticipated victory was nowhere in sight. During 1966 and 1967, there was a steady loss of support both for Johnson and for his handling of the Vietnam issue. The antiwar movement nevertheless was a minority movement and appeared to be strong only because its members were extremely vocal. The major part of the American public, whilst increasingly unhappy with Johnson's handling of the war, still felt committed to a fighting role in South East Asia.

Despite the lack of any real threat which the antiwar protestors posed, Johnson was sensitive to criticism of his Vietnam policy. He thought the criticism treacherous, cowardly and, later, as part of a giant conspiracy to undermine him and shatter his highly prized consensus (Goldman 1969:500). Although the picture is perhaps exaggerated, a biographer who interviewed Johnson after his retirement from politics, portrayed him as a man slipping into a world of fantasy and illusion where he alone was pitted against a host of enemies and where he could barely trust some of his own advisers (Kearns 1976:315–17).

Opposition to Johnson's presidency existed even within his own party. Many people were opposed to the war not because they thought it morally wrong but because they could not see any end to it. In a reflection of Johnson's growing unpopularity, Senator Eugene McCarthy announced, in November 1967, that he would be standing for nomination as the Democratic candidate in the 1968 presidential election. Although his chances of defeating Johnson were exceedingly slim, his announcement indicated just how far the president's popularity had slipped as a result of the war.

Unfavourable media reporting on the conflict became more frequent during 1967 and the administration was faced with criticism from many quarters. There were fewer influential people in the media, or in politics, who gave wholehearted support to the United States' Vietnam policy. Some called for a greater effort to wipe out the NLF and to defeat the North Vietnamese government once and for all and others wanted to stop the bombing and to reach a settlement with the enemy.

By 1967 the war was costing the lives of 816 American soldiers each month (Lewy 1978:73). It was disrupting the economy and was creating division and strife unparalleled in twentieth-century America. Johnson agonized over these facts and struggled to maintain a grip on the nation. But despite a concerted public relations campaign to improve the image of American participation in the war, dissent could not be silenced. A four-man team was set up specifically to provide information for the public relations campaign, but the credibility gap was such that those who opposed the government no longer believed in its pronouncements. In the autumn of 1967 an ambitious propaganda plan to quell the rising tide of disquiet was launched and the US military commander in Vietnam claimed that there was light at the end of the tunnel. Whilst the campaign did not win any new adherents to the government's cause it probably cheered the majority of the population, who continued to support Johnson's war policy and, hence, maintain his shaky consensus. Their support for Johnson's handling of the war was vital and his precarious consensus was balancing on a knife edge at the end of 1967. It only took the events of January and February 1968 to shatter it entirely.

THE TET OFFENSIVE

The Tet Offensive, so called because it took place during Tet, the Vietnamese New Year holiday, was a turning point in the war. On the night of 30–1 January 1968, NLF forces launched a major surprise attack against cities, towns and military installations throughout South

Vietnam. Some thirty-six of the forty-four provincial capitals were attacked and ten were seized temporarily in the most daring and bloody campaign of the war. In Saigon there was a series of separate attacks. Amongst the targets were the presidential palace, the headquarters of the South Vietnamese Armed Forces, the Tan Son Nhut Air Base and the US embassy. The abortive assault upon the embassy by a National Liberation Front suicide squad became a focal point for the world's attention, and although the attack was repelled within a matter of hours the enemy still succeeded in penetrating almost to the heart of the poorly defended embassy. Psychologically the assault was a dramatic affront to American prestige in Vietnam. But despite the early pessimistic reporting of the offensive, and despite its scale, it was, in fact, quickly thwarted in all but Hue, the ancient city of northern South Vietnam. There the NLF seized control of the city and it was not until the end of February that it was retaken by US and GVN forces.

The Tet Offensive did not come as a total surprise to the US and GVN Armed Forces. Intelligence reports had indicated that a major enemy action was likely, but as General Westmorland later confessed, not only was the extent of the offensive unknown but so was its exact timing and the fact that its major targets would be in the cities (Westmorland 1980:413–23, Davidson 1988:479). As Tet was a national holiday and traditionally a time for a cease-fire to be declared, Westmorland thought it an unlikely occasion for the attack. The date of the offensive had been kept secret in North Vietnam but for months public announcements and newspaper articles had been informing the people that decisive and momentous events were soon to occur. The question, therefore, was why the US and GVN were not fully prepared for the scale of the offensive. This tactical error had three main causes (Oberdorfer 1971:119). Firstly, there was bureaucratic inertia. Many of those who should have taken steps to tackle the impending crisis failed to do so because they were unaware of its potential magnitude. Secondly, red alerts were needlessly common and had bred something of an air of indifference. Finally, the prospect that an attack was looming on the horizon would have demanded a dramatic response, causing plans to be drastically altered and forcing often complacent leaders, particularly within the South Vietnamese Armed Forces, to do rather more work than they would otherwise have wished.

As the date of the offensive approached, many US officials became anxious and feared that an attack was imminent. They therefore cancelled the Tet holiday cease-fire in certain areas. The South Vietnamese, however, were reluctant to follow suit and it was not until the very eve of the offensive that a partial cancellation of leave was authorized for GVN troops. Under these circumstances, it is likely that the offensive would have been considerably more successful had it not been for a tactical blunder committed by the NLF. It is probable that the offensive had been scheduled for 29 January and that, for some reason, it was postponed for a day. The message clearly failed to get through to the NLF commander in the northern provinces because his forces struck a day earlier. It thus gave the US/GVN leadership a few precious hours to organize a better defence.

Despite the dramatic impact of the Tet Offensive, it was a military disaster for the revolutionary forces. Thousands were killed. Estimates of the dead were put as high as 45,000 (Davidson 1988:475) and very little territory was seized and held on more than a temporary basis. Ironically, however, Tet proved to be an important episode in the war as a result of its impact in the United States. For the first time it emphasized to the American public that, despite their government's claims, they were not winning in Vietnam. In fact, it appeared that they were losing. Pictures of the fighting were relayed on to American television screens. People were shocked to see NLF forces attacking the US embassy in Saigon and to see a force that they had been told was on the retreat organizing such a breathtaking offensive. No matter that it eventually lost the engagements, the enemy had won a significant battle in the living rooms of the United States.

Shock and anger prompted many individuals to support the war in a fit of patriotic fervour. Then, as disillusionment set in, some came to oppose it for the first time (Roper 1977:674–704). While opposition to the conflict had been growing steadily throughout 1966 and 1967, prior to Tet, a majority still supported the war. Tet temporarily decreased and then subsequently increased opposition so that a slim majority then became critical of Johnson's handling of the war and of his performance as president in general (Roper 1977:674–704). This swing in public opinion was very small but it tipped the balance and was probably made more acute, coming, as it did, hard on the heels of the administration's big public relations drive on the war late in 1967. It did not help matters either when, in the midst of the fighting, administration officials and the military in Vietnam reiterated the same well-worn assurances that the US had the enemy in a corner. It was hard to avoid the impression that the rhetoric was a web of deceit spun by the Johnson administration to hide its failure in Vietnam.

If Johnson had been more honest about the war right from the start and had not allowed the credibility gap to develop, it is probable that the Tet crisis would not have created such a storm. Perhaps people would have seen that, as a result of the dramatic events, the US and GVN had been able, for the first time, to fight more conventional battles, to engage the enemy in a situation in which they could utilize their vast firepower and, as a result, to score some notable military successes.

The administration's initial reactions to the Tet Offensive were not surprising. More men and more money were prescribed. This was an almost inevitable response, especially as global East-West tensions had recently intensified. A US intelligence ship, the *Pueblo,* and its crew had been seized by the North Koreans at the end of January and there were problems in Berlin and the Middle East. Johnson was therefore anxious to head off what seemed to be a giant communist pincer movement. Consequently, the president offered Westmoreland whatever extra forces he deemed necessary to deal with the Tet crisis.

Westmoreland found himself in a difficult position. He did not want to seem too eager for a significant increase in troop strength as it would make his earlier statements about success in the war look poorly judged and unprofessional. Moreover, the men were simply not necessary because the enemy's manpower resources were greatly depleted after the ferocity of the offensive. On the other hand, the JCS were pressurizing Westmoreland to put in a request for a dramatic increase in troop strength. In particular, General Earle Wheeler, Army Chief of Staff, saw the Tet Offensive as an event shocking enough to force the president to end his ban on mobilization of the reserves. This would remove the sticking point which had always limited the number of men available to the military (Schandler 1977:99–102). In order to fight the war in Vietnam, the armed forces stationed elsewhere in the world had been stripped of much of their most experienced leadership and many of their most highly skilled men. In the US, the strategic reserve had been steadily eroded, thereby creating justifiable concern over the military's capacity to quell a major outbreak of civil unrest (Davidson 1988:497). The JCS reasoned that if Westmoreland requested an increase in troop strength of some 205,000 men, Johnson would be forced to authorize a mobilization which would thereby restore the strength of the armed forces. Wheeler and Westmoreland decided that the request for over 200,000 men was not to be designated exclusively for Vietnam, except in the case of a rapidly deteriorating situation. However, in order to get the request approved, General Wheeler painted a gloomy and pessimistic picture of the situation in South East Asia, from which the inference was drawn that the entire request was destined for Vietnam (Schandler 1977:115–16). The military were trying to back Johnson into a corner by forecasting dire consequences should he fail to reverse his decision on the mobilization of the reserves. It was a calculated move and one which ultimately backfired because it led directly to the diminution of the US military role in Vietnam.

Johnson was shocked by the size of the troop request and his response was to set up a task force to investigate the matter. It was headed by Clark Clifford, the highly respected lawyer who was shortly to take over McNamara's job as Secretary for Defense. Following McNamara's disloyal scepticism and his subsequent fall from grace, the president wanted a Secretary of Defense who would agree with him on the fundamentals of his Vietnam policy and who would be able to supply some new, bright ideas. Clifford fitted the bill perfectly as he was generally considered to be a hawk and yet could offer a new perspective as he had not been living with the conflict day in and day out as had Johnson's other advisers (Johnson 1972:392). It was perhaps surprising then that Clifford later wrote that he had begun to be disillusioned with the conflict during late 1967 when he went on a diplomatic mission to visit America's allies. None of them—including many of the so-called 'dominoes' which would fall should South Vietnam collapse—was willing to increase its commitment to the war (Clifford 1969:606–7). For a time he kept his doubts to himself and it was only when he began to investigate the troop request that Clifford became convinced that US policy in Vietnam was heading for disaster. A number of lower-echelon administration officials were anxious to convey their own worries to the new Secretary and so they informed him of the massive impact that the troop request would have upon the already strained US economy and that the prospects for success in Vietnam would still be limited. Listening to their assessments Clifford began to doubt that even 205,000 more men would be enough to ensure victory in Vietnam.

The formal report of the Clifford Task Force, presented on 4 March 1968, nevertheless recommended no fundamental change in strategy. It was basically a compromise between the rival viewpoints held by the JCS and the civilians in the Defense Department. It called for an additional 22,000 military personnel to be sent to Vietnam, provided for a call-up of reserve forces and gave tentative approval at least to the idea of the troop request. While expression of the need to commence in-depth discussions on basic strategic questions was confined to an appendix, much of the report was couched in a manner likely to provoke the president into surveying the wider questions of the war and it was controversial enough to shake Johnson's long-held assumptions.

LBJ was troubled by the Task Force's report, and by the middle of March it was clear that he was not about to authorize the 205,000 man troop request which had been revealed and loudly denounced by the press. The only additional force to be sent to Vietnam was a contingent of 13,500 troops to support the reinforcements deployed immediately after the Tet Offensive. On 22 March, in what was widely interpreted as the harbinger of a new strategy, Johnson announced personnel changes. The most important of these was that Westmoreland was to vacate his post in Vietnam during the summer to become Army Chief of Staff.

Despite the portentous decision not to deploy the 205,000 man troop request, Johnson had not abandoned his established Vietnam policy. Secretary of State, Dean Rusk, was, by early March, pushing forward a new tactic which LBJ found attractive. Rusk believed that the North Vietnamese would respond only to greater military pressure. The main problem was to regain the confidence of the American public and to convince them that such action was justifiable. He believed that a bombing halt would accomplish just this (Schandler 1977:237–40). If the North Vietnamese responded to the pause then Johnson would be seen as a peacemaker, and if Hanoi failed to respond, as was more likely to be the case, the US could thereby resume the bombing on an even greater scale after making it clear to its own domestic critics that it had made sincere efforts to arrive at a peaceful solution. Moreover, as it was the monsoon season in North Vietnam, it meant that few sorties could have been flown irrespective of a bombing halt and therefore the US would lose very little military advantage by pursuing this initiative. Clifford, together with civilians in the Defense Department, realized that Rusk's proposal was merely setting the stage for further escalation and a continuation of the war and they consequently opposed it (Schandler 1977:242).

Clifford anxiously sought a means by which to force Johnson to see his Vietnam policy in perspective. That opportunity came at the end of the month when Clifford encouraged Johnson to convene a meeting of the 'Wise Men'. In an attempt to assuage his doubts and to seek confirmation of his policies, Johnson turned to people whom he believed he could trust implicitly. Seeking encouragement, he solicited the views of a group of highly respected and influential elder statesmen. LBJ had sought their advice only four months previously when, still having faith in the US role in Vietnam, they had endorsed the president's policy. But by the end of March when they met again in Washington, many among them had changed their minds. A majority of the 'Wise Men' had come to disapprove of their country's strategy in South East Asia and of its traumatic implications at home. LBJ was shattered by their reversal of opinion and by the lack of consensus amongst them, especially as it came in the wake of the Clifford Report and from men whose integrity he did not question. Faced with this overwhelming indictment of his Vietnam policy, Johnson took a mammoth psychological step and began to review policies which he had clung to so tenaciously, in the face of daunting criticism, for four years.

With the great weight of opinion leaning towards finding a way out of Vietnam, Johnson reviewed his options. These options were limited because he did not want to acknowledge that America could not win in Vietnam nor that the basic premise upon which US involvement was based was inherently faulty. Convinced, at long last, that the cost of bombing North Vietnam in terms of domestic and international opinion far outweighed any advantage to be gained from it, Johnson decided to curtail the programme. It would be a significant peace offering to the DRV and, he reasoned, if necessary he could always fall back on Rusk's plan and resume the bombing.

It was at this moment that Vietnam policy merged with a decision that LBJ had dwelt upon for many months. The presidential election was fast approaching and six factors loomed large in Johnson's mind as he debated whether or not to stand. First was his health, which had been deteriorating for some time. Second was his poor showing in the opinion polls. Third was the surprising success of Eugene McCarthy, the peace candidate, who in the New Hampshire Primary on 12 March had come within 300 votes of defeating the president. Fourth was the recently announced presidential candidacy of his arch rival, Robert Kennedy. Fifth was the prospect of presiding over a nation in which the cities were consumed by race riots and turmoil, and finally there was the seeming stagnation of his plans for the Great Society and his realization that his grip upon Congress had vanished. Faced with these considerations, Johnson decided not to run. By deciding to withdraw from politics, LBJ believed that his peace proposal would be given more credibility and would be considered more sincere.

Consequently, on the evening of 31 March 1968, Johnson went on nationwide television and, in a speech which rocked the country, he announced, in a conciliatory tone, an unconditional bombing halt north of the twentieth parallel and an effective ceiling on troop deployments to Vietnam. He then went on to talk of the 'division in the American house' and to announce that he would not accept his party's nomination as a candidate in the upcoming presidential elections (Public Papers 1968–9, 1970:469–76).

The Tet Offensive shook the American political system and redirected US involvement in South East Asia. From this point on, the troop ceiling was stabilized. In a move that surprised many, on 3 April, Hanoi responded to Johnson's plea for negotiations and, although it took several weeks before preliminary discussions got off the ground, it signified an important breakthrough.

The remaining nine months of the Johnson administration were spent in feeble attempts to salvage some glory by achieving a negotiated solution to the conflict. This proved impossible and, whilst a good deal of dissent was quietened at home, opposition rumbled on. Many were angered over the continuation of the bombing campaign in the area north of the DMZ but below the twentieth parallel. Johnson had failed to make this limitation on the cessation of bombing clear in his address and war protestors felt aggrieved by the perceived deception. But owing to the positive North Vietnamese response to the initiative, the bombing was not resumed north of the twentieth parallel during Johnson's administration and, on 31 October 1968, the president authorized a complete halt to all sorties north of the DMZ.

Although there was a sudden increase in his popularity after his March announcement, Johnson was, by then, a defeated man, his hopes of a Great Society shattered by the war in Asia. Leading statesman, Averell Harriman, went as far as to say that 'if it hadn't been for... Vietnam he'd have been the greatest President ever' (Kearns 1976:251). Undeniably, Johnson had achieved one of his ambitions: his memory would become immortal along with those of a handful of other presidents. But he would be remembered not for his great works but for plunging his country into a bitter war that it could not win.

Johnson's presidency produced none of the fanfare of which he had dreamed. The five years during which he had been in office had witnessed an unsuccessful conflict, growing discord at home and the disappointing failure to implement the Great Society. The years were punctuated by several key events. There was the Gulf of Tonkin Resolution and the introduction of ground combat troops into Vietnam. Then, in 1968 there was the Tet Offensive—pivotal in the history of the war because it challenged long-held assumptions. No longer were individuals tied to their original positions. The offensive was so shocking that it legitimized reversals of opinion. During the debate that followed, Johnson moved into the camp of the dissenters. It critically altered the balance between the coalition that favoured continuing the war on the accepted basis and those who argued that changes had to be made. Tet did not suddenly produce a coalition favouring a new strategy and, in particular, a halt to the bombing of North Vietnam. What it did do was to add some new and powerful voices to the existing coalition, thereby rendering it triumphant (Thompson 1980:65).

A fundamental shift in policy then occurred. While the US had intervened in Vietnam in order to forestall an NLF victory and win enough time for the GVN to pull itself together, this objective had somehow been lost along the way. Completely defeating the enemy had been substituted for this more limited goal. The impact of Tet changed this and forced the US to return to its original purpose. Thereafter,

Washington sought only to deny the NLF and the North Vietnamese their final victory. This less ambitious objective was a prerequisite of the US's new desire to withdraw from the conflict whilst maintaining its honour and prestige. At the end of March 1968, that goal still lay a long way off and it would take six more years before the US managed to extricate itself from the mire of its own making.

4 Negotiations 1964–73

The diplomatic history of the Vietnam War is littered with failed attempts to find a negotiated solution to the fighting. Literally thousands of initiatives, both official and unofficial, were pursued by a variety of individuals and organizations. Despite their often valiant efforts, it took until 1973 for an acceptable settlement to be achieved and for the US to withdraw from Vietnam.

NEGOTIATING THE UNNEGOTIABLE 1964–8

While there were many attempts to arrange a dialogue between the North Vietnamese government and the Johnson administration, until 1968 none progressed to the point where serious negotiations actually began. Dozens of nations and every aspiring statesman wanted to be the peacemaker who delivered a settlement in Vietnam. Such were their efforts that between 1965 and 1967 White House sources estimated that there were around 2,000 individual efforts to prompt US-DRV talks (Goodman 1978:24). All failed and not even U Thant, Secretary General of the United Nations, who tried to initiate negotiations in 1964, could start the ball rolling. His lack of success was often to be repeated.

On 8 April 1965, Premier Pham Van Dong in a speech to the DRV National Assembly outlined North Vietnam's fundamental negotiating position, known as the Four Points. Firstly, he demanded a recognition of the basic rights of the Vietnamese nation which included peace, independence, the withdrawal of US troops and the dismantling of US military bases. Secondly, he stated that the provisions of the Geneva Accords had to be complied with and that no military alliances were therefore acceptable. Thirdly, he maintained that South Vietnam's political future had to be determined in accordance with the NLF's programme, and his fourth and final point was that peaceful reunification was essential.

Such demands were wholly unacceptable to the United States. The Johnson administration consistently assumed that the Four Points were merely a basis for negotiations and were Hanoi's maximum demands rather than the very minimum conditions that the DRV would accept. The problem for the White House was that at least two of the DRV's Four Points undermined the basis of the American presence in Vietnam. If the US agreed that South Vietnam's political future was to be decided by the NLF, it would have been tantamount to admitting that its client regime was an illegal entity which did not represent the will of the people. Moreover, if peaceful reunification was an aim and Vietnam was, by inference, one country, the justification that the US was in South East Asia to defend and support an independent, sovereign state was immediately nullified (Porter 1975:28–9).

Although it seemed that a dialogue based upon the Four Points would prove sterile, Washington made attempts to initiate talks even if, at times, this was done solely for the benefit of US and world public opinion. The Johnson administration used halts in the bombing campaign *Rolling Thunder* as a device to encourage the DRV to begin negotiations. During the halts, however, no new approaches were made to Hanoi. Washington merely waited for the North Vietnamese to respond positively and for them to revise their Four Points. At no time did this occur.

Hanoi did not respond to the bombing pauses because it claimed *Rolling Thunder* to be wholly illegal. The US wanted the DRV to impose limits on its military action in South Vietnam in return for a bombing halt. However, the DRV would not consider trading in this manner as it suggested that the two actions, because exchanged, were thereby equal. In the eyes of the North Vietnamese it would be equivalent to admitting that their support for the revolutionary movement in the South was also illegal. The DRV dismissed this concept of 'reciprocal' action because it refused to trade the legitimate war in the South for an illegitimate act of terrorism against its own territory. Furthermore, Hanoi reasoned, it could not offer any comparable concessions as it was not pursuing comparable military operations over US territory (Porter 1975:30).

The most promising initiative in 1966 was that organized by Janusz Lewandowski, the chief of the Polish delegation to the International Control Commission. His plan, code-named *Marigold,* sought to create a new negotiating agenda. Lewandowski believed that the great obstacle to the start of talks was not so much the impossibility of reaching a final settlement, but the circumstances surrounding the initiation of a dialogue and the demands that each side made as a prerequisite to negotiations.

His formula was to move beyond this controversial area and to establish some areas of common ground between the United States and the DRV. Despite the initial optimism, however, by the end of July 1966, *Marigold* had been terminated.

On 25 October 1965, the US, together with the other allied nations fighting in Vietnam, issued the Manila Declaration outlining the US position on a peaceful end to the war. Once North Vietnam had withdrawn its forces from the South and had ceased infiltration, the United States pledged to withdraw its own forces within a period of six months. President Johnson also proposed two distinct phases to de-escalation which later became known as the Phase A-Phase B formula. During Phase A, the US would suspend the bombing and in Phase B, US and North Vietnamese forces would begin to withdraw.

It was upon this concept that Harold Wilson, the British prime minister, and Alexei Kosygin, the Soviet premier, began to construct a peace proposal in February 1967 during Kosygin's visit to London. At the heart of their attempt was an interpretation of the Phase A-Phase B formula which called for Washington to stop the bombing if North Vietnam would cease infiltration. Wilson believed that the initiative had a good chance of success but that it was destroyed because of the 'utterly unrealistic time-table' imposed by the Johnson administration (Wilson 1971:364). In fact, while Wilson and Kosygin were busy pursuing their ultimately unsuccessful diplomatic opening, back in Washington Johnson remained extremely sceptical about their entire plan and effectively undercut the initiative by revising the wording of the Phase A-Phase B formula so that instead of committing the US to a bombing halt if the infiltration would stop, the halt was made conditional upon infiltration having stopped. The change of tense made a profound difference.

The first change in the United States' negotiating position came on 29 September 1967. In the so-called San Antonio Formula, Johnson linked a halt in the bombing programme to immediate, productive talks. Infiltration was not expressly forbidden, but the North Vietnamese were requested not to 'take advantage' of a bombing halt. However, it was unrealistic to expect the DRV suddenly to cease supplying its men in the South, and Hanoi remained adamant that the San Antonio Formula still demanded pre-conditions as the price of a bombing halt.

As the Johnson administration considered the war to be proceeding well during 1967, their search for a negotiated solution was not as urgent. Things began to change in 1968 as a result of the Tet Offensive. With its forces from the South depleted, the revolutionary movement decided to shift to a fighting-while-negotiating strategy. Alternatively, it can also be argued that the NLF/DRV, weary of the military stalemate and daunted by the prospect of fighting a long war against such an awesomely powerful enemy, were already looking for some means to push the US towards negotiations. The Tet Offensive of spring 1968 achieved this by providing the political and military breakthrough which initiated negotiations (Porter 1975:32–3, 66–70). In any event, the new strategy of the revolutionary movement hoped that by continuing the war, and at the same time pursuing a skilful negotiating policy, US domestic and world opinion could be exploited in their favour and the negotiations could become a platform for denouncing the US and for sapping its will to continue.

Following a post-Tet reappraisal of America's Vietnam policy, President Johnson ordered a bombing halt north of the twentieth parallel on 31 March 1968. To the surprise of some observers, the DRV responded three days later by agreeing to talks. The North Vietnamese thus opened another front in their war. The attrition of the US's psychological capacity to fight was the goal. Negotiations were essentially part of a propaganda war that both sides utilized. Unfortunately for the US, it was a forum which the North Vietnamese utilized better.

That it took until 1968 for negotiations even to begin requires futher explanation. A number of very basic themes that apply to the period 1964–68 and also, in some cases, beyond, are useful in understanding the seeming dichotomy between efforts to begin negotiations and the diplomatic impasse that actually existed.

The most fundamental reason why talks did not begin was that neither side was sufficiently interested in negotiations to surmount the considerable obstacles involved Both the US and the NLF/DRV thought that they could achieve their objectives on the battlefield In addition, the US feared that, given the weakness of the GVN, a negotiated solution would leave Saigon in a desperately fragile condition and no match for the revolutionary movement. The NLF/DRV, on the other hand, had been forced to relinquish some of their control of the South Vietnamese countryside in response to the massive US escalation in 1965. They therefore considered it vital to recover this lost ground before embarking on serious negotiations.

Although the US did not begin its bombing campaign over North Vietnam with the idea that it would become, primarily, a negotiating tool—a bargaining chip which Washington would give up if the NLF/DRV agreed to talks—it quickly assumed that role. Against the wishes of America's military leaders, who called for all-out strikes against North Vietnam,

Rolling Thunder became the principal weapon in a rapidly evolving strategy of coercive diplomacy. The aim was not to annihilate the DRV's capacity to wage war, as the JCS wanted, but to manipulate the leadership's will and resolve to continue the struggle in the South. This strategy was built upon three basic beliefs (Thies 1980:9). First was that steadily increasing pressure from the bombing would lead Hanoi to question its support for the war in the South. The gradual expansion of the bombing campaign, which started with a very limited number of targets, was expected to leave Hanoi fearful of further destruction of its industrial and communications base. This was a factor considered especially important to a developing nation which had made such a great effort to improve its infrastructure and manufacturing sector. Secondly, the US administration did not question its ability to combine its words and actions in order to send correct and meaningful messages to Hanoi. Thirdly, and in a related vein, it assumed that the force it applied was completely under its control.

Washington's aims were based on erroneous assumptions. Experiences in Europe during the Second World War had indicated that rather than reducing a nation's capacity to fight, enemy bombing campaigns had tended to stiffen resolve. It was unlikely that the North Vietnamese reaction would be significantly different. Moreover, after fighting for six years in the South and after having reached a point in early 1965 when the NLF/DRV leadership believed itself to be on the verge of victory, it was hardly possible that they would have abandoned the revolutionary struggle, especially as it would have entailed a significant risk of creating a secessionist movement in the South which would almost certainly have continued fighting on alone.

A further error in the US administration's strategy arose because Washington assumed that the DRV leadership acted as a 'unitary actor' (Thies 1980:220). This theory sees the enemy government acting as a logical individual who analytically calculates costs and gains and who makes rational decisions based upon the evidence available. It does not make accommodation for divided leaderships, for leaderships which reflect divergent viewpoints, for rationales which are apparent only to the enemy and for the illogical, but powerfully persuasive, emotional dimension to a given issue.

In spite of its assumptions, it proved consistently difficult for Washington to coordinate its military and diplomatic campaign with the fine degree of accuracy needed. This occurred because the implementation of military operations and diplomatic overtures were delegated to separate groups which, hampered by the complexity of the bureaucratic system, then proceeded to implement directives at different times, thus making phasing and coordination haphazard (Thies

1980:312–13). One arm of the administration often did not know what the other was doing and diplomatic messages could easily be ignored because of contradictory, ill-timed military action. Moreover, while the government controlled overall military strategy it was impossible for it to exercise complete operational control in the field. Washington could therefore be pursuing one tactic while the armed forces might, unwittingly, be simultaneously undercutting it.

Had the correct message been received by Hanoi, it was not certain that Washington would have been able to interpret Hanoi's response (Thies 1980:322). The US did not know enough about the DRV leadership and its motivations to ascertain its signals or their meaning. Nor, for that matter, did the DRV appreciate some of the finer points of American politics and, in particular, the growing divisions within the Johnson administration. A cultural abyss separated Washington and Hanoi Bridging it would have demanded that the Americans exercise a subtlety and finesse that they frequently lacked and would have required Hanoi to be more patient with Washington's direct and seemingly heavy-handed approach.

This discussion is in some ways superfluous because a peaceful settlement of the war was simply not possible until 1968 at the very earliest. Even if the mechanics of dialogue had been engineered, a negotiated solution was impossible.

The great stumbling block was that there was no room for compromise and manoeuvre. America was in Vietnam for a political purpose. The NLF/DRVs aim was to liberate Vietnam from foreign domination and, in the process, to install communist ideology. America's aim was to frustrate this. But unlike wars in which a negotiated settlement could be reached by a process of bargaining and compromise, for example by carving up territory, no such neat equations could be found to solve the conflict in Vietnam. It was inconceivable that diametrically opposed ideologies could be manipulated and traded in a similar manner. South Vietnam could not be a half-way house on the road to communism.

The US clung to the hope of finding a solution to the conflict through some form of military compromise with the NLF/DRV. They deluded themselves in this hope because settlement of the military issues would still have left the more important political questions outstanding. There was, therefore, little chance of a negotiated solution because the US refused to agree to a military settlement which contained political provisions. Given the vulnerability of the GVN and the relative strength of the NLF, the United States considered a political settlement to be detrimental to its client regime. Moreover, as it would inevitably involve granting the NLF a legitimate role in the South, it would have meant acknowledging that the aim of stopping communism had been abandoned. The NLF/DRV, on the other hand, refused to agree to any settlement which failed to encompass the political demands of the Four Points. A purely military solution would not have recognized the hard-won gains of the revolutionary organization in the South and its undoubted political support there. Consequently, while each side remained wedded to achieving its fundamental goals in Vietnam, there was little prospect of constructive negotiation because at the heart of the conflict was an unnegotiable ideological struggle.

A significant change occurred in 1968. The post-Tet reassessment of America's role in Vietnam did not indicate a US desire to relinquish its commitment but it did signify that the administration was willing to place limits—however belatedly—upon the extent of US involvement in Vietnam. It also marked a turning-point because, thereafter, the scale of the US presence was gradually cut. This meant a steady weakening of Washington's hand in South East Asia and it forced the US to negotiate before it was left without significant leverage over Hanoi. Thus some form of compromise was inevitable and for practical purposes the US goal of preserving a South Vietnam free from all taint of communism had to be dropped. But 1968 was only the start of this process leading to withdrawal, for it took six more years of costly and destructive war before the United States was finally able to divest itself of its military commitment and before an acceptable compromise was eventually reached.

NIXON, KISSINGER AND VIETNAM

When Richard Nixon became president of the United States on 20 January 1969, hopes were high that a speedy solution could be found to the Vietnam War. During his election campaign, Nixon's supporters had created the impression that he had a secret 'plan' to end the war. In fact, no such plan existed at all.

While the North Vietnamese had agreed to negotiations in April 1968, actual talks with the DRV began only four days prior to Nixon's arrival in the White House. Arguments over the shape of the negotiating table had repeatedly postponed the opening of talks as the GVN refused to sit at a square or rectangular table because they considered that giving the NLF delegation an entire side to themselves confirmed them as a legal entity separate from the DRV delegation. Lyndon Johnson also believed that the South Vietnamese president, Nguyen Van Thieu, was stalling the opening of negotiations in order to scupper any diplomatic breakthrough which might give the democratic candidate a welcome boost prior to the US presidential election (Johnson 1972:517–21). From Thieu's point of view Nixon, a known hard-liner, seemed a far more attractive and dependable patron than the democrat's liberal and, by comparison, antiwar Hubert Humphrey.

If Richard Nixon did not have a fully developed plan to end the war he did, nevertheless, bring a new perspective on foreign policy to the office of the president. It was a perspective he shared with Henry Kissinger, the man whom he chose to be his Special Assistant for National Security Affairs. The application of their ideas was to herald a new age in America's relations with the rest of the world.

Both men considered that they had inherited a crisis in US foreign policy and that it was their duty to restore American power and prestige which had been severely battered as a result of the Vietnam War. At the very heart of the foreign policy crisis, however, was not Vietnam but a changing balance of world power. Towards the end of the 1960s the Soviet Union had begun to achieve nuclear parity with the United States and so, stripped of the advantage of nuclear superiority, the US had to find new levers with which to control the communist bloc. America's unquestioned post-war pre-eminence had vanished and a re-thinking of US foreign policy priorities was essential if the nation was not to over-extend itself. What was needed was a whole new foreign policy agenda.

In light of the new realities of power, Nixon and Kissinger believed that the US had to streamline its policies. It had to ignore peripheral issues and concentrate instead on its relationships with the major powers. Central to this idea was the concept of 'linkage'. Linkage, as applied by Nixon and Kissinger, saw states inevitably bound to one another by virtue of military and political alliances, economics and ideology. The strong nations within this web could therefore greatly influence the actions of the smaller, weaker states. Cordial relations between powerful nations, on the other hand, were maintained by an acceptance of multi-polarity. Great powers had to coexist and peace had to be preserved through the creation and maintenance of political, economic and military equilibrium. The essence of peace was balance. Thus, theoretically, communist North Vietnam could be manipulated by the giants of the communist bloc, while the world's major powers could all live together, quite amicably, providing each concentrated on its own sphere of influence and did not step beyond the bounds of accepted international great power behaviour.

The practical application of these theories concentrated upon discarding non-priority, foreign policy commitments. That meant bringing the war in Vietnam to a conclusion but doing it 'honourably' and in a manner that would not seriously dent America's credibility and affect its relationship with its allies and with the communist bloc. It also meant searching for detente with China and the Soviet Union. This was to be achieved by exploiting China's fear of the Soviet Union, brought about as a result of the Sino-Soviet dispute, and by offering the USSR the prospect of the improved commercial relations and arms control agreements which were essential if the Soviet Union was to undertake long-overdue modernization.

These foreign policy goals appeared quite logical, if oversimplified. What was controversial was the means by which Nixon and Kissinger attempted to achieve them. During Kissinger's years as an academic, he had evolved an elaborate critique of US foreign policy decisionmaking. Bureaucracy, in his opinion, distorted policy and it was only through the actions of outstanding visionary leaders that true progress could be made in the political and diplomatic arena. By virtue of their greater understanding and intellect, such leaders could analyse the world more clearly, could discover order in the midst of chaos, could plan and theorize more astutely and, consequently, could execute more daring and effective policy, providing that they did not have to endure the trammels of conservative, stultifying, bureaucratic meddling. Hardly surprising, given his considerable ego, Kissinger believed himself to be just such a visionary leader. The challenge that confronted him, once appointed by Nixon, therefore, was to fashion the means by which to bypass or suppress the role of the bureaucracy in foreign policy formulation and execution.

Nixon appointed Kissinger precisely because of his views on decisionmaking. The new president was immensely interested in foreign policy. He had some experience and knowledge of it and it was also attractive in that it could be organized by a few people. This aspect of foreign affairs appealed to an often obsessive and withdrawn man who had an almost paranoid concern over secrecy and who felt most confident working with a small coterie of close advisers and sycophants.

Both Nixon and Kissinger wanted to control foreign policy decisionmaking themselves and they considered that secrecy was essential in order to act out their plan for detente and for an end to the Vietnam War. This demanded separating foreign affairs from the established bureaucratic bodies. Consequently, a wholesale reorganization of the machinery for foreign policy decisionmaking was initiated as soon as Nixon began his first term of office.

Perceived as the great obstacle to effective policy execution, the State Department was swiftly bypassed by Kissinger's revised organizational structure. Whole segments of the bureaucracy, in particular the State and

Defense Departments, were neutralized by this procedure. The offices of the Secretary of State and Secretary of Defense, which should have provided resistance to this re-direction of power, were filled by men (Melvin Laird at Defense and William Rogers at State) who were chosen partly because they would pose only a limited challenge to the Nixon-Kissinger strategy (Morris 1977:86–7, 134–6). The new special assistant went further in destroying the previous pre-eminence of the Defense Department in foreign affairs by undercutting Laird through the establishment of his own relationship with the JCS. He thereby ignored the customary role of the Secretary of Defense through whom Kissinger's requests to the JCS should have been transmitted.

While the new procedures did not technically breach constitutional rules, the wide-ranging usurption of powers and the disregarding of well established bureaucratic channels and policymaking forums, reflected Kissinger's and, especially, Nixon's frustration at the limits which the State placed upon the concentration of power. From this position the jump to the approval of extra-legal activities was only very small to a president who had a mania about unauthorized disclosures.

Ironically, Nixon's paranoia about secrecy was exacerbated by the very policy that he pursued. By effectively cutting off a large section of the official bureaucracy from making an effective input to foreign policy, Nixon created a climate in which leaking information to the press, paradoxically, seemed the only method for demoralized employees to contribute to the foreign policy debate (Strong 1986:62). In an attempt to silence the leaks, Nixon, almost certainly with Kissinger's knowledge, ordered that wiretaps be placed upon a number of government employees and members of the press. Such illegal activities were the forerunners, not only of a general clampdown by the intelligence services upon alleged subversive activity in the United States, but also, in the long-term, of the Watergate scandal.

Finding an honourable solution to America's involvement in the Vietnam War was essential to the administration's global strategy. Kissinger believed that 'native idealism' and a belief in America's duty to 'set right the world's ills' (Kissinger 1979:230) had diverted the US into an area and a conflict which was not absolutely vital to US interests. The pursuit of containment had prompted first the Elsenhower, Kennedy and then the Johnson administrations to intervene in Vietnam. But the containment principle had since mellowed. China's disturbing revolutionary zeal had been internalized and channelled into the Cultural Revolution and the threat of communism in South East Asia had receded (Mueller 1987:300–1).

What kept America in Vietnam in the late 1960s were the costs it had already incurred during the fighting. Once the commitment had been made and US prestige had become linked to the fate of the GVN, a quick, unilateral withdrawal was impossible without causing America's allies to question its resolve to play a major part in world politics (Kissinger 1979:1038). Furthermore, the very fact that 31,000 Americans had died in Vietnam up to the point where Nixon took office, meant that a hasty retreat was unpatriotic, politically risky and disrespectful to the memory and to the families of those men who had been killed (Kissinger 1979:235). These factors were the same ones that had motivated the Johnson administration to continue fighting in Vietnam and so, despite the new look to Nixon's foreign policy, many of the assumptions underpinning Vietnam policy during the Nixon-Kissinger era differed little from those of the Johnson years.

It has been argued that the administration did not have an integrated Vietnam policy and that the one that did emerge was *ad hoc* and unstructured (Herring 1984:53–4). This is difficult to reconcile with the facts. Nixon did not have a structured 'plan' to end the war when he came to office but he and Kissinger were in the process of developing a global strategy which inevitably moulded the parameters of their Vietnam policy. The Nixon 'plan' that soon emerged had three main objectives. The government sought to lower the domestic political temperature by withdrawing troops and neutralizing the antiwar movement. It simultaneously shifted the burden of the fighting on to the South Vietnamese Armed Forces (RVNAF), whose combat capability was to be greatly improved. At the same time, the administration, operating within the constraints set by the political situation at home, sought to destroy the enemy's military forces in order to give the GVN time to get its army into decent shape.

A much favoured liberal critique postulates that Nixon wanted to win in Vietnam and that he always held out hope of a victory. Clinging to this illusion, the US did not cut its losses in Vietnam and withdraw. Instead it stayed on for five more years whilst pursuing what was, in all essentials, a losing and contradictory stategy. If American forces were gradually being pulled out of Vietnam, how could Washington believe that it could achieve a more favourable negotiated deal? Time and the US political climate were not on its side. What the administration did in its frustration and in its attempt to counterbalance the withdrawal of its troop strength, was to substitute firepower and, in particular, airpower. It was a policy which produced one of the 'most savage retreats in history (Morris 1977:154).

By mid-1969 the administration's Vietnam policy was being pursued along four main tracks. Firstly, there was an effort to induce the Soviet

Union to reduce its support for the North Vietnamese. Secondly, the administrationm tackled the antiwar movement in the US, Helped by other contributing factors it succeeded in bringing about a temporary reduction of overt dissent. Thirdly, Nixon and Kissinger aimed to frighten the DRV, the Soviet Union and China into believing that they would stop at nothing in order to achieve a 'realistic' settlement of the war. This was known as Nixon's 'madman theory'. He wanted to appear totally unpredictable and uncontrollable and so encouraged rumours that he was so mentally unstable that he was capable of anything. The fourth arm of the new strategy was 'de-Americanization', coined Vietnamization. Vietnamization was a practical application of the 'Nixon Doctrine' which was premised on the belief that native armies would fight in place of American troops. US money and techniques could support the armies of foreign governments or counter-revolutionary organizations which would, henceforth, fight their own wars. There would be no more flag-draped caskets returning home to disturb domestic politics. Americans were no longer going to die for political causes. Nixon and Kissinger resolved to pay someone else to do that.

Vietnamization involved handing over the fighting of the war to the South Vietnamese Armed Forces (RVNAF). This would decrease the level of US dead and injured and would also decrease the number of young men drafted for combat duty. Hence it would have an impact upon the US antiwar movement which was heavily influenced and supported by potential draftees. In addition, Secretary of Defense Laird was undertaking a wholesale rethink of the military budget. Vietnam had seriously drained other vital areas of defence spending and, in order to redress the balance, he structured his financial forecasts on the premise that the American presence in Vietnam was to be cut back sharply. Less money was allocated to the war and Laird therefore provided powerful financial pressures for a reduced commitment of combat troops (Karnow 1984:595).

In 1969, 65,000 troops were withdrawn, in 1970, 50,000 and in 1971 another 250,000. But, despite Vietnamization, Americans continued to be killed in large numbers in Vietnam. In Nixon's first year in office, 10,000 died. Concerned that these statistics would create public pressure for a speedier withdrawal, the new military commander in Vietnam, General Creighton Abrams, was given orders to reduce the casualty rate. Thereafter large operations became less frequent. The number of troops committed to combat duties was dramatically reduced and the burden of the fighting increasingly fell upon the RVNAF.

Kissinger's initial optimism that peace could be achieved swiftly gradually dissolved. Long arduous negotiations became necessary. The frequently postponed talks which opened in Paris in January *1969* quickly developed into a propaganda platform and no progress was made in the 174 sessions held. In fact, the public talks were a facade for secret negotiations which began in August. For the next three years negotiating an end to the Vietnam War consisted of periodic, intensive meetings in Paris between Kissinger and North Vietnamese representatives, primarily politburo member Le Duc Tho. Secrecy was maintained with an almost theatrical flair and Kissinger flew backwards and forwards across the Atlantic without the knowledge of even the most astute and inquiring of journalists.

Until 1972 the secret negotiations proved sterile. The US was unwilling to compromise and talk about a political settlement, while the NLF/DRV had lost considerable ground as a result of over-exposing their forces in the Tet Offensive and were unwilling to agree to a settlement which reflected that weakness. Moreover, the NLF/DRV refused to countenance a 'two-track' approach proposed by Kissinger. Kissinger suggested that this method would allow the US and the NLF/DRV to reach an agreement over military forces, while the revolutionary movement and the GVN would be left to negotiate a political solution to the war once the Americans had withdrawn. The NLF/DRV, however, realized that it was a practical impossibility to separate the various facets of the conflict for any military agreement would inevitably set the parameters for the ultimate political settlement. By insisting on the two-track formula, the US would have avoided addressing the major questions posed by the war. In particular, they would not have been forced to withdraw support for the South Vietnamese president, Nguyen Van Thieu, as the NLF/DRV consistently demanded. Consequently, an insurmountable deadlock in negotiations was created by the US's refusal to drop their support for Thieu and by the NLF/DRVs insistence that his rule was not legitimate and that he therefore had to be removed from power prior to any peace agreement with the United States.

THE BOMBING OF CAMBODIA

As Vietnamization reduced the number of Americans fighting in Vietnam, the White House was concerned that its negotiating position was being eroded. Hanoi would have little incentive to negotiate a settlement if it presumed that Washington would withdraw unilaterally. The remedy, therefore, was to act tough and to indicate, both to Hanoi and to Moscow, that fewer US combat troops did not presuppose a lessening of American resolve. Consequently, 1969 saw the new administration contemplating what Kissinger termed a 'savage blow' against North Vietnam, including the use of a tactical nuclear option (Hersh 1983:128–9, Morris 1977:163–6). It even saw the US Strategic Air Command being placed on 'combat ready status' in order that the Kremlin and Hanoi received the appropriate signs (Hersh 1983:124). The options were part of a plan known as 'Duck Hook' and Nixon threatened to take direct action by 1 November 1969 if the DRV did not respond to his overtures. The president may have been bluffing and 'Duck Hook' no more than an interesting academic exercise, as the administration claimed. On the other hand it may not.

In the event, when the DRV did not respond to his threats Nixon did not not unleash the might of the United States against them. His intuition and, most importantly, the antiwar movement had placed such ferocity out of political bounds (Small 1988:186–7).

Although 'Duck Hook' was not put into operation, the administration had not been quiescent. Unknown to Congress and the American public, in March 1969, the Nixon administration moved to prove how determined it was by beginning the secret bombing of Cambodia. Washington's primary motivation for this new extension to the war was to hinder the NLF/DRV effort to wage war in South Vietnam. This would give the armed forces of the GVN a chance to improve upon their poor performance before the withdrawal of US combat troops left them to fight alone. The bombing of Cambodia, therefore, was designed to purchase more time for the Vietnamization policy to become effective.

For years the NLF's military arm, the People's Liberation Armed Forces (PLAF), and the North Vietnamese Army (PAVN), had used areas on the Cambodian side of the Cambodia-Vietnam border for the siting of extensive sanctuaries. A number of bases flourished, free from heavy US/GVN interference in this supposedly neutral territory. The problem posed by use of the sanctuaries was that Cambodia had successfully struggled to keep itself out of the fighting in South East Asia and it had maintained, through the efforts of its authoritarian monarch, Prince Norodom Sihanouk, a tenuous grip on its neutral status. Sihanouk was obviously aware of the existence of the sanctuaries but turned a blind eye to them because by acknowledging them he would have been seen by the US/GVN to be approving their existence. If, on the other hand, he had acknowledged and denounced their existence he would have opened the way for the US to pressurize him into agreeing to a US/GVN attack. In this manner he would have lost his neutral status in the eyes of the NLF/DRV. Sihanouk maintained this precarious balance until the US bombing of the sanctuaries irreversibly changed Cambodia's international status, shattering its fragile peace and beginning its downward slide into anarchy.

Sihanouk knew of the US bombing of the sancturaries which began on 18 March 1969. This does not mean that he endorsed or even condoned the action, however, because in practice he had little alternative (Shawcross 1979:94). The US action was the result of a unilateral decision. Not only was it unilateral but the bombing programme, code-named *Menu,* was also concealed from the American public and even from the major part of the US government and military. This was done by a complex method of falsifying records. After bombing enemy locations in Cambodia, US pilots would then return to their bases and enter into their logs the geographical coordinates of targets situated inside South Vietnam. The procedure was highly secret and even the superior officers of the men who flew the missions did not know of the planes' true destination because orders for the bombing came through a secret 'back channel' communication system which completely bypassed the conventional network (Shawcross 1979:30–2).

Secrecy was deemed vital because of the furore that was expected to follow revelations of a further extension to a war that was supposed to be winding down. Opposition to *Menu* existed even within those limited sections of the administration that knew of its existence. Secretary of State William Rogers opposed the programme and Secretary of Defense Melvin Laird was also sceptical, although at least some of his doubts were assuaged. Most opposition was based upon political considerations and not upon the questions of whether the bombing was likely to produce successful long-term military results or whether the bombing of populated, neutral territory was morally justifiable.

For fourteen months *Menu* unleased the tremendous firepower of the United States upon hitherto peaceful rural areas. The programme was divided into distinct phases, each one given a code-name such as *Breakfast, Lunch* or *Dinner* and each one concentrated upon areas of pre-supposed enemy activity along the Cambodian-Vietnamese border and inside Cambodia itself. Kissinger claimed that the sanctuaries 'contained next to no Cambodian population' (Kissinger 1979:240). However, this was not true. Many of the areas that came under aerial bombardment contained Khmer villages. Either US intelligence was lamentably and tragically poor or the administration was simply dismissive of the effects of bombing upon the lives of the Cambodian people.

A *New York Times* article published on 9 May 1969 alerted America to the secret bombing. Reaction to the revelation, nevertheless, was rather muted. After an orgy of anti-Johnson and antiwar feeling in 1968,

1969 had seen the peace movement lose much of its dynamism. Later in the year Nixon was to undercut the movement further by staging a dramatic coup. On 3 November, in a televised speech to the nation, he mingled promises of an honourable withdrawal from Vietnam and threats to act tough with an emotive appeal to the 'great silent majority' of Americans. The effect was electric. The nation rallied to Nixon, the antiwar movement lost a bit more of its lustre and not even the public disclosure of a horrific massacre in the village of My Lai could significantly disturb the calm of Nixon's first year in office. Thanks to the carefully cultivated belief that the new president would find an honourable way out of Vietnam, Nixon had won himself a temporary reprieve from the wrath of the antiwar brigade.

While the PLAF/PAVN sanctuaries had been situated just across the Cambodian-Vietnamese border prior to *Menu,* the US bombing had the effect of driving them futher into Cambodian territory. This inevitably created internal political tension within Cambodia, destabilizing Sihanouk and ultimately leading to his overthrow by the right-wing, pro-American prime minister, General Lon Nol, in March 1970. Kissinger claimed that the US had no knowledge of the impending coup (Kissinger 1979:463) but this assertion is questionable especially as US Special Forces teams had been operating in Cambodia during the 1960s with the objective of aiding attempts to overthrow Sihanouk. More significantly, there was interest in a coup at the 'highest levels' of the US government which had resulted in the initiation of a highly classified operation, code-named *Sunshine Park,* to provide support for a coup (Hersh 1983:176–83). Perhaps Washington did not initiate or participate in the ousting of Sihanouk but subsequent US action illustrated that it approved of the coup and was willing to back the Lon Nol government on the grounds that a right-wing regime would support it in the fight against the PLAF/PAVN sanctuaries.

Operation *Menu* did not destroy the sanctuaries and so the logical next step was for Americans to use ground forces on Cambodian soil. Nixon and Kissinger contemplated further measures and finally decided that South Vietnamese forces, supported by the US, would undertake an offensive operation into Cambodia. Nixon then went on nationwide television to announce his decision. He told the American public that the 'incursion', rather than the invasion, was aimed at destroying the PLAF/PAVN headquarters for all of South Vietnam. By the time of the invasion, however, the major leaders had been evacuated. Contrary to widespread belief, the US had correctly identified the whereabouts of the temporary headquarters of the revolutionary forces, and one of the leading members of the NLF has written about just how close the US/

GVN came to wiping out the 'core of the southern resistance' during their operations in Cambodia (Truong Nhu Tang 1986:176–85).

The storm of protest which was generated by the invasion was gigantic. Opposition was strong even within the government and several members of Kissinger's own staff resigned in protest. After a lull in activity, the antiwar movement was re-energized and spontaneous demonstrations took place. One of these, at Kent State University, Ohio, ended in tragedy when four students were killed by the National Guard. Significantly, Congress too began to stir from its lethargy and it passed the Cooper-Church Amendment outlawing the introduction of US troops into Cambodia after 30 June 1970. The Amendment also banned all US air operations in direct support of Lon Nol's troops and also disallowed the sending of American advisers to aid the Cambodian armed forces. Notwithstanding the legally binding nature of the Amendment, Washington found ways to flout its provisions from the outset and in mid-1970 the US began to direct and finance the build-up of Lon Nol's army.

The Nixon administration weathered the 1970 Cambodian crisis but, from then on, the cacophony of dissent over the war grew. It was still centred on vocal minority elements, but the vital political and cultural elites increasingly became hostile to the administration's policy in South East Asia. Under the barrage of criticism Nixon retreated further into the isolation of the White House from where he privately, and occasionally publicly, excoriated their liberal treachery. The antiwar movement had matured during the Johnson years and was able to influence Nixon's policy far more than that of his predecessor. Nixon's memoirs consequently reflect the influence it had upon shaping his Vietnam policy and upon speeding the departure of American forces.

Kissinger's position in the administration was greatly strengthened by the Cambodian invasion. The two political aides closest to the president, Haldeman and Erlichman, were hard-liners who were suspicious of Kissinger's liberal republican background. They transmitted this suspicion to Nixon, and Kissinger's support for the Cambodian invasion could thus be interpreted as an attempt to gain credibility with the president by loyally supporting him in a decision that was almost certain to be unpopular (Szulc 1978:283). After the invasion he tightened his grip upon White House foreign policy. Henry Kissinger then began to emerge as the 'superstar', the man with a dazzling image who dominated the media's coverage of the Nixon administration. Kissinger befriended many influential reporters, leaked selected pieces of information to them, entertained journalists with his wit and charm at press conferences and courted them so that most gave him and his foreign policy highly sympathetic coverage. They returned his flattering attentions by portraying 'Henry', as they affectionately called him, as perhaps the central figure of the Nixon years.

Relations between the United States and the Soviet Union and China showed significant signs of improvement in 1970 and 1971. The long-awaited opening to China was made and, in April 1971, the US ping-pong team made a much publicized visit to China. Preparations for summits with China and the USSR were underway and the president and his special assistant could congratulate themselves on the undoubted progress that had been made towards detente. Vietnam, nevertheless, still loomed large and constantly threatened to overshadow the Nixon-Kissinger detente triumph.

The 1971 South Vietnamese presidential elections presented the next clear opportunity to reach a settlement in Vietnam. The NLF/DRV suggested that the US drop its support for Thieu in the election, thereby allowing the US to relinquish him legitimately as it was unlikely that he would have been re-elected without American backing. Consequently, Thieu would then have been removed as an obstacle to a negotiated solution. The US, however, did not seize the opportunity and they supported Nguyen Van Thieu in the corruption-ridden elections. On 3 October 1971, Thieu was re-elected as president of South Vietnam with an unquestionable majority. It was not surprising: he was the only candidate on the slate.

In the absence of productive negotiations, the war dragged on and Vietnamization progressed hesitantly and not without problems. US intelligence indicated that North Vietnamese forces and supplies were building up for an offensive in 1972, prior to the US presidential election. In order to safeguard his re-election prospects Nixon authorized a pre-emptive strike (Hersh 1983:310). Supplies for the upcoming offensive were reportedly being transported along the Ho Chi Minh Trail, a network of roads and tracks that ran from North to South Vietnam through the jungles of Laos and Cambodia. The president ordered than this trail was to be cut in southern Laos. Operation *Lam Son* 719 was conducted by the South Vietnamese Army (ARVN) with US air support and was considered to be a test for Vietnamization. It was a catastrophe. South Vietnamese troops were routed. They were unable to operate without Americans beside them and *Lam Son* 719 did little more than to reveal the glaring inadequacies of Vietnamization.

War raged in Cambodia despite the Cooper-Church Amendment limiting further US involvement there. The nation's countryside degenerated into a battleground between Lon Nol's government forces supported by US airpower and Thai and South Vietnamese Armed Forces on the one hand and an anti-Lon Nol coalition including the Cambodian communists on the other hand. This coalition was supported by the North Vietnamese. Prior to 1970, the Cambodian communists, known as the Khmer Rouge, had been an insignificant party which had little support amongst the people. Nor had it been given much encouragement by the North Vietnamese who were content with Sihanouk's rule and his benign disregard for their use of his border territory. The DRV's lack of concern for their Cambodian comrades rankled with the Khmer Rouge and heightened their suspicion of Hanoi. This resentment fed upon the memory of the DRV's acceptance of the 1954 Geneva Accords which had neutralized Cambodia and which had failed to recognize the revolutionary movement there. To the Cambodian communists it was an unforgivable betrayal. For the time, however, the Khmer Rouge subdued their antipathy towards the North Vietnamese while they struggled to seize power.

The bombing of Cambodia and the Lon Nol coup wrought a profound change in the fortunes of the Khmer Rouge. Prince Sihanouk, in exile in Peking, found his position so weak that he was forced to ally himself with other opponents of the newly installed Lon Nol government. In practical terms this meant forming an alliance with the Khmer Rouge—a group which he had previously denounced Sihanouk's considerable prestige and the vast numbers of rural Cambodians who were genuinely devoted to their charismatic monarch created an immediate reservoir of goodwill for the Khmer Rouge and, in effect, legitimized them in the eyes of the Cambodian peasantry. The Khmer Rouge adroitly utilized this association, gradually generating their own independent support base until, by 1973, they were in a strong enough position to abandon the facade of a royal alliance. It was then that they began to perpetrate radical and terrible change within the countryside of Cambodia.

The extension of the Vietnam War into Cambodia was not unwelcome to the NLF/DRV. The struggle tied down South Vietnamese troops which otherwise would have been available to fight against the revolutionary movement in South Vietnam and it also diverted at least a proportion of US airpower to another theatre of operations. From Washington's perspective the conflict in Cambodia was a useful adjunct to their involvement in Vietnam for the intensive bombing meant that US planes kept on flying in South East Asia. Because they were not idle, there were therefore no political and economic grounds for reducing sortie rates and withdrawing aircraft from the region. Consequently, Washington was able to divert the bombers elsewhere whenever the need arose and Hanoi could always be reminded that imminent death and destruction from aerial bombardment demanded nothing more from the US military than a new set of target coordinates (Shawcross 1979:217–19).

Even with the considerable support that Lon Nol received from Thailand, the United States and South Vietnam, government forces still found it difficult to hold on to the 50 per cent of Cambodian territory that remained in their hands at the end of 1970. In the midst of all this fighting Cambodia was being transformed. The traditional economy was all but defunct, the capital Phnom Penh was overflowing with refugees and by mid-1972 there were virtually never enough supplies to feed all those who were hungry. Phnom Penh was gradually starving to death. Despite all the horrors to be found in Cambodia during the apocalyptic years of the 1970s this suffering was, as William Shawcross so graphically portrayed, no more than a 'sideshow' to the war in Vietnam.

THE EASTER OFFENSIVE, 1972, AND THE PRELUDE TO PEACE

Following the reversals that the NLF/DRV had suffered as a result of the 1968 Tet Offensive, the revolutionary movement was forced to retreat to a less intense style of warfare. By the end of 1971 it believed that its forces were stong enough to resume the offensive. North Vietnamese leaders therefore agreed to launch a dramatic attack in order to underscore the inadequacies of Vietnamization and to regain ground lost during Tet and as a result of an ongoing US/GVN programme to win the support of the peasantry. During Easter 1972, PLAF/PAVN launched a massive offensive against South Vietnam using conventional military hardware. They succeeded in capturing important territory, in particular the city and province of Quang Tri in the north. The attack provided the ARVN with the opportunity to illustrate its mettle. Unfortunately, despite the bravery of a few elite divisions, it put up a lack-lustre performance. It was saved from disaster only by extensive US airpower which supported South Vietnamese troops and which was decisive in repelling the offensive (Lewy 1978:200).

Of crucial importance at this juncture was the US exploitation of its detente achievement. By 1972 Nixon and Kissinger's manoeuvering had resulted in drawing the Soviet Union and China away from Hanoi. Moscow and Peking both felt that they had something to gain from improved relations with Washington and were thus reluctant to jeopardize their newly established rapprochement simply for Hanoi's sake. Worried by the magnitude of the offensive and bolstered by his diplomatic successes, Nixon authorized a new, aggressive operation, *Linebacker I*. Significant sections of North Vietnam were bombed and he took the unprecedented step of mining the harbour of the DRV's main port, Haiphong. Under the Johnson administration this action was not considered feasible because it posed the risk of antagonizing the Soviet Union and China as the mining option was not one that could discriminate against the North Vietnamese alone. Notwithstanding initial doubts, Nixon was confident enough to assume the risk and the decision was, in Kissinger's opinion, 'one of the finest hours of Nixon's Presidency' (Kissinger 1979:1179). Even though a Soviet ship was hit as a consequence of the US bombing of Haiphong, the USSR made nothing more than a muted protest and the Soviet-American summit scheduled for May was not called off. Neither was China's response especially hostile. The mining and the reaction to it was, as far as Nixon and Kissinger were concerned, a vindication of their detente policy *vis-à-vis* Vietnam.

A combination of factors coalesced to bring a negotiated peace closer in the summer of 1972. Opposition to the war was growing stronger in the US Congress and it appeared that sooner or later funds for the war would be cut. This would have left Nixon and Kissinger in the unenviable position of negotiating without any form of leverage and would have left them no alternative but to withdraw without concluding any face-saving agreement. Better, it seemed, to reach an agreement with North Vietnam rather than to await a less honourable exit. Furthermore, with the US presidential elections fast approaching, the prospect, if not necessarily the materialization, of a soon-to-be-signed peace agreement would enhance Nixon's already high-standing in the polls.

These thoughts were in Kissinger's mind when he went to Moscow in April 1972. His mission was to ascertain how to move decisively against the NLF/DRV, then in the midst of their Easter Offensive, without threatening the forthcoming superpower summit in May. Kissinger's talks with Brezhnev produced 'what was probably the first major turning point in the history of the Vietnam negotiations' (Szulc 1974:36). He informed the Soviet leader that the US would accept a cease-fire in place providing that the DRV would withdraw those forces that it had introduced to conduct the offensive. It was a significant concession because it would mean that PAVN would not have to withdraw its forces from South Vietnam upon successful completion of an agreement. This would enable it to preserve control over the South Vietnamese territory it had liberated. Although Washington had talked about a cease-fire in place as early as 1970, this was always to be followed by a settlement that included provision for the mutual withdrawal of forces. Kissinger's offer in April 1972 was, consequently, the first time that the DRV had been told, categorically, that its troops could remain in the South (Szulc 1974:36–7).

Washington made a second major concession the following month. During the Moscow summit in May, Kissinger announced that a negotiated agreement could incorporate political provisions. Specifically, he suggested that a tripartite electoral commission should be established in South Vietnam and that it should be composed of representatives from the GVN, the revolutionary forces and third party nationalists. It was not a coalition government. Thieu would continue to rule South Vietnam but Washington would allow a political role to the NLF/DRV. Moreover, the concept was sufficiently ambiguous to satisfy those who insisted that Thieu should not be abandoned (Goodman 1978:123). The origins of the Paris Peace Agreement that ended US involvement in Vietnam can therefore be found in the 'conceptual breakthrough' which the May summit produced (Goodman 1978:123).

The NLF/DRV interest in a negotiated settlement in the summer derived, in large part, from the results of the Easter Offensive. Although it had severely shaken ARVN, the revolutionary forces had suffered exceedingly heavy manpower losses. The military leadership had made tactical blunders because they were using unfamiliar conventional tactics for the first time on a nationwide scale. More significantly, conventional tactics meant that troop strength was concentrated and vulnerable to the effects of US aerial bombing, especially since the Americans were using the new, far more accurate, laser-guided, 'smart bombs' (Lewy 1978:200). As a result of the combination of massed troops and effective airpower, the revolutionary movement may have lost as many as 100,000 men (Lewy 1978:198). Convinced by this display of force that they could not win the war when faced with the threat of American bombing, Hanoi prudently decided to come to a negotiated settlement in order to remove this formidable obstacle to victory.

Two additional factors were also pushing the NLF/DRV in the direction of a negotiated agreement at this time. The first was that a considerable amount of new territory had been won during the Easter Offensive. This encouraged the revolutionary forces to feel that the extent of their power in South Vietnam was great enough to allow them to accept Kissinger's cease-fire in place (Goodman 1978:119). The second, far more unpleasant factor was the fear of Nixon's re-election and the inspiration it might give him to step up the intensity of the war. As a result of these converging pressures, on 8 October, Le Duc Tho presented a surprised Kissinger with a draft agreement to end the Americans' war in Vietnam.

THE CHRISTMAS BOMBING AND THE PARIS PEACE AGREEMENT

The draft agreement which the DRV offered appeared to satisfy America's main demands. Of vital importance was the revelation that Hanoi was now no longer demanding that Thieu be ousted from power. Nixon authorized Kissinger to use it as a basis for an agreement and, in a series of intensive meetings, Kissinger and his staff hammered out a revised version of the agreement. It called for a cease-fire in place, a tripartite commission to work alongside the Thieu government, the withdrawal of US troops and the return of all American prisoners of war within sixty days. A timetable for the signing of the agreement was arranged with Hanoi and then Kissinger went to Saigon to request Thieu's compliance. To Kissinger's anger and frustration, Thieu, who had not been informed of the progress in negotiations, would not become party to the agreement. Poring over the draft, his advisers found some 129 points at which they took great offence. Thieu objected specifically to the status of the Demilitarized Zone between North and South Vietnam which, in his view, was not emphasized as an inviolable national boundary. He also rejected the tripartite commission, called the National Council of Reconciliation and Concord, which he interpreted as a coalition government. This verdict was supported by a leading member of the North Vietnamese politburo who, in an interview with a Western journalist, referred to the tripartite commission as a coalition government. Faced with this threat to his rule, President Thieu baulked. Despite Kissinger's determined efforts to woo him, he would not comply even within the extended timetable for signing that the DRV had granted at Kissinger's request. Disillusioned by the US's failure to adhere to the revised timetable, Hanoi disclosed the terms of the secret draft agreement on 25 October.

Although it had seemed as if the US and the DRV were on the verge of concluding a peaceful settlement in October, the negotiations which reopened in November were not encouraging. As the talks proceeded, the US flooded South Vietnam with a billion dollars worth of new military equipment. Operations *Enhance* and *Enhance Plus,* as the gigantic military aid packages were called, were executed with unseemly haste in order to be completed before a negotiated agreement could place a ceiling upon the extent of foreign assistance to the two governments.

Meanwhile the talks had become deadlocked and both parties appeared to be hardening their positions. In response to the stalling of negotiations, on 18 December, Nixon authorized *Linebacker II,* the bombing of Hanoi and Haiphong, more commonly known as the

'Christmas Bombing'. A news blackout on the targets and results of the campaign was ordered in the US, and for twelve days B-52s and tactical fighter aircraft intensively bombed the two largest cities in North Vietnam. Official North Vietnamese figures give the number of dead as 1,643 which, considering the extent of the operation, was a comparatively low figure and which was due, mainly, to the DRV's evacuation of all non-essential personnel.

Linebacker II stopped on 30 December 1972 and on 8 January 1973 talks resumed. This time, however, negotiations were productive and, on 23 January 1973, the Paris Agreement ending US military involvement in the Vietnam War was initialled by Kissinger and Le Duc Tho. The final Agreement was then officially signed four days later. The puzzling fact, nevertheless, was that the Agreement signed in January differed very little on fundamental issues from the draft agreement suggested by the DRV in October. What had happened in the intervening three months and what the Christmas Bombing therefore actually achieved is one of the most hotly debated questions of the Vietnam War.

Current literature offers various interpretations of this period. All interpretations agree that Nixon feared being accused of selling-out Thieu in order to win votes in the upcoming presidential election. Nixon did not want to sign an agreement unilaterally. One view, however, goes further and charges that Nixon purposely sabotaged the agreement by his refusal to put pressure on Thieu to sign. He did this because he considered the provisions of the agreement to be too unfavourable (Porter 1975:127–8, Kolko 1986:438). Nixon simply used the October draft and Thieu's reluctance to sign as a convenient excuse to prolong the negotiations until after the elections whereupon he could push for a better deal. In the intervening period the United States poured a vast quantity of weapons and munitions into South Vietnam and transferred ownership of US military bases to the GVN under operations *Enhance* and *Enhance Plus*.

According to this interpretation when negotiations resumed after the October draft was aborted, Nixon and Kissinger then presented the North Vietnamese with a long list of new demands (Porter 1975:145–54, Kolko 1986:439). In particular, the US demanded significant changes to the nature and function of the National Council of Reconciliation and Concord, requested the withdrawal of all references to the Provisional Revolutionary Government (PRG), the NLFs alternative government, from the text and insisted that there be no movement across the Demilitarized Zone.

To counter the US demands and to compel them to resume their October negotiating position, the North Vietnamese then began to withdraw concessions and to make their own new demands. As a result, the negotiations became deadlocked and the Christmas Bombing took place in order to force Hanoi to accept Washington's new, revised peace terms and to illustrate Nixon's resolve to the rest of the world. The strategy failed, however, because the Christmas Bombing was a political and military failure. According to DRV sources, the US Air Force lost thirty-four of its giant B-52 bombers over North Vietnam, and this astonishingly high figure prompted the military to call for the bombing to be halted because of the vast financial penalties they were incurring (Porter 1975:161–3, Kolko 1986:441). Politically the Christmas Bombing was also ineffective. It created domestic and international outrage and, despite rapprochement with China and the Soviet Union, there was evidence that the bombing was beginning to disrupt detente (Porter 1975:162–3, Kolko 1986:442). Bowing to this pressure Nixon ordered a halt to *Linebacker II*. Now that he had bombed Hanoi and Haiphong and so had used his trump card, Nixon had no new levers with which to pressurize the DRV to accept his revised demands. The US therefore had to settle for the terms which it had previously rejected.

A second interpretation of events concentrates more specifically on internal White House politics. According to this analysis, Kissinger was unsure of his position in the Nixon administration. A number of the president's aides, and even Nixon himself, were hostile to Kissinger and resented his popularity. The special assistant consequently wanted to secure his position in the new government and to improve his chances of being appointed Secretary of State by making it politically impossible for Nixon to drop him. He hoped to achieve this by securing a peace with North Vietnam which would thereby increase his political standing and would give <u>him</u> greater leverage with the president (Hersh 1983:508–9). Kissinger therefore began to follow a more independent path in negotiations with the DRV. Although he did not appreciate the pace and scope of Kissinger's efforts to reach an agreement, Nixon supported his special assistant during the talks. His support was cynical and insincere because he was profoundly reluctant to conclude an agreement. Nixon actively misled Kissinger by permitting negotiations to proceed whilst actually being unwilling to commit the US to an agreement. The reason for his reluctance was that the promise of peace was a valuable political commodity in an election year. Conversely a peace agreement which incorporated concessions by the US could be attacked by his critics and was a distinct liability in the election race (Kalb and Kalb 1974:385).

Nixon probably predicted Thieu's refusal to sign the October draft and encouraged Kissinger to proceed with the negotiations in the knowledge that he himself would not bring pressure to bear upon the South Vietnamese president. According to Nixon's reasoning, the negotiations would subsequently breakdown, there would be no hasty and politically inexpedient peace settlement prior to the election and Kissinger's reputation would take a significant knock (Hersh 1983:595). This seemed an enticing prospect, especially as Nixon thought that the glory of securing a peace agreement should belong to a president and not his overweening assistant.

Once the US presidential elections were over, the re-elected Nixon then moved to find his own way out of Vietnam. But while the US-DRV/PRG negotiations which resumed in November may have appeared to be the critical forum where peace, if it came, was finally going to be concluded, the real negotiations which ended the US role in Vietnam were going on in secret between Thieu and Nixon. Because of the political damage that the charge of abandoning Thieu might have brought—an especially noxious charge when levelled at a president who derived much support from his fierce anticommunism, Nixon was adamant in his refusal to force Thieu into a settlement. Thieu had to be persuaded that the US was not abandoning him and his regime. Consequently, at the end of November 1972, Nixon decided to reach a secret agreement with the South Vietnamese president in which he promised that the US would consider any forthcoming political agreement to be meaningless, would consider Thieu to be the sovereign ruler over all of South Vietnam's territory and would not censure GVN military and political activities contravening a peace agreement. He also undertook to retaliate with US airpower in the event of a North Vietnamese offensive (Hersh 1983:616). In order to prove to Thieu that his promises were credible and, hence, bribe him into allowing America to claim that it had won 'peace with honor', Nixon then undertook the bombing of Hanoi and Haiphong (Hersh 1983:624). The Christmas Bombing, therefore, was aimed not at forcing the DRV to sign the peace agreement, but rather to induce Thieu to sign by proving that the US government was committed enough to the fate of the GVN to risk prompting a political and diplomatic crisis.

This interpretation of events is given some credence by Nixon's actions. Even when he went on television to announce that the Agreement had been signed, he stated that the US administration considered the 'Government of the Republic of Vietnam as the sole legitimate government of South Vietnam'. Moreover, secret letters to Thieu promising US air support against the DRV/PRG emphasize that, even if Nixon's promises and his private negotiations with Thieu were not central to the process of negotiations and to the events surrounding the Christmas Bombing, they must have played a significant role in encouraging Thieu to sign. The question remains whether Nixon's promises were nothing more than lies made for short-term political gain. The question will remain unanswered because, when the time came to test his promises, Nixon was unable to respond as he had been overtaken by the shadow of Watergate.

A third explanation and one that, with slight variations, finds favour with many of the major figures of the day, Nixon and Kissinger included, concludes that it was initially Thieu's truculence and later Hanoi's intransigence that led to the Christmas Bombing. Realizing that Thieu would be opposed to the peace agreement Kissinger decided to keep him uninformed about the negotiations. He feared that Thieu would leak details to the press and would rally South Vietnamese popular opinion against the proposed agreement and so concluded that it was better to present Thieu with a *fait accompli* (Goodman 1978:125) and to assuage his doubts by swamping South Vietnam with military equipment through operations *Enhance* and *Enhance Plus*. Clearly Kissinger had made a giant miscalculation. One writer argues that what then followed was the price of Kissinger's overinflated statesmanship (Morris 1977:191).

Thieu's objections to the October draft and his refusal to sign within the set timetable led the DRV to question the United States' sincerity. The doubt caused pro-war elements in the Hanoi Politburo to raise their concern over the October draft and gave them the opportunity to push for a better settlement. Hence the negotiating deadlock in December 1972 was caused by Hanoi's refusal to accept its own October draft and the Christmas Bombing was undertaken by the US in order to compel the DRV to soften its demands and return to the negotiating table once again. *Linebacker II* achieved this (Herz 1980: ix). Hanoi rushed to conclude a peace settlement, and an agreement similar to the October draft was therefore signed.

Whatever motives gave rise to the complex history of America's last three months of conflict in Vietnam, and the above interpretations are by no means exhaustive, the Paris Peace Agreement signed on 27 January 1973 brought to an end the longest war in American history. It did not, however, bring to an end the fighting in Vietnam. There was, as had been predicted, not a cease-fire but a 'less-fire' and even this was but a temporary lull. War raged on in beleaguered Cambodia and in weary and now divided South Vietnam. There was peace and perhaps some measure of honour for the United States but, in post-US Vietnam, there was still no peace and little room for honour.

5   The war at home

The Vietnam War was not fought solely in South East Asia. Domestic politics in the United States played a fundamental role in defining the nature and scope of the conflict. The antiwar movement, in particular, was to have a decisive impact upon the pursuit of the war and ultimately brought about a re-evaluation of American participation in the struggle against North Vietnam and the National Liberation Front.

THE UNITED STATES' DECISIONMAKING MACHINE

There is no single rationale to explain US involvement in South East Asia. Most influential literature on why America remained unable to extricate itself from Vietnam for such a lengthy period falls into three major categories: the quagmire theory, the stalemate theory and what can be deemed the constraints of bureaucratic politics.

The quagmire theory was the original, widely accepted analysis of America's role in Vietnam (Schlesinger 1967). Variations on this theme are common but their logic is uniform. Vietnam was not always vital to US interests but it became so because of the initial US commitment of prestige and power. When it appeared that each escalatory step was insufficient to achieve the objective of keeping the GVN afloat, another step was taken. In this manner the US sank ever deeper into the quicksand of the war. The 'investment trap' model and the 'slippery slope' theory are both premised on this same belief that escalation followed inexorably from the failure of the previous level of commitment. In essence, therefore, the US became bogged down in South East Asia not because its goals grew ever wider but because the cost of achieving the same goals increased. Believing that the nation was unable to divest itself of its promise to support the South Vietnamese regime and to acknowledge that its earlier commitment of time, money and men had been a failure, successive administrations were literally sucked into the maelstrom of a widening war.

Later literature questioned the 'quagmire theory' and instead suggested the 'stalemate theory' (Ellsberg 1972, Gelb and Betts 1979, Kattenberg 1980). According to the stalemate thesis, the US did not find itself in a quagmire in Vietnam and the key to understanding policy in South East Asia was to be found in the domestic political situation.

Since 1945 US presidents have been caught in a trap largely of their own making. The Cold War mentality was created in part and subsequently encouraged in America by administrations which feared a return to pre-war isolationism and the opportunity which this would afford to Soviet expansionism. In order to encourage support for the United States' post-war internationalist role, the public had to recognize that America had a mission in the world. But in generating hatred of communism and helping to create a climate of hysteria, US governments were also ensnaring themselves in their own rhetoric. The triumphs of communism had to be seen to be fiercely combatted by the US leadership. Failure to do so would lead to a diminution in America's political, military and moral standing in the world and would threaten any incumbent government.

US presidents from Eisenhower onwards feared the spectre of another round of McCarthyite anticommunism. They remembered the furore surrounding the 'loss' of China in 1949 and the effect that it had upon Truman's popularity and they feared that 'losing' Vietnam would have a similar impact upon their own presidency. There was countervailing pressure, however, from those anxious to avoid another Asian land war after Korea, and memories of the beleaguered Truman, criticized on all sides, haunted his successors who had to deal with the Vietnam problem.

Each president knew that Vietnam was potentially critical to his administration. Their strategy, therefore, was to avoid becoming involved militarily while doing just enough to keep the South Vietnamese government on an even keel. At the beginning of each new president's term of office his predecessor briefed him on South East Asia and passed him the 'hot potato' (Gelb and Betts 1979:27–30) which he would endeavour, in turn, to pass on to his successor without the issue coming to a head and presenting him with insuperable problems during his own term of office.

Successive US presidents did no more in Vietnam than that required to maintain the stalemate and they did this at the lowest cost feasible. This strategy was especially clear during Johnson's presidency when the collapse of South Vietnam was forestalled but only in a manner designed to avoid a wider war and domestic criticism from damaging the Great Society.

When Richard Nixon came to office in 1969, he wanted to end the costly US involvement in Vietnam but it was only when domestic considerations were satisfied that the nation could withdraw from South East Asia. In particular, the rapprochement with China, effectively 'regaining' it after a period of over twenty years, meant that US public opinion was that much more amenable to the thought of 'losing' Vietnam, especially if abandoning the South Vietnamese regime was cloaked in the guise of Vietnamization (Kattenberg 1980:250). Between 1968 and 1973, therefore, the Nixon administration did as much to end the war by manoeuvering to reorientate domestic public opinion as it did to end the war by achieving some form of victory.

It has been argued that as the situation in the United States was the principal concern of successive presidents and that as their foreign policy actually prevented the domestic crisis which would have been provoked by the fall of the GVN, then US policy can be held to have been successful. In this sense, although the Vietnam War as a military endeavour failed, the foreign policy decisionmaking process was successful. This was, as Leslie Gelb states, the irony of Vietnam (Gelb and Betts 1979:1-2). Arguably, it also reflects the extent to which intellectual gymnastics can metamorphose the Vietnam War into a conflict that America 'won'.

A third school of thought concentrates more specifically on bureaucratic politics (Gallucci 1975). As the war progressed, the US became locked into its existing policy in South East Asia and serious constructive criticism did not emerge or was not given credence. The mechanics of the decisionmaking system narrowed and restricted US policy in Vietnam so that alternatives were not considered and so that individuals involved in formulating policy exerted a strong and often negative influence which discouraged reappraisals.

During Johnson's presidency, differing viewpoints did exist but they were not substantive and were generally differences over emphasis rather than over fundamental issues. This was because the beliefs of each participant in the policymaking process were premised on the validity of Cold War ideology. Nevertheless, what differences did exist were smoothed over by creating a superficial bureaucratic consensus. Decisions were therefore compromises with which no one, except perhaps the president, in his never-ending search for consensus, was actually satisfied (Gallucci 1975:39, 47).

According to this explanation, the US found itself involved in Vietnam as a result of decisions made incrementally, often as a product of compromise within the bureaucracy. The goals that the administration were pursuing were not static but shifted over time. Moreover, while the decisionmaking process under Kennedy was flexible and open, that during his successor's term of office was more restricted

Two factors were of critical significance in bringing about the narrowing of the bounds of debate during LBJ's administration. First was Johnson's personality. Unable to brook criticism, he effectively restricted policy debates within his own narrowly defined parameters. Second was the role of Dean Rusk (Gallucci 1975:32–33). Secretary of State during the later years of the Kennedy administration and then for Johnson, Rusk's handling of his department ensured that its contribution to the formulation of US foreign policy was severely curtailed, at least after 1963. Conditioned by memories of the Second World War, Rusk had an unquestioned belief in the need for America to exhibit its resolve and avoid appeasement at all costs. In addition, he had a heightened respect for military acumen and this led him to defer to military leaders when he should have been balancing their influence in policy formulation with a countervailing emphasis on a political and diplomatic approach to the conflict. Inevitably, the bureaucratic process malfunctioned because of this lack of balance, so leading to a progressively restricted arena of debate. The State Department became ineffective and inefficient and the centre of foreign policy formulation moved further into the hands of those advocating a military solution.

Whether Rusk's role was pivotal in bureaucratic politics and in the development of US involvement in Vietnam is questionable. But other related aspects of the decisionmaking system certainly did have an impact upon America's role in South East Asia.

All policymakers who had a direct bearing upon the formulation of Vietnam policy accepted the validity of the containment doctrine as axiomatic. This basic premise lay at the heart of the New Frontier. The young men who swept to power along with J.F.Kennedy believed that no problem was too big or too complex for them to solve and that communism, in the form of the burgeoning 'wars of national liberation', had to be halted lest the future should belong to the mortal enemies of the US. Global stability therefore became the essential goal of US policy in the 1960s. But 'system maintenance', which became the watchword for American analysts, was inherently unworkable because it was myopic and hindered ultimately inevitable and often positive change in an era of rapid worldwide political and social transformation.

The intellectual arrogance of the New Frontiersmen detracted from the effective application of their containment strategy. Because thwarting liberation movements was a major priority and because the New Frontiersmen believed all such movements to be part of a Moscow-based offensive, they lumped them together as if all emergent liberation movements could be tackled in the same manner irrespective of their historical roots and whether they were occurring in Asia, Africa or Latin America. Consequently, experts on specific areas were pushed aside in favour of policymakers who thought in global terms (Kattenberg 1980:173–4). A great amount of knowledge and insight into the dynamics of revolutionary wars, including that in Indochina, was thereby lost.

Particularly following the Cuban Missile Crisis in 1961, US policymakers found an increasing premium placed upon the role of toughness, even *machismo,* in foreign policy. The tough, level-headed, determined man was a hero straight from America's cultural past. He was also the dynamic, young, ambitious contemporary man—the kind who, like Kennedy, could go right to the brink of nuclear war. This gave birth to 'crisis management'—to a tendency to tackle problems as they arose and to formulate policy on an *ad hoc* basis.

The New Frontiersmen and those in Johnson's entourage who were mesmerized by their own brilliance and ability to conjure up perfect military and political scenarios with a flourish of mathematical equations were blinded to the failure of their strategy, be it in Vietnam or elsewhere. The fundamental problem lay in a failure of analysis. Their answer to lack of success in Vietnam was simply to do what they were doing already, but to do it better (Kattenberg 1980:188). They confused their thorough and sophisticated management of existing programmes with the actual exercise of policymaking in which they rarely indulged (Kattenberg 1980:207). The preponderance of technocrats within all levels of the bureaucracy naturally gave rise to analysis of the Vietnam War based upon contrived and often artificial formulae which used arbitrary statistics and evaluations bearing little relevance to the reality of war and politics in South East Asia. In 1962, McNamara insisted that 'every quantitive measure we have shows we're winning this war' (Schlesinger 1965:478), but science and the computer could not defeat the NLF and no amount of flip charts, graphs and intellectual wizardry could really predict the outcome of a political and military situation in which so much remained unknown and in which there were an infinite number of variables.

Each of the analyses of why America intervened and remained in

Vietnam may contain a grain of truth. Domestic politics and the need to avoid losing Vietnam were of undoubted importance, but even if the stalemate theory is correct, US presidents certainly did not contemplate the extent to which they would have to commit US prestige, manpower and money in order to maintain the stalemate. In this sense the quagmire theory is valid. Bureaucratic mechanics and politics then added momentum to the evolution of US policy in Vietnam.

CONGRESS AND THE VIETNAM WAR

A fundamental tenet of the American constitution is that the president and Congress, termed the executive and legislative branches respectively, are cast in adversarial roles. The framers of the constitution believed that they could ensure the feasibility and workability of the system by balancing the two branches of government because each would place a check upon the other.

During the Vietnam War, however, Congress failed to fulfil this adversarial role and criticism was levelled at the legislative branch precisely because it did not function as a counterweight to the executive, questioning its Vietnam policy and restraining it when the need arose. In the same way that the initial stages of other wars had witnessed an expansion of presidential authority, the opening years of the Vietnam War saw a growth in executive power. Following the same cyclical pattern, this then gave rise to a reassertion of legislative muscle during the later phases of the conflict (Koenig 1987:85). Accordingly, Congress remained supine while America escalated in Vietnam and it was not until 1968 that significant opposition to the nation's role in South East Asia began to be heard on Capitol Hill. From then on, in the wake of the Tet Offensive, even a majority of congressional hawks opposed sending more ground combat troops to Vietnam.

The need to combat communism following the Second World War dictated that Congress should give universal support to presidential actions which were taken in defence of US security interests. Bipartisan foreign policy was the product of Cold War ideology and it ensured that the president was given unswerving support in the pursuit of containment unless opinion deemed, as in the case of Truman and China, that he was not combatting communism as energetically as he should. Bipartisanship continued until the end of the 1960s when the consensus which had sustained it broke down under the strain of the war (Koenig 1987:97).

During the early years of the Johnson administration, when an official opposition would have been especially valuable, Congress was found to be particularly malleable. This derived, in part, from the skill which Johnson displayed in manipulating Congress and, in part, because, after his years as Senate Majority Leader, he still had many friends there upon whom he could count to support him.

The Gulf of Tonkin Resolution is the best example of the president's handling of Congress during this period. Although Johnson knew that it was not constitutionally necessary to obtain congressional authority in order to pursue an active policy in South East Asia, he believed that it was politically expedient to gain official endorsement from the legislative branch for any military action (Schlesinger 1974:177).

The Republican Party did a good deal to encourage US involvement in Vietnam. Pressure from it to act in South East Asia added to the Kennedy administration's determination to prop up the ailing GVN and contributed to the policies which resulted in US participation in the war (Dietz 1986:55–6). During Johnson's presidency the Republicans carried on the role of the 'loyal opposition'. They were mindful to gain political capital from the way the government was fighting the war but at the same time they supported the president in an effort to maintain the bipartisan consensus on foreign policy. This left them in a dilemma because, whilst their role was to criticize the Democratic president, they basically agreed with the fundamental principles of his policy. They too wanted the US to fight the war in Vietnam. In order to criticize constructively, therefore, they demanded more effective use of US military power.

Paradoxically, although Johnson was a Democrat he found some of the strongest supporters of his Vietnam policy within the ranks of the Republican Party. Unfortunately for LBJ, the base of his national support was the liberal wing of the Democratic Party—those who were ardent exponents of the Great Society. Yet these were the very people whom he was alienating through his foreign policy. Conversely, those who were enthusiastic over his foreign policy were the very people who found his domestic policies anathema. Inevitably, therefore, Johnson pleased no one.

Even as opposition to the war increased during 1965 most congressmen supported the government's Vietnam policy. To many, foreign policy issues were not vital to their re-election and so they tended to follow the lead of the president in classic bipartisan fashion. For some congressmen and senators with military installations and military suppliers in their districts, it was a political necessity to support the war. But for the small but increasing number who opposed the conflict, the avenues for expression of their opposition were few and largely ineffective. Many dissenters operated independently and so diluted their potential political impact. Compounding the faintness of their voice was the fact that most were junior members who were not represented on influential committees.

Criticism of the administration's Vietnam policy nevertheless mounted in Congress during Johnson and Nixon's terms of office and between 1966 and 1972 both houses held numerous hearings on various aspects of the war. But until the early 1970s, Congress did not combat the administration's Vietnam policy productively. This was partly because there was no institutionalized method of doing so, partly because Congress was unwilling to act until public opinion directed it to and also because, to oppose the war and, in particular, to restrict funds to fight the war, would be considered tantamount to endangering the lives of men in the field. Revealingly, once US troops were withdrawn from Vietnam and US POWs had been repatriated, Congress began to slash aid to Vietnam with almost indecent haste.

Congress's attitude to the war did begin to change with the election of Richard Nixon. Democratic opponents of the war now felt free to express their discontent without being disloyal to their party (Mueller 1984:154). But it was the Cambodian invasion of 1970 which did most to generate broad congressional opposition to the conflict (Walker 1987:106). Hitherto, Nixon had been spared from intense hostility to his policies because he had inherited the war and was dealing with a situation not of his own making. But the Cambodian incursion was seen as a widening of the war and as Nixon's novel contribution towards it, and this is why it prompted such violent opposition (Isaacs 1983:493). The president could no longer claim to be tidying up someone else's mess. It was no longer 'Johnson's War' but 'Nixon's War'. Paradoxically, however, while congressional opinion was more hostile towards the war by this time, Nixon's policy of Vietnamization made it very difficult for Congress to mount an aggressive attack on continued involvement in Vietnam (Dumbrell 1989:108).

When opposition to the administration's handling of the war began to emerge in Congress, it crystallized around a number of groups. Early in the conflict there were the Senate doves who argued against the war on moral grounds. In the House of Representatives there were both hawks and doves, but the two most influential factions speaking out on Vietnam were led by Senators John Stennis and William Fulbright. Stennis and his Armed Forces Committee took a hard-line approach and attacked LBJ for not pursuing the war with sufficient vigour. Fulbright, Chairman of the Foreign Relations Committee, led the antiwar fraternity. Once an exponent of the bipartisan rule, Fulbright had even helped guide the Gulf of Tonkin Resolution through Congress. His opinion of Johnson's handling of foreign policy issues began to change, however, particularly after the Dominican Republic crisis of April 1965 when Johnson sent the US marines to the Caribbean island, ostensibly to put down a violent communist revolution which turned out to be little more than an expedient figment of the president's very fertile imagination. Throughout 1965 Fulbright's doubts about Vietnam sharpened until he became one of the most vocal critics of the administration. His views which, over time, became damning, earned him the president's fierce and characteristic enmity. To Johnson, the supreme egotist, Fulbright's criticism was a personal affront and provoked LBJ to nickname him 'Senator Halfbright'.

In February 1966, the Senate Foreign Relations Committee began to hold public, televised hearings on the war and it was evident from the tenor of the discussion that a majority on the committee had deep reservations about the conflict. But despite providing a forum for the articulation of latent opposition, the hearings had little impact upon the formulation of policy. Instead their main contribution to the growing antiwar movement was to illustrate to ordinary people that opposition to the war was not restricted to some lunatic fringe and that respected politicians were willing to argue against the administration's policy. This made no small contribution to the legitimization of dissent.

As Congress became more dovish in the early 1970s, it moved to reassert itself and to regain a role in foreign policy decisionmaking. Thus, in January 1971, the Gulf of Tonkin Resolution was repealed and the Cooper-Church Amendment banned the further use of American ground forces in Cambodia. Following Nixon's orgiastic Christmas Bombing in December 1972, Congress then forbade the use of American troops in Vietnam after mid-August 1973. Congress's most important move, though, was to pass the War Powers Act in November 1973. This allowed the president to undertake emergency military action but made the further involvement of the military subject to congressional acceptance.

To underline the re-emergence of legislative power, congressional approval for the act also coincided with the more effective utilization of its power over appropriations. While it had always retained the ability to authorize levels of finance, it had not exercised this means of control imaginatively until the early 1970s when, despite opposition from the administration, it began to cut appropriations for South Vietnam. What all this amounted to was the beginnings of a reappearance of congressional muscle during the 1970s. Frustrated and emasculated by presidential aggrandizement since the Second World War, Congress was re-entering the foreign policy debate. Vietnam was the primary cause of this political comeback (Walker 1987:110) and Watergate, following hard on its heels, pushed it to centre stage.

THE MEDIA AND THE WAR IN VIETNAM

The nature and effect of media coverage of the Vietnam War is a source of contention. Some have argued that the media played a significant part in foiling the US military and political effort by undermining support for the war at home (Lewy 1978:433–4, Westmorland 1980:553–8). However, the commonly-held view that the media was consistently hostile to the war has been challenged and has been shown to be a myth (Hallin 1986).

Johnson's relationship with the media was one of the weaknesses of his administration. In stark contrast to Kennedy, neither he nor his government ever developed a rapport with the media. At a most basic level, Johnson's treatment of media personnel made the execution of their professional duties extremely onerous (Turner 1985:62–4, 77–8). His press conferences were irregular and his unpredictability made life hard for those reporters sent to monitor the president on his peregrinations. The problem grew to absurd, albeit amusing, proportions when Johnson gave impromptu interviews whilst walking at great speed around the White House lawn, followed by a trail of exhausted and exasperated journalists.

LBJ's poor public image began to develop almost as soon as he became president. His love of secrecy and the wheeler-dealing that had made him such an effective Senate Majority Leader were seen almost as vices in a president. A penchant for secrecy was no advantage when the media and the public wanted a president who was open and honest.

After his election in 1964, LBJ's image gradually deteriorated. His clumsy and ill-humoured television appearances won him no friends and, despite all his great talents and despite his astounding personal career, Johnson nurtured a boundless inferiority complex. He feared and despised the intelligentsia and the cultured circles of the eastern seaboard precisely because he was not one of them and thought, probably correctly, that they derided him for his Texan origins and his undistinguished academic background. He placed the media—or at least the prestige press—within this constituency and his treatment of them was unsure and therefore counterproductive. He looked for the friendship of journalists, thinking that they would thereby endorse his policies. When they did not, he counted them amongst his worst enemies.

Johnson believed it to be the duty of journalists to support the president in foreign policy matters. As his faith in this belief was gradually eroded, Johnson took pains to restrict information to the press. Realizing that public opinion was important, the administration therefore developed a 'policy of controlled optimism' (Gelb 1972:465). They created the impression that the war was being prosecuted successfully. But by creating that illusion they were activating a time bomb because sooner or later, when the results of that success did not materialize, the public would come to doubt the veracity of the government's assertions. Out of this was born the credibility gap.

In the history of wars, Vietnam is unique in the extent to which it was monitored by the media. This was all the more apparent because Vietnam was the first uncensored war. Because of the nature of the war, censorship was considered a practical impossibility. Enforcing the rule would have been difficult because it would have necessitated different jurisdictions for US civilians and third country nationals and, as the war was never officially declared, it would have been hard to justify politically (Hallin 1986:127). Journalists were therefore allowed to accompany military forces in action without being subject to the limitations of formal censorship. They did have to abide by certain commonsense rules, such as discretion when writing about forthcoming missions and troop strength and, in general, this informal control worked well and there were few examples of flagrant disregard for security.

Nevertheless, journalists' reports were poorly received in a White House anxious about the domestic political climate. This media-administration tension was not confined solely to Johnson's term of office. Even Kennedy, the darling of the US media, was irritated by a section of the media's treatment of his Vietnam policy. In 1963, for instance, he requested that *New York Times* correspondent, David Halberstam, be recalled from Vietnam because of his critical reporting (Halberstam 1965:268).

Five periods of overt conflict marked the low points of government-media relations during the war. The first occurred in 1963 when the Kennedy administration became worried by increasingly hostile reports from Saigon. Second was in 1965 when US marines were televised burning the village of Cam Ne. Third was the media coverage of the 1968 Tet Offensive. Fourth was when, in 1971, the *New York Times* published excerpts from the *Pentagon Papers,* which was the Defense

Department's history of the war and which was based on revealing, classified documents. The fifth and final period of intense acrimony was during the 1972–3 Christmas Bombing of Hanoi and Haiphong.

It was under Nixon that the relationship between the media and the administration reached its nadir as sections of the media became more and more hostile to elements of the president's Vietnam strategy. The government was furious when the *New York Times* exposed the secret bombing of Cambodia in 1969 and when it began to publish portions of the *Pentagon Papers*. There was also media outrage at the 1972–3 Christmas Bombing of Hanoi and Haiphong which resulted, according to some critics, in biased and wantonly inaccurate stories particularly from the prestigious journals (Herz 1980). In response to the hostility shown by some journalists Nixon thus inaugurated a wide-ranging programme to pressurize the media into becoming more compliant. To some extent, this proved a success.

Notwithstanding the periods of media-administration controversy, the news coverage of the Vietnam War was not as negative as is often presumed (Hallin 1986:10–11) and what criticism there was did not, as a rule, question the morality of the war but rather questioned the government's optimistic appraisal of the conflict (Mohr 1987:182). Many processes worked in favour of the government, restricting opposing viewpoints and muting the criticism that did emerge. In the early 1960s, the Cold War consensus still predominated. Presidents and reporters therefore shared the same world view. They all believed in America's international role and reduced the complexity of the Vietnam War to the familiar and simplistic battle between 'freedom' and 'communism'. Only gradually was this consensus eroded.

The press in the mid-1960s and, in particular, the prestigious papers such as the *New York Times* and the *Washington Post* differed from today in fundamental respects. A great distinction was drawn between reporting the 'facts' and analysis of the facts. Analysis was left to editorials and columnists while the front page news consisted of official statements. Pronouncements by the administration were the major source of news and these were reported unquestioningly. Moreover the press concentrated on immediate events as the only real news. This meant that day to day events were given a far higher priority than an examination of piecemeal changes in policy taken over a long time period (Hallin 1986:70–4).

Myth has it that television coverage of the conflict in Vietnam had a profound impact upon America's ability to conduct the war and upon the national resolve to fight. The reporting of the destruction of the village of Cam Ne has been cited as an example of television's inadequate and therefore biased coverage (Lewy 1978:53), for whilst a shocked US public watched as marines set fire to the thatched homes of Vietnamese villagers with cigarette lighters, they were not made fully aware that the village was an NLF stronghold and that a maze of tunnels ran under the blazing homes. The reporting of the Cam Ne episode, however, was an exception and, especially up until the Tet Offensive, television coverage was weighted in favour of the US role in Vietnam (Hallin 1986:109).

Television opened up the horror of war to the people back home in a way that had never been possible before. Because it is a dramatic medium it concentrates upon the negative. It was especially hard to capture the Vietnam War on film because of the difficulty of fashioning visually exciting and attention-grabbing pictures based on aspects of the political struggle. In contrast, film of devastated buildings and casualties was far more easy to come by and had far more impact on television screens back home. Yet, even given this incentive to concentrate on the bloody aspects of the conflict, the proportion of film reports, prior to Tet, that showed actual combat was a surprisingly low 22 per cent (Hallin 1986:129). This hardly amounted to an exclusive concentration upon the raw horror of war.

The pressure for good ratings and the very format of television news made it a far from perfect transmitter of what was occurring in South East Asia. Because of the need to compress stories into short, visually stimulating items, facts invariably became distorted (Arlen 1969:7–8) and because commercial networks have to mix information and entertainment there was constant pressure to dwell on emotionally cathartic and militarily-orientated subjects. Understandably, news coverage concentrated heavily upon the US soldier and there was an incentive to thematize coverage by following one story for several days in order to make more entertaining viewing.

It appears likely that television followed rather than led public opinion. Not until after a majority of the population had turned against the war after the Tet Offensive did TV coverage begin to become more critical of the war in Vietnam (Hallin 1986:162–3). Moreover, the possible negative impact of television coverage of the conflict must be tempered by the fact that only a minority—approximately one-third—of Americans watch any television news at all and when they do so they are likely to be somewhat sceptical of the reliability of the information provided (Hallin 1986:107).

The Tet Offensive, in particular, highlighted the media's handling of the Vietnam War and some observers feel that the portrayal of Tet was distorted enough to have a profound and unwarranted impact at home.

With the exception of a few seasoned individuals, the journalists and television reporters in Vietnam had little experience of the war. They knew virtually nothing of the language and had few insights into Vietnamese culture. Few journalists saw actual combat prior to the Tet Offensive. Most were based in the relative luxury of Saigon from where they wrote of the rigours of the war from their hotels. Accompanying military forces for a few hours, they would be flown to the scene of a battle by helicopter and then whisked back to Saigon. They witnessed little combat precisely because most US combat units saw very little combat. It therefore came as a profound shock when the Tet Offensive made the war intrude into their previously peaceful Saigon-based existence.

The fact that the Tet Offensive was directed against the cities where journalists and film crews were based was of great significance. The war was taking place right before their eyes where they could witness battles first-hand. The impact upon the media was immense and the copy and film sent back to the US was a reflection of their shock and of their ability to capture the images of war. The coverage of the attack upon the US embassy in Saigon is a case in point. The embassy was a symbol of the American presence in Vietnam, a supposedly impregnable building. It was, moreover, a matter of yards from the hotel where many media personnel were staying. It was a heaven-sent opportunity for journalists who flocked to the embassy to record the action. Consequently, although the attack was of relatively minor military importance it assumed gigantic proportions to those present and to those back at home who read their reports and watched the film of the events (Braestrup 1977:125).

Images of devastation were relayed to the US from the cities of South Vietnam. In Hue, which was the scene of a major battle during the offensive and which suffered a great deal from the lavish use of firepower, film crews recorded pictures of unparalleled damage. In concentrating upon the scenes of destruction in a few cities, the impression was given that the whole of South Vietnam was a similar wasteland. However, the Tet Offensive did not affect most rural areas and so the coverage of the offensive in the US was not thorough enough to give an overall viewpoint. Furthermore, the wire services contributed to the initial impression of enemy successes by using unverified information on the grounds that to release an inaccurate story first was better than releasing an accurate story last. Only later were these reports found to be unreliable (Braestrup 1977:86).

In the rush for a good, long-running story, the media, especially the television networks, concentrated upon the large battle for the garrison Khe Sanh which raged during the Tet Offensive. As it lasted for seventy-two days and provided the prospect of a US Dien Bien Phu and a focus of interesting material for a lengthy period, it therefore received more emphasis in contemporary reporting than it perhaps deserved. In particular, as the battle went on long after the brunt of the offensive had been contained, the media coverage gave the impression that PLAF/PAVN pressure had not been eased (Braestrup 1977:338–9).

The Tet Offensive and the media's presentation of events changed only a few people's minds about the war. With the initial shock came a sudden surge of support for a more aggressive military line, but as realization of the scale and implications of the offensive gradually sank in, more people than ever before turned against the war and against Johnson's handling of his presidency (Roper 1977:674–704).

Public opinion had been in favour of US action in Vietnam in 1964 but support for the war had been steadily eroded. What the Tet Offensive did was not so much to push a whole section of formerly pro-war individuals into the antiwar camp but to tip the balance, so that whereas a slender majority had supported the war prior to the offensive, a slender majority then became critical of it. The offensive and the media coverage of the action therefore had only a small impact upon the US public and Tet appears as a 'minor ripple in a steadily changing public attitude to the war' (Roper 1977:699).

In the form that it took, it has been claimed that the reporting of the Tet Offensive shaped the climate of public debate (Braestrup 1977:621–2). Crucially, although it had only a limited effect upon US public opinion as a whole, those that it did affect were members of the elite—the press, politicians and officials in Washington. Because elite opinion was shocked by the Tet Offensive, and as they believed that popular opinion had been shaken just as profoundly, the elite felt that some dramatic shift in policy would be needed to assuage public doubt and concern. Yet, as public opposition to the war, in terms of sheer numbers, had shifted only marginally as a result of Tet, this belief was wrong. The media consequently played an important role in changing attitudes to the war because it made decisionmakers assume that media coverage of Tet affected popular opinion.

THE ANTIWAR MOVEMENT

A great deal of mythology surrounds the antiwar movement and its effects are variously described. Some hold that it had little impact upon policymaking because it was perceived by ordinary people to be dominated by unpatriotic, dishevelled hippies and maniacal revolutionaries (Gelb 1976:112). Others endow it with colossal significance, believing that it 'forced the United States out of Vietnam' (Unger 1974:207). Neither view is entirely correct. The movement which was 'spawned and sustained' by the bombing of North Vietnam (Small 1988:32) had a far more complex effect upon America's Vietnam policy. Ultimately it was to set the parameters of acceptable US conduct in South East Asia and restrained the Johnson and Nixon administrations from stepping beyond them.

Antiwar dissent began to coalesce around scattered and diverse groups in 1964 and early 1965. Amongst these were religious groups, pacifists, conscientious objectors, the 'old left' who were the remnants of the discredited Stalinist parties from the 1930s and also the New Left. The broad spectrum of antiwar dissent meant that, right from the outset, it was extremely fluid and incorporated an inchoate mass of people in a shifting and largely leaderless coalition. This was a positive attribute in that antiwar sentiment united people of otherwise widely different and incompatible positions and it also made the movement less vulnerable to external attack (DeBeneditti 1987:27). At the same time, it was also a reflection of its weakness as there was little coordination and overall control, so dissipating energy and making the movement lose momentum and direction.

At its inception, antiwar dissent was dominated by students and it was students who were the vital component of the movement. Almost all major demonstrations took place during the spring and autumn when students were in their colleges and ready to be mobilized (Small 1988:22–3). It therefore fell to SDS (Students for a Democratic Society) as the prominent student group to give a form of leadership to the movement during its early days of dissent.

For years student politics in the US had been uninspiring and establishment orientated With the advent of the 1960s, however, the tenor began to change. A proportion of affluent, white, middle-class children, born into an age of economic buoyancy, became preoccupied, not with gaining a good qualification at college, but with the more glamorous existence of a student revolutionary (Unger 1974:34–5). They were thoroughly disenchanted with life in modern America and could afford to flaunt their disaffection. Such politically inclined students were always in a minority but they were so visible and had such a high profile that other more passive students were frequently overlooked

Born out of a moribund student organization in 1960, SDS, together with the student left in general, grew and began to radicalize very quickly. This was the product of two major influences. First was the inspirational and practical effect of the Civil Rights movement. The second major influence upon student politics was the Vietnam War and it was particularly powerful after 1965 when the Civil Rights movement began to remove white activists from leadership positions on the grounds that the struggle for racial justice had to be led by blacks. This left many white student political activists without a cause and so it was almost inevitable that their energies would be channelled into opposing the expanding war in South East Asia.

During 1964 and 1965, burgeoning antiwar sentiment began to gell around SDS. But the organization's leadership of the movement was transitory and in 1965 it began to turn inward and became wrapped up in its own internal wranglings. At this point it forfeited the leadership of the antiwar movement and, as no other group could effectively assume the responsibility, the movement, henceforth, lacked a unifying leadership.

The left-wing student movement confined an increasing amount of their activity to universities and colleges as the decade wore on. They attacked the educational establishment by sit-ins and by disruptive behaviour. By doing so they believed they could change the politics of the nation and they believed that they were striking at a vulnerable part of the establishment. They failed to realize, however, the error in their reasoning. The universities were considered vital by the students, but this was simply because they were the only area of society in which they, by definition, had any power (O'Neill 1971:283). No matter how many university buildings were occupied and no matter how militant and revolutionary the students believed themselves to be, it was hardly the kind of action that was going to bring the wheels of the hated 'military-industrial complex' grinding to a halt.

SDS degenerated swiftly in the latter half of the 1960s and yet the organization lingered on long after it had ceased to be a key element in the antiwar movement. When it became apparent that SDS and the New Left were failing to bring the war any nearer to a satisfactory conclusion, anger and frustration were expressed in acts of increasing violence. Demonstrations and marches proved to be of no apparent avail and America did not pull out of Vietnam. Misguided and supported by only a minority of the antiwar movement, the turn towards violence was indicative of the New Left's bankrupt political strategy and of its seeming inability to change the course of the war in Vietnam.

This process of increasing radicalization was experienced by other groups. The intellectual left's attitude to the war can be divided into three phases. During the first, lasting from the early 1960s through to January 1965, they perceived the war to be an error in judgement by the administration. In the second phase, lasting from February 1965 to December 1966, it was considered immoral, and from January 1967 as a reflection of the illegitimacy of the political system (Vogelsang 1974:5).

Similar divisions to those which plagued the student left also characterized the intellectual left. In particular there was an increasing gulf between radicals who believed that the existing American political system was defunct and liberals who opposed US intervention in South East Asia but who thought the system tenable (Vogelsang 1974:82).

The dissent of the intellectual left did not take any concrete, coherent form. At the White House Festival of the Arts held by Johnson to woo cultural and intellectual circles in June 1965, a number of critics of the administration's policy voiced veiled and none-too veiled opposition through their contributions, while some simply stayed away. This was one of the high points of the intellectual left's active opposition to the conflict in Vietnam and they never developed a coherent strategy to coordinate their antiwar sentiment nor a programme to achieve peace in South East Asia.

For some in the intellectual left, as in the student left, the antiwar movement was a fashion—a cause to be supported because many of their peers did so. The 1960s in the US witnessed the growth of a strong and distinct counterculture of which one facet was opposition to the Vietnam War. Dissatisfaction and questioning of social and cultural norms would have occurred whether the US was fighting in Vietnam or not and the 1960s would have been a decade of dramatic social change irrespective of the war. The conflict, however, provided a focus around which discontent could coalesce and it gave a *raison d'être* to a generation looking for a cause. For some, therefore, antiwar sentiment was superficial. It was part of the package of radical chic. Amongst certain intellectual and cultural circles, opposition to the war in Vietnam was a condition of acceptance and, to many, commitment to the movement was as transient as the fashions that they followed.

The group that emerged as the clearest manifestation of the counterculture were the hippies. Although their roots were found in the 'beat' generation of the 1950s, the hippie phenomenon became a significant cultural force in the 1960s and especially in the second half of the decade. Their basic aim was to create an alternative culture to the competitive, violent, stress-ridden world of modern America. In its place they proposed a society based on peace, love and drugs which helped to blot out unpleasant reality. But like other sincere movements the hippies soon attracted a whole host of undesirable individuals who wanted a justification to become idle and become involved in the drug scene. The era of the hippies proper did not last long, perhaps only from 1965 to 1966 before it became an escape for a minority of confused, alienated young people and a fashion for the majority of those who professed to be its adherents. By 1967, the integrity of the counterculture was collapsing.

Hippies, ostensibly preaching non-violence, were opposed to the Vietnam War. They joined with the New Left and other antiwar groups in American society to form a very loose, shifting coalition of forces against the war. The forms that dissent took varied from group to group and also altered throughout the war. The initial large-scale forum for the expression of antiwar dissent was the teach-in. On 24–25 March 1965, the University of Michigan held the first of the teach-ins, which were a mixture of lectures and debates denouncing the US role in Vietnam. Teach-ins then followed on many campuses throughout the United States during the summer of 1965, but despite the numbers attending and the antiwar passion that they incited, the teach-in movement came too late to bring about any change in administration policy. Intervention in Vietnam was already a reality and whilst, in 1965, the teach-in was the major focus of opposition to the war, it soon ceased to be a focal point of dissent.

The most popular form of antiwar protest was the demonstration. Marches attracting up to half a million people took place in American cities and upon campuses throughout the war. Generally, the demonstrators were peaceful, or at least the majority of demonstrators were peaceful. A number of protestors occasionally ran into trouble with heavy-handed police but these were usually a minority. Two significant exceptions can be found to this rule. The first was the demonstration in Chicago, staged to coincide with the 1968 Democratic Party Convention. Demonstrators clashed with the police in a series of ugly scenes which, whilst revealing ill-treatment by the police, also put the peace movement in a bad light as a result of television coverage of the events. The second major exception to the non-violent character of antiwar demonstrations was the campus demonstration at Kent State University in Ohio following the sending of US troops into Cambodia in May 1970. The Ohio National Guard was sent on to the campus to deal with the protestors, and when they faced a barrage of rocks, pieces of wood and concrete, the Guard opened fire on the students, killing four and injuring nine. Television cameras recorded the scenes and the nation was shocked to witness the over-reaction of the authorities. Incidents of this kind, however, were unusual in the history of protests against the war in Vietnam.

Several factors helped the movement to become the political and social force it did. First was the administration's clumsy presentation of the war. The credibility gap alienated people and made them more receptive to the criticisms of the antiwar protesters. Second was the rising economic cost of the war. Because of vast governmental expenditure, inflation began to rise and an increase in taxes was inevitable. Moreover, the Civil Rights movement, together with President Kennedy's promises and Johnson's vision of a Great Society, had raised expectations amongst the poor and, principally, amongst poor, black, urban dwellers. But the programmes that were designed to alleviate their poverty were sacrificed to the growing cost of the war in Vietnam. For a time the war itself became an odd form of antipoverty programme in that it increased the demand for war-related supplies and hence increased the demand for labour and especially for black, unskilled labour (Matusow 1984:175). Initially, blacks did not oppose the war as it offered some an escape from the ghetto and many linked the fortunes of the Civil Rights movement to LBJ's administration (Fairclough 1989:115). But the effects of inflation soon undercut the minimal economic gains to society's poorest and the result was a legacy of bitterness and a rising tide of violence and lawlessness in the inner cities. The black riots of the mid- and late-1960s have, in this sense, been attributed, in part, to America's involvement in Vietnam. Alternatively, it has also been argued that Vietnam had nothing to do with the ignition of racial strife because there would have been black poverty irrespective of the war. Money saved would not necessarily have been spent on alleviating hardship and upgrading the ghetto. Instead it would have been spent on tax cuts for the rich. The economic record of post-Vietnam US governments would tend to support this view (Fairclough 1989:121).

The third factor that encouraged the growth of a strong antiwar movement was the effect of generational change. The young people of the 1960s considered themselves free and independent of old-fashioned social and political mores. They thought that they had all the answers and many spurned the ideas and attitudes of their parents as discredited and unenlightened. They therefore fought to distinguish themselves by repudiating the policies which their parents, through their conformity, endorsed The famous and often repeated slogan 'You can't trust anyone over thirty' (O'Neill 1971:279) summed up the fatuousness of the generational divide. Youth's vocal opposition to the war in Vietnam was therefore in part an expression of their need to appear independent and to challenge blinkered old age's control of politics and society.

The draft was one of the most divisive issues in American life during the 1960s. Although there were a large number of exceptions, every male between eighteen and twenty-six was theoretically eligible for service. The military was eager to ensure that everyone believed that they had an obligation to serve. In times of lessened demand for men to fill the ranks, the military, rather than releasing a certain number of men from their obligation, therefore increased the legitimate range of conditions under which individuals could secure exemptions. During the Vietnam War, as manpower needs grew, the list of exemptions contracted accordingly. In this way the draft was manipulated to suit fluctuating demands. The draft was also used in subtle ways to mould the lives and especially the careers of young men. Because draft exemptions could be secured for certain jobs deemed necessary to the nation's well-being, and as students were granted deferments, potential draftees who wanted to avoid service tried hard to fulfil these criteria. This unofficial policy to pressure individuals to follow certain careers, generally in engineering and science and to gain a good education, was known as 'channelling', and until the practice of selective service was abolished in 1969, it ensured that it was the nation's least educated and most disadvantaged who served in Vietnam (Baskir and Strauss 1978:9–18). This was because the sons of many middle-class families were safely enrolled in universities and colleges while their working-class peers could obtain no such exemptions.

Furthermore, the large number of ways in which military service could be avoided were not usually utilized by those lower on the social scale. This was either because of ignorance or simply because recourse to legal advice on exemption was beyond the reach of America's poorer youth.

Approximately 16 million of the 27 million men who were of draft age during the Vietnam War actually escaped the draft completely and, of those who did not, only about 2 million actually served in Vietnam (Baskir and Strauss 1978:31–2). Some 3.5 million were exempted because of their personal status as fathers or husbands, because of their occupations or because they were students or conscientious objectors. Another 5 million were not required for military service because of their physical or mental condition, while 4 million others were lucky enough to secure high lottery numbers when selective service was replaced Under the new system everyone was given a lottery number. The lower the number the more likely the individual was to be called, and the higher the number, the less likely.

Many men cheated the draft by feigning medical conditions or by altering their personal status, for example by marrying more quickly than intended Others escaped by finding refuge abroad, commonly in Canada. There was another category of men, however, who submitted to the draft but who opposed the war and consequently refused to fight. Many could have secured exemptions but instead chose, on principle, to give concrete form to their dissent. For some, opposition to the war and to the draft took the form of a ritual burning of their draft cards. It was an act which became a federal offence carrying with it a possible five-year prison sentence. These and other actions which flouted the authority of the draft boards were orchestrated by the Resistance movement which hoped to bring about an end to the draft and to the war by making the draft unworkable. While it did not cause a breakdown in the system, the action of the Resistance movement was worrying enough for the Johnson administration to seek a way to control it. In 1968 five major figures in the Resistance, including the famous paediatrition Doctor Spock, were indicted on the charge of conspiring to violate the draft. The charges against Spock and his supposed cohorts— none of whom was of draft age—were absurd and a reflection of the administration's desperation to make an example of some suitable, high-profile offenders. All were acquitted, but while the trial proceeded, it became a rallying point for dissent over the war and the draft system which sustained it.

Opposition to the draft was not as intense during Nixon's term of office for two reasons. This was because selective service was abolished and also because the policy of Vietnamization meant that the number of young men called up was significantly reduced The draft still remained a divisive issue in American life but the sharpness of its iniquities was blunted and the scale of its demands was contracting.

Draft resisters and antiwar protestors made good stories and the coverage that the media gave these groups consequently endowed them with a size and influence that was greater than actually warranted (Heath 1975:246). Active opponents of the war always constituted a minority of the American people. As the conflict dragged on, the percentage of the population that considered involvement in Vietnam to be a mistake gradually increased, but it was only a minority that wanted to withdraw unconditionally from South East Asia.

Antiwar protestors, often sporting long, unkempt hair and scruffy clothes, were unpopular with most ordinary Americans who considered them to be deviants (DeBeneditti 1987:27). Some observers even feel that the movement, up to 1968, was counterproductive because the image of the protestors had a negative impact upon the general population's support for dissent (Mueller 1984:151–2). Undeniably, some sections of the media had a penchant for portraying the protestors and the antiwar demonstrations as the preserve of weirdos, revolutionaries and the politically inane. However, as there was hostility towards all deviants, the antiwar movement was not singled out for specific discrimination during the intial, early stages of its growth. Soon after, a section of respected elite opinion began to oppose the war and this gave the antiwar protestors a certain legitimacy and made them more immune to media pillory and popular vilification (DeBeneditti 1987:28).

It was the opinion of the elite rather than public opinion as a whole which had an impact upon America's role in Vietnam. Dovish sympathies were strongest in the elite universities (Small 1988:22, 153) and the students in these august institutions influenced the elite circles in which their relatives and friends moved. Far from being a reflection of majority opinion in the United States, the antiwar movement expresssed the views of a vocal, elite group and, as opposition to the war increased, it was disproportionately centred upon influential, high-profile, establishment circles.

It has been suggested, on the other hand, that those with the least education were most critical of the war (Kolko 1986:172). This is probably true of poor blacks who were alienated from the system *in toto*, but traditional white working-class groups, particularly in Middle America, were, on the contrary, some of Johnson and later Nixon's strongest supporters. Ordinary youths with little of the affluence that allowed their middle-class contemporaries the luxury of dissent and opting out, were often fiercely hostile to the antiwar protestors. They and their lives were not the stuff of which great media stories were made and they did not have a loud voice. They were the 'silent majority' to which Nixon appealed in November 1969. Some may have thought the war to be a mistake, but most were loathe to abandon it.

What, then, did the antiwar movement actually achieve, heavily influenced, as it was, by a young and often privileged section of society? And did it make public opinion 'the essential domino' (Gelb 1972:459)? Firstly, it ensured that the war was a continuously high-profile issue in American life and that the administration's actions were always under intense scrutiny. At no time could Vietnam be forgotten and it forced people to think about the war and to take a stance upon it. Secondly, the Johnson and Nixon administrations claimed that the movement had an impact upon Hanoi, as it encouraged the appearance of weak US resolve. Of course, even if Hanoi did not impute great significance to the antiwar protestors, the very fact that the US government thought that it did, must have had an influence on the formulation of policy (Small 1988:88).

Thirdly, there was the effect that antiwar dissent had on Johnson personally. Always sensitive to criticism, LBJ found it difficult to deal with the incessant pressure of the protestors. His successor, expecting hostility and hardened to it, was far better able to cope, but upon Johnson, one of the most vilified presidents in American history, the protestors took a heavy toll. Even in the White House he could hear the noise of the demonstrators. Whenever he went out he was assailed by placard waving, chanting dissenters whose favourite refrain was 'Hey, Hey, LBJ, How Many Kids Did You Kill Today?'. That Johnson was the object of hatred was especially wounding to a president who wanted to be loved by the people and it probably played an important part in his decision not to run for president in 1968 (Small 1988:149).

The antiwar movement, paradoxically, also contributed to the election of Richard Nixon, both in 1968 and 1972 (Mueller 1984:152–3, Small 1988:132, 159). Not only did it contribute to Johnson's decision not to run, but it also pilloried the Democratic candidate, Hubert Humphrey, for being an accomplice in the war because he was Johnson's vice president. A 'Dump the Hump' campaign was orchestrated which served only to guarantee Nixon more votes. In 1972, the movement also helped to wreak havoc with the Democrats' chances of ousting Nixon by supporting the candidacy of the ultra-liberal, and hence, unelectable, George McGovern who failed so badly that he secured an even lower proportion of the popular vote than Goldwater did in 1964.

On two occasions at least, antiwar dissent had a distinct effect upon the development of US policy in Vietnam. First was in the autumn of 1967. In October a 'March on the Pentagon' was organized by the movement. It was a great success and worried the administration enough for it to begin a big public relations drive on the war. But Johnson oversold the extent of progress in Vietnam and in doing so created an optimistic climate in which the Tet Offensive was viewed with shock and horror. To the extent to which Johnson's decisions of 31 March 1968 were caused by Tet and the reaction to it, the antiwar movement thus won a kind of 'victory' (Small 1988:124).

The second period in which protestors affected policy was October 1969. Highly successful demonstrations and the nationwide protests which were part of a series of actions known as the Moratorium on 15

October, coincided with a critical phase in White House decisionmaking, as Nixon debated whether to escalate the war and to put into operation elements of the 'Duck Hook' plan. The Moratorium, specifically, convinced Nixon that he could not proceed along the path of escalation and consequently the activities of the antiwar movement, whilst not causing the US to withdraw from Vietnam, impelled Nixon to work within guidelines that were more restricted than he would have liked (Small 1988:186–7).

These are two of the most direct instances of the antiwar movement's influence on the construction of American policy. More generally, public opinion and the fear of antiwar activity restrained Johnson from pursuing the war more aggressively in its initial stages. Under Nixon, Vietnamization had to proceed swiftly because it was only through constant withdrawal of troops that he could maintain support for his policy at home and could keep the lid on the antiwar movement.

But it is more difficult to explain why Johnson and later Nixon did react to the movement and to criticism of their Vietnam policy when dissenters were in a minority. Even when, after 1967, a majority of people opposed Johnson's handling of the war, many of these were hawks who disapproved of American conduct of the war and thought that it was not being pursued vigorously enough. Their opposition did not derive from hostility to the principle of US action in South East Asia. The vital fact was that dovish opposition was centred on elite circles. The antiwar movement was dominated by the young elite and it was their elders, profoundly shaken by the Tet Offensive, who came to oppose the war. Johnson and Nixon knew that there was a fund of support in the country, but when most of the influential people, most of the best students and most of the prestige papers were telling them to get out of Vietnam, it was very hard to demur. As has been stated by one analyst of the antiwar movement, the presidents were acting from the gut and not with their brain (Small 1988:234). They were only human and could not fly in the face of all those people who seemed to matter.

Both presidents worried about antiwar protest and were anxious to limit its effect. Both believed it to be communist-led and directed from overseas, but no evidence ever came to light to prove this. Undercover operations designed to disrupt and harass the movement began under Johnson, although they were not directly authorized by the White House (Small 1988:105). They expanded in intensity and scale under Nixon and, taken together with Nixon's legal crackdown upon the movement, had some bearing upon the gradual winding down of antiwar dissent.

Significantly, the catalogue of legal infringements that the president began in order to control the movement, culminated in the Watergate scandal and, in this sense, Watergate can be said to be a product of the Vietnam War.

Although the Cambodian invasion galvanized the greatest demonstrations of the war, and while the movement could still generate considerable support, a number of pressures worked to undermine antiwar dissent in the early 1970s. Much of the fire had gone out of the movement and, in particular, out of the student left. This was partly because fewer men were needed to fight the war and partly because of the new economic climate (Unger 1974:198–9). As a recession began to bite in the early 1970s, students increasingly lacked the affluence which had facilitated their political activism in the 1960s. They had to think about their careers and, in a more competitive environment, the new generation of students had little time for the distractions of politics and antiwar protest.

Many of those who remained in the student left had radicalized so swiftly that they had left the rest of America trailing far behind. As a result, a great dichotomy developed between ordinary people and leftist students who continued in their own ghettoized and ultimately self-defeating spiral of radicalism.

When it was apparent that non-violent tactics were failing to bring about the desired changes, a minority of students, and specifically the factionalized SDS, turned more and more to violence. This process culminated in the co-option of SDS by the 'Weathermen' who took over the organization only to preside over its demise. Weathermen's politics were crude and simplistic and built upon hatred and a violence born out of frustration and a sense of powerlessness. They attempted a few terrorist outrages in order to 'bring the war home', but none achieved anything other than further alienating them from the vast majority of students, the antiwar movement and the mass of the American people. SDS came to a sad and inglorious end, consumed by itself.

Vietnamization and the withdrawal of US troops was a powerful antidote to antiwar dissent. So too was the emergence of detente and the process of negotiating a peace to end the war. Moreover, as support for the war had been a fashion for some, their commitment was inevitably eroded by the 'fatigue factor' (Small 1988:220). People were tired of dressing like hippies and were bored with preaching about peace. The age of liberalism was drawing to a close. The ousting of the Democrats from power in 1968 was not only a reaction to the war. Liberalism had had its day and its unfulfilled promises were thrown back in its face

(Matusow 1984:395). The 'Me' generation of the 1970s was beginning its debut.

It is with justice that those who supported the war consider the antiwar movement to be a 'self-inflicted wound' (Taylor 1972:402, 408). But rather than causing America to lose in Vietnam, as some opponents claimed, the antiwar movement was, to a great extent, a response to America's failing military policies (Small 1988:89). One critic, expressing the views of many others, has taken the Johnson administration to task for allowing the movement so much room to manoeuvre. By not making the war a national emergency and a national crusade, it allowed the movement to gain the moral high ground and allowed the war to lose legitimacy in the eyes of the public (Podhoretz 1982:107). Richard Nixon thinks that it was not the movement that was the 'decisive factor' in the war because all wars generate antiwar movements. Instead, the critical factor which gave stimulus to the movement was the failure of the politicans to provide the people with victories and explain to them the justice of the war (Nixon 1985:15). But the Johnson administration did not rouse the nation's passions over Vietnam precisely because it did not want to generate hostility towards the war. Perhaps Johnson was wrong. Perhaps the war could have been won if he had been determined to pay the political costs and commit the nation to the fighting. On the other hand, who can say that he was wrong and that he had misjudged the mood of the nation? To speculate whether the American people would have been willing to fight a long, full-scale war in South East Asia is a futile and unanswerable endeavour.

The movement against the Vietnam War was unique in American history. It was the first large-scale movement to divide the nation other than on party political grounds, except perhaps for the years of the Civil War. Its achievement in drawing attention to the horrors of the war and the moral questions which it raised, together with its impact upon decision-makers, was fundamental to the making of Vietnam policy. America in the 1960s was an excellent forcing ground for a movement of its kind. That social and cultural change was so dramatic in this decade and that conditions were such that antiwar protest could be voiced so vigorously and on such a wide scale was fortunate for the North Vietnamese and consistently irritating for the US administration. The war in its broadest sense *was* fought in Washington's corridors of power, in the pages of newsprint, upon television screens, on college campuses and upon the streets of Washington, San Francisco and New York. Viewed from whatever political perspective, the movement had a profound impact upon American life, because, in an era of social and political change, it was the war and antipathy to it that helped give expression to some of the greatest changes of all.

6 Politics, economics and religion: a revolution in Vietnamese society

It is impossible to understand the dynamics of the wars in Vietnam and to appreciate why the North Vietnamese fought so hard and for so long against almost immeasurable odds, without some background information on life, politics and the economics of traditional and modern Vietnam. The following pages take a cursory look at some of the most salient elements essential to such an understanding.

ASPECTS OF LIFE IN THE TRADITIONAL VILLAGE

While there is no universally applicable structure to village society in Vietnam and no general history of the Vietnamese village, certain features, nevertheless, were common to all communities prior to the massive changes that accompanied the Vietnam War.

The family was, and still remains, the most important element in Vietnamese society. It was the group to which, above all else, the individual owed his or her allegiance. In contrast to modern ideas in the West, individuals could find their identity, not by assertion of their independence from the group, but through their ties to the family. At the head of the household was the father to whom was shown filial piety and respect in accordance with Confucian principles. Women, by contrast, were assigned a very low status. Patriarchy was well entrenched in Vietnam and polygamy and concubinage were common amongst those who could afford it. In addition to childrearing and household duties, women performed the bulk of the agricultural work. In return they were frequently treated little better than slaves (Mai Thi Tu and Le Thi Nham Tuyet 1978:42–59). The 'Three Obediences' guided a woman's life. As a child she had to obey her father, as a wife her husband and, should she become a widow, she then had to obey her son.

Confucian dogma refused women the right to an education, to a role in politics and the right to make decisions about crucial aspects of her life. But women's role in Vietnamese society had not always been so restrictive. Women had once been prominent figures, and female warriors, like the Trung sisters, had led the fight against the Chinese. It was only with the triumph of Confucian values, transmitted as a result of Chinese colonization, that patriarchy began to be established in Vietnam and only from the fifteenth century that women's lives were so circumscribed (Mai Thi Tu and Le Thi Nham Tuyet 1978:30).

Intimately involved with the rhythm of nature and the seasonal rains and floods which brought life to the soil, the people of Vietnam's rice-growing society developed an acute desire to harmonize themselves with nature and to become one with the natural world. Rituals and ceremonies helped to achieve this and the emperor, the spiritual embodiment of the people, would plough the first furrow of earth each year. Inevitably, in parts of the Mekong Delta where labourers worked on other people's land, where traditional customs had been diluted after their long journey from the Red River Delta and where the demands of collectively organized irrigation were not so onerous, this way of looking at the world was no longer entirely applicable by the early twentieth century. Elsewhere in the south as well as in Tonkin and Annam, such traditional views continued to survive and contributed to what has been described as a 'sociology of rice' (Mus and McAlister 1970:79).

Virtually every household in the traditional village was involved in cultivation. Artisans and craftsmen would cultivate plots of land. Even the rich, while not working the land themselves, would oversee those who did so for them. Involvement to some degree in rice production was therefore something common to all villagers and all were psychologically linked to the land because of it. This has led to a suggestion that villagers could not be divided into classes as there was little culturally to distinguish one group from the next (Hickey 1964:233–4). But, quite clearly, there were inequalities of wealth and landholding which, irrespective of a common interest in rice cultivation and its attendant rituals and beliefs, created a wide enough gulf between families to allow for a loose categorization of households into economic classes.

The very poorest villagers were generally those who owned no land or who farmed plots that were too small to provide them with adequate subsistence. Their poverty was apparent in their dress, their humble, insubstantial dwellings and in the food they had to eat or, more revealingly, did not eat. Above the rural poor was a strata of peasants whose subsistence levels were met by the cultivation of land they either owned or rented. Their homes were more substantial, their clothes of better quality and their food more plentiful. Some of these richer peasants owned enough land to rent a proportion to other villagers and some paid labourers to work on their plots.

At the top of the village socio-economic hierarchy were the landlords. Material living standards for this group were qualitatively different from the poor and middle peasants and it was this group which had political control over the village. It was only the rich who could afford to be powerful figures. It was only they who could make an adequate financial contribution towards rituals and ceremonies and only they who could afford the time to devote to politics. Not everyone who was rich became an influential political leader but wealth and age were prerequisites of high socio-political status. It was impossible for the poor who could make only limited contributions to the village funds to become a major political force in the village. Their voices were rarely heard and they had little influence upon decisions affecting their lives.

Religion was of fundamental importance to the Vietnamese peasant. Their religion was an eclectic amalgam of beliefs, drawing heavily on the Buddhist-Taoist-Confucian heritage from China. Many Vietnamese would have claimed to be Buddhists but added to their Buddhism was a plethora of popular beliefs and practices derived partly from the peoples—the Cham, Khmer and the Montagnards—with whom they came into contact and sometimes absorbed.

Many of the villagers' beliefs involved a basic animism. Spirits were thought to inhabit objects and places. Trees, stones and ponds, for instance, could all contain spirits. In order to maintain harmony between this supernatural world and the natural world, the villager used amulets and talismans, observed taboos and placed his faith in folk medicines. No major decision in life, whether deciding upon a marriage partner or choosing the site for a house, could be taken without consulting horoscopes and divining whether the spirits considered it auspicious.

Each village usually had a number of cults, the most important of which was the universally honoured cult of the guardian spirit of the village. In keeping with the importance of the cult, it was administered by the socio-political elite of the village who would organize elaborate ceremonies and rituals in order to encourage the guardian spirit to look kindly upon the fate of the community and its inhabitants.

By far the most important cult to each individual was the cult of ancestors. It was observed by almost everyone and even by those converted to Catholicism who insisted that they honoured their ancestors, rather than venerated them. Graves of relatives would be tended carefully and in the living area of every home there would be an altar on which would be placed gifts and offerings to the spirits of the departed. On the anniversary of a relative's death there would be a ritual and a feast for the surviving kin. The largesse of the host and the number of relatives invited would reflect the wealth of the family, and the number of preceding generations (following the paternal branch) so honoured was also dependent upon socio-economic status. In newly-settled Cochinchina, only a few generations may have been venerated as some families had lost trace of their lineage in the migration to the south.

The cult of the ancestors was vital to the Vietnamese because it promised them immortality. The individual was not only a member of the family then living, but also a tiny element in a chain that linked past, present and future generations. By venerating ancestors and by creating a new generation (crucially one that included a son who would assume responsibility for the cult) the Vietnamese assured their lineage of continuity. If the cult should, for some reason, be abandoned and the ancestors neglected, they would become errant spirits, unable to rest. Peace in the after life could be achieved only through the proper degree of veneration (Hickey 1964:88).

On a practical level certain material possessions contributed to effective cult veneration. This included a substantial ancestral house, stone tombs and sufficient money to finance feasts and rituals (Hickey 1964:89). Ideally this income, or patrimony, would be derived from inalienable land cultivated by the family exclusively for this purpose. Preferably, this land had to be owned and not rented because renting introduced an element of risk which reduced the security of the cult. But whilst patrimony was important to the cult of ancestors, most Vietnamese peasants could not afford the luxury of adequate finance for veneration. Their tombs were not of stone but of earth, their houses were flimsy and would not last from one generation to the next and, as in one village surveyed in Cochinchina, many had no land and so no secure income for the observance of their ancestor cult (Hickey 1964:90).

CONCEPTS OF CHANGE AND REVOLUTION IN VIETNAM

The veneration of past generations, the search for harmony with the supernatural and the peasants' link to the soil, and through it to the rhythms of the natural world, were the basis of the Vietnamese social contract (Mus and McAlister 1970:88). The emperor was the symbol of this contract, the embodiment of the spiritual life of the Vietnamese. Consequently, more than a political crisis ensued when the French usurped his power during the late nineteenth century. A social and spiritual upheaval tore at the bonds that held Vietnamese society together.

Finding an answer to the crisis and answers to the economic problems which colonial rule entailed were not simple matters. Traditional Vietnamese concepts of change are distinct from Western theories of evolutionary political and social development. Rather than a gradual progression, history in Vietnam was seen as part of a cycle of growth, fruition and decay (Fitzgerald 1972:32–3). Because the political system, known as a 'virtue', was inextricably bound up with spiritual life in an all-encompassing cosmic order, the Vietnamese considered that a particular leadership prevailed because it had the 'Mandate of Heaven'. Consequently, they were very resistant to change. However, once it had been made abundantly clear that the old virtue was exhausted and that a new virtue was prepared to take its place, and would inevitably do so, abuses which had hitherto been accepted were seen as signs of the declining system's unworthiness. The mandate of heaven then swiftly changed and the Vietnamese would, henceforth, show their allegiance to a new virtue (Mus and McAlister 1970:61).

It was incumbent upon this new order to display certain characteristics and undertake certain actions. Firstly, as the nation's spiritual head, the new leader had to be honourable and vigorous and be a man who inspired devotion. Secondly, the new order had to completely replace the old discredited virtue. This entailed wholesale changes to discard all traces of the former order and it also meant that any group aspiring to replace an existing virtue had to produce a programme that offered radical new solutions to society's problems (Mus and McAlister 1970:63).

While the search for an answer to Vietnam's social, political and spiritual trauma began almost immediately after French colonization, it was not until the 1920s and 1930s that the search began to bear fruit. Some of the solutions were unsuited to the task and some were simply too small in scale and/or vision. This left the revolutionary movement the opportunity to apply its prescription of Marxist social change to heal the scars of the Vietnamese nation.

Religious sects emerged in Cochinchina after the First World War in reaction to the momentous changes that were underway in the region. French commercialization of agriculture and the thorough penetration of capitalism into the local economy had created significant problems for the peasantry. As Cochinchina was far from the Vietnamese homeland where traditional Confucian culture was strong, the peasantry were partially released from the mental and spiritual horizons imposed by

Confucian orthodoxy. (Woodside 1976:182–3). There was thus room for the development of extremely popular religious cults such as the *Cao Dai* and the *Hoa Hao* sects which, between them, claimed some 1.25 million followers by the 1930s. On one level the sects were an attempt to reproduce the spirit of collective action and the communal ideal (Woodside 1976:6). Linked to this, the sects were also mutual aid societies and were the peasants' 'rational' response to the threat which the impingement of capitalism posed to already strained traditional ways of life (Popkin 1979:185–7).

The mainspring of the *Hoa Hao's* appeal was a variety of re-energized Buddhism, while the *Cao Dai,* the more popular of the sects, looked to a revived Confucianism. They thus provided old answers to new problems. However, orthodox Confucianism, as represented by the mandarins and the imperial court, had been discredited in the eyes of many Vietnamese. Confucianism as a body of thought lacked the dynamism with which to tackle the onslaught of Western imperialism and the problems which it brought in its train. Finding answers in the past, it was unwilling to gear itself towards the future and search for new and novel solutions (Mus and McAlister 1970:32).

The Confucian heritage played a fundamental role in moulding Vietnam's political development. It did so on several accounts. Firstly, it failed to provide the basis on which non-communist nationalists could build (Woodside 1976:107–8). It therefore helped to contribute to their lack of a coherent ideology and to the emergence of strange phenomena such as the Diem regime's odd and incomprehensible personalist ideology. Secondly, and paradoxically, it prepared the intellectual ground in which Marxism could thrive. Confucianism's concentration upon political, moral and social issues, as opposed to more spiritual questions, made Marxism's lack of concern for otherwordly matters acceptable (Nguyen Khac Vien 1974:46–7). Thirdly, Confucianism stressed the importance of collective discipline and the subordination of the individual to the interests of the group. These Confucian principles, together with the Vietnamese belief in a unified cosmic order, in which the individual is part of a much broader scheme, married well with Marxist concepts of the relationship between the individual, the community and the state. In contrast, Western political philosophy places the individual, rather than the community, at the heart of the political process. Unluckily for American attempts to fashion a liberal, Western-style democratic state in South Vietnam, this was a view that was antithetical to traditional Vietnamese values.

LAND AND LAND REFORM IN THE VIETNAMESE REVOLUTION

The question of land and land reform is central to an understanding of war and revolution in twentieth-century Vietnam. Poor Vietnamese peasants, who constituted the major part of an overwhelmingly rural population, had a keen desire to own and farm their own land. The revolutionary movement, headed first by the Viet Minh and then by the National Liberation Front, answered this desire.

In Tonkin and Annam many peasants struggled to maintain the barest level of subsistence and, whilst it was nowhere near as critical, the problem was also pressing for some of the poorest in Cochinchina. Ownership of land, which was the means of subsistence, the key to power and social status, and the link between the family and the ancestors, was a priority to peasants. A redistribution of land would give them material and spiritual security and would allow them to challenge the existing power structure of the village. More than any other single factor, the promise of land reform motivated rural Vietnamese to join the ranks of the Viet Minh and the NLF (Race 1972:166). It was by no means the only motivating factor, but it was the principal and initial spur that brought many peasants into the revolutionary movement.

It has been argued that if land reform was the major element in creating support for the Viet Minh and, by extension, the NLF, then the revolutionary movement should have been stronger in Cochinchina where there was a far higher percentage of land-hungry peasants (Fall 1967:112). This overlooks the fact that the revolutionary movement had, at one time, been strong in the region. The movement's own premature activity in the early 1940s, and the subsequent repression of the Communist Party and its associated revolutionary organizations, meant that the revolution, until then strongest in the south, took a severe blow. Momentum was lost and it took many years to rebuild the organization in a society in which, moreover, it had to compete for the peasant's allegiance with powerful religious sects.

Following the establishment of the DRV in 1945, the new government ordered a 25 per cent reduction in land rents and cancellation of all rent arrears. It also confiscated land from the French and their Vietnamese collaborators, some of which was redistributed. It was not until 1946, however, and the issuing of another decree, that the government's land policy began to have widespread impact, and not until 1953 that land reform began to be carried out in earnest.

Land reform was the first part of the DRV's programme to revolutionize agriculture. The second phase, collectivization, was begun in 1958. Land reform had two main objectives. It would mobilize the people and encourage them to identify their interests with the interests of the revolutionary government. In addition, it would destroy the existing socio-political and socio-economic hierarchy of the village by depriving the rich of land—the source of their wealth and power. This was especially important as the village hierarchies, dominated by predominantly conservative elements, were an important stumbling block to change. Land reform discriminated in favour of the poorest because, historically, this group had been powerless and excluded from decisionmaking within the community. By promoting the poor to positions of authority, the government intended that this formerly disenfranchized section of society would later be able to hold its own against the recently demoted traditional village leadership. Furthermore, the new hierarchy would have a significant, vested interest in the survival of the political system which had brought it to power.

From 1953 onwards successive 'waves' of land reform were carried out in different regions. Villagers were first classified into five categories. There were the exploiter classes which consisted of landlords and rich peasants, and the exploited classes of middle, poor and landless peasants. It was upon the basis of this classification that the land reform was carried out. Landlords were stripped of their land or were encouraged to 'donate' it, whereupon it was redistributed to the poor. As a consequence of the redistribution, no one in the village had significantly more land than their neighbour. Inequality, nevertheless, remained. Landlords were now at the bottom of the economic pecking order, while the middle peasants, who were often the beneficiaries of land reform, sometimes ended up with a net gain in the amount of land they owned (Moise 1976).

The DRV land reform excited a great deal of interest in the West, albeit after the event. This was probably because the undoubted errors that occurred during the campaign were magnified in order to portray the grim and repressive nature of the DRV in contrast to the pleasant freedoms to be found in non-communist South Vietnam. Allegations of a bloodbath solidified, for some time, into unquestioned fact. Bernard Fall, for example, estimated that some 50,000 were executed and over 100,000 forced into labour camps in a bloody campaign of terror (Fall 1967:156). Later scholarship, however, has cast serious doubt upon the extent of such executions and it is probable that around 5,000 people met their deaths as a result of land reform (Moise 1983:222).

By late 1955 and early 1956 it was clear that the land reform campaign was going seriously wrong and, in the spring of 1956, the Party began to be aware of the dimensions of the campaign's shortcomings and of the gravity of the abuses that were being perpetrated. Significant difficulties were found in the assignment of households to the five socio-economic categories. Specifically, there was uncertainty as to where to draw the line between rich peasants and landlords and whether categorization should take into account attenuating circumstances. For example, some families were classified as exploiters because they rented out their land when, in fact, they did so out of necessity, perhaps because they were too old or ill to cultivate it themselves. In some instances where there were few landlords and rich peasants and where there was therefore a limited amount of land to expropriate and redistribute, middle peasants were falsely classified as landlords or rich peasants in order for their land to be confiscated (Moise 1976:83).

Fierce hatred for the landlords was released under the cathartic effect of mass mobilization and, in the explosive political atmosphere that was generated, innocent people were identified as landlords and traitors. This tendency was encouraged by the short-sighted, and thankfully short-lived, practice of setting quotas for the number of landlords and traitors to be uncovered in each area. Those landlords accused of lesser crimes against the people had their land confiscated and were socially ostracized. Others, guilty of more heinous crimes, were tried at People's Tribunals and were frequently executed. Anyone trying to defend the exploiters, or supposed exploiters, encountered the risk of being denounced as 'connected with landlords' and of being punished accordingly. In this turmoil and confusion, approximately 30,000 peasant households were wrongly classified as landlords and suffered unwarranted penalties (Moise 1983:181).

At the heart of the land reform errors was a grossly oversimplified view of rural society, in which landlords were perceived as wholly bad and in which there was a direct correlation between depth of poverty and degree of virtue. This idealization of the poor and vilification of the rich—a deviation known as 'classism'—gave rise to the persecution of some genuinely worthy but rich people and to the advancement of a number of totally undeserving, poor individuals. Somewhat ironically, the system led to the seemingly absurd spectacle of peasants, who had previously fought with the French, being promoted through the ranks of the new village hierarchy (Moise 1983:198–9). Their redeeming features, of course, were their poverty and their conveniently discovered ability to recite the tenets of class struggle.

The great emphasis which was placed upon class during the land reform campaign was a feature of the Communist Party's policy to broaden the base of its power. During the rent reduction programme it had been discovered that although poor peasants constituted half the rural population, they amounted to only 3.7 per cent of total Party membership. Landlords, on the other hand, comprised 13.5 per cent of Party membership and rich peasants 15 per cent (Moise 1976:80). The Party believed that certain elements of its organization in the rural areas were not truly committed to socialist revolution but were, on the contrary, composed of sections of the traditional elite who had joined the Viet Minh, and sometimes the Communist Party, in an attempt to maintain their local control through a timely alliance with the new order. Prompted in this belief by the laggardly manner in which the 1945 rent reduction decree had been implemented, and concerned lest the old elite, hiding behind the facade of its own revolutionary organizations, should hinder land reform, the Party instructed its cadres to be cautious of 'old organizations', that is, former wartime Viet Minh organizations and Party branches in the villages. In practice this turned into a witch-hunt against Viet Minh leaders, fuelled, no doubt, by the young land reform cadres' resentment of the social standing of heroic members of the wartime hierarchy (Moise 1983:233).

By late 1956 the DRV had responded to the land reform crisis by implementing a three-step correction of errors campaign to resolve the worst abuses. The committee dealing with land reform was stripped of power and Truong Chinh, who was closely associated with the campaign, was replaced as Party secretary. By the end of 1957, the major errors had been corrected and the Party went through a very public period of self-criticism. After a traumatic upheaval in the countryside of North Vietnam, a significant move towards greater economic equality had been achieved.

South of the seventeenth parallel the pattern of landholding was very different. Areas under Viet Minh control prior to 1954 had undergone limited land redistribution, but this was reversed once the Diem government established itself in power. As the war against the Americans and the South Vietnamese government escalated during the 1960s, land reform was carried out in the areas controlled by the NLF. Priority in distribution was given to those who had received land from the Viet Minh. It was granted next to the families of NLF members and thirdly to families with a large number of dependants (Sansom 1970:62–3). The presence of the revolutionary movement, even in areas of marginal NLF activity, had a striking impact upon landholding and tenancy. It forced landlords, who almost universally supported the Saigon regime, to lower their rents and sometimes to flee to the safety of the cities, thus leaving their tenants to pay irregularly, if at all. In fact, by 1966, a direct correlation could be found between downward pressure on rents in the Mekong Delta and the proximity of the NLF

(Sansom 1970:61–2). The nearer one moved to an area in which the NLF had control, the lower rents would become.

In contrast to the extent and equitable nature of the DRV's land redistribution in the North and the NLF's in the South, the land reform programme undertaken by the Diem government in 1956 was far more limited in scale and impact. Diem's Ordinance 57 was applicable to very few peasants and Thieu's 1970 Land-to-the-Tiller law, while more thorough and progressive, was marred by corruption and abuse. Moreover, both merely gave GVN sanction to the transfer of land previously redistributed by the Viet Minh and the NLF. It was hardly surprising, therefore, that it was the revolutionary movement which gained the kudos for land reform.

Land redistribution was only the first phase of the DRV and southern revolutionary movement's plan for agriculture. The second phase, collectivization, received far less emphasis in the South during the years of war with the United States. It was hardly sensible, when stressing the necessity of land reform and the right of each family to own a plot of land, to remind the same people that all the land would one day be held in common. In the North, the process of collectivization was well underway as the war in the South began to escalate in the early 1960s. But as in the South, two decades later, collectivization was already beginning to encounter some early signs of trouble.

SOCIALISM IN THE DEMOCRATIC REPUBLIC OF VIETNAM

When the Geneva Accords divided the country at the seventeenth parallel in 1954, the government of the Democratic Republic of Vietnam was reluctant to resume the war in the South. It hoped that the elections to reunite Vietnam, scheduled for 1956, would take place and, if not, that South Vietnam would crumble under political pressure. Consolidation of the North's fragile economy was given immediate priority.

The DRV assumed formal control over a very difficult situation. The years of war had wreaked havoc upon the colonial economy of Tonkin and northern Annam and the new state found itself with a severe skill shortage. The French had departed with their technicians and engineers and many of the Vietnamese who had skill and expertise, and hence a relatively privileged position within colonial society, took advantage of the provisions of the Geneva Accords to flee to the South. The exodus created a shortfall in the number of skilled workers and temporarily disrupted some areas of the economy (G.Nguyen Tien Hung 1977:42).

Members of the new government and their subordinates had a great deal of political experience and knew all about conducting a revolutionary war, but they had little knowledge of the day to day running of cities and industries. To make matters worse, there was no smooth handover of power. Bitterness bred by a long and difficult war left the French in no mood to aid the new government of their former colony. They simply withdrew, taking everything they could. In Hanoi, this even included the radium from hospital X-ray machines (Fall 1967:153).

Any government faced with the prospect of running the DRV economy would have encountered serious difficulties. In 1954 the DRV had the lowest amount of cultivated land per capita in the world (Thrift and Forbes 1986:70). This would not have been a problem if the DRV had had a large and efficient industrial sector. It did not, and in a country in which 90 per cent of the population depended on agriculture for their livelihood (Thrift and Forbes 1986:70) the restricted amount of cultivated land and the lack of a strong industrial base were two very grave weaknesses.

The DRV's development strategy sought to rectify these major economic problems. First, however, the state had to extend its control over economic activities in order for it to implement its strategy. In the two years following 1954, the state contented itself with restricting and guiding the private sector. It was in no position to assume total control and direction over the economy at this early stage. Then, as the DRV consolidated its authority, it started to change the nature of production relations by drawing agriculture and handicraft industries into the state sector. It also began to absorb large-scale capitalist enterprises, initially by forming joint state-private companies and eventually by transferring them to public management and ownership. In the retail trade sector, state control was complete by 1960 (G.Nguyen Tien Hung 1977:66). In the same year 86 per cent of rural families belonged to government-run cooperatives (G.Nguyen Tien Hung 1977:67) and, by 1965, the state dominated all major sectors of the economy.

Whilst it was extending its control, the DRV began implementing its development strategy. Until 1958, efforts were concentrated upon an ambitious and successful reconstruction programme to repair damage done to the nation's infrastructure and agricultural sector during the war against France. In 1958, a three-year plan, concentrating industrial development upon the production of basic consumer goods, was put into effect (G.Nguyen Tien Hung 1977:138).

Intensive industrialization became part of the DRV's socialist construction programme in 1961 with the drawing up of the first Five Year Plan (1961–5). Investment in industry rose, absorbing 53 per cent of available resources during this period, (G.Nguyen Tien Hung 1977:143) as opposed to 35 per cent of total investment during the years 1955–9 (G.Nguyen Tien Hung 1977:50). Moreover, after 1960, investment was directed most specifically toward heavy industry and, by 1965, a colossal 80 per cent of state investment was absorbed by this branch of the industrial sector (Wiegersma 1988:143).

In drawing up its plans, Hanoi was very much influenced by the models of economic development presented by its patrons, China and the Soviet Union. In the 1950s, when the DRV came to power, the USSR was still the unquestioned leader of the communist world and its own experience of development had encouraged the Russians to regard their strategy as a universally applicable formula, which they advised Hanoi to adopt. Partly because it received aid from the communist bloc and felt under pressure to comply, and partly because the Soviet model of development was the classic and, at that stage, only model of economic development in a revolutionary state, the DRV did concentrate upon an industrialization policy that was, perhaps, unsuitable in a primitive, rural economy (Fforde and Paine 1987:29–30).

The Vietnamese attempted to industrialize and collectivize at the same time. The capital to facilitate development would come not through domestic accumulation but from external sources in the form of aid (White 1983:241). Primarily, collectivization was undertaken in order to establish state control over agriculture and to allow the state to extract the agricultural surplus in order to help finance industrialization and feed the workers in the cities. It also had another motive. Despite land reform, there were reports that the class struggle was reasserting itself in the rural areas, as 'middle' peasants bought the land of poorer peasants during lean times. Beginning in 1958, therefore, the DRV began to push forward its collectivization programme.

During land reform and the beginning of collectivization there was a large increase in agricultural production. Between 1955 and 1959, there was a 47 per cent rise in the production of staple crops such as rice, potatoes and corn (Wiegersma 1988:149). The 1960s, by contrast, saw stagnation and even decline in agricultural output (Wiegersma 1988:150). This can be blamed partly on poor weather conditions and partly upon the exigencies of a wartime economy. Because of these disruptive factors it is difficult to ascertain the true success of collectivization and the degree to which any problems may have affected output. It was possible, nonetheless, to gauge that certain difficulties, common to all collective systems, were begining to emerge. In particular, each household was permitted to cultivate a plot of private land. These plots, when combined, were stipulated to amount to no more than 5 per cent of village land. Villagers, however, spent a good deal of their time working the private plots whilst failing to give the same commitment to the collective's land. Revealingly, yields from the private plots were often two or three times higher than those from collectivized fields (Wiegersma 1988:163). Tools and animals belonging to the cooperative were badly neglected and individuals displayed little commitment to the cooperative and to the crops which they grew and sold to the state at a fixed price. There were, thus, problems of management and motivation.

The stagnation in agricultural production was critical at a time when population was rising and when the state was implementing an ambitious industrialization programme. External aid would have been necessary even if agricultural output had soared, but the failure of staple production to keep pace with the population increase demanded a far heavier reliance upon aid. Approximately 62 per cent of state investment was provided by foreign grants and loans in the period between 1958–60. Once the DRV had consolidated its control and was able to extract the surplus from former private enterprises, this figure dropped to approximately 34 per cent of state investment between 1961–5 (G.Nguyen Tien Hung 1977:89). Virtually all of this aid was from communist bloc nations and, in particular, from China and the Soviet Union.

Despite generous aid from fraternal countries, North Vietnam was experiencing worsening economic conditions by the end of the first Five Year Plan (1961–5). The combination of a far too ambitious investment programme and a meagre rise in agricultural output translated itself into severe problems in the urban and industrial centres. Because there were not enough consumer goods, and especially as the state did not provide enough food, the urban workforce resorted to purchasing food and other goods on the open market. This drove up prices, consequently creating an unbridgeable gulf between the fixed wages paid by the state to its employees and the price of the goods on the open market. To make up for the shortfall in their incomes, workers took second jobs (Fforde and Paine 1987:38–41, 57). Attendance and performance of workers in the urban industrial and public sectors therefore deteriorated accordingly.

Rising levels of food aid, primarily from the Soviet Union, helped Hanoi to overcome some of the very worst problems. In the early 1960s the DRV had been almost self-sufficient in foodstuffs but, by the mid 1970s, 10–15 per cent of its supplies were imported (Fforde and Paine 1987:68–9). On balance, it is extremely doubtful that domestic output would have been adequate to cope with the demands of the DRV's development programme even without a war. It can therefore be assumed that rising food imports were not simply replacing agricultural production lost as a result of the conflict, but were necessary to help the state manage structural changes in the domestic economy and to compensate for the failure of collectivization. Exacerbating the difficulties, the state's non-agricultural sector continued to expand between 1965 and 1975, hence demanding a corresponding expansion in agricultural output (Fforde and Paine 1987:70–1). Rather than attempting to meet this challenge, which was an especially difficult task in wartime, the search for a solution to the problem was postponed temporarily as vast aid packages from the communist bloc served to mask the imbalances.

As was to be expected, the effect of the war on a developing economy was profound. The Second Five Year Plan (1966–70) had to be scrapped and it was replaced by yearly plans starting in 1965. Investment that would otherwise have been directed towards the industrial sector was diverted into repair and construction work and into maintenance of the country's communications network. As a result, resources devoted to industry dropped from a previous yearly average of 53 per cent (1961–5) to an average of 33 per cent during the years of heavy bombing (1965–8) (G.Nguyen Tien Hung 1977:143). The bombing, however, did not decimate North Vietnamese industry. Production did not decline below its 1965 level and, by 1973, output was over 25 per cent higher than in 1965 (Fforde and Paine 1987:4).

Achieving this scale of production in the face of intense bombing required ingenuity and perseverance. The DRV's entire centrally commanded economy was replaced by a more decentralized system in which regions became semi-autonomous economic units. Whenever possible, industrial production and economic activity was moved away from dangerous city locations and into the suburbs or further afield. Factories that could be dismantled were dispersed to rural areas and crucial industries were given refuge in remote countryside and, sometimes, even in caves where they would be less vulnerable to attack. The collectivization programme aided in this process of local level, economic self-sufficiency and, hence, was a critically important ingredient in North Vietnam's defence and its ability to fight the war in the South (White 1983:251). However, there was a price to pay for this dispersal and atomization of industrial activity. The concentration upon heavy industry had to be abandoned and greater emphasis was placed upon the development of light industry.

Worsening economic conditions may have caused the Communist Party's popularity to decline during the 1960s (Fforde and Paine 1987:

37). Since the DRV had come to power there had been little widespread popular dissent. Unrest over land reform had certainly occurred although it was probably not as intense as was frequently believed in the West. Many of those implacably hostile to the regime had left the North in 1954 and the DRV enjoyed goodwill deriving from the Viet Minh legacy. Yet, the government did have its detractors and, in late 1956, a number of intellectuals began to emerge as a focus of dissent. Believing that it could rise to the challenge, Hanoi encouraged the intellectuals to voice their views on the political scene. Unfortunately, the DRV miscalculated the extent of the criticism and, after a few months of quietly accepting an embarrassing stream of censure, free speech was abruptly silenced.

Religious belief was not persecuted under the new regime as initially feared. Buddhism was tolerated as it was the religion of the majority of the population and had, on occasion, provided succour and sanctuary to members of the Viet Minh during the war against the French. The existence of a Catholic minority was more problematic. Many Catholics, of course, had joined the exodus to the South in 1954, but a significant number still remained in the North. Resistance to land reform and cooperativization was encountered in areas where Catholicism was strong but this initial friction subsided as a compromise between Catholics and the state evolved. As a rule, Catholic beliefs and practices were tolerated providing that the individual owed his allegiance, first and foremost, to the state and that he also gave priority to communist principle whenever this clashed with traditional Catholic behaviour. In practice, this meant subduing expensive and often pauperizing observance of religious ritual in the interests of utilitarian, communist rationality (Houtart and Lemercinier 1984:168–74). This was not a discriminatory policy as it applied to non-Catholics as well.

The increasing tempo of the war as the sixties progressed encouraged patriotism and with it people's willingness to bear hardships. This, therefore, helped to dull criticism of the regime. Economic problems and the absence of freedom of speech and dissent were areas in which Hanoi was especially vulnerable, but because of the war and its unifying effect, the government escaped criticism and expression of popular discontent over its handling of these affairs. There were other areas, by comparison, in which the DRV deserved justifiable praise. The provision of education was expanded rapidly both for children and for adults and a successful mass literacy campaign was launched in 1958. Health care was also a priority concern and a basic primary health care system emphasizing preventive medicine was established. In 1955, North Vietnam had one doctor per 150,000 inhabitants. In 1966 there was one for every 8,700 people and one health officer for every 1,850 (Chaliand 1969:50).

While the revolution freed North Vietnam from colonial control and transformed production relations, it did not lead directly to the liberation of women from patriarchal control and from the influence of centuries of Confucian-linked cultural and social oppression. A firm commitment had been made to women's liberation early in the history of the revolutionary movement and, once in power, many of the DRV's policies directly and indirectly improved women's lives. The collective above all else freed women from the patriarchal family economy (Eisen 1984:143). Traditionally, women received no income of their own in return for their long hours of labour in the family's fields. The collective changed this by paying women directly for their work and thus gave them a new-found degree of independence.

Hanoi consistently promoted an image of women both as mothers and as fighters. One drawback to this image was that it frequently meant that women were burdened with two jobs—one inside and one outside the home. Women's contribution to the DRV's war effort was immense. Economically it was vital. Women kept factories operating and, as they had always done, formed the bulk of the agricultural workforce. Women also began to assume lower-level leadership positions in collectives, factory organizations and within the Communist Party. All received military training but, as there was no draft for women, few actually joined the regular army. Those who did were usually involved in extremely dangerous tasks such as bomb diffusing, intelligence work and the medical services (Eisen 1984:106–7). In South Vietnam the situation was somewhat different as a higher percentage of women belonged to the military arm of the southern revolutionary movement and the vice commander of the People's Liberation Armed Forces was a woman, the celebrated General Nguyen Thi Dinh.

The promotion of women into positions of authority, both in the North and South, was a radically new social phenomenon and it did encounter resistance within the conservative culture of traditional Vietnamese society as a whole, and not just amongst men (Wiegersma 1988:209). The war, however, forced attitudes to soften and, perhaps ironically, it was the conflict that did more for women's liberation in Vietnam than the decrees and policies of the socialist state. While men were away fighting the war, women naturally had to assume their roles and responsibilities. Indeed, the years 1968–73 witnessed the highest level of promotion of women to local-level leadership (Eisen 1984:252–3). This necessary assumption of vacant positions gave many women useful experience of life away from the home and gave them a new independence and the assertiveness that accompanied it. What remained in doubt, nonetheless, was how men would accommodate the burgeoning of women's liberation when they returned from the war to resume their former responsibilities.

Hanoi undertook a wholesale re-organization of North Vietnamese society in the 1950s and 1960s. Production relations in all sectors were transformed and the construction of an industrial, socialist economy was inaugurated. The potentially divisive problem of a religious minority was contained, education and health care provision was expanded and an attempt was made to release women from centuries of oppression. All this was not achieved without encountering serious difficulties and without generating some measure of popular discontent. To add to the upheaval, the DRV waged a war in the South and endured ferociously destructive US bombing campaigns. Hanoi received aid from the communist bloc in order to help it fight the war and to sustain its beleaguered economy and its people rallied behind the regime. The aid, however, served to mask massive structural problems within the DRV economy which Hanoi would be left to resolve during the late 1970s and 1980s when it absorbed the economy of South Vietnam. Then, the DRV was faced not only with dealing with its own problems, borne of a too ambitious development programme, but also with the even more complex problems left as a legacy of the southern regime's disastrous economic record.

THE SOUTH VIETNAMESE ECONOMY 1954–73

The South Vietnamese economy was built and functioned almost entirely upon US aid. Moreover, it is not possible to speak of a coherent development programme for the South, especially after 1963. Rather, the GVN appeared to assume that US aid would indefinitely relieve it of the burden of creating an efficient, balanced economy. The vast amount of dollars that the Americans poured into South Vietnam encouraged this assumption, for US policy in Vietnam was directed not towards the development of a viable economy but towards the stabilization of a weak and corrupt one long enough for military solutions to have some impact.

The rulers of the new state of South Vietnam were presented with a difficult challenge in 1954. The economic base of the nation was very weak. There was only a limited industrial sector and the region was heavily dependent upon the cultivation and export of rice. Reconstruction was given priority and it did produce some notable successes. Between 1954 and 1960 rice production recovered from the impact of the First Indochina War and rose from 2.2 million tons to 5.1 million tons (Dacy 1986:5). Building from a very low base, the economy achieved high growth rates and in the period 1957–60 average annual growth reached 7.2 per cent (Dacy 1986:56). The Diem regime also achieved surprising success in integrating more than one million Catholics who had fled from North Vietnam in 1954. The manner of the integration, nonetheless, did create a fund of discontent, as Diem was perceived to be unduly favouring his fellow Catholics. But the fact that the absorption of such a large body of people was accomplished relatively swiftly in a nation with an existing population of around 12 million does suggest a significant achievement.

The primary characteristic of the South Vietnamese economy which inevitably detracted from these apparent successes, was its heavy reliance upon external finance. Between 1955 and 1958 the US provided two-thirds of Diem's combined civil and military budget (Kolko 1986:90). Any estimation of the performance of the GVN economy independent of this level of aid would therefore be impossible.

Vast US aid contributions did not automatically grant American advisers a significant degree of influence over Diem and the formulation of his development plans. Diem's mandarin proclivities encouraged his dislike for all things industrial but, conquering his distaste, he did begin to build a state-owned industrial sector, much to the exasperation of his US advisers who placed their faith in private enterprise. In the years after his fall, Diem's limited development initiatives were abandoned and, as the war increased in scale, the economy swung ever faster into a cycle of dependency, corruption and instability.

A previously critical economic situation was worsened considerably with the expansion of the war and the arrival of large numbers of US soldiers in the mid-1960s. The rural economy was severely disrupted by the fighting and by 1968 agricultural production was 25 per cent below the average for the 1961–5 period (Kolko 1986:224). To avert a crisis, the US imported a large quantity of rice which was sold at a subsidized price. Ironically, the tactic exacerbated the situation as the peasantry then had little financial incentive to produce more rice for domestic consumption.

A potent symbol of the disintegration of South Vietnamese rural society was the rapid growth of the cities. Hundreds of thousands of refugees fleeing from the conflict sought sanctuary in the urban areas. In terms of sheer numbers, Saigon was the recipient of the largest proportion of refugees but other, smaller cities, actually grew faster. The influx of refugees created new difficulties. Cities had neither the amenities nor the housing to accommodate them. Nor did they have sources of employment with which to keep the new population economically productive. The colossal economic pressures of the refugee crisis were temporarily alleviated by aid inputs, by the development of industries and services to cater to the US military presence and by the emergence of a large informal sector. The vulnerability of this economic arrangement, of course, lay in its total reliance upon the existence of US aid and personnel.

Free-spending troops with, in Vietnamese terms, enormous salaries, and a wealthy US military that was eager to build bases and facilities with the help of Vietnamese labour and construction materials, introduced a further destabilizing element into the economic equation. American advisers still had fresh memories of the way in which the US presence in Korea had created run-away inflation and they were concerned not to repeat the experience. Control of inflation thus became the priority of the American aid package because it was believed that inflation would create profound stresses in society and would lead to the GVN's collapse. The rationale for the policy was that inflation would be caused by too much money circulating through the economy and too few goods on which people could spend it, thus leading to spiralling price increases. The United States' answer to this problem was to flood the market with aid-financed consumer goods. These imports would dampen down inflation by counterbalancing the growth in the money supply. Despite concerted efforts, however, inflation continued to worry US advisers. Prior to 1964, annual price increases averaged around 4–5 per cent while from 1965 they varied between 6–60 per cent (Dacy 1986:131). Nevertheless, at no time was there a significant threat of hyper-inflation. Given the massive extent of the US financial disruption of the GVN's fragile domestic economy, this was a noteworthy achievement in itself.

US governmental aid to the GVN was administered through four programmes, the most important of which were the Commercial Import Program (CIP) and the Piaster Subsidy. The CIP functioned by providing dollars with which to purchase and import manufactured goods. Ninety per cent of the commodities had to come from the United States while the remaining 10 per cent could originate from specified third countries. However, because the piaster was grossly overvalued on the official exchange rate, importers and supposed importers could make vast windfall gains through the recycling of dollars.

Manipulation of the CIP created fortunes for many importers. It also meant that the GVN was not receiving the true value of CIP aid because it was not collecting the real piaster equivalent of the US dollars offered through the programme. Inevitably this situation worsened and the windfall gains made by the importers increased as the inflation rate rose while the piaster was not devalued between 1967 and 1972. The South Vietnamese regime, nevertheless, was willing to accept the situation because the CIP functioned as an effective instrument in the distribution of patronage and, especially under the Thieu regime (1967–75), the granting of import licences became a useful method for controlling and keeping powerful individuals loyal to the government. Washington, furthermore, supported the artificial piaster exchange rate and the effect this had upon the CIP because, to do otherwise, would have meant threatening the stability of the corruption-ridden GVN.

The US purchased piasters from the GVN in order to pay its Vietnamese employees and local creditors. This was known as the Piaster Subsidy because it bought at the official exchange rate thereby, in effect, charging itself a higher price for Vietnamese goods and services than was warranted on the open market. Large amounts of aid were funnelled into South Vietnam through the CIP, the Piaster Subsidy and other US aid programmes in order to keep the GVN economy afloat. Whether these were the best means of distributing aid was debatable, but for a time they achieved their purpose.

Industrial development throughout the 1960s was firmly geared towards the American military presence. Service industries flourished and industrial production concentrated principally upon supplying US troops with goods and upon providing the US military with materials for construction. As a consequence, industrial production rose between 1964 and 1967 and dropped thereafter as the American presence was cut and the demand for military construction projects stagnated (Kolko 1986:224).

American economic policy in Vietnam created a weak industrial base vulnerable to the threat of US withdrawal. Commodities purchased through the CIP, and through the GVN's own equivalent of the CIP, were not capital goods to be utilized in the development of industry and agriculture, but were consumer goods which would dampen inflationary pressures. The scale and range of imported consumer goods and their relative cheapness meant that there was little opportunity for domestic industry to compete with its own range of goods in this vital sector. Furthermore, the overvaluation of the piaster discouraged exports by making them expensive for other nations to buy, while it also encouraged imports by making them cheaper. The overall effect of US and GVN economic strategy was therefore antidevelopmental (Dacy 1986:32).

The major growth element in the South Vietnamese economy after 1964 was the public sector and, by 1970, the public and service sectors accounted for two-thirds of the nation's gross domestic product (Dacy

1986:61). GVN expenditure, in real terms, increased by 200 per cent between 1960 and 1973 (Dacy 1986:58–68) and this was furnished almost exclusively by aid. Finding adequate finance for this enormous bill was difficult, even with generous doses of aid, and the GVN, rather than tackling corruption and the siphoning off of funds, made a critical decision to reduce its costs by restricting the salaries paid to its civil servants and military personnel. In a period of high inflation, fixed salaries caused great hardships for many government employees. Significantly, in a nation where there was no effecive tax system, the low salaries constituted an effective tax upon public sector employees (Kolko 1986:227). It was a tax, moreover, which hit disproportionately hard against those who could least afford it and which, in the long-term, was detrimental to the survival of the GVN. Its soldiers and civil servants, after all, could hardly be expected to fight for such a patently unjust society when they themselves were on the point of destitution.

Corruption was institutionalized within the South Vietnamese economy. At the higher levels, corrupt practices were prompted by a self-seeking scramble for lucre and many people close to the regime gained immense fortunes which were salted away into foreign bank accounts. At the lower levels, corruption supplemented poor salaries and was essential in order for families to escape financial ruin. It was corruption that kept the otherwise untenable South Vietnamese nation on the rails and it was American money that oiled its wheels.

Through Vietnamization, the US hoped that the GVN would be able to stand on its own feet militarily. The less publicized but just as critial attempt to Vietnamize the economy and to encourage the GVN to become economically independent was a far more difficult task. Unfortunately, it was also probably impossible, caught as the GVN was between its reliance upon aid and between the demands of fighting a war. It has been estimated that from 1965 to 1971 the US provided 43 per cent of the GVN's total revenues (Dacy 1986:225). Kolko believes that the dependency on US finance was even greater and claims that, from 1966, the GVN's budget was at least 85 per cent aid funded, as much revenue, officially considered as domestically generated, was in fact the product of US funded imports (Kolko 1986:224–5).

It was almost inconceivable that the GVN could become economically self-supporting after its industrial base had suffered years of neglect. Rather than building a strong South Vietnamese economy, the Americans and their Saigon allies had been content to preside over the growth of a vulnerable industrial sector which was intimately tied to the US presence. Successive Saigon regimes, and especially that of Nguyen Van Thieu, had effectively used foreign money to create a false prosperity in the cities and to purchase the support of the growing urban masses through the provision of cheap consumer goods. This did nothing to develop the Vietnamese economy and left the government at the mercy of US aid.

Reliance upon external sources of funding also meant that the GVN did not have to generate its own resources through taxation. Taxing the middle class, and especially the rich supporters of the regime, was considered risky because it might alienate them. Such a policy was very short-sighted as the establishment of an effective tax system would have enhanced the GVN's political credibility. Instead, US aid relieved the South Vietnamese regime from tackling its unpleasant economic problems.

The magnitude of the economy's structural weakness was made apparent in the early 1970s as a recession began to bite. A number of factors prompted the recession. Economic aid as a percentage of GNP was actually falling and this was the primary reason for the deteriorating performance of the economy after 1970 (Dacy 1986:205–6). A US military withdrawal was underway, thus removing a large proportion of the dollars that had formerly buoyed up the market. Worldwide inflation, which increased during the opening years of the decade, also contributed to the falling real value of foreign aid. To compound the hardships, the labour force was growing at a time when the economy was contracting. Industrial and service sectors associated with the US military presence were facing the loss of their market, and the South Vietnamese Army, which by the late 1960s employed over one million, finally stopped expanding. The result was an increase in unemployment and a fall in wages for city dwellers. This created disturbing social tensions in the amorphous, sprawling urban areas.

However, there were some isolated positive economic indicators. Total agricultural output had increased and, by 1970, the real value of rice and other agricultural production exceeded its 1964 level (Wiegersma 1988:198–9). Counterbalancing this, there was a drop in the per capita value of production as output failed to match the growth in the urban population. The sowing of high-yield rice strains and the widespread use of fertilizers financed through US aid was responsible for this increased output. But despite concerted efforts to make South Vietnam self-sufficient in agriculture, food imports rose from approximately 3 per cent of total needs in 1964 to almost 15 per cent of consumption in 1970 (Wiegersma 1988:197). Farmers naturally benefited from the increased yields and, in contrast to the urban dwellers whose wages were falling in the early 1970s, the rural population was enjoying an improvement in its standard of living. However, as in the cities where the prosperity of the late 1960s was always extremely unequal, the new economic progress in the countryside was also unfairly weighted in favour of those who were already rich (Wiegersma 1988:200–1).

Years of neglecting a coherent development strategy in favour of the short-term stabilization of an otherwise unviable economic system had left the GVN economy in a parlous condition to contemplate life without copious US aid. As it became apparent to American economic advisers in the early 1970s that US money was not going to pour into South Vietnam indefinitely, a search was undertaken in order to find alternative means of shoring up the GVN's precarious financial structure. Other sources of aid were sought, a campaign was launched to attract foreign investment and the possibility of a major oil find for a time offered the prospect of salvation. The oil proved elusive and few companies were imprudent enough to invest in a political and military battlefield. South Vietnam was increasingly left to its own inadequate devices. The US military involvement shrank and economic aid was cut. In the cities there was less money, fewer jobs and more simmering discontent. Just as importantly, the bounty with which Thieu had greased the palms of his supporters was beginning to dry up. Foreign aid, the panacea for all South Vietnam's ills and the lubricant for the corruption upon which the GVN relied for its very survival, no longer came from out of a bottomless pit. The shortage of finance revealed the very real limits that the people placed upon their political allegiance to the regime. The consequence was that, in the two years following the American military withdrawal in 1973, the crisis of finance and confidence had deepened to the point where, under a comparatively minor degree of pressure from the revolutionary movement, the whole corrupt edifice came tumbling down.

7 People's revolutionary war

A people's revolutionary war is different from a conventional conflict. In a conventional war the combatants draw their supplies, support and manpower from two separate geographic areas. They then generally endeavour to wage war away from their respective populations. In a people's revolutionary war the opposing sides share the same territorial base and the battle over which type of society is to predominate is fought amongst the people (Race 1972:227–30).

Revolutionary guerrilla warfare is the means by which militarily disadvantaged, politically organized groups, based on socio-economic class lines, have sought to replace existing authority and to introduce wholesale changes in society. In this attempt, unconventional warfare is used to destroy the enemy's military capability and political mobilization of the population is used to win their allegiance and undermine support for the authorities.

The wars in Vietnam are not to be confused with jungle warfare. Jungle warfare, as practised, for example, in the Second World War was not guerrilla warfare, but conventional warfare creatively applied to a jungle environment. Traditional guerrilla warfare is also distinct from revolutionary guerrilla warfare. They share many of the same tactics but guerrillas such as the partisans of the French Resistance operated in support of conventional forces. Their role was thus a tactical one. The role of a guerrilla in a people's revolutionary war, by comparison, is far more clearly strategic.

The Chinese communists' struggle against their nationalist rivals became the classic people's revolutionary war. Mao Tse-tung's political and military concepts thereafter became enshrined as the tenets of revolutionary guerrilla warfare. General Vo Nguyen Giap, North Vietnam's foremost military strategist, acknowledged the considerable influence that the Chinese Revolution had upon the war of liberation in Vietnam (Vo Nguyen Giap 1962:22). But whilst accepting and practising many of Mao's most fundamental ideas, the

Vietnamese made a number of adaptations. Their contribution to the doctrine of people's revolutionary war can therefore be considered important not because it was novel, but because it utilized existing doctrine imaginatively.

A fundamental of revolutionary guerrilla warfare is Mao's theory of substitution. When faced with a militarily superior enemy, the guerrilla has to use what means are available to him. The guerrilla force turns these limitations into advantages. Weapons are replaced by men and unconventional warfare is pitted against conventional warfare. Given the initial weakness of the revolutionary movement's military capability in Vietnam, it was sensible to embrace a concept of substitution. Paraphrasing Mao, Giap emphasized the need to 'defeat material force with moral force, defeat what is strong with what is weak, defeat what is modern with what is primitive' (Vo Nguyen Giap 1970:175–6).

Chinese revolutionaries, however, did not face an opponent wielding the military capability of the United States and elements of their strategy were not totally suited to the wars in Vietnam. The Maoist emphasis upon the pre-eminence of men and politics as opposed to weapons and technological skill led to the 'red vs expert' controversy and elements of this controversy extended to Vietnam. There the revolutionary forces paid homage to the importance of 'redness' and to the human and political element as the decisive factor in people's revolutionary war, but the reality of the struggle against the US forced a far greater reliance upon weapons and the 'expert' use of them than the Chinese deemed ideologically desirable.

Deepening the disagreement was the fact that the Chinese were advocates of self-reliance, holding that a revolutionary movement should support itself. While the guerrillas of the First and Second Indochinese Wars, together with the more conventional North Vietnamese units that fought against the Americans, did endeavour to become self-reliant, for instance by devoting a good deal of time to growing and foraging for their own food, this was increasingly challenged by the rise of professionalism within the armed forces and by the pace and intensity of the conflicts. Moreover, considering the US's technology-based methods of fighting, the Vietnamese were hardly in a position to fight with rudimentary weapons. The revolutionary movement was therefore forced to seek external aid.

The Bolshevik Revolution was city- and worker-based and Marxist-Leninist theory naturally stressed the role of the urban proletariat as vital to subsequent revolutions. But as China was overwhelmingly rural, Mao therefore constructed his strategy around the peasantry and the countryside. Ho Chi Minh also appreciated the potential of the peasant masses as a revolutionary body and it was upon the peasantry that the Viet Minh and later the NLF relied for support. It was in the rural areas, moreover, that their strength was concentrated. But unlike the Chinese communists they did not relegate the cities to a low priority, to be 'encircled' by the revolution. Instead, the Vietnamese stressed the crucial importance of the cities and the necessity of developing urban bases to complement the revolution in the countryside (Vo Nguyen Giap 1971:85).

Because a revolutionary guerrilla force is militarily inferior to its enemy it must preserve its strength by fighting only when the circumstances are propitious. Naturally, this means that the enemy will be engaged only on those infrequent occasions when he is weaker and more disadvantaged than the guerrilla. This necessity gave rise to the Maoist concept of protracted war because it is only by having time that the guerrilla can afford to pass up the opportunity to fight. Whilst acknowledging the viability of this strategy, the Vietnamese added a caveat, maintaining that protracted war was not the only method of struggle and that it could be combined with armed uprisings in the cities if the conditions permitted. Giap claimed that the August 1945 Revolution was just such an example of a revolutionary movement seizing the opportunity to advance outside the bounds of protracted war and he claimed that the adaptability of Vietnamese military and political strategy was highly creative, forming an original contribution to the general theory of revolutionary struggle.

Vehicles prescribed by Maoist doctrine for the triumph of the revolution are the Party, which is the vanguard of the revolution, the army, which the Party controls, and the United Front, which absorbs sympathetic non-Party individuals and organizations, so broadening its base of support. The revolutionary movement in Vietnam utilized these devices very effectively, developing a strong Party and military force and successfully applying the tactic of the United Front. First through the creation of the Viet Minh and later through the establishment of the National Liberation Front, both of which were indirectly controlled by the Party, the Vietnamese revolutionaries fashioned political bodies which attracted many people who agreed on a minimum programme. Whilst this meant temporarily compromising some of its more radical objectives it did grant the revolutionary movement the allegiance of a large number of individuals who otherwise would have been reluctant to affiliate with the Communist Party.

Following a period of preparation in which the political ground is prepared, classic revolutionary guerrilla warfare proceeds through three stages. The initial stage is defence. Emphasis is placed upon building up the movement's political strength, upon small-scale guerrilla operations and upon nibbling away at the enemy's military and political apparatus. The second stage is that of equilibrium when guerrilla forces achieve a form of parity with the enemy and their operations become larger and more aggressive. The third and final stage is marked by a move to large-scale operations more characteristic of conventional warfare. What differentiates each stage is the balance between the armed and political struggle. In the opening phase of the war, the revolutionaries' weaknesses and their need to win the allegiance of the people leads to a greater emphasis upon the political aspects of the conflict. As the revolution's weakness *vis-à-vis* the enemy is redressed and once their political support is secured, the pursuit of a more aggressive, military approach becomes feasible. The earlier political struggle and the small-scale guerrilla operations are not replaced as the revolutionary war enters a new phase; instead they are added to rather like layers on a cake (Tanham 1966:12).

Only in northern Vietnam during the war against the French can the three stages of classic revolutionary guerrilla war be followed with any accuracy. In the south during the First Indochina War and during the struggle for the liberation of South Vietnam, the patterns are more confused. Because the Vietnamese experience was very different from that of the Chinese, they suggested that the three phases of revolutionary warfare could be adapted. Firstly there was the example of the August Revolution which, as mentioned previously, was put forward as an adaptation of the three-stage protracted war doctrine. This became enshrined as the Vietnamese belief in the 'General Uprising'. A second adaption was made when, after 1968, the revolutionary movement feared that it would not be able to pursue the third, offensive stage in the face of mounting difficulties and the ferocity and efficacy of US and GVN firepower. In this context it was suggested that victory could be achieved without advancing from the second to the third stage and that the possibility of a coalition government, which the revolutionary forces would come to dominate, would facilitate their transition to, rather than seizure of, power. To the Chinese the prospective abandonment of the three-stage guerrilla war concept was an heretical affront to their ideological sensibilities.

Three main types of military forces operated on behalf of the revolutionary movement during the wars in Vietnam. At the most basic level there were the village guerrillas. These were men and sometimes women who received a rudimentary political and military training and who engaged in defensive operations in the immediate locality.

Supporting the village guerrillas was a large body of auxiliaries including elderly people, women and children who would not engage directly in the fighting but who would be involved in aiding the guerrillas, for example as porters and lookouts. Those who proved their mettle in the village guerrillas and were keen to do so, advanced into more mobile regional guerrilla units where they participated in a higher percentage of offensive operations. At the top of the revolution's military hierarchy were the main force units, larger groups, akin to conventional military forces, who were highly trained and who, because of their service in the village and regional guerrillas, had considerable combat experience. From 1964, native southern forces modelled on these lines were joined by main force units from North Vietnam. They, however, operated separately from the indigenous forces.

The organizational framework of the military in Vietnam during both wars was highly functional. It meant that there was always a large reserve at the village level ready to replenish the main forces and that this reserve, moreover, had experience. In addition, it ensured that security could reach right down to the 'rice roots' level and that the local community developed a close, binding relationship with the regular military forces (Vo Nguyen Giap 1962:143–4).

In utilizing its military capability, the revolutionary movement had to take into consideration Vietnam's three strategic zones: the cities, the populated plains and coastal areas, and the relatively uninhabited jungle-covered mountains. Each necessitated a different style of waging war. The three military forces, the three adaptable stages of guerrilla war and these three strategic zones gave the conflicts in Vietnam a multi-dimensional aspect. In order for it to be effective, offensives in all three strategic zones had to be closely coordinated and complementary.

In order to launch a people's revolutionary war, the revolutionary movement had to have developed solid rear areas where they could rely on the political support of a large proportion of people. Ideally these were areas in which their guerrilla forces were free to build-up and mature. Obviously, these tended to be situated in remote rural regions. The rear was developed into a base area and from there into a liberated zone where the revolution exercised overall political and military authority. In Vietnam the mountains became solid rear bases and secure jumping-off points for carrying the revolution into the more heavily fortified, densely populated plains (Vo Nguyen Giap 1971:65). At the outset of the struggle the Viet Minh consolidated its strength in the mountains of northern Tonkin and later created a liberated zone there, while in the war to liberate the south, secure bases were established in inhospitable mangrove swamps and in the jungles of the VietnamCambodia border region. From here the revolutionary movement extended its control, establishing bases within more heavily populated areas as the momentum of the war increased. In contrast, the enemy, first the French and then the US/GVN, sought to establish its own secure rear areas in the towns and cities and hence this led to the revolutionaries' concern to strike at the enemy in the cities and destabilize his 'lair' (Vo Nguyen Giap 1971:66).

Of crucial importance to the application of revolutionary guerrilla warfare are the parameters set by time and space. The pace and development of the conflict are determined by these variables and this is why no two revolutionary wars can follow an identical course. Time is the greatest asset of any guerrilla movement because it makes the protracted war strategy possible (Thompson 1969:48). Time allows for advance and retreat as does space which can be exchanged for time. Having space, that is territory and the support of the people who inhabit it, allows the guerrilla forces to withdraw in order to preserve their strength. Threatened by an enemy advance they can abandon space and await a favourable opportunity to reassert their control over surrendered territory. The accumulation of space therefore guarantees more time to the guerrillas. Alternatively, they can maintain control of space by standing, fighting and hence expending manpower (Thompson 1969:49). Because of the military inferiority of the guerrilla this can lead to high losses. In China where there are enormous, remote rural areas, time and space were available in abundance. In smaller Vietnam, geography restricted the space available to the revolutionary movement. Hence space could not be traded as freely for time. Moreover, with the arrival of US high-technology warfare this increasingly became a problem. Helicopters gave the US/GVN forces a new level of mobility so allowing them to penetrate into the heart of the revolutionary movement's secure areas. Combined with the great reach of US firepower, this meant that there was less space available to trade and guerrillas and main force units sometimes had to fight when they would have preferred to have retreated. It also prompted PLAF/PAVN to search for bases out of the reach of US military action. Because there was nowhere immune from attack in Vietnam, they therefore sited bases on the far side of the Cambodian-Vietnamese border where the theoretically inviolable sovereignty of neutral Cambodia for a time granted vital space to the revolutionary forces.

Partially offsetting the disadvantage posed by lack of space was the fact that China became a secure rear area for the Viet Minh. After the triumph of the Chinese communists in 1949, the Viet Minh could rely upon their neighbour for supplies and for sanctuary if the need should arise. Correspondingly, during the war against the US/GVN, North

Vietnam served as a secure rear area for the revolutionary movement in the South. Of course, this did not solve the problem of acquiring and maintaining vital space during the two Indochina Wars, but it helped the revolutionary movement both practically and psychologically.

The guerrilla warfare of the partisan and the revolutionary rely upon pitting surprise and the utilization of basic technology against the strength of conventional arms and tactics, outflanking the enemy by turning his military superiority into a liability. Guerrillas capitalize on their weakness. With few arms they are mobile, whereas their opponent, encumbered with his technological baggage, is far more slow to respond. Because the guerrillas often have the support of the people, their intelligence information is good and they use this to outthink the enemy. They can strike when they know that there is a good chance of success. When the odds are unfavourable, however, they melt into the surrounding country or into the people who support them. As a result, combat rarely takes place other than on terms which they dictate.

The ambush was a favourite tactic of the Vietnamese guerrilla. Both the French and the US/GVN used roads to transport their manpower and extensive armaments and supplies. Ambushing convoys therefore afforded the revolutionaries the opportunity to strike the enemy when he was most vulnerable and at a position of their own choosing. Mining roads, frequently using explosives derived from dud enemy munitions, was an extemely effective tactic and accounted for a good deal of French, US and South Vietnamese casualties and for the destruction of large quantities of equipment.

Harassing attacks were common and accounted for the majority of PLAF/PAVN actions (Thayer 1985:45). These might involve hit and run attacks against village officials or artillery strikes against enemy-held territory. Along with sabotage and small-scale operations against locally-based government troops, such operations sowed fear amongst the enemy, boosted the morale of NLF supporters and created a climate of insecurity in GVN areas. Hamlets controlled by the revolutionary forces were heavily defended and hidden dangers lurked in the most unlikely places, perhaps in fruit trees or chicken coops, awaiting the unfortunate enemy soldier who was inquisitive enough to investigate.

In areas in which the enemy was known to operate, sophisticated traps using primitive materials were employed. A productive tactic was to place a loaded gun or arrow so that it fired across a path when triggered by a trip wire. Sharpened bamboo stakes, perhaps with their tips smeared with excrement, were placed in trenches and then covered with foilage. These were the infamous *punji* traps. Similar stakes were submerged under flooded paddy fields and were placed along the sides of paths and roads at the intended site of an ambush. It must be added, however, that this particularly unsavoury tactic was employed by all sides during the wars in Vietnam.

Both guerrilla and main force units had little with which to combat a barrage of enemy firepower. They therefore contrived to avoid situations in which the enemy could exploit its advantage. On occasions when this proved impossible, the revolutionary forces attempted to neutralize the attack by 'clinging to the enemy'. By staying close to the opponent, perhaps within a matter of yards, enemy firepower could not be used against them without incurring the possibility of causing friendly casualties.

In a people's revolutionary war, the people are the decisive factor: it is for their allegiance that the guerrillas fight and is the people with whom they fight. Political mobilization is the means by which it wins their support and motivates them to fight. The political and military aspects of a people's revolutionary war thus cannot be separated. Without a political dimension there would be no conflict. This Mao expressed in his famous dictum that 'politics is war without bloodshed and war is politics with bloodshed'. As the guerrillas come from amongst the people and because the people support and sustain them, the guerrillas cannot exist without a sympathetic population. According to Mao's theory, the population is for the revolutionaries what water is for the fish, and consequently the critical task for any insurgent movement is to maintain its organization within the population. This is its primary weapon and its guerrilla forces come secondary to it (Thompson 1969:32) because they are born from it.

To aspire to true power the revolutionary movement has to do far more than sow disaffection. It has to illustrate that it is a viable alternative government and it has to consolidate and develop its authority in order that it can challenge the encumbent administration's right and competence to govern. It is true that in the opening stages of the war the revolutionaries have a somewhat easier military objective than that of the government forces, because in order to maintain credibility the government must be prepared to counter guerrilla attacks everywhere while the guerrilla merely has to stage a minimum number of surprise operations in order to appear to be 'everywhere and nowhere' and to reveal the inadequacy of the government's security measures. But it is incorrect to claim that the guerrillas' fortunes do not depend primarily upon their public performance (Fairbairn 1968:175). To become a serious political challenge, it is not enough simply to destroy the government's apparatus. The revolution must create its own, because the very essence of success in people's revolutionary war is to 'outadminister' rather than 'outfight' the enemy (Eqbal 1971:15). To furnish this alternative source of administrative power, the Viet Minh created 'parallel hierarchies' (Fall 1967:133–8), a shadow government which corresponded to existing governmental bodies and which usurped their authority in the liberated zones and which encroached upon it in contested areas. During the war for the liberation of the South, a similar practice developed.

In gaining popular support, the revolutionary movement in Vietnam did not depend on terrorizing the people. Whilst the use of terror might explain the marshalling of a small number into the revolutionaries' camp, it did not account for the support granted by whole communities who, moreover, were convinced enough of the movement's cause to risk their lives for it. The goodwill of the population was vital to the success of the Viet Minh and the NLF and it was upon this 'people factor' (Vo Nguyen Giap 1970:180) that the fate of the revolution depended. Abuses did, of course, occur. In December 1967 the NLF attacked the hamlet of Dak Son, 75 miles north-east of Saigon, where they killed 252 Montagnard tribal people, principally because they had been sympathetic to the enemy (Lewy 1978:245).

During the Tet Offensive around 5,000 people were murdered by the revolutionary forces in Hue (Pike 1970:43–64, Oberdorfer 1971:197–235). Apologists for the NLF/DRV claimed that many of the victims were killed by US airpower expended in the battle to retake the city (Fitzgerald 1972:396–7, Gibson 1986:164–5), but most bodies were discovered in mass graves outside Hue. It is probable that local revolutionary forces, acting independently of the leadership, saw the opportunity that their control of the city gave them to destroy pro-US/GVN support in an area in which they had encountered serious difficulties in extending their political apparatus. Douglas Pike thinks that a limited purge of the old social order took place because the NLF/DRV originally believed that they had seized Hue permanently. However, once they realized that they would have to abandon the city, they systematically began to dispose of witnesses to their crimes (Pike 1970:52–60). Whatever the reason, the Hue massacre is a terrible and inexcusable blot on the record of the National Liberation Front.

Nevertheless, as a rule, the Viet Minh and PLAF/PAVN were mindful to cultivate good relations with local inhabitants. This was in marked contrast to French colonial forces and the US and GVN soldiers who had an unenviable reputation for insulting and often brutal behaviour. Holding that it was beneficial to respect local customs, to treat women courteously, to be mindful not to damage the peasant's home, crops and possessions and to help villagers in small but socially significant ways, the guerrillas developed a strict code of conduct which paid impressive dividends. The revolutionary forces adhered to this code partly because of effective discipline, partly because they frequently operated in their native regions, but most importantly because they could not afford to alienate the people who supported them. Not having to rely upon the goodwill of the population, the enemy, by comparison, believed that it could afford to ignore it.

A very effective programme of violence was employed by the Viet Minh and the NLF. Rather than being indiscriminate terrorism, this rarely stepped outside the bounds of selective terror. Because violence was used to facilitate the vital political struggle, it had specific aims. Primarily, it sought to undermine and discredit the government. Through the assassination of local officials, the revolutionary movement illustrated the government's failure to provide adequate security for its representatives and dissuaded people from assuming positions of leadership in the local administration. Popular pressure led to the selection of corrupt and hated individuals as targets. But just as frequently, such people were bypassed. After all, they did little but discredit the government. Efficient local government leaders were more likely to become victims and especially worthy ones were accorded a high priority.

The violence campaign was successful in disrupting local government. Its impact was such that it led a prominent critic of the NLF to charge that it had wiped out an entire class of Vietnamese villagers—its administrative elite—in a manner approximating genocide (Pike 1966:248). This probably grants the programme a greater degree of effectiveness than it actually warranted. The end-product of the campaign was not to deprive the South Vietnamese regime of representation at the village level because the local leadership adapted itself to the security situation. In practice this meant that officials would be present in the villages during the day but would retire to safer towns and government military outposts at night when the NLF would resume control of the village.

The revolutionary movement made a concentrated effort to ensure that there were no unexplained killings. Assassinations were explained by posters, and leaflets were left on the victims' bodies. In certain cases where people were murdered by common criminals or by non-NLF groups, the revolutionary movement was at pains to deny involvement. Every killing that was not essential to the political struggle was avoided because it questioned their justness and sapped their support. Each government soldier that died left resentful family and friends and therefore the attrition of GVN troops was not an aim in itself (Pike 1966:242). The exceptions to this were the small number of elite South Vietnamese units who the NLF feared and so aimed to annihilate.

As the revolution was built upon the support of ordinary people, the village and the revolutionary organization within it was vital. The Party's organization at this most basic level was called the *chi bo*. In effect it was the political and administrative body of the revolution within the village. During the war against the French it administered villages through its control over Liberation and Resistance Committees which often had a non-Party majority. During the war in South Vietnam the *chi bo* performed a similar function within local NLF committees. Its effectiveness in these roles was due, in large part, to the fact that the *chi bo* was responsive to the local people, addressing their grievances and developing social policies which led to a high level of mobilization and motivation. It consistently sought to solve problems which were considered of importance by the peasants. Most people supported the Party not because of its espousal of abstract Marxist-Leninist ideology but because the Party was seen to achieve real, positive things within their own village. In the revolutionary war in the South, local issues were the things that motivated people to become involved in the struggle and the Party's success was due to its ability to harness these local factors to their own wider, national revolutionary aims (Race 1972:179–81).

Critics of the NLF maintained that it manufactured grievances which it then exploited and that the campaign to generate discontent was a foreign import—a conspiracy from Hanoi and, by inference, Moscow. It would be more accurate to view these grievances as real. They were the product of stresses and strains that had been growing in Vietnamese society for generations and which existing authority was not responding to and, in some instances, was even exacerbating. One school of analysis attributes the success of the NLF to its ability to organize the people, (Pike 1966, Wolfe 1967) as if they could be forced to tow a particular political line because of the efficacy of communist organizational techniques. As Douglas Pike claimed, the winning side in the war would be the one which was best organized. It would win 'victory by means of the organisational weapon' (Pike 1966:111). NLF organizational prowess was indeed formidable, but it was only formidable because the rationale for that organizational effort was readily understandable and supported by a great number of Vietnamese people.

The NLF built upon justifiable grievances, identifying, often accurately, the government and the landlord as the source of the peasants' ills. Heightening the villagers' political awareness, they mobilized support for the revolution. This was achieved through one of the three arms of the political struggle (Pike 1986:234–42).

Dich van was the mode of political struggle in enemy-held areas. It was conducted largely by armed propaganda teams. In rural areas the NLF might take over a hamlet or village at night and hold political meetings and stage entertainment and drama shows heavily laced with political messages. In towns, leaflets might be left on buses and in public places. Cars might be stopped and their occupants lectured on the political situation.

Binh van was carried out among GVN troops, Its aim was to sap morale and to induce defections. Accordingly defectors were treated leniently, the families of soldiers were encouraged to urge them to defect or return home and undercover agents were planted to promote disaffection and undercut the enemy's fighting capability.

Amongst the people that it controlled, the NLF conducted *dan van*. This was an invariably successful programme to maintain support and motivation. It encompassed basic administrative tasks such as finance and recruitment for the revolution's military and civilian bodies. Most critical was the task of sustaining the movement's political momentum. This it did through the creation of self-defence bodies, interest groups and popular organizations which were constructed along the same lines as the Party and were controlled through Party mechanisms (Conley 1967:87–99). The most important were termed functional liberation associations (Pike 1966:113–14, 166–93). One group—the most important—was established for farmers and others for young people, women, students, intellectuals and workers. The associations served as channels of communication between the Party and the masses and as a means of drawing ordinary people into a tighter relationship with the revolutionary movement. Using mass psychological techniques in the form of rallies, demonstrations and campaigns, the associations were an effective way of extending political awareness and binding the people to the NLF. Therefore, political organization, whilst it did not conjure a revolution out of thin air, did help to order and sustain an existing one for the Communist Party in Vietnam.

The wars fought against the French and the Americans in Vietnam differed from each other in a number of ways. But although they were distinct and were fought against two different powers, for the Vietnamese they were, nevertheless, stages in a single revolution. The following pages will outline a brief history and some of the major features of this maturing revolutionary movement.

THE RESISTANCE

The Resistance is the name given by the Vietnamese to the war fought against the French between 1946 and 1954. It differed somewhat from the later war to liberate the South because its political content was not as overt (Vo Nguyen Giap 1962:44–5). This was because the conflict was occurring in a long-colonized nation where the issue of nationalism was of primary importance.

To attract as many people as possible to their cause, the Communist Party adopted a united front strategy. This gave them a wider constituency of support than would otherwise have been the case if they had followed a narrow, sectarian line. As a result, although the Viet Minh was established under the aegis of the Communist Party and was predominantly communist-led, it did incorporate other organizations and individuals who shared broadly similar aims and could agree on a minimum programme.

In order to encourage non-communists to join its ranks and to forestall claims that the Viet Minh was simply the Communist Party masquerading in the guise of the nationalist movement, the Indochinese Communist Party was dissolved in November 1945 and was replaced by Marxist Study Groups. Partly because the Viet Minh had become so closely associated with the communists, another less politicized front, the Lien Viet, was created in 1946 to broaden the movement's appeal (Pike 1978:78–9). Like the Viet Minh, within which it existed until it was incorporated into a wider front in 1951, the Lien Viet was controlled by the Party. However, the united front was not intended to dupe people. Most peasants, for example, knew that the Viet Minh was run by the Communist Party because people they had known to be prominent communists within their locality before the war immediately assumed leading positions within the new organization (Trullinger 1980:27–34).

It was not so much that the Party was attempting to hide its controlling hand, but merely that it was trying to illustrate to would-be allies that it would consider and incorporate their political demands—at least in the short-term. In 1947, the Viet Minh responded again to the need to downplay its communist orientation by incorporating non-communists into the cabinet. The dissolution of the ICP had resulted in the communists losing some of their control over the Viet Minh and to rectify this they reconstituted the ICP under the name of the Lao Dong Party (Vietnamese Workers' Party) in February 1951, with Ho Chi Minh as its father figure. Henceforth, the Lao Dong Party was to form the nucleus of power within the Viet Minh.

The importance of a united front policy in strengthening the Viet

Minh's support base was vital. However, the strategy also had its drawbacks as it meant that a degree of flexibility had to be shown in the drafting of policy. In a nation of poor and landless peasants, the promise of land reform was an important method of ensuring ordinary men and women's allegiance to the revolution. Conversely, if the Viet Minh had pushed the issue of wholesale land reform to the fore, they would have alienated many better-off individuals. In order to gain a wide spectrum of support the Viet Minh therefore compromised upon certain aspects of their social programme, thus creating an unresolved tension between the demands of the class struggle and the expediency of the united front (Kolko 1986:4).

Once the Viet Minh had gained sufficient strength, the policies dictated by the united front were dispensed with and in 1953 steps were taken which were a practical reflection of the fact that the united front was no longer essential to the survival of the revolutionary movement. The struggle with the French was nearing its height and the Viet Minh, realizing the necessity for an expansion of its military potential, began to implement more radical policies (Kolko 1986:59–61). This enabled them to mobilize a large number of highly motivated peasants for their 1953–4 military offensive.

The victorious army at Dien Bien Phu was very different from the armed forces of the revolutionary movement during the Second World War. The forerunner of the People's Army of Vietnam (PAVN) was established on 22 December 1944, when a handful of revolutionaries, armed with poor weapons, formed an Armed Propaganda Team in the mountains of Tonkin. Despite the inauspicious beginning, PAVN's numbers swiftly rose and its proficiency increased Equipment still remained in short supply however. The Japanese and Chinese had provided a limited number of weapons, but much of PAVN's equipment had to be scavenged from the enemy, and because of this scarcity, early artillery units had an astonishingly high ratio of men to equipment (Tanham 1967:42).

The lack of artillery forced PAVN to concentrate on infantry tactics and the absence of vehicles created a heavy reliance upon porters. Indeed, it was estimated that one Viet Minh division conducting a relatively simple operation needed 40,000 porters (Tanham 1967:71). Not only had the porters to transport munitions and artillery stripped down into small pieces, but they also had to carry sufficient provisions for themselves. Whilst the lack of vehicles rendered the movement of military supplies arduous and time-consuming it did, nonetheless, have an advantage in that Viet Minh supply trains crossing the jungle were virtually invisible from the air. Nowhere did this produce more spectacular results than at Dien Bien Phu when, in a mammoth logistical feat, large pieces of artillery were carried through dense jungle and literally dragged up mountainsides in order to present the French garrison with a deadly and unexpected challenge.

It was not until the arrival of the Chinese communists at the Vietnamese border in 1949 that the Viet Minh's weapon supply problems began to be allieviated, and it was only as the war began to draw to a close that they received a significant amount of heavy artillery. It was this artillery that undoubtedly contributed to the French débâcle at Dien Bien Phu.

With the arrival of Chinese aid, PAVN began to develop larger units. Prior to 1950 the largest military unit available was a regiment (Tanham 1967:41). Thereafter, as artillery gradually became more available, larger operations and larger units were feasible. Nevertheless, throughout the war PAVN remained very different from a conventional army. An emphasis upon egalitarianism led to the granting of no official titles or rank insignia (Pike 1986:134). Egalitarianism was a reflection of the role of politics within PAVN. The revolutionary movement appreciated that political awareness was essential in order to motivate the soldier to fight and to make him efficient and dedicated. Politics was, as Giap stressed, 'the soul of the army' (Vo Nguyen Giap 1962:55). But the revolutionary movement encountered difficulties in creating a politicized fighting force. In particular, the Resistance needed competent leaders. Those whose educational background made them suitable candidates did not usually originate from the politically and ideologically desirable toiling masses. Coupled with the pressures of the united front strategy, the Resistance hierarchy therefore had to disregard class-origin criterion in the selection of leaders during the early stages of the war. However, once the class-struggle associated with land reform commenced, these individuals ceased to be promoted and were often transferred to non-essential operations (Turley 1975:141).

Ideally the revolutionary movement looked for individuals who had a high level of political awareness and who were good military tacticians with considerable flair for leadership. Men possessing the appropriate qualities were in short supply and so the Resistance adopted a policy used after the Russian Revolution. Unsure of the loyalty of former Tzarist officers, the Bolsheviks introduced political commissars to work alongside military officers. Their task was to supervise military leaders and to provide a political dimension to their activities. A similar scheme was practised by PAVN and commands were divided between the military and political officers. Taken together with party committees which existed within the armed forces, this ensured that the Party exercised political control within PAVN.

The revolution's military force in 1954 was a politicized, unorthodox army which had partially overcome some of its initial weaknesses largely thanks to Chinese aid. The PAVN that fought in the South against the Americans and the Saigon regime was even more highly politicized and, although a little more orthodox after undergoing a period of modernization, it was, if anything, even more of a dedicated and formidable fighting force.

THE WAR IN THE SOUTH

Although over 100,000 Viet Minh supporters regrouped to North Vietnam under the provisions of the Geneva Accords (Pentagon Papers Vol. I 1971:247), a number of covert Viet Minh and Communist Party activists remained in the South. These people were to provide the initial leadership of the group which became known in the West as the 'Viet Cong'. Their role was not to relaunch a new struggle but to follow the party line which stressed peaceful political struggle pending the elections to reunify the country scheduled for 1956.

It has been claimed that the Party realized immediately after Geneva that these elections would never take place (Honey 1963:14–15) and that they began to ferment strife in South Vietnam from the outset, merely utilizing Saigon's refusal to participate in the elections as a pretext to grant legitimacy to their own illegal, aggressive activities. However, the Party's actions in the South are not consistent with this belief. The primary emphasis was given to the political struggle and the Party structure was re-organized and, in effect, made less important. Hanoi probably realized that a refusal to comply with the Accords and hold elections was a possibility but hoped that international pressure would force Saigon to comply or, alternatively, that the shaky regime would collapse in any case.

Unexpectedly President Diem, with US help, shored up South Vietnam and then proceeded to carry out a thorough campaign of repression against those who had been associated with the Viet Minh. The Party staggered under this repression and by 1958–9 its political apparatus in the South was facing decimation (Race 1972:97–104). Notwithstanding the order of the Party leadership in Hanoi to refrain from armed struggle, an unofficial assassination campaign was launched in order to forestall the imminent annihilation of the Party. Southern cadres consistently called for Hanoi to authorize a resumption of the armed struggle but their pleas fell upon deaf ears. The socialist state of North Vietnam was busy organizing its economy and was mindful that its allies, China and the Soviet Union, would look unfavourably upon the outbreak of hostilities. They thus resisted demands that the Party fight violence with violence in the South.

A number of commentators claimed that the war in South Vietnam began as a result of orders from Hanoi. The organizational mechanics, particularly the establishment of the National Liberation Front in 1960 to orchestrate the struggle, were undertaken under the aegis of North Vietnam but it was forced to authorize the armed struggle directly because of pressure from southern revolutionaries (Devillers 1962, Chen 1975:243–4), and if it had not done so there loomed the possibility of a radical secessionist movement in the South that would have taken up arms in its own defence irrespective of orders from Hanoi (Kolko 1986:103–6). R.B.Smith argues that if Hanoi had, at this juncture, decided otherwise, the revolutionary movement in South Vietnam would 'not have grown up when it did' (Smith 1983:16–17). On one level this is correct. A revolutionary movement in the South that did not have the DRV's support would have been very different and quite probably not nearly as successful, but this is not the same as saying that no revolutionary movement would have emerged.

Assessments as to the extent to which Hanoi controlled and dominated the war in the South varied dramatically during the 1960s and supporters of the revolutionary movement were fond of proclaiming the NLF's autonomy. This was quite wrong because the NLF was the Party's front organization. The NLF was dominated by the Party which, in the South, was reformed as the People's Revolutionary Party (PRP) in January 1962. Ostensibly this was because the goals of the Communist Party in Vietnam—in the North, socialist construction and in the South, liberation struggle—were sufficiently dissimilar to warrant that the Party in the South be independent from the Lao Dong Party of the DRV (Thayer 1975:47). It probably also owed a great deal to the need for the revolutionary movement in South Vietnam to appear distinct from Hanoi in the eyes of the international community.

Although the PRP was a southern Party in that its members were natives of the South, it was closely associated with the Party in the DRV. In 1960 the Lao Dong Party's regional organization in South Vietnam had been upgraded through the creation of a Central Committee Directorate for Southern Vietnam, more commonly known as the Central Office for South Vietnam or COSVN. This restored the importance of the regional apparatus to the level it had enjoyed during the Resistance. Hanoi appointed its own influential personnel to this committee which, after the creation of the PRP, served as a standing committee for the new Party's own Central Committee (Thayer 1975:47). COSVN, moreover, was responsible directly to the Lao Dong Party. This was a vital link between the revolutionary movement in the South and the Party in the North and by the mid-1960s COSVN personnel and the NLF and PRP Central Committees were virtually synonymous (Thayer 1975:49). At the very highest level general policy directives were decided by the Politburo and Central Committee of the Lao Dong Party in Hanoi and were then forwarded to its Central Committee Directorate for South Vietnam, whereupon they were endorsed and disseminated to appropriate NLF/PRP organs which, exercising a degree of autonomy, then drew up plans based upon the directives (Thayer 1975:51–2).

While the higher echelons of the NLF comprised a large proportion of PRP members, lower levels had a higher percentage of non-Party members. As it was essential for the Party to maintain some form of control over the NLF, the Front did not actually have a separate vertical chain of command. Instead, it depended upon its corresponding Party body. Furthermore, while the NLF had its own military wing, the People's Liberation Armed Forces (PLAF), it commanded these units only in name (Race 1972:122). True control lay in the hands of the PRP, although this distinction Was rendered meaningless where, as was often the case, the PRP and the NLF were represented by the same people.

That Party members dominated the NLF owed less to a communist conspiracy than to the fact that they were often the most highly motivated and dedicated political activists. Nevertheless, as the NLF became increasingly identified with Hanoi and as Party domination became an obvious fact, the need arose to broaden political opposition to the US and the Saigon regime. This was achieved through the creation of the Alliance of National, Democratic and Peace Forces which incorporated a number of major nationalist figures who were not members of the NLF. Its political platform differed from the NLF's in that it had more of a southern perspective and was liberal rather than revolutionary in approach (Truong Nhu Tang 1986:140). The Alliance became a partner with the NLF and coordinated policy with them, and when in 1969 the revolutionary movement formed a Provisional Revolutionary Government (PRG), a number of its members were given ministries in the new shadow cabinet.

The formation of the PRG was closely associated with the start of peace talks. Primarily the NLF wanted to gain domestic and international credibility and to be able to negotiate on the basis of having an alternative and, they claimed, legitimate government waiting in the wings. The incorporation of non-communist elements in the PRG was consequently a reflection of the need to gain progressive, world support for this supposedly independent body. However Truong Nhu Tung, the disillusioned non-communist justice minister of the PRG, has since questioned the sincerity of the Party commitment to the PRG (Truong Nhu Tang 1986:194). He cites the deteriorating relations between the Party ideologues and their NLF/Alliance allies in the PRG as indicative of the Party's bad faith and their interest in the united front only as a short-term tactic to be used for more sinister ends. In his opinion, once the PRG had been utilized and sufficient political capital extracted from it, the Party dispensed with it with Machiavellian efficiency. Certainly, the swiftness with which the NLF, the PRP and the PRG were absorbed within the DRVs political structure once reunification was achieved in 1975, does seem to indicate that efforts to prove the independence of the southern revolutionary movement and its prospective government were little more than a charade. But given that the intimate workings of the NLF were so heavily influenced by North Vietnam and given that the North had made such sacrifices in order to pursue the struggle, Hanoi was hardly likely to countenance anything other than its own plans for South Vietnam. Perhaps the only surprising thing was that people like Truong Nhu Tang were unwise, or perhaps naive enough to believe differently.

During the early 1960s the struggle was southern-based to the extent that it was conducted by native southerners. An increasing quantity of supplies nevertheless came from the DRV as the tempo of the conflict accelerated. Up until mid-1961 Hanoi could probably furnish the NLF with adequate material support but, as the scale of US military assistance to the GVN grew, the necessity of procuring aid from fraternal countries became pressing (Smith 1985:37). China and the Soviet Union increasingly stepped in to make up the shortfall in supplies for what the revolutionaries called their 'special war' against the US backed Saigon regime. A 'special war' was characterized as one in which a neo-colonial power sought to wage war through the auspices of a comprador native regime whose troops served as proxies. The NLF proved consistently successful in this war, making great gains at the expense of the Diem government and capitalizing on the people's antipathy towards the regime. Paradoxically, Diem's presidency was actually a boon to the NLF, and immediately following the coup that overthrew him, the revolutionary movement became temporarily disorientated and perplexed as the object of their most fierce hatred had vanished. Soon recovering their momentum, however, the NLF made dramatic gains in the countryside in the months after the coup as the GVN's administrative structure in the rural areas reeled under the impact of the political upheaval.

During the war a heated debate developed over whether the DRV had sent PAVN units to the South before the arrival of US ground combat forces, or whether the DRV had responded to US escalation. It is now abundantly clear that PAVN units arrived in South Vietnam before March 1965.

At the Ninth Plenum of the Lao Dong Party in December 1963 critical decisions were taken which fundamentally altered the DRV's role in the conflict (Smith 1985:221). Whilst not authorizing the deployment of entire units, the plan that emerged called for the intensification of the struggle in the South. Once upon this path of escalation it was only a short time before PAVN units were fighting in the South.

Hanoi introduced its forces because they wanted to end the war within the foreseeable future. The GVN was in a parlous state, vulnerable to the slightest pressure. The DRV therefore perceived an opportunity to deal a crushing blow to the uncompromising post-Diem Saigon juntas (Chen 1975:254–5). Incorrectly surmising that the US would not intervene militarily, Hanoi decided to introduce PAVN units and to employ them in offensive operations in order to assure victory in a truncated protracted war. Other factors were also important in this decision. Undoubtedly the developing Sino-Soviet dispute encouraged Hanoi's allies to mute any calls for restraint and obliged them to support the DRV's expanded role in the conflict (Smith 1985:255). More controversially, it has also been suggested that Hanoi was suspicious of the NLF/PRP apparatus and, believing that it had too much autonomy, was determined to take control of the military struggle and to secure a quick victory whereupon it could put its southern house in order.

Under the triple pressure of the PLAF guerrillas, PAVN and PLAF main forces and, most importantly, its own internal weaknesses, the GVN's disintegration accelerated during late 1964 and early 1965. It was because of the imminent collapse of its ally that the US then intervened in force. In 1965 US combat troops first arrived in Vietnam. The NLF/DRV had not foreseen this escalation and it presented them with a dilemma. They could retreat, abandoning large, offensive operations and return to a more defensive, low-intensity guerrilla warfare with the concomitant loss of morale and momentum that this would have entailed for the revolutionary movement and the chance it would have given to the South Vietnamese to improve their performance. This reasoning, of course, was premised on the belief that the appallingly inept South Vietnamese government and army could not possibly get any worse and could only improve. The alternative to resuming the defensive was for the NLF/DRV to match the US escalation, step for step, and pit their forces against the American's technologically superior military with the inevitable manpower losses that this would involve (Thompson 1969:55–6). Believing that guerrilla warfare could only deliver a stalemate when counterposed against US firepower, the NLF/DRV took the only decision seemingly open to them—they escalated

Once US forces were actively participating in the struggle, the 'special war' was transformed into a 'limited war' and Giap adapted military strategy to suit the new conditions. Called Regular Force Strategy, Giap's idea was to combine two basic tactics, the 'coordinated fighting method' employing medium-sized operations against important targets, and the 'independent fighting method', which encompased a host of frequent small actions (Pike 1986:226–7). This strategy was utilized by PLAF/PAVN for three years and culminated in the 1968 Tet Offensive.

Until Tet, PLAF assumed the major role in combat (Pike 1986:46). A few northerners worked with PLAF as officers and technicians but as the US strategy of attrition depleted indigenous forces, they began to be replaced by soldiers from the North. In fact, troops from the DRV outnumbered native southerners in PLAF main force units by 1967 (Kolko 1986:184). By their nature, however, the regional and especially the village guerrilla units were not subject to this same transfusion of personnel from the North.

PAVN and PLAF main force units tended to be based in the relatively uninhabited region of the Vietnamese-Laotian and Vietnamese-Cambodian border. There they baited an all too willing US military who were drawn away from the vital Delta and coastal provinces where the political and guerrilla forces were left a free hand to work amongst the people. In fighting the Americans, PLAF/PAVN faced fearsome technology which was extremely difficult to adapt to. The helicopter, for instance, created initial problems for the revolutionary forces. Offsetting the US/GVN's technological predominance was PLAF/PAVN's greater mobility, their superior intelligence sources, their adaptability, their high morale and their military planning which often involved repeated rehearsals of operations on models of their intended targets. As a result, a large proportion of PLAF/PAVN operations were faultlessly executed.

The Vietnamese who fought for the revolutionary movement were generally highly motivated. This was necessary in order to endure the hardships of combat. PAVN soldiers who infiltrated into South Vietnam came along the Ho Chi Minh trail which led from the DRV through the jungles of Laos and entered the South at various points across the Cambodian-Vietnamese and Laotian-Vietnamese border. During the early and mid-1960s the trail was little more than a series of rough paths cut through the jungle and mountains and the arduous journey for prospective PAVN would take up to six months and would claim between 10 and 20 per cent of them, mainly through disease (Van Dyke 1972:37–41). As the war accelerated, the trail was turned into a sophisticated network of roads along which troops and supplies were transported. Then the danger to life came not so much from disease but from the ferocity of US bombing which pummelled the trail almost incessantly.

Once in South Vietnam, life in the jungle and swamps was little easier. Perpetually malnourished, PAVN and also PLAF units were subject to irritating skin diseases, to stomach and bowel infections and, above all, to debilitating malaria. Called the 'jungle tax', malaria may even have proved more effective in attriting the revolution's forces than the enemy (Truong Nhu Tang 1986:160–2).

Surviving in the harsh environment was extremely tough even for those who were leading figures in the revolutionary movement. For those who operated in the particularly dangerous Vietnamese-Cambodian border region where the revolutionary forces maintained the various branches of their headquarters, there was the especially serious threat of bombardment from B-52s. Because these planes could not be seen or heard and because the sheer quantity of ordinance that they dropped was so massive and their capacity for destruction so immense, the fear that they generated was legion. Truong Nhu Tang, who lived through numerous such bombardments, described the raids as 'undiluted psychological terror' (Truong Nhu Tang 1986:167).

The revolutionary movement adapted to life in the jungle and to life in villages controlled by the enemy because it had to. Paradoxically, it was forced by its own weakness to assume tactics which ultimately provided it with great strength. An example was the use of tunnel warfare (Mangold and Penycate 1985). Practised both by the Viet Minh and the NLF, the development of vast tunnel networks and complexes, often stretching for miles, was the natural response of militarily weak guerrillas who wished to remain within territory controlled by a technologically superior army. When hiding above ground proved impossible, the guerrillas found sanctury beneath their villages and fields. In the dark, dank and airless labyrinths that were carved from the earth, hospitals, workshops, stores, living quarters and kitchens were created, providing a refuge, albeit an uncomfortable one, for many guerrillas, some whom did not emerge into the light for years. Against this variety of warfare, the US/GVN had few answers. A highly skilled body of troops known as 'tunnel rats' was assembled in order to take the war into the tunnels, but these specialized soldiers operating in a very dangerous environment, did not have any real impact upon the revolutionaries' use of tunnel warfare and the explosives which the conventional forces used to destroy tunnel complexes were largely ineffective. Tunnel warfare therefore remained one of the many successes of the revolutionary movement and a powerful example of the way in which commitment can sustain people enduring apparently unbearable conditions.

There was little monetary reward for PAVN soldiers fighting in the South. Pay was very low. A soldier's monthly salary purchased him the equivalent of twelve bottles of beer (Pike 1986:138). For PLAF the desire for personal advancement may have been a significant factor in attracting people to fight. Implementing a policy of promoting men from the ranks, PLAF offered the peasant the prospect of an education and a career. This was in stark contrast to the GVN Armed Forces whose officer corps was inflexibly drawn from the middle and upper classes.

As many as 850,000 PAVN and PLAF soldiers may have been killed in the war (Thayer 1985:103). Despite this very high loss rate, morale and commitment were surprisingly high. Some North Vietnamese troops preparing to travel South to join PAVN forces had the motto 'Born in the North to die in the South' tattooed on their bodies and some, fully expecting to meet their deaths, took part in their own funeral rites before they departed.

Although US/GVN attempts to promote defections did succeed in encouraging a significant number of lower-level PLAF personnel to abandon the revolutionary movement, this naturally proved less successful amongst PAVN troops whose defection would effectively cut themselves off from their familes in the North. Moreover those that did defect were generally at the bottom of the PLAF hierarchy and were the least politically aware.

Not all those who joined PLAF did so voluntarily. Arguably, perhaps 30 per cent were coerced into fighting (Berman 1974:69) and, as the war escalated between 1964 and 1967, PLAF recruiting policies became more draconian (Pike 1969:7). What degree of force this actually implied is debatable and many joined the revolutionary forces because of pressure from the village and the family and because they were expected to do so (Berman 1974:73). Once in the PLAF, enthusiastic and more reluctant soldiers were fashioned into true revolutionaries through the force's political training. This was not so much brainwashing as the creation of an environment in which politics and the revolution became of paramount importance (Berman 1974:79). The soldier was encouraged to identify with the unit and to integrate himself with the primary group, and the efficacy of these pressures owed a great deal to the fact that they harmonized well with the troops' interpretation of traditional social and cultural relations (Berman 1974:106).

Central to the creation of an ideologically and politically effective fighting force was the role of the cadre. Cadres within the armed forces consistently sought to develop political awareness and to give the combatants support and encouragment to view their role and actions within a political framework. They were there to provide a clear political line and to exhort the military to analyse its weaknesses and improve upon them. To the soldier, the cadre was a friend, a teacher and a leader. To the military leader he was a co-commander and adviser, although, as the war developed, the balance of the command swung away from equal responsibility shared by military and political officers and devolved more clearly upon the military commander.

Most political cadres were members of the Communist Party and, as in other sectors of society, the Party at its most fundamental level was constructed upon the basis of a group of three individuals, known as the 'three-man cell', who supported each other ideologically and psychologically. Completely separate from the political three-man cells were the military cells. Every soldier belonged to a cell and it was the cell to which he owed his allegiance and which bound him to the revolutionary forces. Consequently, it was the cell which formed the fundamental building blocks of the armed forces and it was the cadre system which formed its political backbone (Berman 1974:93, Conley 1967:147).

As a rule, the morale of PLAF/PAVN was high. This derived from the force's political orientation, from a strong *esprit de corps* and from the fact that PLAF/PAVN troops believed themselves to be elite forces, in contrast to the lackadaisical GVN military. Revolutionary fighters were accorded prestige and those who died became martyred heroes. Guaranteed of an afterlife, what mattered was not so much that they had died but the manner in which they had died (Berman 1974:31–8). The soldier's belief in the cause of revolution and his willingness to sacrifice his life for it rendered PLAF/PAVN an implacable opponent.

In order to conduct such a fierce war in the South, North Vietnam had to mobilize itself for total war. Every individual was encouraged to play some role in the struggle, even if this amounted only to looking out for spies. By making people feel part of the fighting and by emphasizing the importance of personal commitment, North Vietnamese society was buttressed to face the pressures of the war. The US bombing of DRV territory was the greatest of these pressures but North Vietnam adapted well to it. Lines of communication were kept open by constructing temporary bridges from pontoons of bamboo and roads were repaired by women, girls and old people. The success of repair-teams in keeping open roads that were repeatedly bombed and apparently made impassable kept traffic moving, and although vehicles in many heavily attacked areas had to move at night and in darkness, the road and rail transportation systems did not grind to a halt. Essential petrol and oil storage depots were dispersed and small tanks of petroleum were positioned along all major routes, thus ensuring that there would be few supply problems (Van Dyke 1972:207–10).

As well as damaging the DRV's military and industrial capacity, US bombing inevitably caused civilian casualties. The Vietnamese responded to this by adopting both active and passive defences. Soviet-supplied anti-aircraft artillery was used, especially towards the end of the war around particularly vital areas. Major cities were evacuated of all but essential personnel and a variety of shelters and trenches were constructed in all areas liable to attack. In addition to large shelters, one-man shelters were found in Hanoi at frequent intervals along almost every road in the city (Van Dyke 1972:67–77). In villages, trenches criss-crossed between the houses and led out to the fields, while in regions subject to the most intensive bombing, particularly the area just north of the Demilitarized Zone, a shelter system of such sophistication was developed that people could spend most of their lives underground (Van Dyke 1972:71–2).

In its liberated areas in the South communities were turned into combat hamlets fortified by trenches and bamboo fences. The NLF administered the liberated zones and also strove to carry out its trade and taxation policies in contested areas. NLF taxation was highly progressive, and operated according to a sliding scale. The rich could expect to pay a high proportion of their earnings and profits while a peasant family could expect to contribute 10–20 per cent of its gross income (Sansom 1970:222). After 1964–5, as NLF taxes increased in order to fund the widening war, there was a perceptible decline in support for the revolutionary movement (Sansom 1970:237). In early 1967, a mere 18 per cent of NLF finances were derived from the taxation of agricultural production (Kolko 1986:128) but, even so, this still represented a burden to the peasantry.

NLF trade policies were intended to separate the economies of the liberated zones and GVN-controlled territory. The revolutionary movement discouraged the purchase of such wild luxuries as nylon shirts, arguing that spending money on consumer goods merely served to help the US/GVN and keep Saigon's economy afloat (Sansom 1970:223). However, the flow of goods to and from GVN and NLF areas continued and the NLF were forced to turn a blind eye to it.

Moreover, by the end of 1965 the revolutionary movement was beginning to encounter shortages of locally generated produce as areas under its control became depopulated as a result of enemy bombing (Sansom 1970:225). This consequently resulted in a relaxation of a number of restrictive trade policies.

A significant amount of NLF income was derived from the US and the GVN. Gross corruption and woefully poor management led to the siphoning off of money and materials, particularly from a large number of aid projects. Inevitably, some of this money found its way into the coffers of a grateful NLF and, to a great extent, this symbiotic relationship helped sustain the revolutionary movement at a time when the war was disrupting its own independently derived sources of income and supplies.

By 1967 it was apparent that the war had reached a stalemate. The US/GVN could not defeat the NLF politically and yet PLAF/PAVN could not defeat their opponent militarily. The NLF/DRV therefore decided to launch the Tet Offensive in order to hasten an end to the war. Its aim was to trigger a General Uprising and the overthrow of the Saigon regime. At the very least, it was hoped to have a dramatic impact upon the development of the war. Yet because it actually had a profound effect upon US decisionmaking, a number of commentators imputed that this was its major aim. It was not, and no evidence has come to light to indicate that opinion in the US was one of Tet's primary targets (Karnow 1984:537).

Various interesting interpretations have been placed upon the offensive. Sansom claims that it was an act of desperation on the part of the NLF/DRV. Because the war was destroying customary ways of life, the peasant was becoming obsessed, not with politics and with the justice of the Revolution's cause, but with basic security for himself and his family. These people were being driven from their homes in NLF controlled territory and were seeking refuge in the cities where US/GVN forces did not employ lavish firepower. In order to illustrate to these refugees that the cities were not secure and in order to pressure them to return to their villages, the NLF/DRV therefore undertook their city-orientated Tet Offensive (Sansom 1970:241).

Even more interesting, but even more questionable, is the suspicion that the DRV authorized the offensive in the hope that the NLF would be crippled by its losses and that the DRV could step into the breach and assume total control over the movement in the South. This is largely what happened, but it is unlikely that the DRV planned it this way. Certainly, the mauling of the NLF weakened it and facilitated the DRV's swamping of the South's revolutionary movement after the 1975 reunification of Vietnam, but this was an unintentional fillip for the DRV rather than any malicious and cynical betrayal of the NLF in 1968. After all, the indigenous political apparatus was the revolutionary movement's greatest asset.

Tet proved to be a disastrous miscalculation. General Giap had argued against the offensive from the beginning but he was overruled by elements in the Hanoi leadership who insisted that the time was propitious for an aggressive military assault to overthrow the GVN and to spark an uprising of the supposedly oppressed and restless population of the South who were waiting for a signal to act (Davidson 1988:449–50).

Although he had opposed the offensive, it fell to Giap to plan it. Unfortunately his direst predictions were borne out. Thousands of the revolutionary movement's finest soldiers died in the campaign and the indigenous PLAF, which bore the brunt of combat, was dealt a debilitating blow from which it never fully managed to recuperate. Native cadres, with their intimate knowledge of the South and with their links to the local population, were irreplaceable and, thereafter, the NLF's rural organization had to operate at a reduced level. New US/GVN efforts to woo the population, the severe, war-induced dislocation of the countryside and the peasants' suspicion that the NLF had lost the mandate of heaven, all contributed to a marked lowering of the revolutionary movement's profile in many areas in the years following the offensive.

As a result of PLAF losses during Tet, PAVN had to take over much of the fighting. But because of the weakness of the movement, it proved extremely difficult to persevere with regular force strategy. The NLF/DRV therefore adopted two new approaches. First was the talk-fight policy, which prompted them to agree to negotiations with the US. The second was a new military strategy promoted by General Giap and which Pike has termed 'neo-revolutionary warfare' (Pike 1986:227–8). Much to the horror of the Chinese, it stressed that victory was possible within stage two of guerrilla war. Giap considered it vital to avoid the concentration of troops which would make them vulnerable to air and ground attack and, instead, to rely on more defensive actions, punctuated by larger offensives termed 'military highpoints' (Pike 1986:228).

The NLF/DRV pursued this strategy until 1972 when they launched their Easter Offensive. A conventional military assault using modern weapons, the offensive was conducted primarily by PAVN who carried out approximately 90 per cent of the combat action (Pike 1986:49). In undertaking the Easter Offensive, the NLF/DRV were trying to hasten an end to the war. Pacification efforts, together with the war's disruption of life, had loosened the bonds which tied the people to the NLF and the revolutionary movement feared a further transformation of politics and society. Furthermore, the organizational system which had initially linked Hanoi and the South had been eroded and local and regional forces were frequently cut off from high-level Party control for extended periods (Kolko 1986:186). After Tet this was increasingly a problem and Hanoi was impatient to reassert its dominance over the southern movement. The prospect of an offensive to coincide with an election year in the US and, with luck, to achieve the same level of political impact as Tet, therefore tempted the NLF/DRV to launch their Easter 1972 campaign.

Although US combat forces no longer operated in Vietnam, American airpower played a crucial role in halting the offensive. It was partly owing to the knowledge that US airpower could decimate the conventional forces which increasingly operated in the post-Tet environment that led to the DRV's decision to secure the United States' departure from Vietnam though a negotiated peace. Reasoning that it could now successfully achieve its objectives through a temporary political settlement, Hanoi initialled the Paris Peace Accords on 23 January 1973. Once the US had left Vietnam the NLF/DRV were only a few short steps away from their never relinquished goal of reunification.

8 America's war: the strategy and tactics of the United States' military in Vietnam

With the exception of the activities of the Office of Strategic Services during the Second World War, direct US military involvement in Vietnam dates from 1950 when, as a result of the establishment of the Military Assistance Advisory Group (MAAG) in Saigon, US Air Force personnel, including military advisers and aircraft maintenance experts, were sent to Indochina to aid the French. Following the Geneva Accords and the withdrawal of France from South East Asia, MAAG was to assume the training of the armed forces of the newly created South Vietnamese government.

The first combined US/GVN air operations took place in 1961. From then on, the US Armed Forces (USAF) were to undertake a growing operational support role. The scale of the involvement eventually exceeded the capacity of MAAG to implement and oversee it and so Military Assistance Command, Vietnam (MACV) was established in February 1962. This was to remain the controlling body for US forces during the subsequent conflict.

The head of MACV was COMUSMACV (Commander, United States Military Assistance Command, Vietnam) who, in the chain of command, was subordinate to the Commander in Chief of forces in the Pacific. The command structure in Vietnam was criticized as conflicting and inefficient because COMUSMACV did not have control over all operations in the Indochina theatre. Multiple lines of responsibility for individual services and a highly fragmented and uncoordinated logistics system were features of the US presence in Vietnam right up to, and even beyond the dramatic escalation of 1965. Organizational confusion and the failure of the logistics system to keep pace with a snowballing support requirement was primarily due to the unplanned nature of escalation which inevitably gave rise to *ad hoc* arrangements which were only systematically integrated once the size of the American commitment rendered centralization imperative.

The counterinsurgency concept was supposedly central to America's early military role in Vietnam. Counterinsurgency was the Kennedy administration's new weapon in its arsenal to fight the 'brushfire wars' which appeared to be breaking out in many developing nations as the 1960s began. The US perceived these wars to be part of a Soviet plan to achieve global domination by exploiting the stresses that developing nations were experiencing as they modernized and adapted, often very poorly, to the post-colonial world. Using guerrilla warfare techniques, their native proxies sought to overthrow neutral or pro-Western governments (Blaufarb 1977:66–7). Such a belief was confirmed in 1961 when Soviet premier, Nikita Krushchev, pledged his support for wars of national liberation.

The Kennedy administration was determined to rise to the challenge. Rather than depending on Elsenhower's none-too-credible 'massive retaliation' with nuclear weapons, the new buzz words were 'flexible response' which was calculated to deal with everything from nuclear to guerrilla warfare. The answer to insurgency, Kennedy hoped, lay in the development of the multi-faceted counterinsurgency doctrine. Its main objective was to strengthen the beleaguered government in question and to improve its performance. Social and economic measures would improve the popularity of the regime and remove the discontent upon which the insurgency thrived. To ensure that this could be achieved without too much interference, counterguerrilla forces employing the same kind of unconventional tactics as the enemy were to be trained to deal with the insurgents.

President Kennedy took a keen personal interest in counterinsurgency and in assembling suitable forces to undertake it (Sorensen 1965:631–3, Schlesinger 1965:309–10). He set up a Special Group to deal specifically with the new doctrine and its implementation and requested that the JCS provide the requisite equipment and supplies. The Special Forces, a branch of the military specializing in counterguerrilla operations, were expanded and Kennedy authorized them to wear the famous green beret as a sign of his favour and to symbolize their elite status. However, the special forces remained very small in scale and outside the mainstream career structure of the military. Furthermore, the counterguerrilla units that the US did evolve could not fight insurgents on their own terms because the US counterguerrillas always tended to remain dependent upon external support, supplies and command (Cable 1986:154).

For a time, counterinsurgency became extremely fashionable within the armed services. It gave the army, in particular, a new lease of life after the nation's faith and finance had been diverted to the nuclear battlefield. Fortunately counterinsurgency came along to save it and to give the army a chance to prove its mettle in modern warfare. But what interest the military had in counterinsurgency always remained superficial. The army never really wanted to create counterguerrilla forces and so it paid lipservice to the concept while never implementing it (Hilsman 1967:578–9, Krepinevich 1986:51).

Fulfilling a commitment to counterinsurgency would have demanded far too many changes in training, tactics and equipment for the armed services to stomach. Therefore, rather than developing units with a specific counter-insurgency capability, the army insisted that it would train its regular forces to become competent counterguerrillas, thereby effectively dismissing the fundamental differences between conventional and unconventional warfare (Blaufarb 1977:80–2). Inevitably, these regular forces were totally inappropriate in a counterinsurgency context and 'flexible response' became simply the first step in a process of conventional military escalation. The blow that this dealt the United States' counterinsurgency capability was fatal.

Far more to the military hierarchy's liking was a slightly more creative application of tactics to deal with mid-intensity, or conventional warfare. Their basic and mistaken premise was that the conflict with the NLF and the DRV was a conventional war and that the enemy could be defeated by standard means. They could not believe that a home-grown insurgency was possible and sustainable. It always had to have external sponsors (Cable 1986:145) and the guerrilla was perceived merely as a partisan who operated in support of regular forces. It was these forces that the Americans sought to fight. In Vietnam this led them to develop a 'border fixation' (Cable 1986:134) and to fight the war, not as if it was a politically-charged civil war, but as if it was a test-run for the long-awaited and meticulously trained-for traditional war of fronts against Warsaw Pact nations on the plains of Europe.

Even if a few had reservations about the relevance of such an approach, their doubts were assuaged by implicit faith in the might and invincibility of the US Armed Forces. No great effort had to be made to understand the Vietnamese or the dynamics of the conflict because the belief in the efficacy of technology was so great that 'technowar' would prevail regardless (Gibson 1986:98–9). Clearly, it did not.

Although the Americans did not assume a major combat role until 1965, they had been directly involved in the fighting for a number of years as they had performed what was ostensibly a training role for the

South Vietnamese Armed Forces (RVNAF). In practice, this was interpreted as a licence to engage in limited, defensive combat providing that a South Vietnamese trainee was present in order to be instructed. However, the premium placed upon defensive action was gradually dropped in favour of a more aggressive approach. The shift in emphasis was a reflection of deepening US involvement in the war and was a feature of the general escalation leading to the assumption of an overtly offensive role in 1965.

The first American ground combat troops arrived in Vietnam in March 1965 and were given the responsibility of defending US bases and crucial installations within South Vietnam. This was known as the base defence strategy. Soon after it was replaced by the enclave strategy which widened the area of operations for US forces. But both approaches came under fierce criticism from the military because they forced them to assume the defensive. General Westmoreland, COMUSMACV (1965-8), suggested a more dynamic policy and requested, and then received, permission to take the war into the Central Highlands where he believed that he could 'find, fix, fight and finish' the enemy. Ultimately, it was his appropriately termed 'search and destroy' operations that became the unchallenged strategy for winning the war.

In essence, there were two wars running concurrently in Vietnam and success in one inevitably contributed to successs in the other. The first war was fought on a military level and the second war was the political struggle in which, for many years, the National Liberation Front appeared to be the only serious contender. By concentrating efforts upon the military conflict, the US left its enemy to make headway on the political battlefield and, indeed, PLAF/PAVN actively encouraged this misplaced utilization of resources by drawing US troop strength away from populated regions and into areas of limited tactical or political importance.

US strategy came in for some heavy criticism from those who believed that the military should have been fighting the war in the villages and using its forces to improve local security. This would have meant giving the 'political' war priority. Westmoreland, however, had other ideas. As he was later to claim, he did not have enough troops to maintain a presence everywhere (Westmoreland 1980:189). And as he thought that the greatest danger came from regular PLAF/PAVN units, what he tried to do was to fashion a shield against these forces whom he called the North Vietnamese 'bully boys' (Westmoreland 1980:187). In this manner he would enable the US/GVN political war in the village to be conducted without interference. But Westmoreland and the rest of the army brass had seemed to miss the point. Up until 1968, North Vietnamese regulars were fighting in support of the NLF and if it had not been for the NLF's political apparatus in the villages there would not have been a war in the first place. Whilst this network remined intact, the NLF could still go on recruiting people to fight. In addition, until 1967, at the very earliest, the US/GVN did not actually pursue a concerted political war at the local level anyhow and so Westmorland's military shield came to function very nicely as a shield behind which the NLF could continue its productive political work.

America's grand military strategy in Vietnam was simple: they wanted to kill as many enemy soldiers as possible. This was the concept of attrition and it was chosen in preference to a politically orientated strategy because it seemed more clear-cut and because America had all the equipment to accomplish it. Having vast armed forces and a breathtaking array of sophisticated military technology was a remarkable incentive to the pursuit of such a war (Komer 1972a: 48). American military action in Vietnam was consequently seen to be a cut-price solution to a deeper socio-political crisis.

Because the conflict was not a war of fronts and because victory could not be achieved simply by holding territory, the US used the number of deaths it inflicted as an alternative measuring stick. The axiom that underlay American strategy was that the enemy could be defeated by attrition of his combat strength. The Tet Offensive revealed the weakness of this notion because it highlighted the dichotomy between the military's consistent reporting of steady progress in the war and the fact that PLAF/PAVN were able to mount such a large-scale attack. At the heart of this contradiction was the mistaken faith in attrition and the methods used to measure the success of this strategy.

What Westmorland and the Joint Chiefs of Staff were aiming for was the critically important 'cross-over point'. This was the juncture at which the enemy would lose more soldiers than it could replace on the battlefield. To achieve this, the US presence in Vietnam had to grow because, as the enemy increased in strength, more and more men were required in order to improve the rate of attrition. It therefore became increasingly obvious that America's strategy was literally to grind the enemy down through the utilization of its vast armed forces and the power of its weapons. However, the US failed to recognize the inherent ability and willingness of the NLF/DRV to replace their losses. Because North Vietnam's population was composed predominantly of young people and was growing rapidly, US forces and the RVNAF would have had to have secured a kill ratio far in excess of that which marked even the high points of allied military activity during the war (Thayer 1985:90).

Confusing the picture still further were the US methods of assessing enemy strength. Controversially, intelligence estimates counted only regular soldiers and full-time guerrillas in the figures. They did not include the large number of part-time guerrillas nor those people belonging to the enemy's extensive political infrastructure. Inevitably this resulted in an assessment that greatly understated PLAF/PAVN capability and which was exposed by a CIA analyst as an important reason for the underestimation of the enemy's ability to mount the Tet Offensive. Obviously, if the enemy was stronger than was presumed, then that vitally important cross-over point moved further out of reach.

Aside from ignoring the war's political perspective, the theory also failed to recognize that the guerrilla had the option to engage in combat when the situation appeared favourable, or alternatively, to retreat and sink back into the surrounding countryside if it did not. This meant that PLAF/PAVN could determine the level of attrition that they experienced. The fact was that the enemy would not stand and fight in the way that the Americans wanted and, revealingly, less than 5 per cent of total enemy actions between 1965 and 1972 involved ground assaults in which PLAF/PAVN forces came into direct contact with allied troops (Thayer 1985:45).

It was only very occasionally that US forces and the South Vietnamese Army (ARVN) could initiate contact with the enemy in a situation in which they were likely to retain the advantage. A complete absence of tactical surprise marked the majority of US operations (Lewy 1978:60–1, Davidson 1988:406). The American method of fighting the war demanded a large supply of equipment, thus making operations noisy and difficult, especially in the wet season and, when there was a lack of air mobile support, very slow in an environment in which stealth, speed and silence were hallmarks of the successful guerrilla. It was not smart planning, for instance, to advertise the arrival of the Americans by 'prepping' an area with heavy artillery fire prior to an operation, nor to broadcast military plans by requisitioning and building up supplies for an offensive, nor to anchor a hospital ship off the coast a few hours before an amphibious attack. To add to these rather elementary problems, the NLF possessed a highly sophisticated intelligence network and there were informants at all levels within the South Vietnamese political and military structures. As such, even highly classified operations were often foiled and the ever-elusive enemy would disappear into thin air.

The armed forces of the US and the GVN had an apparent advantage over their enemy. They had a greater quantity of sophisticated weaponry and, throughout the war, the military generated a flow of advanced technology to help fight the war. New additions to the armoury included improved munitions, night-time viewers and such dubious devices as 'people sniffers' which could identify the locations of people in the jungle by detecting urine concentration. How to tell whether it was enemy urine was a fraction more complicated and the wily enemy learnt how to confuse the 'sniffer' by hanging buckets of urine in the trees (Davidson 1988:405).

Technological superiority, therefore, did not automatically mean that the US possessed a great advantage. Its armoured units could not operate effectively at night and they lacked mobility and demanded vital time for maintenance and repair (Krepinevich 1986:170). Furthermore, PLAF/PAVN quickly adapted to the use of equipment like armoured vehicles and tanks and, by 1965, they were using suitable, armour-damaging weaponry (Starry 1981:45–47). The emphasis upon the use of greater quantities of superior machinery also had another drawback since it demanded an exceptionally large logistical operation. The American way of fighting the war meant that vast, comfortable bases had to be built and maintained and colossal quantities of materials had to be imported. Each day the equivalent of 96lb of supplies had to be imported for every American in the theatre (Cincinnatus 1981:64). Keeping this structure functioning demanded a large number of men. Therefore the US Army's 'foxhole strength'—that is the men who were ready to fight—was always limited and the majority of troops fulfilled a support role (Thayer 1985:93). As a result, even at the height of US involvement, only some 80,000 men were available for combat duties out of an American presence which totalled over 500,000 (Gabriel and Savage 1976:353).

Awesome and overwhelming firepower was fundamental to the way that the US fought the war. Greater use of firepower usually meant more enemy dead. In addition, the horrific slaughter of the First World War had pressured the US Army into honouring the dictum 'expend shells not men'. The principle made good sense, especially in the context of a conflict which had domestic critics. Consequently, a sincere effort was made to replace manpower with firepower. In a sense, therefore, infantry came to be employed as a 'fixing force'—as bait to lure the enemy whereupon he could be decimated by artillery and aircraft strikes.

'Search and destroy' operations were the principal vehicle of the attrition strategy. They typically involved wide sweeps through a given area. US forces would then utilize their vast firepower potential whenever the enemy was engaged, regardless of whether or not there was any significant strategic value to be gained by victory. This was the army's method of creating front lines, even if such militarily defined front lines were almost invariably transitory, as opposed to the more enduring but less visible lines denoting success or failure in the political arena. It was a policy that led to famous battles like that for 'Hamburger Hill' in 1969, so named because of the number of men who fell victim to enemy fire. Infuriatingly for those who had seen their comrades die in the attempt to dislodge PLAF/PAVN from the hill, it was later abandoned because it had little strategic value.

Militarily and politically, 'search and destroy' operations were a failure. Once an area was cleared of enemy troops and installations by US forces, the South Vietnamese Army (ARVN) would step in to maintain the region's continued security. Frequently, however, this back-up role never materialized or was just too ineptly handled and insufficiently coordinated to resist the re-establishment of PLAF/PAVN forces. Moreover, while the US Army may have destroyed the enemy's military control, little was done to undermine his highly resilient local political apparatus and, more importantly, to capture the support of the people.

Operation *Cedar Falls* in January 1967 was indicative of the problems besetting US strategy. It was one of the largest operations of the war and aimed to destroy the headquarters of the NLF's Military Region IV, which directed operations in and around Saigon and which was based in the 'Iron Triangle' jungle area, north-west of the city. At least on paper, *Cedar Falls's* achievement appears noteworthy. Mass evacuations deprived the enemy of his support base. Bulldozers and ploughs flattened installations, fortifications, and destroyed the extensive underground tunnel network used by PLAF/PAVN. They also levelled the houses of many non-combatants. Large caches of weapons were seized and over 720 NLF personnel were reported killed for a loss of seventy-two Americans. Notwithstanding this statistical victory, in a matter of weeks, US intelligence noted that the area was once more the scene of high PLAF/PAVN activity (Lewy 1978:65).

The contribution that US firepower made to pacification—to the political offensive—was largely negative (Lewy 1978:96–105). The expenditure of large quantities of munitions understandably generated immense fear amongst the people. Firepower was not discriminating in the suffering that it caused and it was the villager and his quality of life rather than the enemy and his ability to wage war that all too frequently bore the brunt of US action. Many officers, concerned to protect the lives of their men, responded to the threat of minor skirmishes with the enemy in an exaggeratedly aggressive manner. Civilians inevitably became caught in the cross-fire and any carefully nurtured pacification gains were wiped out in an instant. All too often, the expenditure of munitions was needless, destructive, brutal and consequently dysfunctional. The absurd logical conclusion of such a short-sighted strategy has been recorded in the immortal words of a US Army officer who is reported to have said in the aftermath of the battle for Ben Tre during the February 1968 Tet Offensive that 'It became necessary to destroy the town in order to save it'.

The military gave upbeat reports on the progress of the war because the strategy of attrition helped to encourage inefficient methods of monitoring and evaluation. In the absence of front lines which could register success or failure by the distance they had shifted, the US Armed Forces came to rely upon body counts, quantification of sortie rates and the expenditure of ordnance as a measure of their success. An assessment of utilized firepower was no indication of political or military advance and the body counts which revealed the number of PLAF/PAVN personnel that had been eliminated were equally unreliable.

Inevitably, the strategy of attrition led to enormous pressures upon units and their commanders to kill as many enemy troops as possible. Assessment of units depended on their performance in the body count stakes. This technique of managing the war was exemplified by commanders like Lieutenant General Julian Ewell who used kill ratios to establish elaborate grading procedures (Ewell and Hunt 1974:212–13). Padded claims of enemy dead were thus the inescapable result. The Systems Analysis Office of the Defense Department estimated that the body count was probably exaggerated by at least 30 per cent (Enthoven and Smith 1971:296) and even a majority of generals who served in Vietnam considered that it was a misleading and inflated indicator of success (Kinnard 1977:74).

Obsession with securing a high body count gave rise to a whole host of malpractices. Junior officers reported fictitious enemy kills in order to impress their superiors who, in many cases, knew of the deception but were unwilling to question the statistics because a high body count reflected well on their own leadership. Such was the pressure to produce an adequate death toll that some units were requested to submit enemy casualty figures before a battle (Cincinnatus 1981:90). More disturbingly, men in the combat environment were not encouraged to discriminate between PLAF/PAVN forces and non-combatants. Innocent civilians therefore were killed and their deaths added to the tally of enemy dead.

Duplication of the count was exceedingly common as each unit or service wanted to claim the 'kill' as its own. At times the demands for results was so great that there would be wrangles over parts of bodies (Cincinnatus 1981:89) and some units went as far as to dig up rotting enemy corpses in order to include them in their body count (Cincinnatus 1981:90).

Statistics like the body count could only be accepted as proof that the US was pursuing a winning strategy in Vietnam because they correlated with and were given credence by the military's reporting from the field. Negative or even realistic verdicts of the war were not common because criticism of the way the military hierarchy was conducting the war would do little to enhance an officer's career.

During the Vietnam War the officer corps of the US Army was busy divesting itself of its traditionally honoured standards of professionalism. This phenomenon was set within and contributed manifestly to the far more disturbing, general disintegration of the US Armed Forces as the war progressed. Indeed, by the early 1970s, a far-reaching breakdown in the conduct and discipline of US troops was clearly evident.

The crisis in US Army discipline was on a global scale and drug abuse, in particular, was a problem not confined exclusively to Vietnam. Both in Europe and in the United States, drug abuse was widespread amongst army personnel. It was in South East Asia, however, that the crisis became the most acute. In the later years of the war, between half and two-thirds of lower-ranking enlisted men were smoking marijuana, and in 1971 an official report estimated that over a quarter of the US Army stationed in Vietnam were occasional users of narcotic drugs (Gabriel and Savage 1978:49). The extent of drug usage and addiction was indicative of crumbling control within the army and also of corruption and profiteering amongst certain South Vietnamese officials.

The frequency of mutiny, or of 'combat refusal' as it was called in the emasculated terminology used in Vietnam, was gaining momentum as the war drew to a close. Moreover, it is possible to surmise that many mutinous outbreaks were never reported and that a tacit agreement was secured between troops and officers who undertook to lead so-called 'search and evade' operations. Basing their figures on the number of official refusals in a division that was acknowledged to be good, Gabriel and Savage estimated that there may have been over 200 mutinies in 1970 alone (Gabriel and Savage 1978:45).

'Fragging' emerged as a major problem in Vietnam. An incident was usually orchestrated by a group of men angered by what they considered to be an officer's disregard for their safety in combat. Alternatively it was prompted by drug-related or racially inspired issues. The victim was then assaulted by means of an explosive device, commonly a hand grenade or fragmentation bomb which could, but did not always, inflict serious injury and even death. Naturally, these incidents must have seriously affected the ability and willingness of officers to command in Vietnam.

Linked to combat refusal was a steeply rising desertion and AWOL (absent without leave) rate, which, despite the relatively low US KIA (killed in action) statistics, actually surpassed the highest figures reached during the Second World War and the Korean conflict. Furthermore, such rates rose over time, notwithstanding the gradual reduction in the intensity of combat as a result of the ongoing Vietnamization of the war.

Racial antagonism lay behind a number of fraggings and contributed, quite significantly, to tensions within the army. Black consciousness spilled over from the civilian world although both blacks and whites considered that the racial climate within the armed forces was better than at home (Fiman 1975:45). Nevertheless, the racial divide further undermined the effectiveness of the military's fighting capability even though racial antagonism and cases of self-imposed racial segregation were limited, in the main, to support troops in rear base areas (Moscos 1975:34)

Contrary to contemporary popular belief, blacks did not die in vast numbers in Vietnam. In 1965 24 per cent of deaths in the American Army were those of blacks. In 1966, this proportion had fallen to 16 per cent (Baskir and Strauss 1978:8). Given that blacks comprised approximately 13 per cent of the US population this was a higher percentage of army deaths than their proportion of the population would warrant. However, in all services, blacks accounted for 12.3 per cent of all combat deaths in Vietnam and so did not suffer an unfair burden of sacrifice (Lewy 1978:155).

The military hierarchy liked to portray the decomposition of the army in Vietnam as the product of the 'permissive society'. Certainly, popular political currents which challenged the validity of the US role in South East Asia must have had reverberations within the armed forces and some influence upon the morale of combat troops and their willingness to fight in a domestically divisive conflict. At least on one level this was illustrated by the steady growth of small antiwar movements within the forces. Yet the emergence of such groups and the incidence of previously limited or unknown disciplinary problems were not a cause of the army's progressive disintegration but merely concrete manifestations of an internally generated crisis.

The functioning and morale of the combat unit is rarely influenced by social and political developments in civilian life. Rather it is a product of the unit's own leadership and internal dynamics. Unit cohesion, which ultimately makes for an effective fighting force, is determined by the quality of the officer corps, which, by its professionalism and courage, inspires respect, trust and obedience amongst subordinate men, hence bringing about an *esprit de corps* and a camaraderie within the unit which knits it into a well coordinated and formidable military team (Gabriel and Savage 1978:36–7).

In the context of the Vietnam War, a series of factors worked to lower the quality of officers, to alter the perception that combat troops had of their commanders and, as a concomitant, to bring about the collapse of the unit.

Most important was that the fundamental character of the officer was seen to be changing from one cast in the traditional warrior mould to one represented by the paper shuffling, desk-bound, managerial officer with whom it was very difficult for the man in the combat unit to identify and therefore respect. The army, in essence, was being bureaucratized and transformed into a giant corporation and its employees, the officer corps, were becoming hypnotized by 'career management' (Gabriel and Savage 1978:17–25).

This became a problem because the officer no longer made a career out of leading his men into combat but instead made a career out of managing his career (Kinnard 1977:112). They had to serve in all the right command posts, attend all the right courses and make the right impression on all those people who counted. The situation deteriorated to the point where half of those generals who had served in Vietnam considered that careerism was a problem while a further third thought that it was a serious problem (Kinnard 1977:110). Coming from the hierarchy of the US military itself, this was a worrying indictment of the army's career structure. Vietnam did not cause the transformation or the decline in professionalism, it merely highlighted and accelerated the process (Gabriel and Savage 1978:23). It also proved to be no way to fight a war.

Consequently, the traditional military ethos was challenged by the lower-ranking man's resentment and unfavourable opinion of his superior officers. Such a tendency was stimulated by two important developments. The first was the growth of the officer corps which, by 1971, comprised 15 per cent of total army strength compared to 7–9 per cent during the Second World War and the Korean War (Gabriel and Savage 1978:31, 62). The second was the tactical nature of the war which demanded a circular rather than linear logistical pattern, thereby creating an awareness amongst combat troops of the existence of large numbers of high-ranking officers leading comparatively well protected lives well away from the battlefield (Gabriel and Savage 1978:11–12). Far from sharing the risks of combat and incurring greater losses than the men it led, the officer corps was not seen to be willing to accept a rate of sacrifice commensurate with its privileges, and, indeed, although officer deaths as a percentage of all KIAs was higher in Vietnam than in the Second World War, overall accounting for 8.4 per cent of all deaths, they were far less significant when the inflation of the officer corps is taken into account (Gabriel and Savage 1978:66).

Some men came to detest their commanders and there was often great bitterness amongst combat troops at the risks they had to take in battle while senior officers watched from their 'eye in the sky' and directed the conflagration from the safety of their helicopters (Cincinnatus 1981:81).

Unit cohesion also came under severe strain as a result of troop rotation. A twelve month tour of duty was decreed for all soldiers in Vietnam, although, of course, those wishing to stay longer could volunteer to do so. It was believed that the year long tour would limit opposition to the war at home and would improve morale because it gave each man a goal (Westmoreland 1980:387).

The effect that this policy had upon the maintenance of unit cohesion and primary group ties was profound because the soldier was sent home just as he was becoming fully integrated into the unit and his allegiance attached to his comrades. Indeed, the turnover of personnel through rotation and injury was so rapid that the average rifle company became an entirely new body of men within nine or ten months (Palmer 1984:170).

The inevitable emphasis that came to be placed upon the soldier's DEROS (Date Expected Return Overseas) undermined his commitment to long-term projects and to the war in its widest sense. An essentially individualistic perspective of the war was therefore promoted and the soldier came to see his release from combat as wholly separate from victory in the conflict. Unlike in the Second World War, winning the war was peripheral to the US troops who fought in it and the essential goal was merely to stay alive until the twelve month tour of duty was completed.

Rotation meant that combat experience became a rare commodity as more seasoned troops were constantly being removed from the unit. As a veteran pacification expert is credited to have said, 'We don't have twelve year's experience in Vietnam. We have one year's experience, twelve times over.' Having a unit comprised of raw recruits to Vietnam inevitably increased the casualty rate as it took time to become accustomed to combat and to learn the best ways of self preservation. Killed in action statistics therefore said much about the policy of rotation. Forty per cent of combat deaths involved soldiers who were in their first three months of their tour. Only 6 per cent of KIAs involved men in their final three months (Thayer 1985:114). Although this may have been influenced by 'short-timer's fever', which was the desire of those approaching their personal DEROS to avoid all risks (Moskos 1975:31–2), the dangers associated with the absence of combat experience were, nevertheless, manifold.

Exacerbating this already serious problem was the strong desire of the army to push as many career officers as possible through what became revolving door command posts. This was true even of general officers. Over half of the 183 generals who commanded in Vietnam served for less than a year (Kinnard 1977:115) and company and battalion commanders held their posts for an average of six months (Westmoreland 1980:389). This was ridiculous, firstly because leadership demands experience, and secondly because the officer was placed in a position in which many of the men in his unit knew more about combat in Vietnam than he did.

Pressure from officers concerned to improve their chances of promotion by having their 'ticket punched' contributed to the rapid turnover as did the army's desire to 'blood' as many young officers as possible. They wanted, it seems, to prepare and train them for the next war rather than that fought in Vietnam.

It is hardly surprising that an increasingly undisciplined army should have been accused of war crimes. The accuracy of such accusations is a source of controversy, particularly as the definition of a war crime is unclear and the international law of war is especially difficult to apply in the context of guerrilla warfare and counterinsurgency. Moreover, much of what is termed a war crime is dependent, not upon any absolutes, but upon the moral justification which a particular conflict acquires. It is a legitimization of behaviour which, in practical terms, is often assumed by the victor.

International treaties on the law of war bind all states which have ratified them and the United States and North and South Vietnam all confirmed the Geneva Convention. However, the situation during the Vietnam War was complicated by the insistence of the US and the GVN that the struggle was a case of international aggression, while the DRV claimed that it was a purely internal civil war. In the event, treaties such as the Hague and Geneva Conventions proved inadequate to cope with the conflict, characterized, as it was, by the United States' application of sophisticated military technology juxtaposed with the enemy's guerrilla warfare tactics.

In general, uncodified rules determine acceptable military acts as those which inflict human suffering on a scale or in an intensity which is not out of proportion to the military success likely to be gained by the act. Needless to say, very few contenders are likely to agree upon what is, in essence, an arbitrary equation of human misery and military value. As a result, the gap that has always existed between the theory of the law of war and its actual relevance was especially large during the years of struggle in South East Asia.

Particular areas of US strategy came under harsh criticism. Obviously, the use of indiscriminate firepower was one, as was the policy of refugee generation. Controversy also centred on the practice of defoliation and the use of incendiary weapons, fragmentation bombs and riot control agents.

Defoliation was first practised by the British in an effort to suppress the insurgency in Malaya following the Second World War. It was also conducted on a wide scale in Vietnam. Early in 1962, the USAF began defoliation operations along highways in order to destroy the vegetation which formed a welcome cover for ambushes. The main thrust of the programme was to improve aerial reconnaissance and to restrict the movement of the enemy during daylight hours. A more limited aim of the programme was crop destruction which was designed to deprive the enemy of food supplies.

Chemical defoliation led the ecological assault on South Vietnam's forests. In addition, enormous Rome ploughs levelled forest land and aerial bombardment replaced it with thousands of craters. This combination partially damaged over half of South Vietnam's forest land and completely devastated 4 per cent (Westing 1983:375). In addition, 41 per cent of the mangrove forests were destroyed by chemical warfare (Westing 1983:377) and three-quarters of these have been affected so badly that regeneration is likely to take fifty years or more (Westing 1983:379).

Ecologically, politically and militarily the herbicide offensive was a catastrophe. Although only a fraction of the total cultivated area was sprayed, it was the civilian owner/cultivators of the land who were the principal ones to suffer, while the impact upon the enemy's food supplies at all times remained minimal. More disturbing were the long-term affects of defoliation upon the population. Dioxin, a component of Agent Orange, a herbicide used in Vietnam, was found to be toxic to humans and highly teratogenic and carcinogenic. Admittedly, this was not realized at the time and the defoliant was also available for use in the US. The dioxin issue, however, remains contentious. The Vietnamese claim that babies are now being born with genetic abnormalities produced by the toxin while the US, because the issue is so politically explosive, insists that there are no incontrovertible studies which prove this to be the case. The weight of evidence, nevertheless, points to the significant possibility that the Vietnamese people are suffering long-term, dioxin-related health problems (Westing 1983:372).

Incendiary weapons including white phosphorous and napalm were in widespread use by US forces during the conflict and the horrific injuries that they caused made them the object of condemnation. Napalm is a petroleum fuel that was especially effective in destroying enemy bunkers together with the people that they contained. Likewise, white phosphorous was employed to mark targets and to set fire to flammable ones. It also has a reputation for causing unwarranted suffering as it tends to continue burning and smouldering long after initial contact with the skin. When used in conjunction with napalm, its consequences were devastatingly lethal. The mortality rate of those suffering from napalm and white phosphorous burns was very high and the true extent of deaths arising from such injuries may never be known as many victims were far too badly burnt to receive hospital treatment and hence be officially recorded as mortalities arising from the employment of incendiary weapons (Lewy 1978:244–6).

The use of fragmentation bombs in Vietnam also attracted criticism. Those which acquired the worst reputation were refined fragmentation bombs known as CBUs (Cluster Bomb Units) which were, primarily, anti-personnel devices. Within the shell of a large bomb were many far smaller 'bomblets'. Thus, when the container impacted, explosive projectiles were hurled in many directions. The consequences for any individual within range were dire and, inevitably, such munitions which inflicted high enemy casualties and inflated the body count were viewed as a necessity by military authorities, irrespective of the approbium levelled at their use.

A similar rationale was made for the controversial application of Riot Control Agents (RCA), amongst which CS gas was the most widely employed. By causing physical distress, the US armed forces claimed that RCA could disorientate the enemy and therefore enable them to distinguish combatants and non-combatants with a far greater degree of accuracy. The proficiency of CS gas in clearing tunnel complexes was stressed and certainly its use did facilitate the sifting of enemy soldiers and cadres from the large number of civilians who also sought refuge in the tunnels. In reality, however, RCA were primarily used to dislodge the enemy from his positions and defences, thereby making him a far more cost-effective target for US firepower (Lewy 1978:250).

Some antiwar critics of US action in Vietnam were fond of claiming that America was conducting a war of genocide in Vietnam. This was not true. US military strategy and tactics did not amount to an official policy of genocide (Lewy 1978:301–4). It was never the intent of the

US government or armed forces to wipe out the Vietnamese people or any significant part of them, even though the use of devastating military hardware suggested that this may, indeed, have been the case.

Armed with an enormous destructive capability, it was unavoidable that US forces would kill and maim the innocent. Operating in an environment in which it was not always clear who was the enemy, where racism accorded only limited value to Vietnamese life and where there was incessant pressure for a high body count, the US troops took no pains to control the impact of the war on the civilian population. There appeared to be an assumption that because the killing was done from a distance by high technology, it was somehow 'cleaner' and more morally acceptable than killing done at close quarters where it was possible to see the victim's face (Baritz 1985:50, 54).

US troops showed little respect for the lives of the Vietnamese. Racism played a large part in determining this conduct. The 'Mere Gook Rule' tended to apply to all Vietnamese, enemy or not. Many US troops, brutalized by the war and unable to tell who was friend and who was foe, came to hate the local people, whom they derisively referred to as slopes, dinks, slants and gooks (Cincinnatus 1981:92-9). An unoffical code was observed by many, 'If it's dead and its Vietnamese, it's VC'. It offered, in other words, a carte blanche to kill indiscriminately.

Harrowing acts of violence perpetrated upon the civilian population are related in the many books written by those who fought in Vietnam or compiled from interviews with veterans. Raised in a culture which eulogizes the gun and the aggressive spirit of the Wild West, a minority of young American soldiers became drunk with the power that their weapons gave them. They became, quite literally, small gods (Baritz 1985:295-6). They had the power to destroy and the power to take life and they killed because it gave them a kick.

A general disregard for the safety of the Vietnamese led to a whole catalogue of complaints and accusations. Cyclists were run off the road, pedestrians hit by vehicles racing through villages, communities were assaulted by unprovoked sniper fire from passing convoys, girls and women were raped, goods stolen and livestock butchered without reason. This failure to appreciate either the lives or the rights of the Vietnamese increased as the war progressed and was probably influenced, to a limited degree, by the lowered induction standards of the US Army both for men and officers. Desperate for new recruits, the army scoured the inner cities of America and allowed the recruitment of those men who had failed the army's undemanding intelligence tests.

The officer corps too, tolerated previously unacceptable standards of entry as draft deferments for those in higher education limited the supply of talent. Rather than maintaining standards and making do with a restricted number of officers, the army made the mistake of drawing into the corps men who were not adequate to the leadership task (Westmorland 1980:498–9, Gabriel and Savage 1978:10). This was a critical decision in a war which required especially tight control over troops operating amongst civilians. Poor leadership, unfortunately, was to prove a vital and, it has been claimed, the most important element leading to the incidence of atrocities (Lewy 1978:330).

Between 1965 and 1973,201 army personnel were convicted by court martial of serious offences against the Vietnamese. Between 1965 and 1971, seventy-seven marines were also convicted (Lewy 1978:324). These figures bear little relation to the extent of brutality in Vietnam of which the worst example was the My Lai massacre. On 16 March 1968, Charlie Company, a unit of the Americal Division, took part in a 'search and destroy' operation directed against an enemy concentration supposedly centred upon the village of Son My in Quang Ngai province in northern South Vietnam. Although no enemy forces nor hostile fire was encountered in the hamlet of My Lai, the unit butchered all the inhabitants, who were predominantly elderly people, women and children. In all, some 200 people in My Lai and a total of about 400 within the area of Son My lost their lives. Despite a year-long cover up, twelve men were charged following an enquiry into the case although only one, Lieutenant Calley who led Charlie Company, was convicted and even he was released after serving a fraction of his sentence.

It is unlikely that other atrocities on the scale of My Lai actually occurred at the hands of US troops in Vietnam. However, cases involving a more limited number of victims almost certainly did and were never reported and brought to public attention.

However, apologists for the violence of US troops in Vietnam pointed to mitigating factors. Firstly, many combat soldiers who saw buddies killed by booby traps laid by women and grenades thrown by children, came to direct their anger and frustration not upon enemy troops who could rarely be found but upon civilians whom they believed to be NLF collaborators. Secondly, while the ROE (Rules of Engagement) defining acceptable military conduct were faultless in their construction, the understanding and application of such procedures was, until after the My Lai massacre, rarely high upon the military's agenda and many officers as well as lower-ranking men had scanty knowledge of their provisions (Lewy 1978:234–7). Failure to ensure that the ROE were adequately understood and complied with led to claims of negligence against US commander General William Westmorland (Lewy 1978:241). Such charges are debatable and mirror the questions raised by the

Nuremburg Trials. Even if legitimate, they cannot absolve individual men from responsibility for their crimes. Torture, rape and brutal murders are atrocities and crimes against humanity whether they are sanctioned by commanders or undertaken on the order of a superior officer. It is not an adequate excuse to blame the army for inculcating murderous intent and for producing brutalized automatons as a result of its training.

The abysmal conduct of a minority of soldiers in Vietnam gave the rest a bad name. The media generated an image of a merciless, doped-up killer who returned home to become a crazed psychopath, haunted by his memories of the war. Most soldiers in Vietnam, however, were just ordinary young men, whose average age was nineteen. Many were frightened by the thought of fighting and many of them sincerely believed that they were taking part in an honourable war to save Vietnam and its people from communism.

Not all those who went to Vietnam were forced to do so through the draft. The majority of those who served were volunteers to the armed forces and, overall, draftees accounted for a third of all KIAs. However, draftees actually died in greater proportion to volunteers who were given safer jobs (Gabriel and Savage 1978:73), and in the army, which took the bulk of the draftees, they accounted for 96 per cent of all deaths. (Thayer 1985:114).

All wars produce heroes. The Vietnam War was no exception to this because it too had its share of men who displayed outstanding bravery. Despite antiwar critics who portrayed the North Vietnamese as untainted by the American vice of brutality, the US did not maintain a monopoly on the abuse of human rights. The testimonies of US POWs who were held in both North and South Vietnam reveal that torture was practised and that prisoners were routinely kept in atrocious conditions and given totally inadequate diets and medical attention. The courage and determination of a number of these men who held out and refused to denounce US policy, despite repeated torture, is a powerful reminder to those who opposed the war that many who served in Vietnam did so with pride and with an immense faith in their country and in the righteousness of its ideals.

THE SOUTH VIETNAMESE ARMED FORCES

Whatever criticism may be directed at US conduct in Vietnam, their allies, the South Vietnamese Armed Forces (RVNAF), were guilty of far greater abuses and a significantly higher degree of incompetence.

Problems permeated all aspects of the RVNAF and corruption and a sheer lack of ability undermined the strength of the army as a fighting force. There were fundamental flaws in the construction and functioning of ARVN. At the heart of the problem was the political orientation of the armed forces and the US Army's blunder in moulding ARVN into a pale shadow of itself.

Initially the US believed that the main threat to the GVN would come from a Korean-style invasion across the Demilitarized Zone. To produce a conventionally orientated force capable of dealing with this scenario, they shaped ARVN into a replica of the American Army. This became known as 'mirror imaging'. But, as the Americans were destined to fail in their military objective, even less success could be expected from a far inferior force fashioned along similar lines and employing the same well-worn tactics.

Although ARVN did not benefit greatly from the availability of firepower until after 1968, as more and more military hardware became available to the South Vietnamese, they, like their US counterparts, came to depend upon it rather than upon more traditional infantry manoeuvres. They were taught, in other words, to fight a 'rich man's war'. This was fine as long as US aid continued to flow, but once it began to falter ARVN was unprepared and unable to adapt.

The quality of leadership was of paramount significance to the functioning of the RVNAF. Officers were rarely appointed for their ability. Political considerations determined the composition of the officer corps (Lewy 1978:169–77). Thus, important army and air force posts were granted to men who came from small, formally educated elites and to those professing the strongest allegiance to the government. Their military aptitude was almost irrelevant. This verdict was borne out by US generals who candidly assessed one-third of ARVN's general officer leadership to be inadequate (Kinnard 1977:87).

Poor leadership resulted in a poor army and there was a significant correlation between the quality of ARVN commanders and the performance of troops (Thayer 1985:61–2). Desertion rates in combat units commonly ran at an average of 30 per cent a year (Thayer 1985:75). Many men saw this as their only means of escape from the bad conditions of service under ARVN and the low pay which never managed to catch up with inflation. Unlike their US counterparts, no rotation system operated and South Vietnamese troops were inducted for the duration of the conflict or until their death or serious injury, which ever was the sooner. Furthermore, soldiers operated away from their native provinces and little provision was made for them to visit their families. This resulted in desertion or the migration of the soldier's family to camps near military bases.

Low morale and inadequate leadership fashioned the ARVN into an army which would be considered poor by most standards. Disregard for good conduct and the value of life led to wide-scale abuse of the civilian population (Lewy 1978:177–82). Looting and all its accompanying depradations were not unusual and the South Vietnamese also gained an unpleasant reputation for the torture of enemy captives. Even in day-to-day operations, many ARVN units failed to fulfil their function of maintaining local security. The role of back-up for US forces, particularly in providing long-term security once an area had been cleared of enemy troops, was seldom accomplished in any satisfactory manner. Indeed, it was often suggested that ARVN commanders tended to conduct 'walks in the sun' or, more descriptively, 'search and avoid' operations in areas in which the enemy was known not to be present (Lewy 1978:87). Not all South Vietnamese Army units were bad; a minority were excellent, a slightly larger minority were dreadful but the bulk were barely adequate.

Throughout the war, the US and South Vietnamese did not share a unified command and only in the field of intellegence was there any effort at integration. During the Second World War, a single Supreme Allied Commander had responsibility for all Allied forces within a particular theatre. In Vietnam, COMUSMACV never exercised operational control over the RVNAF, although approximately 60,000 Free World Military Assistance Forces (which included Australian, New Zealand, Filipino, South Korean and Thai contingents) generally did come under the operational control of the US military commander within a particular region. The exception were the troops provided by the Republic of Korea which furnished almost 80 per cent of non-US/GVN forces. These forces remained under the control of their own commanders who worked within the parameters set by the Free World Military Assistance Council.

Criticism was levelled at the division of command between the US military and the RVNAF, and calls for a greater subordination of the services of each nation to the control of a single commander were frequently voiced. The failure to put such a suggestion into practice was justified on three grounds. Firstly, that if the US dominated the leading positions in the allied command, as was almost inevitable, then it would be accused of outright colonialism (Westmorland 1980:171). Secondly, that the South Vietnamese were reluctant to relinquish control over their armed forces given their political importance (Krepinevich 1986:195) and, thirdly, it was believed that integration would expose US forces to a greater degree of danger as the RVNAF were, allegedly, riddled with NLF informants.

When political considerations in Washington led to a concerted programme of Vietnamization in 1968–9, ARVN, with all its weaknesses, was substituted for the US Army and it reluctantly took on a greater share of the combat burden. Yet without the help of the Americans, large-scale operations frequently ended in near disaster. Thus, while Vietnamization was accomplished in the sense that the RVNAF assumed a level of combat formerly undertaken by US forces, the handover was not a success. The average South Vietnamese soldier and officer and the efficiency of each unit did not bear comparison even with the shoddy standards of US forces during the period. Moreover, where the US had failed, it was hardly likely that South Vietnamese forces could succeed and, despite whatever morale-boosting praise was heaped upon the RVNAF, the reality of Vietnamization was gloomy indeed.

THE WAR IN THE AIR

In budgetary terms, the Vietnam conflict was an air war. Air operations claimed the largest chunk of the US $150 billion spent on the war. In FY 1969 47 per cent of the budget was absorbed by this arm of the conflict and only 30 per cent by the land war (Thayer 1985:25). For this massive outlay, allied aircraft flew around 3.4 million combat sorties in the Indochina theatre between 1965 and 1972 (Thayer 1985:79–80). Forty-two per cent of these were flown against targets in South Vietnam, 22 per cent against those in the DRV, 28 per cent against those in Laos and 4 per cent against those in Cambodia (Thayer 1985:80–1).

The air war in the South was characterized by the development of air mobility and the air assault concept. A new dimension was added to the conventional battlefield by the use of helicopters to ferry troops and equipment from one otherwise inaccessible area to another. The application of advanced technology and the use of the helicopter made this battlefield far more fluid and the war witnessed a rapid development in the sophistication of the helicopter. However, the innovative concept of air mobility did have its detractors. While the units may have been mobile in the air they were not light and mobile once on the ground and this put them at a distinct disadvantage when faced with the ultra-mobile PLAF/PAVN (Krepinevich 1986:112–13). Another criticism was that the helicopter undermined the tenacity of the troops who, with the knowledge that they could make a speedy withdrawal, were understandably unwilling to stand and fight (Palmer 1984:168). Most damning of all, however, was the assessment of veteran pacification expert, Sir Robert Thompson, who thought that the helicopter contributed to the failure of US strategy in Vietnam because it made the ultimately inadequate 'search and destroy' operations possible (Thompson 1969:136).

Fixed-wing aircraft were used extensively in South Vietnam primarily to attack areas of supposed enemy activity and enemy concentrations which threatened allied forces. One of the best and most successful examples of the use of multi-layered firepower in South Vietnam was that orchestrated to relieve the siege of Khe Sanh during the Tet Offensive. In January 1968, the North Vietnamese Army surrounded the garrison of Khe Sanh in the north-west corner of South Vietnam. The siege lasted seventy days and a tremendous amount of firepower was expended before the US finally saved the garrison. Aerial bombardment of enemy positions totalled almost 100,000 tons (Nalty 1973:105). This is a tonnage which is double that dropped in the Pacific theatre during 1942 and 1943.

The bombing of North Vietnam was the second arm of the air war and can be divided into five phases (Thompson 1980:41–3). The first three are the escalating stages of the *Rolling Thunder* programme. From its inception, the operation concentrated upon interdiction, that is halting the infiltration of troops and supplies into the South, and upon destroying the DRV's logistical system. This lasted throughout the entire period of the *Rolling Thunder* operation while other layers of action were later added to it.

For one month, from 29 June 1966 to the end of July 1966, a concerted attack was made upon the country's POL (petroleum, oil and lubricants) storage facilities. Then, between the spring of 1967 and April 1968, a third more aggressive phase was launched in which very few military or industrial targets of any worth were spared.

The fourth phase of the air war against North Vietnam began after Johnson ordered a partial bombing halt on 31 March 1968. Thereafter bombing was restricted first to the area south of the twentieth parallel and then to the area south of the nineteenth. This phase continued until November 1968 when the bombing was completely halted. Thereupon the fifth phase began and this was characterized by sporadic bombing, culminating in the 1972 Christmas Bombing of Hanoi and Haiphong.

Rolling Thunder, which was the largest campaign of the war, had three important objectives. The first was to raise the morale of the South Vietnamese. The second was to reduce the infiltration of enemy personnel and supplies into South Vietnam and the third was to bring the DRV to the negotiating table by imposing forfeits should they resist. Only the first of these objectives was ever achieved to any appreciable degree.

The bombing of North Vietnam was a source of great controversy between the JCS and the politicians in Washington. The JCS and a few civilian policymakers complained that political considerations were hindering the success of bombing as significant restraints were placed upon the number and location of targets deemed acceptable by the White House. What they wanted was an all-out strike against major targets and the opportunity to, in the words of General Curtis Le May, bomb Vietnam, 'into the stone age' (Halberstam 1972:462). But President Johnson stubbornly refused to authorize strikes against targets near the Sino-Vietnamese border for fear of incurring China's wrath and bringing it far more directly into the fray. Washington was also reluctant to authorize targets situated within the environs of the densely-populated Hanoi-Haiphong urban connurbation as it wished to avoid antagonizing an already hostile assessment by international public opinion of US conduct in the war.

The concept of 'gradualism' permeated the thinking of policymakers in Washington. By mounting the pressure of bombing in incremental phases, Washington hoped that Hanoi would be frightened into negotiating because it dreaded the devastation that would accompany the next escalation of the campaign. This view was annoyingly obtuse to the military mind and thus there was no clear-cut consensus on what was to be achieved and the best way to go about it. All agreed that bombing was necessary but that was where the consensus abruptly ended (Thompson 1980:25–6). Consequently, as the campaign progressed, greater and greater divergences of opinion emerged between factions in the military and policymaking hierarchies.

The strategy of escalating bombing failed for a number of reasons. Firstly, high-ranking military figures believed that 'gradualism' undermined the campaign from the start (Westmoreland 1980:542, Taylor 1972:403–4). In particular, it allowed the DRV time to build its defences and acclimatize itself psychologically and physically to the bombing. The military also complained that 'political restrictions' hampered the effectiveness of the bombing. However, this is not a sustainable argument because, by early 1968, virtually all restrictions were inoperative and almost all targets specified by the JCS had been either destroyed or significantly damaged (Thompson 1980:71).

The real reason for the failure of *Rolling Thunder* was that the US failed to appreciate just how much punishment the DRV was willing and able to absorb. North Vietnam did not possess an extensive industrial sector which would have rendered it susceptible to air attack. On the contrary, it possessed an underdeveloped, peasant-based economy which, as a result of imports from the Soviet Union and China, did not have to manufacture its own military equipment. Therefore, bombing of industrial targets could have had little impact upon the overall ability of the NLF/DRV to wage a war in the South. Furthermore, those targets that did exist, particularly petroleum, oil and lubricant storage depots, were dispersed around the countryside and, ironically, bombing may in fact have helped to mobilize the North Vietnamese people and so to strengthen the mechanisms by which the DRV controlled its citizens (Van Dyke 1972:78–110).

When pitted against a country like the DRV, stategic airpower was weak and the failure to perceive this amounted to a 'colossal mistake in political-military judgement' by American decisionmakers (Thompson 1980:29–30). *Rolling Thunder* had little practical influence upon the conduct of the war in the South. The army of guerrillas and the predominantly low-technology PAVN units needed few external supplies to support and sustain them and, therefore, during the initial phases of the bombing campaign, the offensive in the South could have continued with extremely limited external support. Moreoever, it was ironic that while the US was pursuing interdiction by the bombing of North Vietnam and the Ho Chi Minh Trail that ran through Laos, the majority of PLAF/PAVN supplies were entering the South across the border with Cambodia. They were transported overland after being shipped and unloaded at the port of Sihanoukville. When Lon Nol came to power, nevertheless, this convenient arrangement was swiftly halted.

The scale of the *Rolling Thunder* campaign was enormous. By December 1967, after thirty-four months of bombing, over 850,000 tons of high explosives had been dropped on the relatively small geographic area of North Vietnam. To place this in perspective, such a quantity of ordnance exceeds the 500,000 tons of munitions which were dropped in the Pacific theatre by both sides during the entire Second World War.

Major strike forces were rarely stationed in South Vietnam. Most bombing missions were flown either from the aircraft carriers of the US Seventh Fleet stationed off Vietnam, or from bases outside the country. The best-known aircraft involved in the aerial bombardment of the North was the B-52 stratofortress. The B-52 was originally intended to drop nuclear bombs from high altitudes, and with its carrying capacity of 30 tons of ordnance it had a terrifying destructive capability. Although they initially flew from Guam, the B-52s came to be based in Thailand, from where they launched their offensive air strikes, principally against the movement of men and supplies along the Ho Chi Minh Trail and across the Demilitarized Zone.

Most sorties were flown by tactical fighter aircraft on armed reconnaissance missions. Because there were so few fixed targets of value, most pilots on sorties had to scout around for likely quarry, usually convoys or trains. In 1967, for example, 90 per cent of all sorties involved planes sent on armed reconnaissance missions (Thompson 1980:92).

There was immense competition between the Seventh Air Force and the navy's carrier-based airplanes of the Seventh Fleet as to the number of sorties flown. Interservice rivalry exists in any war but in Vietnam it was acute, especially between the air force and the navy. Both wanted to fly the greatest number of sorties because this would prove that they were a more effective force that was entitled to a larger share of the military budget. Competition created ludicrous situations. To keep up the sortie rate planes would fly even when supply problems meant that they had no bombs or that they did not have a full load (Gallucci 1975:84). The imperative to maintain the service's contribution to the air war also led to aircraft carriers remaining on station for such long periods of time that they fell so far behind on their maintenance schedules that the impact was still being felt in the mid-1980s (Palmer 1984:160). Moreover, as North Vietnam was carved up so that each service had specific areas of responsibility, aircraft were effectively channelled into route packages. It did not take much analysis for the North Vietnamese to arrange their air defences accordingly (Thompson 1980:77) and by the early 1970s Hanoi was extremely well fortified by the very latest Soviet SAMs (surface to air missiles).

Pressure to 'use it or lose it' was also placed upon the force of B-52s which was controlled by Strategic Air Command. Sortie rates had to be consistently high or the number budgeted and planned for would be reduced. What happened, therefore, when bombing was halted in one area was that the designated sorties were switched to another area, even if no suitable targets were available. This led to such an absurd situation that one targeteer of B-52 strikes felt it less hazardous to life on the ground to supply the coordinates of imaginary 'underwater storage areas' in the giant Tonle Sap lake in Cambodia (Tilford 1987:74).

Despite the scale of air operations in Vietnam they failed to achieve their goals. What they did succeed in doing was inflicting incalculable suffering upon many people. Nonetheless, terror bombing in a manner reminiscent of the Second World War was not intended. The exception to this may have been Nixon's Christmas Bombing in 1972 because, although the figure of 1600 dead compares favourably with the death tolls experienced, for example, in Dresden, this was only because the cities had been quickly evacuated.

Generally, collateral damage was the inevitable result of the uncontrollable movement of missiles away from their intended targets and the consequence of strikes directed at targets which were purposely sited within highly populated areas because it was hoped that this would bring them some degree of immunity from attack (Lewy 1978:404). It is not reasonable to maintain, though, that the US's use of airpower was, as has been asserted, the 'most restrained in modern warfare' (Lewy 1978:416). This may have been the intention but the breadth and intensity of air operations rendered it a totally impossible objective. The application of airpower in Vietnam cannot not be construed as anything other than a ruthless misapplication of power.

A fascinating new perspective on the war has emerged in recent years. It argues that Vietnam was a 'winnable' war and that it was incorrectly perceived and mishandled from the start. The movement to prove that America could have won in Vietnam was led first by General Harry Summers. In a remarkable book (Summers 1982) he postulates that the US was deluded into thinking that the conflict was a revolutionary guerrilla war when, in fact, it was a conventional war all along. The real enemy was the DRV and it was to the borders of North Vietnam that America should have taken the battle. Norman Hannah argues that a 1962 agreement to neutralize Laos was one of the root causes of America's military failure in Vietnam. He maintains that although the Laos Accords broke down, a 'tacit agreement' was arrived at between the DRV and the US. The North Vietnamese would control south-east Laos and America would not try to end this, providing that the revolutionary movement did not destabilize what was left of neutralized Laos in the north-west of the country (Hannah 1987:73). What the US hoped to do through this agreement was to put Laos on the 'backburner', pending a solution to the Vietnam War (Hannah 1987:60). The problem was that the US gained next to nothing from this transaction while the revolutionary movement was allowed the use of a part of Laotian territory through which ran the Ho Chi Minh Trail. Although America bombed the Trail and attempted to interdict supplies, they did not use ground forces to halt the stream of supplies entering South Vietnam. This thesis points to Laos as the 'key' to the Vietnam War and US military men, including Summers and Bruce Palmer Jr., have stressed the need to have cut the infiltration route through Laos.

There are facts which lend credence to the Summers argument that Vietnam was a conventional war and to the importance of Laos in the pursuit of this kind of war. The North Vietnamese, after all, defeated Saigon in 1975 through a conventional attack. But the flaw in the logic is that whilst the war may have ended in the manner of a conventional war, it did not begin and progress that way.

Salvaging some more life for the pseudo-revolutionary war thesis is a view admirably expounded by Timothy Lomperis who sees two distinct phases to the war. It was a revolutionary war prior to spring 1967 and primarily a type of conventional war after the PLAF had been decimated in the Tet Offensive. Paradoxically, he thinks, the Americans actually won the first phase which they should have lost and failed in the second phase which they should have won because they chose not to participate in it (Lomperis 1984:173). It is a persuasive argument on one level because, theoretically, they could have thwarted the conventional assault upon South Vietnam and they should not have been able to quell the political struggle in the South prior to 1968. But these conclusions can be reached only by ignoring the fact that it was not the Americans and their three years of combat that defeated the indigenous revolutionary forces. They accomplished this feat themselves by undertaking the foolhardy Tet Offensive. America had secured a victory but it was won by default. More importantly, it is not possible to claim that the US could have won the conventional war. In a sense they *had* been defeated by the southern revolutionary movement because although they had acquired a partial military advantage by mid-1968 they had been politically defeated. The war created a political climate in the US that made the pursuit of victory impossible. America could not contain the conventional attack that brought down Saigon because it had lost the political war at home. It is therefore wrong to claim that the military could have won in Vietnam because the armed forces do not operate independently of the wider society.

The revisionist school of Vietnam War historians responds that the political war could have been won if only the politicians had handled the conflict differently. But they did not and it is only with the benefit of hindsight and defeat that America's military men can look back and decide that they understood the political situation better than the politicians.

The military failure of the United States in Vietnam is hardly surprising. They failed to analyse the dynamics of the struggle and to respond adequately to its political character and the nature of the battlefield which was the minds of the people. Instead they tried to turn it into their own kind of war—one with big battles, the pushing back of fronts and the physical but not political attrition of the enemy.

It was almost inevitable that the United States should see the application of its military might as an easy solution to a complex social and political crisis. For a nation which is, at times, obsessed with power and with the tangible manifestations of that power as the motive force in the world, military action was an all too obvious answer to the threat of communism in South Vietnam. It was not until

1967 that this approach began, very gradually, to be altered and alternative remedies sought. Until then, and perhaps even beyond, the fearsome military capability of the US was used only to destroy and to alienate, and while the battle for the hearts of men and women was being won by the National Liberation Front, it was being ignored by the United States from a height of 30,000 feet.

9 Pacification and the attempt to build a viable South Vietnamese state

Pacification is the term given to the efforts of the Saigon regime and the United States to create a strong, independent and viable state in South Vietnam. Its aim was to encourage the population to identify its interests with the survival of the GVN, to bind the government and the people together and hence to cut away at the NLF's support base. Seeking a rejoinder to the NLF's political programme, the allies sought to undertake a political and social programme of their own. The problem was, however, that the US/GVN consistently tackled pacification as one facet of a war, while the NLF placed their political and social programme at the heart of the revolution. The failure to perceive this crucial difference rendered the majority of pacification programmes ineffectual and the attempt to build a nation ultimately sterile.

Because of the failure to take on board the counterinsurgency concept and because of basic misconceptions about the nature of the war, the US firmly adopted a military approach and relegated pacification or WHAM, the 'winning of hearts and minds' as it was known, to a low priority. This was exacerbated by the mindset of the Americans in Vietnam who saw not one war—a political war with a military component—but three separate wars: a military struggle, a war to pacify the countryside and a war to build a nation, which it appeared to tackle as three distinct, albeit related, conflicts (Thompson 1969:149).

After Diem's fall, the political and military situation in South Vietnam deteriorated to the point where extensive military measures were essential to ensure the survival of the GVN. Pacification was accorded little importance during this period, and even in 1966, a year that was supposed to see a renewed emphasis upon wooing the people, only US $600 million was spent on this vital aspect of the anti-NLF struggle at a time when the war claimed a budget of US $21 billion (Komer 1986:148).

Compounding the over-emphasis upon the military struggle was the fact that allied military operations severely hampered pacification efforts (Lewy 1978:95–105). The US/GVN reliance upon firepower resulted in many civilian casualties. Naturally it was difficult for a military commander to judge precisely how much force to use in an engagement. Too little and he would endanger his men and too much and pacification would be severely hampered. The province chief was faced with a similar predicament when controlling disorder. He could apply too little force, so allowing the insurgents to win a small victory and for the government's credibility to be shaken. Conversely, too much would alienate the people and give rise to charges of repression. The intensity of force to be applied was thus a basic dilemma of counterinsurgency (Tanham and Duncanson 1969:114).

Because of the brutal nature of the war and because it was carried out in an under-developed society, the exact numbers of civilian casualties will never be known. Reliable figures are difficult to obtain and estimates vary significantly. The most authoritative assessment of the death and destruction wreaked in South Vietnam posits that over 250,000 civilians died and that over 900,000 were wounded (Lewy 1978).

Very few remained untouched by the war. Millions of people were displaced by the fighting. Between 1954–75 over half of South Vietnam's population was uprooted. For some, this happened more than once (Wiesner 1988:345). They were not refugees in the strictest sense because they did not cross international boundaries. Instead, they were called displaced persons.

During 1964–5 it was NLF policy to push unsympathetic villagers, and primarily Catholics, out of areas that they controlled. Their motivation was two-fold. They would rid themselves of troublesome elements and would also burden the GVN with the task of accommodating the refugees physically and economically (Wiesner 1988:59). However, as NLF areas began to be depopulated under the impact of the fighting, the revolutionary movement became anxious to preserve its manpower base. Accordingly, it reversed its policy in mid-1965 and ceased the creation of refugees (Wiesner 1988:101). Instead, it concentrated far more upon driving people back into the villages by staging attacks upon refugee sites (Wiesner 1988:225–8).

US/GVN military forces generated the greatest number of refugees. Especially during the early stages of US military involvement, the creation of refugees was seen as an indicator of success (Krepinevich 1986:225) and it was only in 1967–8 that the generation of refugees as a policy objective began to be abandoned. Until then it was actively encouraged because it was thought to deny the revolutionary movement access to the people.

Commonly, the armed forces would remove families from areas of suspected, or known, enemy activity and would then transfer them to politically safer territory. This was a short-sighted policy. Not only did it introduce possible NLF partisans into GVN-controlled regions, but it also prompted many neutral peasants to assume anti-GVN sentiments and to become receptive to enemy propaganda. This was particularly true as the provisions made for the refugees were frequently less than satisfactory. Because military operations were secret, the civil authorities often had no advance warning and so no time to prepare for an influx of refugees (Wiesner 1988:75). Camps soon overflowed. Many were insanitary and depressing and a poor advertisement for life under the GVN. Welfare benefits and payments for war-related damages were extremely limited and adequate sources of employment were not always available.

Sometimes refugees could return to their villages but ongoing military operations and the desire to restrict the revolutionary movement's access to people meant that many had to be forcibly relocated. They were moved from temporary camps to resettlement sites. A few of these sites were model communities and were superior to the villages from which the peasants had come. Many, however, were not, and, in general, forced relocations were counterproductive to pacification goals (Wiesner 1988:144, 243–4).

Most displaced persons were not forcibly moved from their homes in a literal sense, but were people who, of their own volition, were escaping from the horrors of the war. Others who crowded into the cities of South Vietnam were not refugees at all, but migrants attracted by the prospect of life and employment in an urban environment. Some of these migrants and refugees were bitterly disappointed. All too many people drifted into a life of drugs and crime, and women and girls became prostitutes in order to keep their families from financial ruin. Hundreds of thousands lived off the fat of the American military by providing menial services. For some, gaining a meagre subsistence meant scavenging on dumps for scraps of food and whatever the Americans, in their affluence, deemed fit to throw away.

War created a new South Vietnam. While many who migrated to the towns did enjoy a higher standard of living and liked their new fast, varied life, there were just as many who yearned to return to their villages and were resentful of the disruption to their traditional way of life. US/GVN military policies, consequently, created few supporters amongst ordinary people. It was hardly credible for the allies to imagine that they were winning the war for the goodwill and allegiance of the people when, as part of that war, they had evacuated peasants from their homes and had flattened houses and their inhabitants. Exactly how they hoped to defeat the NLF by defoliation of crops, napalming and bombing of villages and the traumatization of the South Vietnamese countryside can only be explained by the fact that the US/GVN, despite all their pronouncements to the contrary, must have considered the support of the population to have been peripheral to the outcome of the conflict.

Between 1954 and 1967 a bewildering variety of pacification programmes were orchestrated, the most important of which were based around the concepts of encadrement and population regroupment.

Encadrement involved the sending of trained personnel into villages to help improve security and encourage political mobilization. This individual, personal approach to winning hearts and minds tried to mimic the success of NLF cadres and, when appropriately executed, also produced some limited gains for the GVN. This was particularly true after 1964 when more thorough training began to be provided and the cadre programme operated under the name of 'Revolutionary Development'.

Cadres were sent into existing villages and also into new settlements where the population had been regrouped. This was the second major pacification approach and was pursued primarily because it was thought that this method offered the best means of separating the guerrillas from the people who supported them. As the US/GVN were patently failing to increase the political distance between the NLF and the masses, and as it could not develop a political programme to accomplish this, it hoped, instead, to substitute a physical barrier between the revolutionary movement and the people. From the long list of such programmes a number of the most significant can be extracted to shed light on the process of pacification in rural Vietnam.

Shortly after the GVN had been established as an independent state, Ngo Dinh Diem launched the Civic Action campaign. Heavily influenced by the US pacification expert, General Edward Lansdale, who had been instrumental in the thwarting of rebellion in the Philippines, Civic Action entailed some resettlement in areas that had witnessed intense Viet Minh activity and also a cadre programme in which pro-government individuals would live amongst the villagers and promote support of the GVN. Unfortunately, the programme was dogged with problems. It was too small in scale to be effective and many of the cadres were unsuited to their task. As many were Catholic zealots from North and central Vietnam, there was a cultural gap between them and the population, thus making it difficult for them to be accepted into the community. This, of course, was a prerequisite of the cadre programme.

To make matters worse, a number were undisciplined and corrupt and an associated vigorous Communist Denunciation Campaign, which resulted in the mistreatment of many totally innocent people, may actually have proved to be a source of support for the NLF (Nighswonger: 1966:36).

In 1957 agglomeration camps became the next weapon in the GVN's strange political war and, in 1960, they were superseded by the more ambitious Agrovilles. Both were resettlement programmes which hoped, by placing dispersed families in one key area, to improve security, to increase the government's surveillance capacity and to reinvigorate local government through administrative reforms and aid packages to improve local services.

The Strategic Hamlet concept launched in 1961 was also based upon the theory of resettlement. Drawing on the British experience in Malaya a plan was drafted by the pacification expert, Sir Robert Thompson, and was ostensibly adopted by the Saigon regime although, in reality, it used the plan as a facade to acquire US acceptance of its own more questionable pacification ideas (Blaufarb 1977:104). To apply the lessons of Malaya to Vietnam, moreover, was not wise. The two conflicts were not comparable and resettlement worked in Malaya because it separated the majority Malayan population from the guerrillas who were drawn mainly from the minority Chinese community. Political divisions therefore reflected a racial cleavage and hence it was feasible to separate the guerrillas from the people. In Vietnam, by contrast, the guerrillas and the people all belonged to the same ethnic and social community and it was impossible to differentiate between them because the people *were* the guerrillas.

Exacerbating the problems caused by the unsuitability of the Strategic Hamlet concept in the Vietnamese context was the fact that Thompson's plan was not applied properly and what was achieved was accomplished with far too much haste. The essence of the programme was to improve the village's self-defence capability by fortifying it. Once security had been established, social improvements could be made in order to win the support of the inhabitants, who would then become a source of intelligence for the GVN. Logically, it was essential to begin the programme in a relatively secure area and to move outwards, gradually extending the sphere in which the government retained overall control. However, in practice, strategic hamlets were constructed in totally inappropriate areas where there was little chance of them being adequately defended. People were forcibly uprooted from their homes and ancestral graves and herded into unprepared compounds where they were instructed to build a new hamlet and construct defences from sharpened bamboo poles and barbed wire. Often the supplies and finance that they were supposed to utilize failed to materialize. Furthermore, in the Delta area where settlement patterns were traditionally dispersed, the movement of people into an arbitrarily located strategic hamlet meant that some peasants had to walk miles to tend their fields. Strangely this programme was supposed to win support for the GVN. The NLF had a simple retort to the strategic hamlets. They called them concentration camps. Unfortunately for the GVN, their inhabitants generally concurred.

After the Diem coup, the Strategic Hamlet programme was abandoned and no new pacification programme immediately replaced it. The 'New Life Hamlets' which began to be promoted in the Delta in January 1964 did indicate that a few lessons had been learned from the failure of Strategic Hamlets. In particular they eschewed forcible removal of people. Despite this obvious concession to peasant sensibilities, the resettlement approach was still dogged with problems. The turnover of province chiefs in the turbulent post-Diem period meant that there was a lack of continuity and added to the inadequate supervision and coordination which had always plagued regroupment policies. Moreover, the cadre responsible for implementing the programme and for maintaining political support for the initiative within the community, frequently lacked commitment and dedication. There were thus human problems of motivation which no amount of US aid and finance for laudable public works could overcome (Tanham 1966:57).

However, in this seemingly unremitting catalogue of pacification failures there were some successes. The US Marines' counterinsurgency doctrine was considerably more sophisticated and relevant than that of other branches of the armed forces and this was put to good use in their Combined Action Platoons (CAP) which operated in northern South Vietnam. Beginning in 1965, small teams of marines integrated themselves with existing Vietnamese paramilitary forces in local villages, where they subsequently lived and worked. Bringing with them a greater professionalism, better weapons and the superior military backup and support that American forces inevitably granted to their fellow countrymen, the CAPs proved successful in raising morale and in improving village defences.

Despite the apparent success of the CAPs, it proved to be the only large-scale programme of its kind. The army did employ a superficially similar scheme, the Mobile Action Teams (MATs), but these involved only short-term deployments of men. The army was unwilling to make the necessary commitment of time that had been crucial to the success of the CAPs. As for the marines' approach to pacification, it came in for some scathing criticism from the army hierarchy, and the CAPs were consequently abandoned when the marines reorientated their mission and concentrated instead upon fortifying the Demilitarized Zone and tackling infiltration from the North.

The Highlands of South Vietnam were of vital significance as base areas and entry points for the revolutionary forces. Approximately three-quarters of a million Montagnards, or Highland people, divided into numerous different tribes, inhabited these regions and their allegiance was an important factor in the war. Land Development Centers were constructed for some of the tribal people in the late 1950s and, unlike similar resettlement programmes in the South, the Centers did not generate profound discontent, primarily because the culture and traditional settlement patterns of the Montagnards were very different from those of the lowland Vietnamese who had taken great exception to forced regroupment.

In the early 1960s the US began to make concerted efforts to rally the Montagnards to the GVN's cause. This was organized by the Special Forces, who operated first under the auspices of the CIA and later under MACV. Under the CIA the programme concentrated upon creating village defence systems. This approach proved to be an extremely effective pacification technique. However, once responsibility for the programme was transferred to MACV, the emphasis of operations was shifted towards border surveillance and offensive forays into enemy base areas (Krepinevich 1986:71–5). Naturally this had a detrimental impact upon pacification. Notwithstanding this, pacification programmes were expanded and did attract a large number of Montagnards. Volunteers joined Civilian Irregular Defense Groups (CIDGs) which were trained by US Special Forces and US-trained South Vietnamese Special Force units. The Highlands were soon dotted with military camps garrisoned with 50,000 full-time Montagnard soldiers (Blaufarb 1977:259). Their allegiance, it must be pointed out, was won not because of ideological motivation but principally because, for the often primitive tribespeople, the US/GVN could provide them with a regular income. The Montagnards proved to be tenacious fighters, notwithstanding the fact that they were actually mercenaries who evinced great dislike for the lowland Vietnamese who historically treated them with utter contempt and whose handling of the minority peoples was poor enough to spark a widespread rebellion in 1964.

Despite the relative success of the CAPs and CIDGs, pacification programmes, at least until 1968, did not bring forth expected results. The NLF was not undercut and the South Vietnamese people did not appear to like the GVN any more than they had done previously. Some very basic problems lay at the root of pacification failure. Some were elementary and could easily have been put right given the necessary will and effort. Some, however, were apparently insoluble.

At the heart of the problem was the GVN. It could not adequately govern, administer and develop the nation. This was especially true when it was simultaneously fighting a war (Joiner 1967:540–1). Moreover, the US did not appear to appreciate the extent of Saigon's administrative and political weakness. It has been suggested that this oversight was one of the most important reasons for the failure of US policy in Vietnam (Goodman 1984:89, Komer 1986:12).

The Diem government inherited a complex problem from the French. The functions of central government had been extended significantly during the colonial period and the Vietnamese had been relegated to lowly positions in the administrative hierarchy. The administration that resulted was constantly overstretched and burdened by bureaucracy. But rather than face the enormous challenge of remodelling the administration, Diem was content to work within and adapt the system which he had inherited, so confining himself to perpetuating the lack of an effective nationwide administrative structure (Joiner 1967:544–5). Almost as if to aggravate the situation, Diem abolished the traditional village councils in 1956 and authorized that village leaders be appointed, not by the people, but by the government. It was a decision which, along with enforced resettlement programmes and the regime's political clampdown, illustrated Diem's dictatorial tendencies and the unfortunate tendency of the GVN to control rather than win the support of the people. Judging by its actions, the GVN seemed to consider that a political community evolved not as a result of mutual dependence, trust and goodwill between government and governed, but by virtue of the government's will to impose one, if necessary through unpopular policies and a generous application of its power.

Local and national GVN administration did not inspire respect and support in the rural areas because the GVN was divorced from the people. Basically the government was urban-orientated. Staffed at its higher levels by individuals who had been educated in and who lived in the cities, and who often refused to serve in the provinces, the upper echelons of government did not really know a great deal about, and were not terribly interested in, the countryside in which the war was being waged (Tanham 1966:5–7, 49). A social and cultural gulf therefore separated the government from the Vietnamese people.

Initially the US did little to counteract this bias. Until 1962, few Americans ventured into the villages to assist with pacification, and US development programmes concentrated upon large-scale projects which had only limited bearing upon the lives of the peasantry (Tanham 1966:7).

When the US/GVN did try to reach the villages, the GVN attempted to find solutions to rural problems through vast inputs of aid. Theoretically, this would obviate the need for rural political organizations and so would neutralize any opposition to the government's monopoly of official power (Goodman 1970:672-3). Paradoxically, this was counterproductive because the GVN thereby discouraged the people from taking an active part in the political process and from feeling that the government actually represented them. Given that the breakdown of traditional society had left a vacuum in which people searched for new forms of political expression, the failure of the GVN to create a climate and provide suitable mechanisms for the development of a political community was a grave error. Indeed, it is significant that resistance to communist pressure was especially fierce in those villages populated, for example, by Catholics, by supporters of the politico-religious sects or where Buddhism was especially strong (Tanham 1966:51, Race 1972:189). In these instances, religion was the factor which bound the community together.

Diem and his brother, Nhu, appreciated the efficacy of communist ideology and the Party's all-encompassing embrace in answering a need within the social and political psyche of the Vietnamese people. Nhu responded by attempting to fashion political organizations and develop control techniques that mirrored those of the communists (Duncanson 1968:314-15). To this end he established the National Revolutionary Movement, the only officially authorized political party, to function as an alternative to the NLF, as well as the small Can Lao (Revolutionary Workers' Party) which provided its leadership. He hoped that these organizations, when armed with his Personalist ideology, would be able to infuse the people with anticommunist ardour and that the Strategic Hamlet programme, and the concomitant control it offered over the people, would be an efficient means of applying the ambitious plan (Blaufarb 1977:110). Nhu's strategy, nevertheless, contained a fatal flaw. The revolutionary movement's ideology and organization worked so well because they struck a cord with the peasantry. Nhu's, however, relied upon the imposition of organization from above and he controlled no system that rivalled the communists rural cadre network. Hence Nhu was attempting to orchestrate a revolution without the apparatus of a revolution (Nighswonger 1966:69) and without the requisite support amongst the people.

As government officials were appointed rather than elected they were far more eager to curry favour with their superiors than to consolidate support among the people they ruled. The aid that those running pacification programmes thus dispensed did not take into consideration the needs and desires of the villagers as the first priority. Frequently, in the rush to bring economic benefits to local communities, it was not ascertained in advance what form the villagers would like the aid to take. Construction projects would be sited in inappropriate locations and the gifts that were dispensed might be given to the wrong people and not to those most in need. Rather than creating a body of grateful peasants and a fund of goodwill, the misapplication of aid could in fact magnify the people's sense of helplessness and alienation. It is significant, in this respect, that the NLF were not completely averse to government-financed projects when they were built by contractors. When built by the villagers, however, their attitude was hostile because self-help projects might increase the people's identification with the regime (Nighswonger 1966:168–72).

Pacification programmes aimed to improve the image of both the US and the GVN. Troops would involve themselves in 'civic action' which basically amounted to good deeds in the villages. Washing children's hair, handing out sweets, digging wells and clearing rubble from bomb sites were just some of the activities. In all too many cases, however, indiscriminate use of firepower and a minority of abusive US and GVN troops were able to counteract any good works undertaken. The attitude of some ARVN soldiers towards the rural population was reprehensible and consequently counterproductive (Lewy 1978:177–82). Rapes, beatings and looting were not uncommon and the Ninth ARVN division, which operated in the Mekong Delta in 1971, gained such a bad reputation for stealing livestock that it was nicknamed the 'chicken division' (Lewy 1978:178). Understandably, the conduct of GVN and US troops made a considerable number of friends for the NLF, and abuses and atrocities committed against members of an individual's family were the most likely reasons to motivate someone to become an extremely ardent and determined NLF activist (De Sola Pool 1967:559). Under these circumstances, no amount of civic action could atone for the atrocities of the few and the racism of the many.

Both US and GVN military and even civilian officials were apt to believe that the rural population did not really know what they wanted. Instead, their interests were considered best served by US and GVN officials, irrespective of whether their actions were contrary to the people's wishes and detrimental to the pursuit of pacification.

This dismissive attitude was all too prevalent in the handling of pacification efforts. For example, when the US established a military camp near Hue in 1968, they bulldozed graves, thereby causing grief and anguish to the ancestor-honouring villagers (Trullinger 1980:133–4). In 1967 Jonathan Schell reported on operation *Cedar Falls* in the jungle-covered Iron Triangle area north-west of Saigon, which had long been an NLF stronghold. His reports were a terrible indictment of pacification in Vietnam. Several thousand villagers were evacuated from the area and their homes destroyed along with the NLF fortifications. They were then herded into a giant compound where they and their assorted animals could find shelter under vast gaily-coloured tents and listen to propaganda and songs broadcast from loudspeakers mounted on a truck. There was inadequate food and water and they were subjected to the indignities of open latrines and a roving pesticide controller armed with an insecticide sprayer. Astonishingly the US commander surveyed the operation and pronounced it 'wonderful'. The evacuees were not so impressed and there was something ludicrous about the signs declaring 'Welcome to Freedom and Democracy' and 'Welcome to the Reception Center for Refugees Fleeing Communism' (Schell 1961:94). It hardly seemed a promising method of enticing the people away from the NLF.

It was therefore hardly surprising that the South Vietnamese people felt little personal affinity with the GVN or that they failed to commit themselves wholeheartedly to its survival. In 1966, only one-seventh of those ordered to report for induction into the armed forces actually complied (Lewy 1978:93), and, at the village level, the NLF could rely upon attracting five to ten times as many active participants to their cause as the GVN could (Race 1972:160). This arose because the NLF proposed real changes in society whereas the US/GVN did not.

It was common for GVN officials to consider peasant grievances to be the product of communist agitation. Most believed that the peasantry would be content with their lot if it were not for the evil influence of subversives (Race 1972:39–40). Consequently, their priority was to attack the symptoms rather than the causes which gave rise to the revolutionary movement. Thus, while the NLF's social strategy was 'pre-emptive' in that it sought to eradicate causes for discontent, the GVN resorted to a 'reinforcement strategy' designed to improve and consolidate the prevailing social structure (Race 1972:150, 155–6). In addition, when evaluating its officials, the GVN placed a greater emphasis upon 'conflict aggravating' actions such as tax collection and enforcement of the draft, as opposed to 'conflict minimizing' social welfare functions. This ensured that the former were more thoroughly and effectively carried out and so helped the GVN to acquire a heavy-handed and uncaring image (Race 1972:160).

Saigon and Washington's pacification programmes were based upon providing an *increment* of wealth, while the revolutionary movement championed a wholesale *redistribution* of wealth. Of fundamental importance was the fact that under the US/GVN approach the poorest would still remain the poorest despite being better off in absolute terms (Race 1972:176). Economic stratification would therefore be perpetuated. Consequently, it was inevitable that the GVN found its most ardent supporters amongst the richer members of society. In his study of a South Vietnamese village, James Trullinger identified approximately 5 per cent of the population as supporters of the colonial government during the Second World War. In the period 1961–5, roughly the same 5 per cent were pro-GVN (Trullinger 1980:40, 91). Interestingly, these people were members of the extended families of four or five large landowners, two wealthy tradesmen and a number of civil servants. All lived in substantial homes and enjoyed a standard of living which was considerably superior to that of ordinary villagers (Trullinger 1980:73–4).

As it depended on the people and grew from the people, the revolutionary movement was, of necessity, responsive to their wishes. The GVN, on the other hand, was seen to operate in support of a social elite. Lax and sloppy administration was tolerated because, thanks to US aid, the GVN did not have to fend for itself. In the short-term it could afford poor standards. In a survey conducted in rural areas under GVN control in 1969, the population catalogued the failings of the administration, listing them as amongst their most basic and serious problems (Goodman 1970:677–9). Injustice and corruption were rife. Money to cover resettlement expenses and pay for war related damage was frequently delayed. Often it could only be obtained through resort to bribery and, in some cases, it never found its way to the rightful recipient at all. Moreover, even when corrupt officials were identified, it often proved impossible for local people to amass enough influence to enforce their removal. To compound the injustice, securing their removal usually meant that they were simply transferred to another province.

Pacification efforts were naturally hindered by corruption. Fertilizer and agricultural equipment might be stolen to be sold on the black market or used on an official's private farm. The same was true of building materials and food supplies. Apart from having a debilitating effect upon the US/GVN's political war, corruption facilitated the siphoning off of funds and materials directly to the NLF (Tanham and Duncanson 1969:120–1) and, ironically, funding for pacification may have aided the revolutionary movement as much as it did the Saigon regime.

That the GVN failed to address corruption within its civilian and military organizations owed less to its lack of interest in the matter than to the fact that, even with the necessary will, it would have been hard-pressed to tackle the problem without seriously damaging its political support. Too many of its key supporters had vested interests in the preservation of the existing system. This begs the question as to how unstable governments can reform themselves when faced with a military and political crisis (Blaufarb 1977:87)? Clearly, reform is needed in order to generate popular support and yet that very process might induce such turmoil within the regime and alienate its supporters to such an extent that it ceases to be viable as a functioning government. Ultimately this dilemma presents a colossal and perhaps insurmountable hurdle for aspiring counterinsurgents.

The GVN's failure to undertake adequate land reform measures until 1970 must be set within this context. Farmers in the South evinced an 'extraordinary desire' to own land, and acquisition of land was by far the highest priority of peasants (Bredo 1970:739–40). Notwithstanding this, the land reform that Diem undertook in 1956 fell far short of peasant demands and its ultimate effects were minor (Callison 1983:46–51). Ordinance 57 allowed landowners to retain 100 hectares plus a further 15 hectares to finance ancestor worship. The limit of 100 hectares was, in the Vietnamese context, extremely high. In Long An, for example, the average agricultural unit was a mere 2.5 hectares (Race 1972:58). Moreover, clauses were also included to permit the owner to retain the choice land, to keep a further 30 hectares if they farmed the land themselves and to keep lands converted to industrial crops.

Under Ordinance 57 and under an agreement with the French which approved the purchase of French-owned land, some 670,000 hectares, or approximately 33 per cent, of the tenanted land in South Vietnam was technically released for redistribution. However, by 1968 only 276,000 hectares had been redistributed (Bredo 1970:742) benefiting a maximum of 10 per cent of South Vietnam's tenant farmers (Sansom 1970:57–8). Ironically, as the insurgency intensified during the early 1960s, Diem abandoned land reform at the precise moment when it might have been politically expedient (Nighswonger 1966:38). Instead he chose to substitute a draconian programme of control over the population. Furthermore, in the post-1954 period, the GVN had enforced the return of lands granted by the Viet Minh. The goodwill which this dissipated and the failure of the Diem land reform to respond to the peasants' keenest desires left the revolutionary movement free to reap a copious amount of political capital from their own progressive land policies.

Ordinance 57 was not enforced properly because of poor

administration and because the GVN lacked the political will, muscle and appreciation of the importance of land reform. Why the US failed to give land reform the highest priority is more problematic. It has been suggested that the US did not consider that land-based grievances were of great significance (Sansom 1970:229) and that they did not appreciate the importance of land in a traditional, rice growing society. Further, because the NLF laid special emphasis upon land redistribution, the Americans took an ideologically opposed stance, refusing to believe that anything the NLF did could actually be wholeheartedly supported by the peasants (Sansom 1970:233–6). Certainly land reform did not figure prominently in major, top-level US policy discussions and it was not the subject of intensive analysis until later in the war. However, in some instances the US *had* appreciated the importance of land. US advisers in South Korea, Taiwan and Japan had advocated far more progressive land reform policies than Ordinance 57. There, land reform was seen to contribute to stability because these countries had more diversified economies. South Vietnam, on the other hand, was heavily dependent upon the cultivation and export of rice. By redistributing land, it was thought that the peasants would consume the rice that had formerly been exported. This would create economic problems and would seriously threaten the economic wellbeing of the pro-US elite. Land reform was thus sacrificed in favour of the need to ensure the continuation of large-scale rice exports (Wiegersma 1988:175–7).

The lack of progress in pacification cannot be laid solely at the door of the GVN and its poor administration. The US also played a significant role because, up until 1967, it did not give the requisite administrative and bureaucratic backup to pacification. A variety of US agencies operated in Vietnam. The State Department, the Agency for International Development (AID), the United States Intelligence Agency (USIA), the Department of Defense and the Central Intelligence Agency (CIA) all operated independent programmes. This was the problem. Independence meant no overall management and coordination, leading inevitably to *ad hoc* measures and inefficiency. US and GVN programmes got in each other's way and, in turn, American agencies got in each other's way. Moreover, most of the US's civilian agencies were not equipped or structured in order to deal with the war in Vietnam. They retained peacetime funding and operating procedures which lacked the dynamism to react with speed and effectiveness to a fast-moving war situation (Komer 1986:64, 83–4).

As there was no unified management of pacification and as no one had a large stake in it, no bureaucratic interest spoke up for it.

Accordingly, the military was left to fight the war in its own way without significant demur (Komer 1972a:76). In this sense it has been argued that the conflict, rather than being overmanaged by Washington, was actually undermanaged. This was because, in practice, the conduct of the war was delegated to the military and because the civilian leadership did not possess the machinery to exert control and direction over the armed services running the war in Vietnam (Komer 1972a:76, Komer 1986:82–3). In a related vein, rather than the US advisory role being too large, it has been claimed that it was not large enough and that its emphasis upon technical assistance detracted from the need to improve GVN performance (Komer 1986:127).

The administration of pacification in Vietnam was altered radically when, in May 1967, all the various programmes were placed under the control of a new organization, CORDS (Civil Operations and Revolutionary Development Support). Robert Komer, a forceful and energetic proponent of pacification and effective management techniques, was appointed as its head. Komer, a civilian, became a deputy to Westmoreland, the US military commander in Vietnam, and was accorded the status of an ambassador. CORDS was placed under MACV because it was intended that the vast resources of the military would thereby be channelled into pacification. However, while the new body was a civilian-military hybrid, subordinate to MACV, in reality most of the senior CORDS staff were civilians, thus giving civilians a far greater influence over pacification than had hitherto been the case (Komer 1972b:50).

The pacification programmes that were launched under the auspices of CORDS were not distinct from previous programmes. The difference lay in the fact that they were more comprehensive and were carried out on a more ambitious scale. Of special importance was Komer's decision to assume responsibility for South Vietnam's paramilitary units, the Regional and Popular Forces (RF and PF). Under CORDS their role was greatly expanded and their supply of weapons improved. By 1970 approximately half a million men belonged to the 'Ruff-Puffs', as they were called. But despite the impetus given to pacification by the bureaucratic shake-up, the success of pacification depended ultimately upon the Vietnamese. Americans operated merely as advisers and the ratio between GVN and US personnel devoted to pacification was 100:1 (Komer 1972b:51). Pacification would succeed only in so far as the South Vietnamese people sympathized with its objectives and, if they did, only in proportion to the effort expended by Saigon.

The establishment of CORDS may have made pacification more effective but it was extremely hard to ascertain exactly how successful it was. Throughout the war it was consistently difficult for the Americans to discover people's political persuasion. In order to avoid compromising him or herself with either side, most villagers kept their political cards close to their chests. This was especially true in contested areas where there might be a US/GVN presence in the day, but NLF control at night, once the US/GVN troops had retired to their bases. Many, therefore, bided their time. They were *attentistes,* or fence sitters, who cautiously waited for the mandate of heaven to reveal itself so that they could give enthusiastic support to the winning side at an appropriate moment. Their action was not opportunism—it was a matter of survival.

The vast cultural gap that separated the Americans from the Vietnamese and the difficulty of unearthing an accurate picture of political sentiment created difficulties for US analysts who were characteristically eager to reduce the subtleties of politics in the village to neat formulae. Applying their sophisticated managerial techniques, they devised the Hamlet Evaluation System (HES). A hamlet's security status was graded on a six point scale from A, secure, to F, which was NLF controlled. Grades were based upon eighteen political, social and economic factors, but tended to reflect factors such as the amount of resources poured into the community and who ostensibly controlled it, rather than the underlying political sympathies of the villagers. In 1970, a more sophisticated and reliable system, HES/70, was adopted. It was intended to produce a more accurate picture by removing the element of subjective judgement and personal bias that local officials inevitably injected into the former evaluation system. Nevertheless, HES/70 still concentrated on those superficial factors that were readily discernible and hence quantifiable.

Coinciding with the advent of CORDS, more concerted and productive efforts were made to bring 'democracy' to Vietnam. Democratic institutions modelled on those in the US were adopted under the new constitution in 1967. Provision was made for an executive, a legislature and the requisite judicial checks and balances. Admittedly a legislature had existed prior to this time, but it was merely a token concession to democracy and the executive continued to follow its own path untrammelled.

In the presidential elections provided for under the new constitution, Nguyen Van Thieu was elected as president. The fashioning of an effective National Assembly, however, was more difficult. The bitter war had polarized the population but had not resulted in a greater mobilization of the people into parties operating within the official political milieu. Basically this was because the GVN lacked a political community (Goodman 1973:5), and if there was political mobilization in the countryside, it was mobilization in favour of the NLF. Revealingly, people saw elections as a process of competition amongst the elites (Goodman 1973:18) and most leaders of nationalist political parties considered that their main opposition came from other party leaders or from leaders of factions within their own party. This perception began to alter, however, after the shock of the Tet Offensive (Goodman 1973:53). Belatedly, the NLF became their principal political opponent.

A profusion of parties and independent candidates vied for power. Most had limited appeal. Some were based on religious groups and many were restricted to specific geographical areas (Goodman 1973:53, 62–3). In the countryside, party politicians lacked support and, although a number began to extend their organization, their appeal was limited because many lacked the kind of platform to attract villagers and because religious groups could succeed in enlarging their political support only by undertaking a programme of religious conversion (Bullington and Rosenthal 1970:658). Without the bargaining power that support in the rural areas would have granted to members of the new National Assembly, the executive constantly sought to subvert the new constitution by assuming far greater powers than officially sanctioned.

The regime's neglect to broaden its base of support further undermined the chances of democracy functioning in Vietnam. Prior to 1968, it sought simply to consolidate its existing, very restricted political underpinning and the main preoccupation of successive Saigon regimes was not the defeat of the NLF but the pursuit of their own internal power wranglings. They were committed, above all else, to forestalling challenges to their rule and authority, primarily from within the armed forces. This did not create a propitious climate in which to conduct pacification, and vital measures that were needed in order to bring about a greater degree of success in the prosecution of the war were not given top priority. In particular, the GVN refused to authorize a full-scale manpower mobilization. The Tet Offensive was dramatic and shocking enough to change this sloppy approach to pacification and to the war in general and, henceforth, the battle for internal power was subordinated to the battle against the NLF.

There is another interesting perspective on what, ultimately, proved to be a failure of democracy in Vietnam. According to this interpretation, the failure was the consequence of fundamental historical and cultural factors and, significantly, other nations in South East Asia have also succumbed to authoritarian rule. The basic problem in Vietnam was that there was no tradition of parliamentary democracy. In the West, by contrast, it has taken generations to evolve. Socio-economic divisions and political and social traditions made Vietnam infertile ground for democracy to thrive. In particular, the influence of Confucianism, with its emphasis upon the community as opposed to Western, liberal democracy's emphasis upon the individual, ensured that democracy and the democratic process were not readily assimilated into the Vietnamese political environment (Duiker 1983:71–2, 76).

If the triumph of democracy in South Vietnam had been dependent upon the size of the propaganda campaign orchestrated in order to promote it, then the US and the GVN would have won a decisive victory in South East Asia. The US campaign was tailored according to its audience, amongst which were three major target groups: the communists and their adherents in the South, the people and the government of the DRV and, finally, the non-communist South Vietnamese (Chandler 1981:4–5).

Inevitably the US encountered some difficulties in cross-cultural communication when formulating its propaganda. For instance, leaflets featuring pictures of a bikini-clad girl may have stirred the imagination of the Americans who designed them, but, in the cultural context of Vietnam, they did little to entice guerrillas out of the jungles (Chandler 1981:16–20). The cultural gulf was widened because the majority of officers involved in propaganda work lacked any great depth of knowledge about Vietnamese society and history, and few were bilingual (Chandler 1981:239–40). Lacking expert knowledge, those in charge of propaganda at the grass roots level resorted to reproducing broad themes and to using standardized leaflets. This cut down the incidence of mistakes but it also tended to reduce effectiveness because the themes may not have been entirely appropriate for specific groups and specific occasions (Chandler 1981:230–9).

The Americans had a penchant for dropping leaflets. Between 1965 and 1968 they dropped an amazing 1.9 billion propaganda leaflets over North Vietnam (Van Dyke 1972:84). Tons were released from cargo aircraft flying over the sea and were then carried by the wind over land. Others were dropped from fighter aircraft. The messages on most claimed that the North Vietnamese people had been duped by the Communist Party and that they were pawns of the Chinese (Chandler 1981:103–7). The USIA's 'Voice of America' and the GVN's 'Voice of Freedom' broadcast radio propaganda into North Vietnam. Despite its scale, however, the US propaganda campaign had little impact because the DRV's own variety of propaganda proved even more efficacious in strengthening the state's ideological 'shield' (Chandler 1981:148,151).

Five major appeals formed the basis of psychological operations (PSYOPS) conducted against PLAF and PAVN forces in South Vietnam and along the Ho Chi Minh Trail (Chandler 1981:44–69). One played upon fear and showed gruesome pictures of mutilated bodies. This proved counterproductive because it angered the revolutionary forces who perceived the US/GVN's exploitation of the dead as callous. Other more appropriate themes capitalized upon the hardships of life in the jungle and encouraged the often hungry, tired and uncomfortable soldier to question his faith in a communist victory and to ask whether he had been deceived by the communists. The most potent appeal was based on the soldier's concern for his family and the worry and uncertainty that resulted from being separated from them and so unable to fulfil his family responsibilities.

In addition to leaflet drops, the US broadcast messages using vast loudspeakers fixed to helicopters and aeroplanes. Amongst the most disturbing to the NLF and North Vietnamese forces were the sounds of crying women and children which were supposed to deepen their feeling of homesickness and worry about their family. Also productive was the use of a 'quick reaction' approach. A known PLAF or PAVN unit would be targeted and leaflets designed specifically for it. For instance, if a unit was known to have taken heavy casualties this could be used as a powerful weapon in the psychological war. Even more demoralizing was when a defector could be persuaded to appeal directly to individual members of his unit. The message was then transmitted over loudspeakers to the disconsternation of his former comrades. The success of 'quick reaction' initiatives lay in the application of suitable propaganda to specific target groups. As such, it demanded more effort and better intelligence than was otherwise available and so, despite its advantages, it was always overshadowed, at least in scale, by the emphasis upon the relatively indiscriminate use of leaflets bearing broad-based appeals (Chandler 1981:82–8).

The aim of such propaganda was to induce the enemy to defect or at least to induce a lowering of morale. Because their ideological commitment may have been more durable than that of native southerners, and because defecting would mean cutting themselves off from their families, the propaganda campaign did not persuade a large number of North Vietnamese to surrender (Chandler 1981:95–6). For the PLAF, the Chieu Hoi or 'Open Arms' programme, on the other hand, was effective in encouraging at least low-ranking personnel to change sides. Defectors, known as ralliers, to the government were treated leniently and were placed in detention centres for a few weeks, during which time they were supposedly politically-reorientated and prepared to resume a normal life in society. Although established in 1963 it was not until 1968 that the programme really began to take off as a result of a reward scheme. Financial incentives were paid for surrendered weapons and to those taking advantage of the third-party inducement programme which paid money to individuals who encouraged defections. The higher the status of the defector the greater the reward. The figures illustrate how the material incentive affected the Chieu Hoi programme. In 1968 there were 17,836 ralliers while in 1969 there were 47,088 (Lewy 1978:91–2).

Statistics, nevertheless, do not tell the whole story because the programme became the victim of corruption. People sought to claim rewards for ralliers who were not NLF members at all and the same individual might rally repeatedly. This was only possible, of course, because there was no adequate means of administering the programme. A number of guerrillas even took advantage of the scheme by defecting and so enjoying a welcome rest from the rigours of combat. Upon being released they would then return to their units.

The American propaganda campaign in the South aimed to improve the image of the GVN and the US, and to tarnish that of the revolutionary movement. Neither Saigon nor Washington enthusiastically promoted the use of the person-to-person propaganda which was utilized so well by the NLF, although there were a number of drama teams who, like their counterparts in the revolutionary movement, spiked their shows with a heavy dose of politics. Instead, reliance was placed upon leaflets, posters, radios and televisions which, thanks to US aid, appeared in some of the remotest areas of South Vietnam.

As it was important to portray the GVN as an independent, sovereign government, propaganda had to be seen to emanate from the GVN itself. However, as the GVN was not capable of managing such a large campaign, the US took over a great deal of what Saigon should have undertaken itself. Consequently, the US and the GVN succeeded in generating a sizeable credibility gap. The leaflets, for instance, that were purported to have been sent by the Saigon regime, were far too slick and sophisticated for a shambolic entity like the GVN to have produced and, what is more, many were thoughtlessly printed with US codes which were quite meaningless in Vietnamese (Chandler 1981:215–21). To guess where the leaflets had emanated from was thus no great intellectual exercise.

Notwithstanding these oversights, the leaflets and the other facets of the general propaganda campaign in South Vietnam after 1968 coincided with an improvement in the fortunes of the GVN so that the appeals of the campaign began, at last, to contain a vital element of truth. This considerably increased their effectiveness, although the propaganda campaign was never sufficient to have a really decisive impact upon popular political allegiance.

PACIFICATION IN THE POST-TET ENVIRONMENT

The Tet Offensive proved to be of vast significance to the progress of pacification. Native southerners of the PLAF bore the brunt of combat and it was their ranks which were decimated in the fighting. Consequently, the indigenous political organization was severely damaged and was never able to recover its former strength. This loss was crucial because those who died in the offensive were the link between the revolutionary movement and the people. Henceforth the NLF limped on. It was still the most coherent and powerful political group within South Vietnam, but it remained almost a shadow of its former self.

The failure of the Tet Offensive to furnish the revolution with a decisive victory was a blow to many of its supporters and must have encouraged *attentistes* to place more confidence in the GVN. It seemed that the revolutionary movement might not have secured the mandate of heaven after all. Not only did an NLF victory seem more questionable, but as the US/GVN improved its military position, it became increasingly dangerous to fight for the revolution. Moreover, people in the NLF controlled areas did not enjoy the benefits US aid could bring and they could no longer rely upon paying lower taxes. Accordingly, while peasants frequently viewed the NLF government as of 'superior quality', in practice they were lured by life in the safer and more prosperous GVN areas (Popkin 1970:662–3).

Vietnamization of the war was spurred by the Tet Offensive. Because President Thieu realized that America's commitment to Saigon was beginning to falter and because the impact of the offensive had severely shocked South Vietnam and its leaders, the GVN was finally motivated to act. A long-postponed decision to authorize the drafting of men of military age was taken and Thieu became personally interested and involved in the pacification programme.

The spur given to pacification by the combined effects of the establishment of CORDS and the galvanizing impact of Tet was reflected in the increased proportion of the US/GVN war budget allocated to pacification. In 1965, US $582 million were spent on pacification while in 1970 this figure was US $1.5 billion (Komer 1972b: 55). This increase, however, was partially offset by inflation and the fact that the total war budget had risen.

Hoping to capitalize on the Tet-induced weakness of the revolutionary movement in the countryside, Thieu launched an Accelerated Pacification Campaign in November 1968 and established a People's Self Defense Force. By 1970 this armed militia in the villages numbered 3 million men and functioned rather like an anti-NLF police force.

These initiatives were part of a new rural strategy for South Vietnam which emerged in mid-1969 and which had three major aims. First was an attempt to maintain a more secure local environment and to relaunch a more vigorous attack upon the NLF's political organization. The second objective was to reinvigorate village life and the third was the desire to carry out land reform and encourage self-help projects (Grinter 1975b: 63).

Operation *Phoenix,* deriving its name from the Vietnamese *Phuong Hoang* or 'all-seeing bird', was intended to eliminate the NLF's political organization known as the Viet Cong Infrastructure (VCI) in South Vietnam. Once NLF activists had been neutralized, either by being killed or placed in prison, the mechanisms for the recruitment of new supporters and guerrillas would consequently be destroyed and the revolutionary movement would wither away.

In theory, the programme was supposed to be discriminating and was supposed to be executed with precision and neatness. *Phoenix,* however, became the subject of intense criticism and its detractors condemned it as an assassination programme. It probably amounted to such, although it was maintained that those who died as a result of the programme did so in combat situations while trying to resist arrest. Giving the programme a generous interpretation, the assassination of enemy operatives in the context of a bitter war is not an unreasonable objective, but what was unacceptable about Operation *Phoenix* was that it was not selective but instead brutal, indiscriminate and deformed by corruption.

In 1967 the CIA had the sensible idea to gather together all the intelligence upon the VCI which had been collected by various, independently operating agencies. The responsibility for acting upon this pooled intelligence was given to the Vietnamese. Eventually Operation *Phoenix* grew out of this suggestion but, almost from the outset, the programme was marred by problems. In particular, the Vietnamese intelligence agencies were reluctant to cooperate in the sharing of information and in the coordination of their actions (Blaufarb 1977:247). Most district chiefs, moreover, displayed a distinct lack of commitment towards *Phoenix*. Efficiency in ferreting out NLF cadres would earn them the enmity of the revolutionary forces and would thereby make them certain targets. In addition, revealing the extent of NLF activity in their district might reflect badly upon them and so jeopardize their careers (Herrington 1982:194–5).

Stupidly, CORDS added to the difficulties by establishing quotas for the number of neutralizations to be achieved in specific areas. Inevitably, enthusiastic but inefficient Vietnamese teams were not discriminating about exactly who they eliminated and a large but unknown number of innocent people lost their lives in order to swell the number of 'VC kills'. Consequently, the worst aspects of the programme arose from the unfortunate juxtaposition of US managerial technique with GVN incompetence and inefficiency (Blaufarb 1977:246). Between 1968 and 1970 over 40,000 individuals were neutralized under the auspices of *Phoenix,* almost half of these being killed (Colby 1978:272). Most were low-level VCI The percentage of innocent people included in these statistics will never be known.

Because *Phoenix* operated outside the law, suspects could be subjected to 'administrative detention' even when there was not enough evidence to take them to court (Szulc 1978:234–5). Abuses did occur in the programme (Herrington 1982:196–7) and torture was used routinely in the prisons. The unreliable confessions extracted by these means were then used as a source of intelligence.

Phoenix lacked tight overall coordination and there was a shortage of facilities to house prisoners. This resulted in some suspects being released almost immediately after capture. Bribes could be paid to local officials to ensure a prisoner's release (Goodman 1970:678) and individuals might be arrested simply in order to give the officers in charge the opportunity to gain extra money. Indeed, the actual application and administration of Operation *Phoenix* was so bad that, in 1969, it came out top in a list of problems with which the rural population living in GVN areas felt that they had to contend (Goodman 1970:677–8). Nevertheless, despite its record of mismanagement, corruption and brutality, *Phoenix* did have the desired effect (Herrington 1982:195–6): it weakened the southern revolutionary organization and caused alarm in the higher echelons of the movement (Karnow 1984:602–3). Coinciding with the problems faced by the NLFs political organization in the wake of the Tet débâcle, *Phoenix* made an important contribution to the eclipse of the NLF and to the increasing political neutralization of the South Vietnamese people.

The economic aid that came courtesy of the US increased standards of living in the South Vietnamese countryside in the late 1960s and early 1970s. 'Miracle' rice strains, fertilizers and mechanization helped to make farmers better off. A land reform which, at long last, was legislated into existence in 1970 as the Land-to-the-Tiller law was genuinely progressive, in contrast to Diem's Ordinance 57 (Callison 1983:81). Although it was inevitably disfigured by corruption and fraud it was a vast improvement. However, it was an improvement that came far too late to have any real impact upon the war. It could not steal any thunder from the NLF and frequently simply legitimized in GVN law what had been accomplished by the revolution in practice. A minority was swayed by the reform, and because they now owned land which was recognized as their own private property by the GVN, they had a vested interest in the survival of the Thieu regime. Indeed the new law reduced tenancy from 60 to only 10 per cent of cropland in three years (Thayer 1985:242). However, it could not generate a groundswell of support for the government. Many people had already received land from the NLF and most were concerned far more with security and staying alive than with owning land. By 1970, land reform, which formerly could make or break the fortunes of opposing sides, was no longer a burning issue.

That the NLF no longer commanded the depth or breadth of support that it previously had was clear by the beginning of the 1970s. Between 1968 and 1970 the revolutionary movement's popularity declined in the villages and the intensity of its operations was reduced (Trullinger 1980:143). In 1968 the Hamlet Evaluation System estimated that 77 per cent of the population lived in relatively secure areas while, in 1971, that figure had soared to 97 per cent (Lewy 1978:192). Indeed, recognizing that pacification was having some impact, PAVN/PLAF forces concentrated half of their attacks against pacification targets during their three-day military 'high point' in April 1970 (Komer 1972b: 61). However, it would be incorrect to interpret what was essentially a swing away from the revolutionary movement as a swing in popular support towards the GVN. Much of what was considered the product of successful pacification in the post-1968 period was won almost by default. With the revolution's indigenous political apparatus damaged by the losses of the Tet Offensive and its victory no longer seemingly assured, it was not surprising that many people, heartily sickened by years of bloody conflict, should choose to tread a more careful, neutral path.

In many senses the revolutionary movement proper had been unable to deliver victory in South Vietnam. From 1968, with its forces spent, the fighting was assumed by regular troops from the North, and when the final denouement came it was delivered by a conventional military assault upon which the successes or the failings of the GVN's pacification efforts had but a tangential bearing. But, despite the PLAF's more restricted role in the aftermath of Tet, they had served a vital purpose. They had sapped the will of the US to continue fighting the war and the slow but inexorable American withdrawal that Tet initiated ensured that PAVN would eventually be free to fight in a more conventional manner.

Ultimately pacification did fail in Vietnam because it failed to build a nation. Most of the US/GVN socio-political responses to the NLF were irrelevant to the challenge posed. Six major politico-military strategies operated in Vietnam during the war (Grinter 1975a: 1118–27). There was the social mobilization and organization building strategy, the improvement of local government and administrative reforms promoted by the British, the authoritarianism and power concentration practised by Diem and later by Thieu, the building of democratic institutions advocated by certain, more liberal Americans, the stability and economic development option and, finally, the military occupation approach practised by the US Army. Of these, only the first two failed to be applied in one form or another on any major scale by the US/GVN. The problem was that the remaining strategies were either inappropriate or mismanaged and that the social mobilization approach, which was the most vital and which was the one that the NLF/DRV adopted, was almost completely ignored.

To a great extent, nation building in South Vietnam was doomed from the outset. Successive regimes could not fashion a nation and win support because the means of doing so were inimical to their own survival. The GVN was an artificial creation which hid behind a facade of legitimacy financed by the United States. It is not unfair, therefore, to say that South Vietnam, as a legitimate national entity, existed only on the balance sheets of the US treasury.

Because the revolutionary forces of the mid-1960s commanded incomparably more popular support than the GVN and because the movement was so well entrenched and its adherents so numerous and committed, the US/GVN effort to quell the revolution's advance and to avoid a humiliating defeat entailed wrenching South Vietnamese society apart. Traditional life was irreparably damaged. Vast areas of land were depopulated and the brutality of war spared few villages. Refugees flooded into overcrowded city slums where most joined an amorphous mass of wretched humanity and some became part of a rootless lumpen proletariat cut off from their culture and its values by the shock of the war. For these people, the survivors and yet the victims of the years of struggle, politics and pacification seemed irrelevant. The NLF had lost control of them and the GVN, for whom all the suffering had been caused, could count on nothing but their apathy. America's sons had died in order to keep the GVN afloat and to create this human wasteland. North Vietnam had been pummelled by bombs and had sacrificed much of its youth in order to prevent a United States victory. But in the cities, towns and villages of South Vietnam, it was the people and the scarred land on which they lived that had paid the highest price of all.

10 The war in five capitals—the international context of the Vietnam War

The Saigon regime could not have existed for long without the patronage of the United States. Conversely, the revolutionary forces in the South would not have proved such a serious threat if it had not been for generous material support from China and the Soviet Union. Despite these realities, the relationships between the various nations intimately involved in the conflict cannot be understood by a cursory appraisal of their relative status in the world. Saigon and Hanoi were not subservient to the greater powers and relations were frequently troubled by the frustrations common to patron-client linkages. Saigon remained infuriatingly reluctant to heed US advice, while Hanoi, far from being a tool of Peking and Moscow, steered a course independent of the giants of the communist bloc.

Paradoxically the greatness of a nation's power and the control, at least of the mechanical and financial means by which the struggle was fought, could not, in the context of the Vietnam War, always be translated into effective leverage over the conflict's political dimensions.

WASHINGTON AND SAIGON

In the autumn of 1972, Henry Kissinger was appalled to find that the South Vietnamese president, Nguyen Van Thieu, was unwilling to comply with a US request to ratify an agreement arranged with North Vietnam. Thieu's stubborn refusal to oblige was not the first time that real tensions had emerged between America and its client regime. Relations between the two governments had been bedevilled with problems from the very beginning.

The problems had deep-seated roots. Although the US-GVN relationship was not a formal alliance, the link was exceedingly close owing to the inescapable fact that the GVN relied upon American support for its very existence. However, the degree of political intimacy and understanding was always limited by a vast cultural gap. The Americans had one perspective and one way of doing things and the South Vietnamese had another. Dynamic Americans barked commands, reduced the world and its ills to a neat set of statistics and browbeat the Vietnamese with the sheer forcefulness of their impeccable logic. Seeming to agree, the South Vietnamese would smile, nod their heads and then proceed to ignore completely any requests they found distasteful. Admittedly, however, this was sometimes the result of genuine misunderstandings brought about by a failure to communicate.

The cultural gap was very wide and at times generated great animosity between lower-level American personnel and their South Vietnamese counterparts and also between those in the highest echelons of the GVN and US governments, including certain US ambassadors and South Vietnamese leaders. Basically, the allies neither respected nor trusted each other (Goodman 1984:89). It was not the best foundation upon which to build an alliance and to fight a war.

As South Vietnam was a former French colony, America was concerned lest it should appear as a nee-colonial power and a successor to Paris. The image of subservient Asia and the dominant West, of the white man as ruler and the yellow-skinned race as the ruled, cast its subtle influence over US-GVN relations. President Diem especially was keenly aware of the historical context in which the US-GVN relationship operated and his frequent refusal to comply with US requests probably reflected an element of protest against the lingering overtones of the white man's rule in Asia.

It may seem paradoxical that while the GVN was so dependent upon the US, it also felt able to disregard a good deal of Washington's advice. Saigon retained this degree of independence because it was confident of the United States' commitment to its survival. As American prestige had been wagered and Washington had pledged to uphold democracy in Vietnam, Saigon was sure that the US would not withdraw from Vietnam whatever it did, or rather failed to do. Although the problem had existed for a number of years, it mushroomed into an almost insoluble one in the early 1960s. Hitherto, the US commitment to the GVN might still have been terminated without incurring significant costs. But as US aid began to pour into South Vietman without the GVN undertaking the reforms specified by the Kennedy administration, Saigon assumed that American support was guaranteed irrespective of their actions (Grinter 1974:843). As a result, there was no direct correlation between the strength of the United States and its ability to pressurize the GVN and, instead, a direct correlation arose between the extent of US involvement in the conflict and the bargaining power of the ruling South Vietnamese regime. The more the US became embroiled in Vietnam and the more it invested in the war, the more confident the GVN became of US resolve and, consequently, the less influence Washington could wield (Cooper 1971:426).

Periodic requests were made for the GVN to undertake political reforms and to tackle the corruption which permeated South Vietnamese society. Westmoreland claimed that he was able to influence ARVN leadership to a satisfactory degree (Westmoreland 1980:315) and the US did use the disbursement of aid and its management of pacification as a bargaining tool. As a result, it funded some programmes and not others, prompted changes in certain initiatives and leant on the government to remove at least a proportion of the most outrageously corrupt officials (Komer 1972a:30). But this was just the tip of the iceberg. Despite all the exhortations, the GVN adamantly refused to carry out the wholesale changes that were needed in order to win itself some measure of popular support. The justification was that the regime was so fragile that its imminent demise would be triggered by political changes and any disturbance to the system of graft that furnished its narrow band of adherents with the necessary financial incentives. Fundamentally, therefore, the GVN was too weak to comply with US demands and Saigon cultivated, in the words of Bernard Fall, 'an unassailable position of total weakness' (Fall 1967:399). Ironically its weakness, *vis-à-vis* the Americans, was in fact its strength.

To support its claim that the GVN was a separate, sovereign state which needed help from a friend in order to resist an external threat, the US made great international efforts to highlight the independence of the Saigon regime. If the GVN was assumed to be a puppet of Washington, then the US justification that it was fighting to preserve the legitimate government of South Vietnam lost its credibility.

Paradoxically, however, while the White House wanted Saigon to appear independent it did not wish it to act independently. Because the Americans had little faith in the GVN, they effectively fought the war for it and took over functions that should have been undertaken by the South Vietnamese. Although GVN incompetence may have been of understandable concern to the US, ultimately the American assumption of control over the war rebounded because it deprived the GVN of much-needed experience and sullied its nationalist credentials, which were such an essential requisite if the regime's claims to legitimacy and support were to amount to more than whistling in the wind.

Even though the US controlled the purse strings, it could not exert total control over South Vietnamese leaders. Diem was anything but a puppet and to President Kennedy it appeared that the only way to achieve the reforms that Diem refused to carry out was to replace him. Short of this ultimate sanction, the US lacked virtually any leverage and making the GVN respond to its wishes was an intractable problem. In reality, US power was restricted to the ability to change governments but not to change their policies (Grinter 1974:839). Indeed, it was only after the US began its Vietnamization programme, following which it dawned upon the GVN that the US commitment may not have been as boundless as first assumed, that the Thieu regime became a little more amenable to American suggestions.

Kissinger was furious when, in 1972, Thieu began to object to a settlement allowing a peaceful US withdrawal. In fact, by insisting that the agreement would be detrimental to the South Vietnamese government, which it undoubtedly would, Thieu was looking after the best interest of his regime and was clearly illustrating to his nation that his government did have a voice of its own and that it could distance itself from Washington. This display of defiant independence, however, came far too late for Thieu to win any prizes for his nationalism but it did display to the US and the South Vietnamese people that, if nothing else, Thieu would place the future of his government before the demands of US political and diplomatic expediency. Notwithstanding the fact that the US had been insisting for years that the GVN was an independent, sovereign government, when it finally acted like one it was outraged at its temerity.

Despite long experience with its own truculent ally, Washington consistently presumed that Hanoi remained subservient to Moscow and Peking. But in the same way that many misjudged the relationship between Washington and Saigon and believed that Saigon had no voice, however faint, the US considered the leverage that the USSR and China exercised over the DRV to be far greater than it actually was.

HANOI, PEKING AND MOSCOW

The North Vietnamese government was never merely a puppet of the Soviet Union or China. It always remained independent and as far as the Sino-Soviet dispute was concerned, Hanoi pursued its own interests rather that adopting a neutral position. It did, on occasions, veer to one side or another but this was dictated not by pressure from Moscow or Peking but by the exigencies of the North Vietnamese situation.

The DRV and the National Liberation Front fought the Vietnam War against the background of the Sino-Soviet dispute. This was the overarching issue in the communist world at the time and it had a major effect upon the conflict because it profoundly affected relationships between communist states and later between communist nations and the West.

Whilst Vietnam assumed the proportions of a major issue to Moscow by the mid-1960s, South East Asia and, more specifically, Vietnam had not always been of great interest to the Soviet Union. Stalin's foreign policy sought to encourage communist uprisings throughout the world. Accordingly, Moscow-trained Vietnamese communists assumed contol of the Indochinese Communist Party in the 1930s (Duiker 1981:46–8). Unlike Ho Chi Minh and others who had formed the Party and who placed a greater emphasis upon the role of a united front in the revolution, the Stalinist recruits sought to agitate exclusively amongst the urban proletariat. Given the socio-economic class structure pertaining at the time, this means of creating a revolution appeared distinctly unproductive and it was not until Ho's return to Vietnam in 1941, whereupon he reassumed control of the Party, that the ICP's approach was reorientated towards the united front, nationalism and the land question (Duiker 1981:66–9).

After the Second World War Moscow did not advocate cataclysmic change in Vietnam. The Soviet Union's interest in a communist Western Europe prompted it to pressurize the Vietnamese to consider the revolution in France before the revolution in their own country. In practical terms this meant that communist uprisings in Vietnam had to be restrained lest they should alienate the potential sympathizers of the French Communist Party.

The Soviet Union's attitude to revolution in Vietnam began to change with the establishment of the People's Republic of China in 1949. The triumph of the Chinese communists made the position of the Viet Minh seem far more promising. Consequently, in January 1950, shortly after the Chinese formally recognized the DRV, the Soviet Union followed suit. This was a concrete expression of Moscow's changing policy towards Vietnam and, henceforth, South East Asian affairs were awarded an increasingly high profile in the Kremlin.

While the USSR showed interest in the fate of the Viet Minh, its practical role in the conflict remained extremely limited. By contrast, during the early 1950s the DRV received material support and considerable ideological succour from the new, vast communist state on its northern border. Many of the social and economic policies applied by the Viet Minh in the areas that it liberated from French control bore a distinct Chinese imprint. Between 1950 and 1952 the DRV took Chinese advice in overhauling its finance and taxation system and, after 1953, fundamental elements of the Viet Minh land reform campaign were based upon the Chinese experience (Chen 1969:253, 258).

Ideological and political support provided the DRV with a great source of strength, boosting morale and reinforcing the belief that they would ultimately be triumphant. But just as importantly, the Chinese provided vital weapons to fight the war especially in the final phases of the conflict. With this aid the Viet Minh was able to fight with heavy armaments at Dien Bien Phu. Whilst the scale of the aid package, which had risen from 10–20 tons a month in 1951 to 1500 tons a month in early 1954 (Tanham 1967:68–9), was dwarfed by the US aid enjoyed by the French, it did enable the Viet Minh to act more decisively than otherwise and was a major contribution to the French collapse.

In addition to war material, the Chinese also sent advisers, technicians and medics, some of whom were present at Dien Bien Phu. It has even been suggested that Chinese troops assisted the Viet Minh during the battle (Duncanson 1968:177, Lancaster 1961:299). This loan of skilled Chinese workers was more an effort to emphasize solidarity rather than an attempt to become intimately involved in the fighting of the war, and at no time did it seem likely that the Chinese would intervene directly in large numbers in the conflict.

China and the Soviet Union supported the Viet Minh because of ideological principle. Nonetheless this did not mean that they consistently viewed the conflict in a favourable light. The war, on occasions, interfered with their own national interests. In particular, China feared being drawn into another Korean-type war and wanted a period of stability in which it could concentrate upon internal economic development. The Soviet Union was also antipathetic to the continuation of the war against the French. Firstly it feared that the conflict might spark off a major war. This was particularly worrying since the threat of massive retaliation from the US was still a credible prospect. Secondly, the Soviet Union was opposed to the attempt to build a European Defence Community in Western Europe during the early 1950s and they thought that ending the war in Indochina would lessen the likelihood of France joining the organization (Zagoria 1967:40). Thirdly, the USSR did not want to be concerned about a war in South East Asia. Following Stalin's death in 1953, a power struggle had ensued in the Kremlin and this rendered Moscow more concerned about internal matters and unwilling to divert its attention to the war in Vietnam (Papp 1981:7).

Both Moscow and Peking therefore had an interest in bringing the war to a close and they gave practical application to this interest by playing important roles in the negotiating process of the 1954 Geneva

Conference. Moscow, in particular, was instrumental in initiating moves to begin negotiations (Chen 1969:294) and jointly with Great Britain assumed the chairmanship of the conference. But owing to the closer relationship established between Hanoi and Peking, the North Vietnamese appear to have followed the Chinese lead during the conference far more than that of the Soviet Union (Chen 1969:308).

By 1954 the Viet Minh had seized control of a sizeable amount of territory in Vietnam. The Geneva Accords nevertheless did not adequately reflect the strength of the Viet Minh and many observers felt that they were entitled to better terms than they actually received. Specifically, the dividing line between the North and the South was established at the seventeenth parallel—somewhat higher than might have been expected. Yet the Soviet Union and China did not object to these provisions. Indeed, they were instrumental in encouraging the DRV to accept the terms in order that the war could be ended and hence their own national interests satisfied.

The Viet Minh resented the fact that its allies were pressuring it to accept a settlement and this underlined to the DRV that its foreign policy was too reliant upon Moscow and Peking (Chen 1969:294). The realization that allies would surrender Vietnam's best interests in favour of their own was a bitter lesson that the North Vietnamese learnt by heart. It was one which they never forgot and which the newly-established government in Hanoi sought to avoid repeating. Therefore, in the post-1954 period, the DRV, strengthened by its internationally sanctioned status as a sovereign regime, began to carve, tentatively at first, its own independent path in the communist world.

Moscow and Peking's concentration upon their own interests was re-emphasized in 1956 when the South Vietnamese government, backed by the US, refused to take part in the elections scheduled by the Geneva Accords to reunite the country. The DRV's allies passively accepted the situation and refused to make it an international issue. The Soviet Union, as co-chairman of the Geneva Conference, was in an especially prominent position and would have been able, quite justifiably, to galvanize world opinion and denounce the GVN's stubborn refusal to comply with the Accords. Both China and the Soviet Union, however, were content with the status quo and so remained silent. Despite its bellicose rhetoric, China was eager to court US favour and the Soviet Union was mindful not to upset the stability of the region and so disturb the South East Asian nations it was assiduously courting (Smith 1983:31). In 1957 Moscow proceeded to compound its injury to the DRV by proposing that both North and South Vietnam be admitted to the United Nations (Ulam 1968:699). Clearly this was interpreted as

Soviet recognition of the division of Vietnam as an irreversible feature of the international political scene.

THE SINO-SOVIET DISPUTE

Significant differences between the USSR and the People's Republic of China (PRC) began to be revealed in the late 1950s. The basic source of this dispute was a diverging attitude towards the United States. In the post-Stalin era the Soviet Union's hardline political stance was mellowing and it was gradually adopting a policy of accommodation with the West. By comparison, China was fiercely hostile to the US. Washington continued to support Chiang Kai-shek in his truncated, nationalist Chinese republic in Taiwan and still refused to soften its attitude towards the communist government in mainland China. While Washington refused to extend the hand of friendship, the PRC had little incentive to abandon its militancy. Consequently, Peking pursued a policy of at least rhetorical confrontation with the US and was critical of the Soviet Union's compromising relations with the arch enemy of communism.

In 1956, at the Twentieth Congress of the Soviet Communist Party, Nikita Krushchev made a historic speech in which he expounded the policy of peaceful coexistence, claiming that war could be avoided and that there could be a peaceful transition to socialism. In addition, he attacked the cult of personality that had grown up around Stalin and made the first serious criticism of the dictator's policies. His statement raised problems for the DRV and it questioned the universal applicability of Krushchev's interpretation of Marxism-Leninism. Specifically, it objected to the concept of peaceful coexistence, arguing that wars could not always be prevented. It maintained that the transition to socialism could not always be peaceful and it also felt uneasy about the attack on the cult of personality which had unwelcome implications for the DRV's own reverence for its leader, Ho Chi Minh (Smyser 1980:7–9).

In accordance with Krushchev's peaceful coexistence policy, Moscow maintained a cautious line on Vietnam, and while the DRV began to receive a substantial amount of aid from the Soviet Union, the North Vietnamese kept their distance from Moscow to ensure that they did not become too closely associated with its revision of accepted Marxist-Leninist tenets. However, while China liked to portray itself as a supporter of revolutionary militancy, it too was cautious about encouraging the DRV to adopt an aggressive policy following the GVN's failure to hold elections in 1956.

It was against this background of Soviet and Chinese passivity that the DRV took the decision in 1959 to adopt a military strategy in South Vietnam. It has been argued that the North Vietnamese launched the armed struggle because a climate favouring this kind of action was emerging within the communist world (Smith 1983:16–17, 162). However, Moscow was doubtful about armed revolution and the Chinese, despite their fiery words, did not appear to have actively encouraged the DRVs decision. Indeed the DRV had learnt from bitter experience that it could not listen exclusively to the advice of its allies. It had to look after its own interests, first and foremost, and it would not have launched the armed struggle at the behest of Moscow or Peking if this would have prejudiced the success of an immature revolutionary movement in the South. Nor is it likely that it would have postponed a decision to act if faced with Soviet and Chinese criticism. The move to armed struggle was primarily a decision based upon the objective assessments of local conditions which in turn were analysed within the context of the world situation (Smyser 1980:28–30).

Although the DRV maintained a balanced position between China and the Soviet Union from 1957 to 1960, Hanoi began to move closer to Peking as the Sino-Soviet dispute deepened. Krushchev's peaceful coexistence did not marry well with the armed struggle while, by contrast, Peking's avowed militancy and ideological purity had a potent appeal to a government at war. In a reflection of the USSR's ambivalence towards the mounting struggle in Vietnam, the formation of the NLF in 1961 was not announced in the Soviet Union for over a month and in the intervening period Krushchev revealingly referred to the First Indochina War as a successfully concluded war of national liberation (Papp 1975:148).

China's greater moral support for the conflict as the 1960s began masked areas of Sino-Vietnamese controversy which were later to sour relations between the two nations. Five major issues were to be the source of friction between China and the DRV and all existed as the new decade began (Lawson 1984:2–7). Firstly, Peking and Hanoi had differing attitudes towards negotiations. Initially the DRV wanted negotiations to take the form of bilateral talks with the US. Peking, on the other hand, favoured the multilateral format of the Geneva Conference in 1954. This would have enabled it to have assumed a role in the negotiations. Peking then reversed its position on negotiations in response to the intensifying Sino-Soviet dispute. Peace talks were no longer welcome because they might have granted a role to the Soviet Union. In addition, the Chinese did not actually want the war to end. The conflict tied down the United States, proving the strength of a revolutionary movement when pitted against the corrupt, reactionary Americans and it also deflected US military might away from any adventures against mainland China in support of Chiang Kai-shek. As no talks took place until 1968, however, China's hostility towards negotiations did not cause a significant problem. When the DRV decided to adopt a talk-fight strategy in the wake of the militarily damaging Tet Offensive of 1968, this naturally changed and the PRC evinced hostility towards the initiation of talks.

A second source of friction was China's perception of North Vietnam's intended role in Indochina. Peking believed that Vietnamese domination of the area was a distinct possibility and, fearful of an aggressive, expansionist power on its southern border, the PRC was always wary of the DRV's long-term goals. This latent tension was to flare into overt hostility following the triumph of the DRV and the reunification of Vietnam in 1975. Until then it simmered gently.

As was to be expected, the Sino-Soviet dispute furnished further areas of controversy between China and North Vietnam. Peking would have liked to have seen the DRV take a far more critical view of the Soviet Union. While the USSR pursued a policy of peaceful coexistence it was natural for the DRV to assume a more pro-Peking line, but as Moscow's attitude to the conflict began to change in the mid-1960s and as the Soviet Union started to supply large amounts of munitions to the DRV, it would have been illogical for Hanoi to adopt a more hostile posture towards the USSR.

As a corollary to Sino-North Vietnamese differences over the Soviet Union, controversy emerged over attitudes towards the United States. As the Sino-Soviet dispute escalated in 1968–9, Peking began to view Moscow as its main enemy and America as its ally in the fight against the evils of Soviet revisionism. The position was, of course, an absurd contradiction for the DRV which was fighting the US in South Vietnam using weapons supplied by the Soviets.

The fifth area of disagreement, and one which was constantly at issue, was the strategy for pursuing the war. Peking advocated a protracted war strategy but as the conflict developed Hanoi increasingly began to adapt the concept. A traditional guerrilla war was difficult to pursue when the opponent had the technological power of the Americans. Believing that this technological advantage could seriously sap the strength of the revolutionary forces by inflicting heavy casualties, the DRV favoured a compressed version of protracted war (Taylor 1976:50–1). Such a strategy was anathema to the Chinese who were doubly annoyed because a more aggressive military strategy would require just the sort of weapons that the Soviet Union could supply.

During the early 1960s these areas of Sino-Vietnamese controversy did not develop into major divisive issues and between 1960 and 1964 Hanoi swung increasingly towards Peking. The nadir in Soviet-Vietnamese relations and the corresponding highpoint in the rapprochement between China and the DRV occurred in 1963 and 1964. The USSR continued to provide economic aid but, in line with its policy of peaceful coexistence, it did not attempt to match China in the provision of funds and armaments for the war in the South (Smyser 1980:66–7) and in the period 1963–4 China became virtually the sole external supplier of arms to the NLF (Chen 1972:809).

In March 1963 the estrangement between Moscow and Hanoi was given a concrete ideological basis when the Lao Dong Party denounced 'modern revisionism' and thereby clearly identified itself with the Chinese position. By the summer of 1964 the DRV was heavily involved in the Sino-Soviet dispute and was committed to the Chinese camp. Indeed relations between Moscow and Hanoi had deteriorated to the point where Krushchev became willing to abandon Soviet interests in South East Asia and to relinquish the co-chairmanship of the Geneva Control Commission. Interestingly, the Kremlin may also have been encouraged to assume this attitude because of a desire to dissociate itself from an impending regional conflict between China and the US over Vietnam (Papp 1981:19, 34).

A thaw in Soviet-Vietnamese relations began with the fall of Nikita Krushchev in late 1964. The DRV began to assume a more neutral position in the Sino-Soviet controversy as Moscow adapted its line on peaceful coexistence. Although the new Soviet leaders remained faithful to the broad concept of detente they attempted to enhance their image in the socialist world by assuming a more revolutionary stance. This obviously entailed more rhetorical and material support for the North Vietnamese and in early 1965 Alexi Kosygin visited Hanoi to underline friendly relations and also, perhaps, to link the Soviet Union to a revolutionary movement that appeared to be on the verge of a momentous victory (Papp 1981:46).

The swing to China and then the move back to a more neutral stance illustrated that Hanoi was not manipulated by either the PRC or the Soviet Union. It was not forced into a close relationship with China in the early 1960s but chose to associate closely with Peking because the Chinese political line served its needs far better than that of the USSR. Ideally, the DRV would have preferred to remain completely independent but this was not possible given the need to secure supplies for the war and given the existing political alignment within the communist camp. Certainly Hanoi did not agree with aspects of China's sectarian policies during this period and was critical of its dogmatic approach to military tactics, but as the Chinese, in contrast to the Soviets, were supportive of the war in the South, Hanoi found it expedient to align itself with the more militant Chinese (Smyser 1980:78).

The fall of Krushchev and the commencement of a more flexible policy in the Soviet Union allowed the DRV to redress the balance and chart a more independent course. As the war was beginning to escalate rapidly in early 1965, Hanoi found itself in greater need of armaments and was prompted to move away from the protracted war tactics advocated by the Chinese. Such pressures argued in favour of a closer relationship with the Soviet Union.

The escalation of the war revealed the latent differences between Hanoi and Peking, and Sino-Vietnamese cordiality began to disappear in 1965. Animosity flowed from the DRV's partial rejection of protracted war in the post-1965 Vietnamese context. In September 1965 Lin Piao, one of China's foremost politicians and theorists, published a major article in which, speaking for the Chinese leadership, he criticized Hanoi's strategy and offered advice on the way the war ought to be conducted. As a rule, however, Chinese methods of offering advice were more subtle and indirect. Their media, for example, refused to inform the people of large-scale battles and concentrated instead upon the pursuit of guerrilla warfare (Lawson 1984:103). Not surprisingly, the Chinese were horrified by the massive Tet Offensive and so in a fit of ideological pique they completely curtailed all press coverage of the war (Lawson 1984:106).

Despite the downturn in Sino-Vietnamese relations, the Chinese continued to provide equipment for the conflict. This was restricted to a level of support commensurate with the conduct of a guerrilla war (Taylor 1976:58). Emphasis was placed principally upon the supply of light infantry equipment, and a large number of Chinese soldiers were stationed in North Vietnam in order to help with logistical work, maintain lines of communication and supply technical advice. At one point in 1968 there may have been as many as 170,000 Chinese in North Vietnam (Smyser 1980:96). By contrast, Soviet aid was orientated towards the provision of heavier armaments. Artillery, rockets, tanks, helicopters, fighter aircraft and anti-aircraft missiles were all supplied in varying quantities to the DRV. Several thousand military technicians were also seconded in order to maintain and advise upon the use of the equipment (Smyser 1980:95–6).

As the war in Vietnam expanded during early 1965, the Soviet Union proposed a form of 'united action' with the Chinese. Specifically this would have involved the creation of an air corridor for Soviet planes over Chinese territory, the transportation of supplies and men overland from the USSR to Vietnam, the Soviet use of air bases in south-west China and trilateral talks between the three communist nations. The proposal flew in the face of the 'three no's' policy formulated by Mao: no united action, no Sino-American war and no peace talks (Chen 1972:809–11). He insisted that the Soviet Union's proposals for a coordinated Sino-Soviet effort to aid the DRV be dependent upon Moscow relinquishing its policy of peaceful coexistence. A serious debate over united action emerged within the Chinese leadership with one faction opposing the Maoists and arguing in favour of cooperation. The debate was finally settled in the autumn, however, when Mao and his party prevailed (Smyser 1980:88, 90–2).

To counter Peking's inflexible attitude the DRV also developed a 'three no's' policy. They refused to sanction China's repudiation of united action, refused to endorse Peking's no negotiation stance and, haunted by the memory of Chinese occupation in the aftermath of the Second World War, resolved to resist overt Chinese intervention in the conflict with large numbers of troops (Chen 1972:811–12).

A number of reasons help explain the Chinese reluctance to participate in united action with the Soviets (Lawson 1984:167). After the stream of polemics and the denunciation of Soviet revisionism, cooperation with Moscow would have appeared to have been an embarrassing betrayal of Peking's revolutionary purity. The Maoists also felt that the DRV and the National Liberation Front might be corrupted and sell-out to the US if Moscow was allowed a greater role in the conflict. In addition, close cooperation might offer the Soviet Union an opportunity to extend its debilitating influence into Chinese military and domestic affairs. Although an agreement was signed with Moscow authorizing the transport of Soviet equipment across China by rail, even this limited compromise was soured thanks to Chinese denigration of the scale and quality of the aid so supplied (Taylor 1976:42).

Of vital significance in dissuading Peking from embracing united action was the fear of war with the United States. In the early 1960s, China had made fierce rhetorical pledges, promising action in Vietnam in the event of direct US intervention. In the summer of 1965 military preparations were underway, probably as a means of warning the US to curb its escalation. At no time, however, was a war atmosphere encouraged in the PRC and, as the US build-up continued, China realized that Washington was not to be frightened away from its commitment to Vietnam. It therefore distanced itself from its earlier promises to send volunteers to help fight the war (Taylor 1976:48).

Despite all the loud noises Peking made about its militancy as compared to the Soviet Union's treacherous passivity, Mao and his clique did not want a war. Harbouring bitter memories of Korea and the way in which China was drained as Moscow sat back and watched the carnage, the avoidance of another war with the US was a top priority. Accordingly, those few Sino-American clashes that inevitably took place during the Vietnam War when US planes strayed into Chinese air space, were always accorded exceedingly cautious diplomatic treatment (Taylor 1976:48–9).

China's domestic politics were the main point of issue during the Cultural Revolution. Foreign policy issues, nevertheless, were important and the American involvement in Vietnam was a catalyst which exposed political differences within the Chinese leadership, principally because the war raised important questions about the nation's relationship with the Soviet Union (Zagoria 1967:63). For Mao and his adherents, China's involvement in the Vietnam War was less a matter of preserving China's security interests and far more a useful vehicle for pursuing its fight against the Soviet Union for the leadership of the world revolutionary movement (Taylor 1976:58). As a result, the interests of the NLF/DRV were occasionally sacrificed by China in the pursuit of its struggle with Moscow, and the Cultural Revolution, in general, had a deleterious impact upon the DRV's war effort. Beginning in 1966, for example, Soviet aid shipments destined for North Vietnam were increasingly jeopardized by the activities of the Red Guards. Missile shipments were delayed in order that the weapons could be copied, Russian specialists were harassed and some shipments even had their Soviet markings replaced and Chinese ones substituted (Smyser 1980:97–8).

Sino-Soviet animosity was building up to a crescendo throughout 1967 and 1968. Relations deteriorated to the extent that China began to perceive the USSR, rather than the US, as its main enemy. The Brezhnev Doctrine of limited sovereignty and the practical application that this was put to in the Soviet invasion of Czechoslovakia in 1968 generated unease in Peking, especially as the Sino-Soviet border had become the scene of increasing tension. Complementing the Chinese belief that the Soviet Union posed a real threat to their security was their perception of a diminution in the danger presented by the United States. This arose principally because the US policy of Vietnamization was thought to amount to an American retreat and because the US had begun to search for an opening to China.

The height of the Sino-Soviet dispute was reached in 1969. Violent clashes occurred between Chinese and Soviet troops along their disputed border in the spring and early summer and, in August, the US detected a 'stand-down' or alert of the nuclear weapon-carrying Soviet Air Force in the Far East (Kissinger 1979:183). Overt hostilites created problems for North Vietnam primarily because the passage of Soviet war supplies through China was interrupted. This meant that material had to be shipped by sea which naturally entailed more delays. As an added incentive, Peking may have seen this as a move likely to increase the chances of a Soviet naval confrontation with the US.

Whilst the Sino-Soviet dispute had hitherto been of benefit to the DRV in that it gave them room to manoeuvre between the two sides, playing one off against the other because both desperately wanted the support of such a high-profile revolutionary movement, the crisis that erupted in 1969 was of a different magnitude. Consequently, the DRV sought to mediate in the dispute and used the funeral of Ho Chi Minh to initiate the beginnings of a dialogue. In their attempts to reduce the tension they achieved some notable success (Lawson 1984:166).

North Vietnam's relations with the USSR were warm after 1965. Correspondingly relations deteriorated between Peking and Hanoi. However, China's more pragmatic foreign policy, which emerged as a result of its changing perceptions of the Soviet Union and the US, encouraged it to accommodate a more flexible line on the Vietnam War. In particular, its attitude towards negotiations softened considerably. After denouncing negotiations and insisting upon the pursuit of protracted war, and after criticizing the DRV for adopting a talk-fight stragegy in April 1968, by the end of the year Peking had relented and accepted that negotiations were a necessary evil. As the Soviet Union was now China's primary enemy it was sensible to develop an anti-Soviet axis with the United States. In the pursuit of their aim, negotiations were essential. Furthermore Maoist sensibilities were no longer under such overt attack from the DRV which, as a result of the losses incurred during the 1968 Tet Offensive, had resumed a form of protracted war. The comforting knowledge that Mao's theories on revolutionary guerilla war had been vindicated, at least in a circuitous way, made the acceptance of hitherto heretical negotiations appear that much more palatable.

North Vietnam's close relationship with the Soviet Union was inevitable as the DRV needed Soviet arms to fight its war. Until the late 1960s, when it adopted a more restrained attitude to the US, China actually wanted the war to continue because it bogged the US down and proved the viability of revolutionary movements. The Soviet Union, on the other hand, was not so keen on the continuation of the conflict. To this end it made a number of diplomatic efforts to achieve a negotiated settlement of the war. Amongst the most significant of these were politburo member Alexander Shelepin's visit to Hanoi during the US's second major bombing halt ostensibly to encourage the DRV to begin talks, and also the Wilson-Kosygin initiative in 1967.

Soviet efforts to initiate a dialogue may have been an effective propaganda measure and may not have had real substance. Certainly the USSR did reap significant benefits from the conflict. It gave a boost to budding revolutionary movements and proved that the US, despite its power, was not invincible. The Soviet Union could look with satisfaction upon the situation in Vietnam as the US began to withdraw and, while Vietnamization did worry them for a while and created doubts about the ultimate success of the revolutionary forces and fears that 'neoimperialism' might prevail, Moscow breathed a sigh of relief when *Lam Son* 719 proved Vietnamization to be hollow (Buszynski 1986:49).

Most importantly, the United States sunk billions of dollars into the war. Part of this might otherwise have been spent on improving and increasing America's military capability. As a result of the vast financial drain of the conflict and of Soviet efforts to update its equipment, by 1969 the Soviet Union had, for the first time, achieved nuclear parity with the United States. The achievement marked a decisive turning point in the global balance of power. Henceforth the USSR was able to deal with the US as a superpower of equal stature.

On the other hand the conflict also had its drawbacks for the Soviet Union. It exacerbated tension with China although, to a great extent, this would have surfaced irrespective of the struggle in Vietnam. More significantly, it caused a serious deterioration in Soviet-American relations which had been slowly improving during the early 1960s. A degree of amity was only reintroduced with the opening of the 1970s, when the emergence of detente heralded a search for a new basis for Soviet-American relations.

Sino-North Vietnamese cordiality was much improved after the failure of the Tet Offensive forced the PLAF/PAVN to reduce the scale of their operations. Fraternal solidarity was strained once again, however, when the large-scale Easter Offensive angered the Chinese for its flagrant breach of Maoist military dogma.

The United States reacted with force to the offensive. Nixon authorized *Linebacker I*, the mining of Haiphong harbour and the bombings of hitherto restricted targets in North Vietnam. Perhaps unexpectedly, Chinese and Soviet reaction to these potentially provocative measures was muted even though one Soviet ship was sunk as a direct result of the action. Although Soviet and Chinese military aid had furnished the materials for the offensive, both Moscow and Peking were anxious not to deflect the moves towards detente by making the offensive and the American response to it an issue of controversy. For the DRV, the warming of relations between Moscow and Washington and the Sino-American rapprochement of 1971–2 came as a profound shock and there was bitterness at the perceived betrayal (Chen 1972:815). The failure of their allies to place pressure on the US to curtail its militarily damaging action during the Easter Offensive must have brought back unhappy memories of Geneva and underlined to Hanoi that, whatever Moscow and Peking's presumed commitment to the success of the revolution in Vietnam, they would always place their own national interests above international proletarian solidarity.

Both of Hanoi's biggest patrons were pleased when the Paris Peace Accords were signed. It is unlikely that either applied any significant degree of coercion in order to encourage the DRV to reach a negotiated settlement. Peking did use its influence to encourage Hanoi to drop its demand that a negotiated settlement be conditional upon Thieu's resignation, and in 1972 Moscow did act as an intermediary conveying Kissinger's views to the DRV (Szulc 1974:43–5). But whilst this did amount to an important role for the Soviet Union and China, it did not indicate that Hanoi was responding to their express command. Neither could afford the opprobrium that would accrue to a power forcing the heroic Vietnamese into a deal that they did not want, and nor is it conceivable that, after years of bitter fighting, Hanoi would accede to pressure from those who had, in effect, sold them short in 1954.

What all this points to is the inescapable conclusion that the North Vietnamese and, by inference, the revolutionary movement in the South were no tools or dupes of Moscow or China. They were fiercely independent and if, at various times, they did side with one of the two communist giants it was simply because this served their own ends. There were no easily identifiable pro-Chinese or pro-Soviet factions within the DRV leadership and North Vietnam had no great emotional attachment to one as opposed to the other (Lawson 1984:175).

Viewed dispassionately, the DRV actually profited as a result of the Sino-Soviet dispute. Had there been no controversy and had Moscow and Peking worked in concert, world politics would naturally have been radically different. In the unlikely event that both had been opposed to the pursuit of a people's revolutionary war, it is possible that Hanoi would have been more restrained and less able to embark on a war in support of the southern revolutionary forces (Smith 1985:255). Under the circumstances created by the Sino-Soviet dispute, the affection of the NLF/DRV was an especially valuable commodity within the world revolutionary movement so enabling Hanoi to play one side off against the other. To benefit from this, however, the Vietnamese had to tread a cautious line in order to retain their room for manouevre and to ensure that they did not become irretrievably committed to either camp. To this end they developed a series of tactics designed to charm their patrons whilst simultaneously safeguarding their independence (Lawson 1984:47).

The essence of North Vietnam's approach was balance. The DRV's media coverage given to Moscow and Peking was comparable in terms of quantity and form. Delegations to and from the DRV were similar in size and importance and, with the exception of Yugoslavia, all communist nations received fulsome praise. To reinforce this diplomatic and ideological equilibrium the Vietnamese placed enormous emphasis upon the need for unity within the communist world. Effusive thanks were given to the Soviet Union, and China and Vietnam were said to be as close as 'lips and teeth'. In reality, nevertheless, there was not so much real warmth behind the words as a real appreciation of the value of deft diplomacy and political flattery. It was no coincidence, for example, that the warmth of Hanoi's praise for one or other of its supporters varied according to the schedule for renegotiation of military and economic aid agreements (Lawson 1984:175–6).

North Vietnam's independence was its strength. In the context of the Sino-Soviet dispute this granted a small and comparatively powerless nation a great deal of influence and surprising degree of latitude in the formulation of its strategy. In the same way that Washington found that its capacity to influence Saigon bore no relation to the control it exercised over the material factors of the war, so Moscow and Peking, because they acted separately, found that their power to influence Hanoi was not commensurate with their financial stake in the struggle. Throughout the war, leverage was never intimately related to a nation's intrinsic power. This was one of the reasons why it was difficult to make facile assumptions about international relationships and their impact upon the conflict. Perhaps the most obvious erroneous belief was the view that Kissinger and Nixon claimed to share in 1973 when they hoped that Chinese and Soviet persuasion would induce Hanoi to abide by the Paris Agreement. If they really believed this, it was a gross error of judgement. Washington's wealth of experience in dealing with a churlish and often intractable Saigon and the time and money they spent analysing the communist world should have sharpened their perceptions and made them significantly more sensitive to the limitations of power.

11 The end of the war and its aftermath

The last thing that the Paris Peace Agreement brought to Vietnam was peace. In the days prior to the Agreement PLAF/PAVN had seized territory in order to claim it as their own. The GVN responded by launching a counteroffensive immediately afterwards. The Americans may have departed from Vietnam, but the war did not.

Militarily drained by the Easter Offensive, the NLF/DRV temporarily assumed the defensive after the 'cease-fire' had been concluded (Kolko 1986:485), and the DRVs economy was reorganized along peacetime lines (Porter 1975:175–6). The revolutionary forces prudently wanted to recuperate and to avoid major clashes with the GVN, especially as RVNAF was replete with the bounty provided by the US under *operations Enhance* and *Enhance Plus*. Rather than continue the war at the same level of intensity, the material disadvantages of PLAF/PAVN forced them to rely upon destabilizing the Saigon government primarily through political mobilization. But Thieu was doing a masterly job of alienating his own people, irrespective of enemy activity and, ironically, the weaknesses of South Vietnamese society posed the biggest challenge to the survival of the regime (Kolko 1986:459).

Worldwide economic problems had exacerbated South Vietnam's own. The cities were overcrowded and many people were unemployed. In the rural areas, the Land-to-the-Tiller law had not propelled the peasants into the government fold and, in a series of moves during 1972 and 1973, Thieu had abolished the election of village and hamlet officials and had authorized the district chiefs to appoint suitable people. These counterproductive measures were undertaken because the regime believed, probably justifiably, that certain village chiefs had been collaborating with the NLF/DRV, but it still did little to improve the image of the government and its legitimacy in the eyes of many.

In characteristically ham-handed fashion, the GVN inaugurated a disastrous 'rice war' in the Mekong Delta in August 1973. Concerned that the enemy was receiving rice from local farmers, Thieu decreed that all rice supplies should be confiscated from families in areas adjacent to NLF/DRV territory. They were allowed to keep one week's supply and were given a ration to be collected at weekly intervals from GVN stores. The rest was purchased by the government at a price which was substantially below that obtained on the free market. Not surprisingly, the rice war was exceedingly unpopular amongst peasants who lost out not only to the government but also to the corrupt officials who managed the programme. It was a poorly conceived and dreadfully implemented policy and one which, ultimately, proved prejudicial to the GVN's cause in the Delta (Kolko 1986:466–7).

Large numbers of refugees, generated both before and after the 'cease-fire', were crammed into GVN controlled territory where there was not enough employment or land to make them self-sufficient. Many wanted to return to their native villages which were in the hands of the NLF/DRV and provisions in the Paris Agreement did facilitate this. Thieu, however, was adamant that movement should be stopped wherever possible. In effect, this doomed large numbers of people to unproductive lives in wholly inadequate camps and resettlement communities. Such restrictions consequently created a core of discontent within the population and thus constituted a serious liability to the GVN (Wiesner 1988:352–3).

Thieu's concern to halt movement into enemy areas was understandable, primarily because it would confer a greater legitimacy upon the rule of the NLF/DRV. The more people and the more territory one side could contol, the greater would be its claim to be the legitimate government of South Vietnam. Such reasoning provided Thieu with his initial motivation to assume an aggressive stance in the post-cease-fire war (Snepp 1980:58). Other pressures may also have motivated Thieu to act. He may have wanted to encourage the fighting so that the United States could not emotionally and psychologically disengage from the conflict (Porter 1975:184). If there had been a temporary peace, Washington might have been allowed the opportunity to view a resumption of hostilities as a separate war from the one in which it had fought. Thieu may have considered it advisable for the inevitable North-South showdown to occur quickly, before the US had time to distance itself from the conflict and to divest itself of responsibility for the GVN (Porter 1975:260). Nevertheless, as Thieu was always quite convinced that the US would never actually abandon Vietnam, these factors are open to doubt.

What emerged in the summer of 1973 was an aggressive GVN military policy which, in a somewhat contradictory fashion, was underpinned by Thieu's 'four no's. There was to be no coalition government, no legitimate role for the communists in South Vietnam, no negotiations with them nor any form of territorial concession. So, although ARVN was busy trying to capture land from the enemy, because the regime was committed to retaining all its own territory at whatever cost, it spread its forces very thinly so that it could maintain a presence everywhere. Particularly as the war increased in tempo during 1974, this meant that the GVN assumed a posture of static, passive defence while the PLAF/PAVN was free to mass and strike at poorly defended areas at will. It was no advantage for ARVN to be everywhere because it merely rendered it weak everywhere. Unable to break the pattern of twenty years, there was a massive flaw in ARVN's military planning which granted its enemy an important advantage.

The revolutionary forces did not sit idly by for long. In October 1973, the NLF/DRV authorized a change in strategy. Reliance upon political mobilization was scaled down and a more aggressive military policy was begun (Porter 1975:260). By May 1974 the defensive position assumed after the Paris Agreement was scrapped and the war was put into higher gear. By this time the balance of forces was changing very rapidly. As part of its preparation for a renewed offensive the DRV had sent further men and equipment into the South. The extent of this aid is controversial. At the time, the US and GVN claimed that some 75,000 men and 400 tanks were sent to the South after the cease-fire. A build-up of this scale is commonly accepted by various authorities on the war, but it has also been argued that the greater part of the build-up took place prior to January 1973 and that claims to the contrary were distortions used by the GVN and the US to illustrate Hanoi's bad faith (Porter 1975:202, 268).

Apart from the increased size of PAVN's military capability, other factors were decisive in swinging the military balance of forces in its favour. Firstly it had modernized its logistical system. New roads were built, the Ho Chi Minh Trail was widened and improved, and a pipeline was built so that forces in the South did not have to depend upon unreliable sources of fuel. Secondly, the disintegration of South Vietnamese society proceeded apace during PLAF/PAVN's period of defence and recuperation and when they resumed the offensive they were able to savour and exploit the regime's self-inflicted wounds. Thirdly, and most significantly of all, there was the situation in the United States. Washington, which had made and sustained the GVN, was divesting itself of the burden of supporting its artificial creation. This could mean only good news for the NLF/DRV. What they did not realize, nevertheless, was just how fast America was distancing itself from South Vietnam and just how swift its client regime's consequent degeneration would be.

Momentous changes were taking place in the US during 1973 and 1974. In part they were a product of the Vietnam War. What is undeniable is that they helped determine its outcome. Congress's years of pliant acceptance of the executive's iron hand on foreign policy and its direct manipulation and ignoring of the legislature, especially over Vietnam, were coming to a stormy and bitter end. Watergate was the issue over which this disaffection came to a head.

Inevitably the scandal and the increasingly terse relations between Congress and the president had a profound impact on Vietnam policy. It may be that Nixon and Kissinger never intended to commit themselves to the survival of the GVN. Perhaps they signed the Paris Agreement in the knowledge that Saigon would fall and that a negotiated settlement would provide the US with little more than a convenient interval in which it could distance itself from the fate of the GVN. But this question will never be answered because domestic politics overtook and paralysed the administration's execution of foreign policy. Nixon may even have been prepared to resume the bombing of North Vietnam in mid-April 1973, as has been claimed, but whatever plans he had were scuttled when he discovered that the Watergate issue was about to explode into a crisis (Lewy 1978:203–4).

On 31 July 1973, Congress had voted to end all bombing in Indochina. As if this was not a big enough repudiation of American commitment, Congress also refused to authorize the requested level of aid for South Vietnam. In 1973 aid had totalled $2.2 billion and in 1974, $900 million. The administration requested $1.6 billion for fiscal 1975. They got $700 million—less than half that supposedly necessary. That aid declined so drastically was partly thanks to those in the Pentagon who wanted to see the money better spent. This was especially pressing as finance was becoming restricted and as the Soviet Union was reputed to have forged ahead in the development of its strategic nuclear arsenal. The faction seeking to cut the amount of precious resources wasted by the profligate GVN formed a *de facto* alliance with those in Congress who saw the cut-backs in aid to Thieu and his regime as part of a larger cost-cutting exercise to get the national budget back in shape. It was to be the workings of this alliance rather than the effects of the antiwar lobby which fashioned Congress's more frugal attitude to South Vietnam (Kolko 1986:505).

At the same time as aid was being reduced to the GVN, China and the Soviet Union were cutting back on military aid to the DRV although, during the same period, the scale of economic aid did rise.

Lessening military aid did not entail any problems for PLAF/PAVN, however, because this was offset by the absence of US airpower and interdiction which had previously destroyed a proportion of the supplies sent south (Kolko 1986:474).

For the GVN, by comparison, the cut-backs in aid were devastating. Their impact was felt in four main ways. Firstly it compounded the economic problems. The rural economy had come to depend on capital; upon the use of fertilizers in order to grow high-yielding varieties of rice and upon gasoline to run motor driven equipment. Coupled with the rising price of oil and the world economic recession, aid reductions had a serious impact upon the standard of living of many farmers who had so recently come to relish an aid sponsored jamboree. It also impacted upon urban dwellers already suffering withdrawal symptoms after the free-spending American troops had vanished.

The second effect was psychological. South Vietnam felt that it was being abandoned and that the US no longer considered it worth saving. This attitude, and the creeping advance of hopelessness that accompanied it, was just as serious as the physical problems created by declining aid inputs (Hosmer 1980:9–10). The third area in which the reduction in American money was felt was in the military sphere. In terms of equipment and ammunition expenditure, the South Vietnamese still had a decisive advantage over their enemy. But, in real terms, less money led to a tightening of military belts. Ammunition, although still available in large quantities, was rationed and there was a shortage of fuel. What this meant was that ARVN could not fight the war in the way in which the Americans had and in the way in which it had been trained to fight. It could not use air and artillery support in an unrestricted fashion because it was just too expensive and it could not always rely upon helicopters and vehicles to transport troops and equipment for the same reason. ARVN was perplexed. It had, in the words of one South Vietnamese official, 'forgotten how to walk' (Hosmer 1980:88). Unfortunately, it did not remember soon enough.

Morale in the armed forces was gradually crumbling. The pay of soldiers, at all times ridiculously inadequate, reached a new low. In 1974 the average married ARVN soldier received only a third of the amount necessary to support his family at subsistence levels (Kolko 1986:468). Not only did falling levels of aid affect the amount of money in his pocket, it also meant that fighting became more dangerous for him. Less firepower was translated into a greater reliance upon the soldier rather than the equipment. Deaths inevitably increased (Hosmer 1980:98). More demoralizing still, the shortage of funds led, for example, to the tardy removal of wounded from the battlefield as ambulances would remain until there was a full complement of casualties in order to make the journey more cost-effective in a period of growing fuel shortages (Hosmer 1980:34–5). The cost in human terms was a long wait and perhaps someone's life. Needless to say, morale and the soldier's willingness to fight were seriously impaired as a result.

It was not as if those in Congress who determined the level of assistance to the GVN were giving totally inadequate funds. They were giving enough for a competently run army to fight a war. This was precisely the problem because ARVN was anything but competent. It had an astounding genius for mismanagement of most things—especially its money.

The fourth effect of the reduction in aid was that the legend of Thieu took a sharp knock. Many top people had supported him because it seemed that he was the man with the ability to divest the US of a good deal of its riches and the one able to dispense those riches with appropriate disregard for their intended use. Thieu's hold over the US treasury was no longer quite so magical and he could no longer grease quite as many palms with quite as much money. The effect was sobering. Thieu's political empire, built on foreign treasure and venal politicians and military men, was crumbling all around him.

Whilst the revolutionary forces were appearing increasingly threatening externally, by the autumn of 1974 the regime was also beset by internal problems. In the cities anti-Thieu groups had emerged. In particular, in July, Catholic priests had begun a People's Front Against Corruption. This resulted in Thieu making some suitable gestures when, in October, he began a crackdown on corruption, sacking ten cabinet ministers and a large number of lesser figures. Even so, this did not satisfy the campaigners as Thieu and members of his family were prime movers implicated in the sordid business.

In this atmosphere of growing social crisis and increasing military pressure, desperate measures began to be contemplated. A truncated South Vietnam was considered. The northern part of the country could be abandoned to the enemy and a giant redoubt made of Saigon and the Mekong Delta. Thieu, sticking to his 'four no's' would not hear of it and despite rumours and plots to overthrow him, the president would not be budged. He remained, until the end, a master of intrigue and the controlling hand in the burlesque world of Saigon politics.

It was against this background that the NLF/DRV decided to launch an offensive aimed at overthrowing the GVN. Realizing that US airpower was unlikely to return to complement RVNAF's defence, the Party in Hanoi decided that the time was right to bring the war to a successful conclusion. According to their plans, 1975 was to be a year of preparatory military strikes and 1976 was to be the time to topple the South Vietnamese regime. What they did not anticipate, nevertheless, was the swift momentum of the GVN's collapse once they had set it in motion.

The débâcle began with a PAVN attack on Ban Me Thuot in the Central Highlands on 10 March 1975. By the next day it had seized control of the city. Thieu then began to make a series of truly spectacular and terrible decisions which delivered victory to his enemy without them really having to fight for it. True to form, the GVN had set about destroying itself.

As if in a scene from a military strategist's nightmare, Thieu ordered the Central Highlands to be abandoned within two days. The withdrawal that began on 16 March was a catastrophe. The departure was totally chaotic. ARVN units were abandoned by their commanders and whole companies dissolved with lightning speed. Panicking civilians then joined frantic soldiers in a hideous exodus to the coast. As PAVN bombed the column, trucks literally ground people into the road in the rush to escape. The GVN's air force even did its bit by mistakenly attacking the retreating army and civilians. Of the 60,000 troops that began the withdrawal from Pleiku in the Highlands, only 20,000 made it to the coast and of 400,000 civilians only 100,000 survived (Davidson 1988:778–9). But worse was to follow.

On 12 March Thieu had ordered the elite Airborne Division defending northern South Vietnam to move to Saigon. He did this principally for political reasons, fearing that the commander of the region had designs upon his office. Militarily the move was yet another disaster. As if to sow further confusion Thieu then authorized that northern South Vietnam be abandoned and that a defensive line be drawn at Danang. He then considered that Hue, further north, should be held. Thieu may have been a skilled politician but, as a military leader, he was proving to be the very worst liability that the GVN possessed.

Mass hysteria erupted as troops and civilians surged into the coastal cities. Hue and Danang, where 2 million people congregated, witnessed scenes of unrivalled hysteria. No one was in control. Terror reigned. An unabated series of killing, raping and stealing began and troops brutally murdered defenceless civilians in the orgy of violence released by the panic. In their haste to escape to ships waiting to evacuate the armed forces, soldiers shot at any one who stood in their way, killed one another to ensure themselves a place and drowned while trying to swim to safety.

The success of the revolutionary forces owed less to the fact that they defeated RVNAF in battle than to the fact that the GVN crumbled before them. Commanders abandoned their units and troops disappeared leaving behind expensive military equipment supplied by the US. In total, US $5 billion worth of military hardware was to fall into enemy hands.

In many instances the revolutionary forces did little more than to step into the void created by the dissolution of the RVNAF and its civilian counterparts. There were some cases of bravery and heroic rearguard actions by a few South Vietnamese units but these were the exception. RVNAF was being defeated as much by its own weaknesses as by the force of North Vietnamese arms.

Although the DRV had planned to conquer the South in 1976, they quickly reappraised their strategy in light of their rapid advance. Concluding that the GVN was in the process of implosion, it was decided to press on with the offensive and to overwhelm the South in the current campaigning season.

The relentless disintegration of the RVNAF and civil society proceeded apace throughout March and April. Right up until the last moment, the GVN leadership believed that the US would send its airpower to the rescue. After so many years and the outlay of so much prestige and money, they could not believe that America would abandon them (Hosmer 1980:38–42). In January, in a bid to buttress Thieu's image and restore his reputation as the man who held the key to America's coffers, the US administration requested a supplemental aid request for South Vietnam (Kolko 1986:511–12). But as the disaster unfolded, Congress grew more averse to wasting money on a lost cause. In March, therefore, the request was turned down. This action did not doom the GVN. It was already disintegrating. It may have lowered morale a little more, but at such a late stage, money could not have saved South Vietnam (Kolko 1986:534). The North Vietnamese offensive had exposed the artificiality of the GVN and had triggered its demise. By the end of April there were eighteen PAVN divisions poised outside Saigon. When they entered on 30 April 1975, Thieu had fled and the government left in charge surrendered unconditionally.

Several factors played a crucial role in the final days of South Vietnam. There was, as Ngueyn Ba Can said, a 'psychological collapse' (Hosmer 1980:56) as a result of the pressures of the war. This pyschological disintegration was nationwide and affected important individuals such as President Thieu himself, ultimately leading him to make serious errors of military judgement. The abandonment of the Highlands was one of these strategic errors as was the withdrawal of the Airborne Division from the northern provinces. These moves set in motion an irreversible train of events.

Thieu made rash decisions because the GVN had no comprehensive military plans to use as guidelines. Neglect to draw up plans and make adequate preparations was partially the product of RVNAF's legendary unprofessionalism, but it was also thought to be defeatist and unpatriotic (Hosmer 1980:112). Yet even if suitable plans had existed it would have been highly unlikely that the RVNAF could have carried them out. The calibre of the forces' leadership was poor and after years of deferring to US political and military control, the American withdrawal had produced a leadership vacuum (Hosmer 1980:87).

The units that ARVN's inadequate leaders commanded were demoralized and often understrength. Troops too were affected by the nation's psychological collapse and their fighting ability suffered accordingly. Most importantly, the average ARVN soldier could not appreciate why he should risk his life to preserve a government that did little for him (Lewy 1984:3). Thus, when he found himself on the verge of battle with the enemy, frequently abandoned by senior officers who were busy making good their escape, it was not surprising that the soldier should think less of his government and rather more of the safety of his family. Concern for relatives in the path of the advancing revolutionary forces was a very real problem because some families accompanied soldiers and set up camp near to them. The priority that the troops gave to the safety of their family as opposed to their commitment to the armed forces was known as the 'family syndrome' and it was a major contributor to the military's collapse (Hosmer 1980:126–7, Kolko 1986:527). It was particularly acute as memories of the slaughter in Hue during the Tet Offensive drove people into a blind panic, fearful that they too would share the same grisly fate.

There were a considerable number of Vietnamese who were legitimately afraid for their safety in the event of a NLF/DRV victory. This applied especially to those people who had worked closely with the Americans in intelligence and political work. Unfortunately the evacuation of such individuals was handled extremely badly by the US embassy in Saigon. The removal of high-risk collaborators was delayed so long that the evacuation process became caught up in the rapid advance of the revolutionary forces and entangled in the chaos. In the absence of a well orchestrated plan, people who were not in danger were evacuated to safety and thousands, to whom the Americans had an obligation and who were in real danger, were abandoned. In many instances, the US even failed to destroy important intelligence dossiers and files on their South Vietnamese collaborators (Snepp 1980:473). The evacuation and the final withdrawal of America from Vietnam was, in the opinion of one CIA operative who watched it first hand, an 'institutional disgrace' (Snepp 1980:474).

South Vietnam was finally conquered by an invading army from North Vietnam. It was not defeated by indigenous revolutionaries from the South, although this distinction may not have been so clear to those Vietnamese who argued that North and South Vietnam were one country. General Van Tien Dung's account of the offensive that he led against the GVN clearly reveals that it was a conventional military offensive that toppled the Saigon regime (Van Tien Dung 1977).

It has become accepted wisdom that the native revolutionary forces were defeated during the Tet Offensive in 1968, and that, thereafter, the war was a traditional conflict. This is not entirely true. The NLF was still a powerful force in some areas of the country and what influence the NLF had lost had not been transmuted into support for the GVN (Lewy 1984:9). Kolko goes further in stressing the importance of the NLF by claiming for it a role of 'immense strategic value' in the fall of South Vietnam (Kolko 1986:536). Specifically, he points to the contribution that local forces made to the policing of liberated areas and to the support of conventional units. It remains true, nevertheless, that PAVN, which planned and carried out the offensive, would have won irrespective of the complementary role played by local militia and guerrillas.

That the war was won in its final stages by conventional forces, and that the world witnessed North Vietnamese tanks rumbling through Saigon's streets, led to the assertion that a people's revolutionary war had failed and that claims to the contrary were a 'fraud' (Lomperis 1984:173). Superficially this is true. But PAVN could win the conventional war only because the people's war had politically defeated the United States. This is not, of course, the same as saying that the revolutionary forces won the war, but their role in preparing the political and social context for the final denouement was immense and indispensable.

The failure of the NLF to deliver final victory in the South has led to an interesting perspective on the war and the post-war period. The struggle was between rival ideologies which sought to establish and consolidate their own claim to national legitimacy. The GVN, quite clearly, never achieved this. However, because it was not a native South Vietnamese movement which won the war, it has been suggested that the new revolutionary government also lacked legitimacy (Lomperis 1984:164). Considering how much the war altered the society of South Vietnam and how difficult it has been to integrate the two halves of the country, there may be an element of truth in this argument.

POST-WAR VIETNAM

The NLF/DRV inherited a chaotic situation in the south. Because they had not anticipated such a speedy victory they had not drawn up plans to manage the interim period between the collapse of Saigon's authority and the establishment of the revolutionary government's writ.

Once they had consolidated their control, the new rulers had gigantic problems with which to contend. The economy was in appalling shape and was held together only by foreign aid. The cities were full of people they could not sustain. Approximately 34 per cent of the nation's population lived in urban areas (Duiker 1980:5) and Saigon had between 3.5 and 4.5 million inhabitants (Thrift and Forbes 1986:53). The social fabric of the south had been irretrievably wrenched apart and, especially in the cities where there were as many as half a million prostitutes (Eisen 1984:45) and all the vice-ridden trappings of a culture mesmerized by the West and degenerated by poverty, it appeared that the new government faced an almost insoluble problem.

The integration of the south into the northern economy was initially intended to proceed over a number of years, but by the middle of 1976 the transition to socialism in the south was greatly accelerated. The new government was finding it very difficult to establish control over the private sector. Furthermore, the corrupting ways of life in the south were said to be having a deleterious effect upon the attitude of cadres and, by implication, upon the society of the more frugal and regimented north (Duiker 1980:11). Consequently the south began to be propelled along the path taken by the north twenty years earlier.

Political integration proceeded quickly. The PRP was absorbed within the Lao Dong Party and, in July 1976, the Vietnamese Communist Party was formed. The NLF too was absorbed within its northern counterpart, the Fatherland Front. However, in the process of integration the southern-based organizations lost a large proportion of their power. The government of the NLF, the PRG, for instance, did not come to rule the south and its representation in the national government was derisory (Truong Nhu Tang 1986:264–70). Because they were thought to be more ideologically committed, uncorrupted and free from pro-southern regional bias, leadership of united Vietnam became the preserve of the old guard revolutionaries from the former DRV.

There was some sporadic resistance to the new government, particularly from vestiges of RVNAF who continued to fight on and from US-trained Montagnard tribesmen, but whilst it rumbled on throughout the late 1970s, it was little more than an irritation and posed no real threat to the new regime.

From the outset, the newly established Socialist Republic of Vietnam encountered economic difficulties. Not only did it have to contend with the problems of the northern economy which had long-standing structural imbalances, but the southern economy was in a terrible condition and a significant section of the population, accustomed to years of US aid and the flexibility of the free market, were proving reluctant socialists. Collectivization was one of the worst casualties, especially in the Mekong Delta where farmers owned their land and had a comparatively high standard of living. After over a century in which individualism had been taking root in Cochinchina, few people wanted to farm collectively. Collectivization in the Delta was therefore a failure (Beresford 1988:63). By the end of 1985, 90 per cent of households had joined collectives but these were not full cooperatives as in the north (Beresford 1988:64). In southern Annam, or the north of the former South Vietnam, the war's social transformation of the countryside had not been as thorough as in the Mekong Delta. People were poorer, the level of commercialized farming far more limited and the communal ideal a little stronger. Collectivization in this environment was far easier (Beresford 1988:62).

Low productivity in the agricultural sector and imbalances, shortages and draining poverty characterized the Vietnamese economy. Aid was vital to alleviate some of the very worst conditions. Although a form of 'reparations' had been discussed between the US and the Vietnamese both during and after the war, the discussions amounted to nothing and the US did not give war-torn Vietnam any aid. Moreover, it encouraged other nations to join an economic boycott in order to protest against post-war Vietnam's foreign policy. As a result, Vietnam came to tie itself ever further to the Soviet Union because it alone was willing and able to provide vital assistance. In return the Soviet Union was granted Vietnam's political support and the use of the vast US-built naval bases at Danang and Cam Ranh Bay.

The government hoped to develop Vietnam into an industrial socialist state and to improve its very low standards of living. It aimed to do this through tight regulation of the economy and through the redistribution of people from densely populated areas. This latter policy was also pursued on a more limited scale in the DRV prior to unification but in the post-war period it took on a new urgency. New Economic Zones were created in lightly populated areas, particularly in the Central Highlands and in border regions in southern Vietnam. Since 1975 over half a million people have moved to the Central Highlands particularly from the overcrowded Tonkin Delta. Around 350,000 of these have migrated since 1981 (*Far Eastern Economic Review* 25 May 1989:42). The policy was not without significant problems, however. There were claims that the government was pressurizing families to migrate (*Far Eastern Economic Review* 25 May 1989:42) and it has also created tension with the Montagnard peoples, as many of the new settlements were situated on tribal lands. Some even thought that the influx of lowland Vietnamese was encouraged not solely because of economic imperatives but also because it would be a powerful antidote to the tribal discontent which made the Highlands a focus of opposition to the Communist Party's rule (*Far Eastern Economic Review* 25 May 1989:42).

In the late 1970s Vietnam's economic crisis deteriorated to the point where the sixth plenum of the VCP (Vietnamese Communist Party) in 1979 instituted a number of liberal reforms which encouraged the private sector and, especially household production, to grow. Then, in 1986 in response to the disastrous economic situation, the VCP undertook a political shake-up. Three of the old guard revolutionaries who were generally committed to the ideological purity of the revolution resigned and Nguyen Van Linh was appointed to lead the Party. His appointment was significant because Linh was the man who had overseen the introduction of a pilot programme of liberal economic measures in the south. The reforms that he has since presided over have attempted to replace central planning with a more deregulated economy, to provide financial incentives to improve poor performance and output and to create some room for a free market to operate.

There is a tendency for those who supported the American's role in Vietnam to look, somewhat smugly, at the disasters that have befallen the Vietnamese economy since the communists won in 1975. While it is true that many of the problems have been of the government's own making, many are not. Vietnam is a small, poor, under-developed country. Its per capita income in 1985 at $220 (Todaro 1989:52) is amongst the lowest in the world. It was poor before the war and its economy was savaged during thirty years of bitter fighting. The prosperity that was apparent in South Vietnam during the years of American involvement in the war was not only the result of the Mekong Delta's fertility. It also came courtesy of US aid and the spin-offs of the US military presence. Once this disappeared, the economy began to contract. The Vietnamese government cannot possibly hope to recreate such days of abundance even with Soviet aid.

There are some positive signs on the economic horizon. Tough new measures introduced since March 1989 appear to be having some impact in reducing government spending, reducing the budget deficit and curbing hyperinflation. However, after years of unmitigated economic gloom it is too early to assess the long-term success of these measures.

Complimenting the more favourable financial forecast is the international context for Vietnam. Since 1979 Vietnam has been penalized financially for its foreign policy. The work of international aid agencies has been curtailed and Vietnam has been economically ostracized in the West, primarily as a result of its invasion of Cambodia in 1978 and also because Vietnam defaulted on its loans in 1985. There are indications, nevertheless, that this is beginning to change. The IMF and the World Bank are returning to Vietnam, and the country's South East Asian neighbours, after years of hostility, are softening their attitude. Thailand, in particular, is leading the way towards an accommodation with Hanoi. Vietnam's neighbours have been motivated to reverse their approach because of the increased likelihood of a relaxation of the restrictions that the West has placed on commerical relations with Indochina. The reason for this more promising commercial climate is Vietnam's changing policy towards Cambodia.

There was no peace following the war for the unification of Vietnam. Long-standing ethnic antagonism between the Cambodians and the Vietnamese flared into border clashes within months. The Cambodian communists, called the Khmer Rouge, had overthrown the government of Lon Nol in 1975 and had proceeded to impose a barbaric reign of terror upon the people of Cambodia, which claimed the lives of as many as 2 million. Whilst both newly installed governments were communist in name, no fraternal love was lost between them. The leadership of the Khmer Rouge, headed by Pol Pot, hated the Vietnamese communists for the perceived injuries and slights they had inflicted upon their Cambodian comrades and also because Vietnam was, historically, an aggressive power which had expanded at the expense of Cambodian lives and soil. Massacres of ethnic Vietnamese living in Cambodia, then termed Kampuchea, and massacres of people living just across the border was the first phase of Pol Pot's vengeance and a reflection of his desire to use the anti-Vietnam card to unite the country behind his rule.

Arguments over disputed territory, Vietnamese protests over Khmer Rouge abuse of ethnic Vietnamese and armed clashes in border regions strained relations to such a point that Vietnam invaded Kampuchea in December 1978, overthrew the Pol Pot regime and installed its own Hanoi-backed government. This action earned Vietnam international condemnation and caused it to be placed in economic quarantine by the West.

Vietnam's Cambodian entanglement had another dimension. It was a manifestation of resurgent Sino-Vietnamese antipathy which had been submerged during the Second Indochina War. China had always been fearful of an expansionist Vietnam on its southern border and it was concerned that Vietnam was going to build a Hanoi-dominated Indochinese federation. Consequently, Peking encouraged Pol Pot's activities because such diversions were a useful means of restraining the spread of Vietnamese power throughout South East Asia. To Vietnam, therefore, the invasion of Cambodia was undertaken not only to relieve them of Pol Pot's irritating behaviour, but also to ensure national survival by removing the Chinese menace from Cambodia (Duiker 1986:66).

Direct conflict broke out between China and Vietnam in reaction to Vietnam's invasion of Cambodia. Relations had been deteriorating very fast since the end of the Second Indochina War. In March 1978 Hanoi had decreed the nationalization of all large-scale private enterprises. The target of this measure was the powerful Chinese business community in Ho Chi Minh City, formerly Saigon, which Hanoi suspected had a dubious loyalty to the Socialist Republic of Vietnam. The PRC stated that its nationals were being persecuted by the regime as refugees began to flee across the border into China and to leave Vietnam by boat. Following Hanoi's establishment of firmer links with the Soviet Union and its joining of CMEA (Council for Mutual Economic Assistance), a furious China then decided to cut off aid to its former client.

Intending to pressure Hanoi to desist from its policy in Cambodia and to teach it a lesson, in February 1979, Chinese troops crossed the Sino-Vietnamese border and devastated the town of Lang Son before being pushed back by fierce Vietnamese resistance. China's action did not force the Vietnamese out of Cambodia and thereafter relations between Vietnam and China have been hostile and there have been intermittent clashes along their mutual border.

In addition to restricting foreign aid, Vietnam's role in the renewed fighting in Indochina drained its already fragile economy. Hanoi has been obliged to maintain one of the largest standing armies in the world in order to pursue its policy in Cambodia and to strengthen its border with China. The cost of the Vietnamese occupation of Cambodia has been high because of the loss of aid and contact with the West and also because it has absorbed a high proportion of the national budget. Admittedly much of the cost has been borne by the USSR but a good deal of this money could have been far better spent. In many respects what has become known as the Third Indochina War is the continuation of traditional animosities and hostilities that have simmered and periodically flared up in the region for centuries. But both this conflict and Vietnam's war against the French and later the Americans have been influenced by the global struggle between communism and the West and by the ideological split between China and the Soviet Union. The war between Cambodia and Vietnam has even been seen as a war by proxy—as a struggle between the Soviet-supported government in Hanoi and the Peking-backed Khmer Rouge (Duiker 1986:91–3). Logically, it was only when there was a thawing of Sino-Soviet relations that an accommodation could be reached and the Vietnamese could end their occupation of Cambodia.

In the summer of 1989, tension in mainland South East Asia was lessening. Vietnam pledged to withdraw its forces from Cambodia by September 1989 and Sino-Vietnamese hostilities ceased. In late 1988 China ceased shelling Vietnam and Hanoi removed its anti-aircraft guns from the sensitive border region. In December 1988 the border was opened to trade and one month later the first high-level meeting for nine years took place between the two countries.

Withdrawal from Cambodia will effectively end Vietnam's economic quarantine and lessen the burden on its shaky economy. This must obviously be a vital consideration for Hanoi. But even though Vietnam is pulling out the threat from Pol Pot has not been contained and it is not certain that Hanoi's client regime in Phnom Penh will be able to hold its own against an opposition coalition which includes Prince Sihanouk and the internationally denounced Pol Pot.

Arguably one of the main reasons influencing Hanoi's decision to withdraw from Cambodia and helping to bring about a reduction in Sino-Vietnamese antipathy is the changing context within the communist bloc. Economic considerations are of importance to Peking. It wants to divert resources away from the military as a major feature of its reform campaign. More important is the growing Sino-Soviet rapprochement. Soviet president Mikhail Gorbachev is anxious to encourage improved relations with China. War by proxy in Cambodia would not promote this and the Kremlin is unwilling to go on paying for a war that Hanoi appears incapable of winning outright. China for its part is hesitant to derail improved relations by involving itself in further acrimonious disputes with Vietnam (*Financial Times* 24 January 1989). With luck a solution to Vietnam's foreign policy problems will help to alleviate some of the pressures on its chaotic economy and reduce the exodus of economic migrants.

Many of the people who have fled from Vietnam since unification have been fleeing from barely tolerable economic conditions. In general, the first to leave were ethnic Chinese who were persecuted by the regime, especially during the early period of overt hostilities with Cambodia and China. Many fled over the border into China and many left by sea. Since then countless Chinese and Vietnamese have left Vietnam,

The end of the war and its aftermath   271

primarily by boat. They have become known as the boat people. The exact numbers of refugees leaving in this manner is not known, as many of the unseaworthy craft in which they departed sank in the notoriously unpredictable seas and a further, inestimable number, have been brutally killed by pirates. A generally accepted approximate figure, however, is that over 2 million have tried to escape from Vietnam (*Far Eastern Economic Review* 30 March 1989:24).

Most refugees claim political persecution but increasingly they are economic migrants who, up until 1988–9, have been guaranteed political refugee status by the West because of the communist victory in Vietnam and the political background to it. America, in particular, after years of predicting the horrors that would accompany a North Vietnamese victory were morally obliged to receive refugees. But, almost fifteen years after unification, the numbers fleeing are once again rising, probably as a result of the intensity of the economic crisis. Hong Kong received almost 13,000 refugees in 1987, over 21,000 in 1988 and the projected total for 1989 is as high as 50,000 (*Financial Times* 3 March 1989). Moreover, most of these refugees have come from northern Vietnam. Since it has been a communist state since 1954 there are less grounds for claiming political persecution as the motivation for leaving. In response, in June 1988, Britain ordered screening of the new arrivals and the forcible repatriation of those who were not political refugees. So far, only those who did so voluntarily have been returned to Vietnam. Hanoi, for its part, insists that it will accept only those who wish to return and that once back in Vietnam the returnees will not be mistreated

Vietnam's South East Asian neighbours have also faced difficulties in coping with the influx of boat people, and Malaysia, only a few days' sailing away, has been particularly hard hit by refugees from southern Vietnam. After years of accommodating the refugees their attitude has hardened. In 1988 Thailand began an unofficial policy of pushing off and redirecting boats full of refugees that landed on its shores (*Far Eastern Economic Review* 23 February 1989:27–8) and, in March 1989, the member states of the Association of South East Asian Nations (ASEAN) announced that the boat people would no longer be eligible for automatic resettlement.

It is a measure of Vietnam's economic and political malaise that so many people have paid fortunes to escape and have risked their lives in overcrowded, unseaworthy vessels. An indeterminate proportion of the boat people have been legitimate political refugees fleeing from persecution. Although the bloodbath anticipated by some in the West thankfully never materialized after reunification, thousands of people were placed in re-education camps. Military leaders, important civil servants and an assortment of characters that the new regime considered to be politically undesirable were detained, some for many years. There are constant reports of inadequate conditions in Vietnamese prisons and abuse of human rights. Doan Van Toai, in his book *The Vietnamese Gulag,* has given a graphic and horrifying description of life in detention. Written by a man who was a supporter of the NLF and who was wrongly imprisoned, his work is a sad reflection on the political atmosphere in post-liberation Vietnam (Doan Van Toai 1986). His is not the only indictment of Hanoi's political activities. Others too bear out his portrayal of the new Vietnam. Some claim, like Nguyen Long, that the people are held in 'near slavery' (Nguyen Long 1981: ix). The picture may be overdrawn and overly gloomy because so much is written by those who were sympathetic to the former regime in South Vietnam. Notwithstanding this, there is enough evidence of human rights violations to seriously discredit the Hanoi regime. The Socialist Republic of Vietnam may be the end result of a struggle against centuries of social and economic injustice and the product of a war fought against foreign imperialism, but it faces a long and difficult task to prove itself worthy of the sacrifices made on its behalf. It is only to be hoped that it will not fall victim to the disease that so often afflicts worthy causes—that revolutions betray those who believe in them and communist parties in power think that the justice of their cause grants them the liberty to trample on those values and those people whom they supposedly fought for.

AMERICA AND THE LEGACY OF THE VIETNAM WAR

After Saigon crumbled before North Vietnam's tanks, the nations of South East Asia did not succumb, in succession, to communism. Cambodia and Laos 'fell', but this was only to be expected as Indochina had become one large theatre of operations during the latter stages of the war. Yet none of the larger states in the region was toppled. On the contrary, a number of nations enjoyed a giant economic boom and consolidated their political stability in the post-war years. The dire predictions of the domino theory did not come to pass.

Many of those who supported the war in Vietnam blame Congress for the collapse of the GVN. The reduction in aid is variously described as 'ignoble' (Podhoretz 1982:172), as 'a spasm of congressional irresponsibility' (Nixon 1985:165) and as the 'root cause' of South Vietnam's defeat (Colby 1978:287). This 'stab in the back' theory is not an adequate explanation. South Vietnam collapsed because it was artificially created and maintained. When the US did not supply the correct quantity of aid and support to maintain it, the GVN imploded. As Jonathan Schell aptly expressed it, South Vietnam 'did not so much collapse as fail ever to be born' (Schell 1989:18). Whatever power the GVN wielded came directly from the United States and without American money and American military force it was unsustainable.

For all those to whom the war was abhorrent and to those who realized that the United States was trying to mould a nation and a foreign culture so that it would fit snugly into America's global vision, the collapse of South Vietnam was the inevitable culmination of misguided policies. America's creation could not survive without it. Conversely, for those to whom the war was fought 'for the sake of an ideal' (Podhoretz 1982:197) and who believed in the necessity of saving Vietnam from communism, the withdrawal from South East Asia and the reductions in aid to the GVN can only be interpreted as the abandonment of a protege and a morally indefensible renunciation of commitment.

With hindsight, the Vietnam War was not a 'great' event in American history. It did not force change so much as catalyse change (May 1987:9). Since the high point of US power in the years immediately following the Second World War, America's stature in the world has been in relative decline. Vietnam threw this into relief (Komer 1987:314). According to ex-president Nixon, the war left America 'crippled psychologically'. But this is not entirely accurate. There was a dovish consensus amongst the young and amongst elite opinion in the aftermath of the war, but this was shattered by the Iran hostage crisis and the Soviet invasion of Afghanistan (Koenig 1987:96). Thus, whilst the administration of Jimmy Carter had witnessed a form of neoisolationism, the election of Ronald Reagan signified that a resurgent, more self-confident America was ready to begin coming to terms with the war and its defeat in South East Asia.

The 'Vietnam syndrome' has not curtailed US willingness to use force to achieve its objectives. The rate of military employments since 1975 has been consistent with the 1945–75 period (Zelikow 1987:46). Yet there is a significant difference in that the type and scale of force have been altered. Since Vietnam, US administrations have chosen to use numerically small forces in a less intrusive manner (Zelikow 1987:45). Moreover, America has moved away from worldwide commitments and has concentrated far more specifically on clearly defined spheres of action/interest in Central America, the Caribbean, the Middle East and North Africa (Zelikow 1987:37).

In some measure these changes are a product of the war and,

incontrovertibly, the memory of Vietnam has led to public abhorrence of protracted war and to a reluctance by the military to get its own troops involved in inconclusive wars in Central America (Koenig 1987:101, Taylor and Petraeus 1987:260–1). Clearly, this had a formative effect upon the Reagan administration's policy in Nicaragua and El Salvador. An overt US presence has to be restricted in El Salvador and Reagan battled with Congress over funding for the Contras who fought the Sandinista government of Nicaragua. Such constraints even prompted sections of the administration to conduct the clandestine funding of the Contras. This was exposed as an important element in the Irangate scandal. A significant motivation for this extra-legal activity was the desire to circumvent Congress. The legislature, stirred from its lethargy by Vietnam and Watergate, now plays a more important role in foreign policy decisionmaking and appears to be an equal and, sometimes, the senior partner in this area of policymaking (Walker 1987:117).

Yet it is not just Vietnam that has changed attitudes and American military responses. The perception of the communist threat has dwindled and, with it, so has the imperative of containment (Mueller 1987:302). A lessening desire to become entangled in foreign wars is consistent with the fear of more 'Vietnams' but also with the relaxation of rigid containment doctrine.

This is not to say that America was not profoundly affected by Vietnam. For a time, defeat created a crisis of national confidence. After an outlay of 58,000 lives, $150 billion and incalculable emotional energy, Vietnam could not be forgotton so easily. America wanted a victory in a war in order to recoup its self-esteem, but no administration could afford to pay the costs in lives and money. Reagan found the answer in the invasion of the tiny island of Grenada (Schell 1989:41).

For the US military, coming to terms with Vietnam has been even more difficult. Understandably, the armed forces are not enamoured of the Vietnam War and if they have learned any lessons from the conflict they are probably not the most appropriate ones (Krepinevich 1986:269). The counterinsurgency doctrine took a hefty knock with the defeat. Despite the fact that it was not implemented correctly or on a wide enough scale, counterinsurgency was discredited in the minds of the military and even its name was changed. After Vietnam it increasingly became known as low-intensity conflict (LIC). Moreover, once the expedition into the jungles and paddy fields of South East Asia had ended, the military saw fit to dispose of counterinsurgency as an 'abberation' created by the unique Vietnam situation (Waghelstein 1987:129). Troops and officers received even fewer hours training in the controversial subject and there was a renewed emphasis on training for the kind of war that America fought well. The capability of the Special Forces was expanded fractionally in response to the Central American political and military situation, but for a few years after the end of the Vietnam War counterinsurgency languished in the doldrums (Waghelstein 1987:129), the victim of the military's need to blame defeat on anything but hallowed traditional tactics.

The Vietnam War has been rehabilitated politically and the spate of films on the conflict are helping to rehabilitate it culturally. But while the embarrassing memories are dulled by frequently voiced claims that the US could have won if only things had been done differently, the men who served in Vietnam have not been cast in the role of America's prodigal sons. There is a lingering suspicion about the mental health of Vietnam veterans which was encouraged by their portrayal in the media. Reagan may have claimed the war to be 'noble', but the Vietnam veterans are still not treated as heroes. They did not receive the same kind of preferential treatment as their the Second World War counterparts and post-service mental and physical care for them has been far less than optimal. Veterans suffering from the effects of herbicide use and, specifically, the use of Agent Orange had to fight inordinately hard in order to get their plight recognized, and it was not until November 1982 that those who died in Vietnam were honoured by a memorial in Washington. Even this was dedicated amidst an acrimonious debate about the suitablity of the design and the designer. Shamefully, President Reagan did not attend the ceremony.

Part of the problem is that the veterans' organizations which run programmes for veterans, determine priorities and which wield vast powers have been unwilling to take on board the Vietnam veteran. Instead, they remain overwhelmingly commited to the interests of those men who fought in the Second World War (Bonior 1984:99–117). The needs of those who served in Vietnam are thus downgraded.

Presidential interest in righting the slights done to the veterans of the war in South East Asia has been limited. Lack of concern and action consequently meant that America 'did not honour its debt to the Vietnam veterans' (Bonior 1984:188). Perhaps most damaging of all to those who lost sons, brothers, husbands and fathers in the war, is the thought that their sacrifice is unappreciated and in vain. Those who died in combat against Germany and Japan were seen as heroes fighting for a noble and successful cause. In stark contrast, not only did America lose the war in Vietnam but the cause for which they died was also dragged through the mud. For those who lost family and comrades in the fighting, their loss must be that much more difficult to bear because it seems unacknowledged and ultimately pointless.

*

The defeat of the US in Vietnam gave heart to revolutionary movements throughout the world. It illustrated that the weak could defeat the mighty. Yet the conflict contained uncomfortable lessons for those practising a people's revolutionary war. There was nothing inevitable about a PLAF/PAVN victory. American military policy tore South Vietnam from its roots. Conceivably, it could have carried on doing so and completely transformed the country. If a people's revolutionary war is waged by the people and is a product of their society, then the insurgency can be controlled by completely altering that society. The US had the power and the money to accomplish this in a small nation like South Vietnam, but it did not have the political will to see it through.

If America has to learn one lesson from Vietnam, it is that it is impossible to conduct a long and painful war without creating and maintaining public support for the endeavour. But as people tire of war and killing and the accompanying economic hardships, and as a democratic society can always vote a less militant government to power, the likelihood that America could fight a long war is questionable. When it comes to wars, the US has not got military staying power.

There is a major school of thought that believes that the US military would have won if it had not been for the restrictions imposed by the politicians and if the presidents, and especially Johnson, had rallied the nation behind the war. Presuming that this had been achieved and that the nation had been behind the war, it is debatable how long it would have remained supportive of a conflict so far away, so destructive of men and materials and so damaging to America's image in the world. But this is one of the controversial and ultimately specious 'what ifs' of history. The thesis is, more than anything, a contribution to that revisionist school of history which seeks to remould Vietnam into the war which America could have won. Apparently only by this means will the US be totally liberated from the mental discomfiture imposed by its defeat. Perhaps by reinterpreting the war in this manner it will learn to unlearn the lessons of Vietnam. With history rewritten and the Vietnam War analysed, dissected and discarded, America may free itself of its debilitating failure and see fit to act, once again, to create the world in its own image.

Bibliography

Ambrose, S.E. (1984) *Eisenhower,* New York: Simon & Schuster.
Arlen, M.J. (1969) *Living-Room War,* New York: Viking Press.
Baritz, L. (1985) *Backfire: A History of How American Culture Led Us Into Vietnam and Made Us Fight the Way We Did,* New York: William Morrow.
Baskir, L.M. and Strauss, W.A. (1978) *Chance and Circumstance. The Draft, the War and the Vietnam Generation,* New York: Random House, Vintage Books.
Beresford, M. (1988) *Vietnam: Politics, Economics and Society,* London: Pinter.
Berman, L. (1982) *Planning a Tragedy: The Americanization of the War in Vietnam,* New York: W.W.Norton.
Berman, L. (1984) 'Waiting For Smoking Guns: Presidential Decision-making and the Vietnam War 1965–1967', in P.Braestrup (ed.) *Vietnam As History: Ten Years After the Paris Peace Accords,* Washington: University Press of America.
Berman, P. (1974) *Revolutionary Organisation: Institution Building Within the People's Liberation Armed Forces,* Lexington, Massachusetts: Lexington.
Blaufarb, D.S. (1977) *The Counterinsurgency Era: US Doctrine and Performance, 1950 to the Present,* New York: Free Press.
Bonior, D.E. (1984) *The Vietnam Veteran,* New York: Praeger.
Braestrup, P. (1977) *Big Story. How the American Press and Television Reported and Interpreted the Crisis of Tet 1968 in Vietnam and Washington. Vol I,* Boulder, Colorado: Westview Press.
Braestrup, P. (ed.) (1984) *Vietnam As History: Ten Years After the Paris Peace Accords,* Washington: University Press of America.
Bredo, W. (1970) Agrarian Reform in Vietnam: Vietcong and Government of Vietnam Strategies in Conflict', *Asian Survey,* 10 (8):738–50.
Bullington, J.R. and Rosenthal, J.D. (1970) The South Vietnamese Countryside: Non-Communist Political Perceptions, *Asian Survey,* 10 (8):651–61.
Buszynski, L. (1986) *Soviet Foreign Policy and South East Asia,* London: Croom Helm.
Buttinger, J. (1969) *Vietnam: A Political History,* London: Andre Deutsch.
Cable, L.E. (1986) *Conflict of Myths: The Development of the American Counterinsurgency Doctrine and the Vietnam War,* New York: New York University Press.
Callison, C.S. (1983) *Land-To-The-Tiller in the Mekong Delta. Economic, Social and Political Effects of Land Reform in Four Villages in South Vietnam,* Berkeley, California: University of California Press.
Chaliand, G. (1969) *The Peasants of North Vietnam,* Harmondsworth: Penguin.

Chandler, R.W. (1981) *War of Ideas: The US Propaganda Campaign in Vietnam*, Boulder, Colorado: Westview Press.
Charlton, M. and Moncrieff, A. (1978) *Many Reasons Why: The American Involvement in Vietnam*, London: Scolar Press
Chen, K.C. (1969) *Vietnam and China, 1938–1954*, Princeton, New Jersey: Princeton University Press.
Chen, K.C. (1972) 'Hanoi vs Peking: Policies and Relations—A Survey', *Asian Survey*, 12 (9):806–17.
Chen, K.C. (1975) 'Hanoi's Three Decisions and the Escalation of the Vietnam War', *Political Science Quarterly*, 90 (2):239–59.
Cincinnatus (1981) *Self Destruction: The Disintegration and Decay of the United States Army During the Vietnam Era*, New York: W.W.Norton.
Clifford, C.M. (1969) 'A Vietnam Reappraisal: The Personal History of One Man's View and How it Evolved', *Foreign Affairs*, 47 (4):601–22.
Colby, W (1978) *Honorable Men: My Life in the CIA*, London: Hutchinson.
Conley, M.C. (1967) *The Communist Insurgent Infrastructure in South Vietnam: A Study of Organisation and Strategy*, Washington DC: United States Government Printing Office.
Cooper, C.L. (1971) *The Lost Crusade: The Story of US Involvement in Vietnam From Roosevelt to Nixon*, London: MacGibbon & Kee.
Cooper, C.L. (1972) 'The CIA and Decisionmaking', *Foreign Affairs*, 50 (2): 223–36.
Cotter, M.G. (March 1968) 'Towards a Social History of the Vietnamese Southward Movement', *Journal of South East Asian History* 9 (2):12–24.
Dacy, D.C. (1986) *Foreign Aid, War and Economic Development. South Vietnam, 1955–1975*, Cambridge: Cambridge University Press.
Davidson, P.B. (1988) *Vietnam at War—The History: 1946–1975*, London: Sidgwick & Jackson.
DeBeneditti, C. (1987) 'Lyndon Johnson and the Antiwar Opposition', in R.A. Divine (ed.) *The Johnson Years, Volume Two: Vietnam, the Environment, and Science*, Kansas: University of Kansas Press.
De Sola Pool, I. (1967) 'Political Alternatives to the Viet Cong' *Asian Survey*, 7 (8):555–66.
Devillers, P. (1962) 'The Struggle for the Unification of Vietnam', *China Quarterly*, 9:2–23.
Dietz, T. (1986) *Republicans and Vietnam 1961–1968*, New York: Greenwood Press.
Divine, R.A. (ed.) (1987) *The Johnson Years, Volume Two: Vietnam, the Environment and Science*, Kansas: University of Kansas Press.
Doan Van Toai (1986) *The Vietnamese Gulag*, New York: Simon & Schuster.
Duiker, W.J. (1975) *The Comintern and Vietnamese Communism*, Athens, Ohio: Ohio University, Center for International Studies.
Duiker, W.J. (1976) *The Rise of Nationalism in Vietnam 1900–1941*, Ithaca, New York: Cornell University Press.
Duiker, W.J. (1980) *Vietnam Since the Fall of Saigon*, Athens, Ohio: Ohio University Press.
Duiker, W.J. (1981) *The Communist Road to Power in Vietnam*, Boulder, Colorado: Westview Press.
Duiker, W.J. (1983) *Vietnam: Nation in Revolution*, Boulder, Colorado: Westview Press.

Duiker, W.J. (1986) *China and Vietnam: The Roots of Conflict,* Berkeley, California: University of California Press.
Dumbrell, J. (1989) 'Congress and the Antiwar Movement', in J.Dumbrell (ed.) *Vietnam and the Antiwar Movement,* Aldershot: Avebury.
Duncanson, D.J. (1968) *Government and Revolution in Vietnam,* London: Oxford University Press.
Dunn, P.M. (1985) *The First Vietnam War,* London: Hurst & Co.
Eisen, A. (1984) *Women and Revolution in Viet Nam,* London: Zed Books.
Ellsberg, D. (1972) *Papers on the War,* New York: Simon & Schuster.
Enthoven, A.C. and Smith, K.W. (1971) *How Much is Enough?,* New York: Harper & Row.
Eqbal, A. (1971) 'Revolutionary War and Counter-Insurgency', *Journal of International Affairs,* 25 (1):1–47.
Ewell, J.J. and Hunt, I.A. Jr (1974) *Sharpening the Combat Edge: The Use of Analysis to Reinforce Military Judgement,* Washington D.C.: Department of the Army.
Fairbairn, G. (1968) *Revolutionary Warfare and Communist Strategy,* London: Faber & Faber.
Fairclough, A. (1989) 'The War in Vietnam and the Decline of the Civil Rights Movement', in J.Dumbrell (ed.) *Vietnam and the Antiwar Movement,* Aldershot: Avebury.
Fall, B.B. (1963) *Street Without Joy: Insurgency in Indochina, 1946–1963,* 3rd Ed. London: Pall Mall Press.
Fall, B.B. (1967, 2nd rev. ed.) *The Two Viet-Nams: A Political and Military Analysis,* New York: Praeger.
Fifield, R.H. (1973) *Americans in Southeast Asia: The Roots of Commitment,* New York: Crowell.
Fiman, B.G. (1975) 'Black-White and American-Vietnamese Relations Among Soldiers in Vietnam', *Journal of Social Issues,* 31 (4):39–48.
Fitzgerald, F. (1972) *Fire in the Lake: The Vietnamese and the Americans in Vietnam,* Boston: Little, Brown & Co.
Fforde, A. and Paine, S.H. (1987) *The Limits of National Liberation: Problems of Economic Management in the Democratic Republic of Vietnam,* London: Croom Helm.
Gabriel, R.A. and Savage, P.L. (1976) 'Cohesion and Disintegration in the American Army', *Armed Forces and Society* 2 (3):340–76.
Gabriel, R.A. and Savage, P.L. (1978) *Crisis in Command: Mismanagement in the Army,* New York: Hill & Wang.
Gallucci, R.L. (1975) *Neither Peace Nor Honor: The Politics of American Military Policy in Vietnam,* Baltimore: John Hopkins University Press.
Gelb, L.H. (1972) 'The Essential Domino: American Politics and Vietnam', *Foreign Affairs,* 50:459–75.
Gelb, L.H. (1976) 'Dissenting on Consensus', in A.Lake (ed.) *The Vietnam Legacy: The War, American Society and the Future of American Foreign Policy,* New York: New York University Press.
Gelb, L.H., and Betts, R.K. (1979) *The Irony of Vietnam: The System Worked,* Washington D.C.: Brookings Institution.
Gibson, J.W. (1986) *The Perfect War—Technowar in Vietnam,* Boston: Atlantic Monthly Press.
Goldman, E.F. (1969) *The Tragedy of Lyndon Johnson,* New York: Knopf.

Goodman, A.E. (1970) 'The Political Implications of Rural Problems in South Vietnam: Creating Public Interest', *Asian Survey*, 10 (8):672–86.
Goodman, A.E. (1973) *Politics in War: The Bases of Political Community in South Vietnam*, Cambridge, Massachusetts: Harvard University Press.
Goodman, A.E. (1978) *The Lost Peace: America's Search for a Negotiated Settlement of the Vietnam War*, Stanford, California: Hoover Institution Press.
Goodman, A.E. (1984) 'The Dynamics of the United States—South Vietnamese Alliance: What Went Wrong?', in P. Braestrup (ed.) *Vietnam As History: Ten Years After the Paris Peace Accords*, Washington: University Press of America.
Grinter, L.E. (1974) 'Bargaining Between Saigon and Washington: Dilemmas of Linkage Politics During War', *Orbis*, 18:837–867.
Grinter, L.E. (1975a) 'How They Lost: Doctrines, Strategies and Outcomes of the Vietnam War', *Asian Survey*, 15 (12):1114–32.
Grinter, L.E. (1975b) 'South Vietnam: Pacification Denied', *South East Asian Spectrum*, 3 (3):48–70.
Grinter, L.E. and Dunn, P.M. (eds) (1987) *The American War in Vietnam: Lessons, Legacies and Implications for Future Conflicts*, New York: Greenwood.
Halberstam, D. (1965) *The Making of a Quagmire*, New York: Random House.
Halberstam, D. (1972) *The Best and the Brightest*, London: Barrie & Jenkins.
Hallin, D.C. (1986) *The 'Uncensored War': The Media and Vietnam*, New York: Oxford University Press.
Hammer, E.J. (1966) *The Struggle for Indochina 1940–1955*, Stanford, California: Stanford University Press.
Hammer, E.J. (1987) *A Death In November: America In Vietnam, 1963*, New York: Dutton.
Hannah, N.B. (1987) *The Key to Failure: Laos and the Vietnam War*, Lanham: Madison Books.
Heath, J.F. (1975) *Decade of Disillusionment: The Kennedy-Johnson Years*, Bloomington: Indiana University Press.
Herring, G.C. (1984) 'The Nixon Strategy in Vietnam', in P.Braestrup (ed.) *Vietnam As History: Ten Years After the Paris Peace Accords*, Washington: University Press of America.
Herring, G.C. (1986) *America's Longest War, the United States and Vietnam 1950–1975*, 2nd ed., New York: Knopf.
Herrington, S.A. (1982) *Silence Was a Weapon: The Vietnam War in the Villages*, Novato, California: Presidio.
Hersh, S. (1983) *The Price of Power: Kissinger in the Nixon White House*, New York: Summit Books.
Herz, M.F. (1980) *The Prestige Press and the Christmas Bombing 1972: Images in Reality in Vietnam*, Washington D.C.: Ethics and Public Policy Center.
Hess, G.R. (1972) 'Franklin D. Roosevelt and Indochina', *Journal of American History*, 59:353–68.
Hess, G.R. (1987) *The United States' Emergence as a South East Asian Power, 1940–1950*, New York: Columbia University Press.
Hickey, G.K. (1964) *Village in Vietnam*, New Haven: Yale University Press.
Hilsman, R. (1967) *To Move a Nation: The Politics of Foreign Policy in the Administration of John F.Kennedy*, Garden City, New York: Doubleday.
Hodgkin, T. (1981) *Vietnam—The Revolutionary Path*, Houndmills: Macmillan.
Honey, P.J. (1963) *Communism in North Vietnam*, Oxford: Holywell.

Hosmer, S.T. (1980) *The Fall of South Vietnam: Statements by Vietnamese Military and Civilian Leaders,* New York: Crane, Russak.
Houtart, F. and Lemercinier, G. (1984) *Hoi Van: Life in a Vietnamese Commune,* London: Zed Books.
Irving, R.E.M. (1975) *The First Indochina War: French and American Policy 1945–1954,* London: Croom Helm.
Isaacs, A.R. (1983) *Without Honor: Defeat in Vietnam and Cambodia,* Baltimore: John Hopkins University Press.
Johnson, L.B. (1972) *The Vantage Point: Perspectives of the Presidency 1963–1969,* London: Weidenfeld & Nicolson.
Joiner, C.A. (1967) 'The Ubiquity of the Administrative Role in Counterinsurgency', *Asian Survey,* 7 (8):540–54.
Kahin, G. McT. (1979) 'Political Polarization in South Vietnam: US Policy in the post Diem Period', *Pacific Affairs* 52 (4):647–73.
Kahin, G. McT. (1986) *Intervention: How America Became Involved in Vietnam,* New York: Knopf.
Kalb, M. and Kalb, B. (1974) *Kissinger,* London: Hutchinson.
Karnow, S. (1984) *Vietnam: A History,* Harmondsworth: Penguin.
Kattenburg, P.M. (1980) *The Vietnam Trauma in American Foreign Policy 1945–75,* New Brunswick, New Jersey: Transaction Books.
Kearns, D. (1976) *Lyndon Johnson and the American Dream,* New York: Harper & Row.
Kettl, D.F. (1987) 'The Economic Education of Lyndon Johnson: Guns, Butter, and Taxes', in R.A.Divine (ed.) *The Johnson Years, Volume Two: Vietnam, the Environment, and Science,* Kansas: University Press of Kansas.
Kinnard, D. (1977) *The War Managers,* Hanover: University Press of New England.
Kissinger, H. (1979) *The White House Years,* London: Weidenfeld & Nicolson.
Koenig, L.A. (1987) 'The Executive Office of the President', in G.K.Osborn *et al.* (eds) *Democracy, Strategy, and Vietnam: Implications for American Policy Making,* Lexington, Massachusetts: D.C.Heath.
Kolko, G. (1986) *Vietnam: Anatomy of a War 1940–1975,* London: Allen & Unwin.
Komer, R.W. (1972a) *Bureaucracy Does its Thing: Institutional Constraints on US-GVN Performance in Vietnam,* Santa Monica, California: Rand Corporation (R-967-ARPA).
Komer, R.W. (1972b) 'Impact of Pacification on Insurgency', *Journal of International Affairs,* 25 (1):48–69.
Komer, R.W. (1986) *Bureaucracy at War. US Performance in the Vietnam Conflict,* Boulder, Colorado: Westview Press.
Komer, R.W. (1987) 'The Long-Term Significance of the Vietnam Experience', in G.K.Osborn *et al.* (eds) *Democracy, Strategy and Vietnam: Implications For American Policy Making,* Lexington, Massachusetts: D.C.Heath.
Krepinevich, A.F. Jr (1986) *The Army and Vietnam,* Baltimore: John Hopkins University Press.
La Feber, W. (1975) 'Roosevelt, Churchill and Indochina, 1942–1945', *American Historical Review,* 80 (5):1277–95.
Lancaster, D. (1961) *The Emancipation of French Indochina,* London: Oxford University Press.
Lawson, E.K. (1984) *The Sino-Vietnamese Conflict,* New York: Praeger.
Lewy, G. (1978) *America in Vietnam,* New York: Oxford University Press.

Lewy, G. (spring 1984) 'Some Political-Military Lessons of the Vietnam War', *Parameters*, 2–14.
Lomperis, T.J. (1984) *The War Everyone Lost—and Won. America's Intervention in Viet-Nam's Twin Struggles,* Louisiana: Louisiana State University Press.
Mai Thi Tu and Le Thi Nham Tuyet (1978) *Women in Viet Nam,* Hanoi: Foreign Languages Publishing House.
Mangold, T. and Penycate, J. (1985) *The Tunnels of Cu Chi,* London: Hodder & Stoughton.
Marr, D.G. (1971) *Vietnamese Anticolonialism 1885–1925,* Berkeley: University of California Press.
Matusow, A.J. (1984) *The Unravelling of America: A History of Liberalism in the 1960s,* New York: Harper & Row.
May, E.R. (1987) 'Great Events and US Polities', in G.K.Osborn *et al.* (eds) *Democracy, Strategy, and Vietnam: Implications for American Policy Making,* Lexington, Massachusetts: D.C.Heath.
McAlister, J.T. Jr (1969) *Vietnam: The Origins of Revolution,* London: Allen Lane.
Mohr, C. (1987) 'The Media' in G.K.Osborn *et al.* (eds) *Democracy, Strategy and Vietnam: Implications For American Policy Making,* Lexington, Massachusetts: D.C.Heath.
Moise, E.E. (1976) 'Land Reform and Land Reform Errors in North Vietnam', *Pacific Affairs,* 49 (1):70–92.
Moise, E.E. (1983) *Land Reform in China and North Vietnam: Consolidating the Revolution at the Village Level,* London: Chapel Hill.
Morris, R. (1977) *Uncertain Greatness: Henry Kissinger and American Foreign Policy,* London: Quartet Books.
Moskos, C.E. Jr (1975) 'The American Combat Soldier in Vietnam', *Journal of Social Issues,* 31 (4):25–37.
Mueller, J. (1984) 'Reflections on the Vietnam Antiwar Movement and on the Curious Calm at the War's End', in P.Braestrup (ed.) *Vietnam as History: Ten Years After the Paris Peace Accords,* Washington: University Press of America.
Mueller, J.E. (1987) 'Vietnam and the Mellowing of Containment: Implications for US Foreign Policy Attitudes', in G.K.Osborn *et al.* (eds) *Democracy, Strategy and Vietnam: Implications for American Policy Making,* Lexington, Massachusetts: D.C.Heath.
Murray, M.J. (1980) *The Development of Capitalism in Colonial Indochina (1870–1940),* Berkeley, University of California Press.
Mus, P. and McAlister, J.T. (1970) *The Vietnamese and Their Revolution,* New York: Harper & Row.
Nalty, B.C. (1973) *Air Power and the Fight for Khe Sanh,* Washington D.C.: United States Air Force.
Ngo Vinh Long (1973) *Before the Revolution: The Vietnamese Peasants Under The French,* Cambridge, Massachusetts: MIT Press.
Nguyen Long (1981) *After Saigon Fell: Daily Life Under the Vietnamese Communists,* Berkeley: University of California Press.
G.Nguyen Tien Hung (1977) *Economic Development of Socialist Vietnam, 1955–1980,* New York: Praeger.
Nguyen Khac Vien (1974) *Tradition and Revolution in Vietnam,* ed. D.Marr and J.Werner, Berkeley: Indochina Resource Center.
Nighswonger, W.A. (1966) *Rural Pacification in Vietnam,* New York: Praeger.
Nixon, R.M. (1985) *No More Vietnams,* New York: Arbor House Publishing.

Oberdorfer, D. (1974) *TET! The Turning Point in the Vietnam War,* (orig. published 1971) New York: DaCapo Press.
O'Donnel, K.P. and Powers, D.F. (1972) *'Johnny We Hardly Knew Ye': Memories of John Fitzgerald Kennedy,* Boston: Little, Brown.
O'Neill, W.L. (1971) *Coming Apart: An Informal History of America in the 1960's,* Chicago: Quadrangle Books.
Osborn, G.K., Clark IV, A.A., Kaufman, D.J. and Lute, D.E. (eds) (1987) *Democracy, Strategy and Vietnam: Implications for American Policy Making,* Lexington, Massachusetts: D.C.Heath.
Osborne, M.E. (1969) *The French Presence in Cochinchina and Cambodia. Rule and Response (1859–1905),* Ithaca, New York: Cornell University Press.
Osborne, M.E. (1974) 'Continuity and Motivation in the Vietnamese Revolution: New Light From the 1930s', *Pacific Affairs,* 47 (1):37–55.
Palmer, B. Jr (1984) *The 25-Year War: America's Military Role in Vietnam,* Lexington, Kentucky: University Press of Kentucky.
Papp, D.S. (1975) 'The Soviet Perceptions of American Goals in Vietnam: 1964–1965' *Soviet Union II,* 145–61.
Papp, D.S. (1981) *Vietnam: The View From Moscow, Peking, Washington,* Jefferson, New Carolina: McFarland.
Paterson, T.G. (1978) 'Bearing the Burden: A Critical Look at JFK's Foreign Policy', *Quarterly Review,* 54 (2):193–212.
Patti, A.L.A. (1980) *Why Viet Nam? Prelude to America's Albatross,* Berkeley: University of California Press.
Pentagon Papers (1971) *Pentagon Papers: The Defense Department History of United States Decisionmaking on Vietnam, vols 1–5,* Senator Gravel Edition, Boston: Beacon Press.
Pike, D. (1966) *Viet Cong. The Organisation and Techniques of the National Liberation Front of South Vietnam,* Cambridge, Massachusetts: MIT Press.
Pike, D. (1969) *War, Peace and the Viet Cong,* Cambridge, Massachusetts: MIT Press.
Pike, D. (1970) *The Viet Cong Strategy of Terror,* Saigon.
Pike, D. (1978) *History of Vietnamese Communism,* Stanford, California: Hoover Institution Press.
Pike, D. (1986) *PAVN: People's Army of Vietnam,* Novato, California: Presidio.
Podhoretz, N. (1982) *Why We Were in Vietnam,* New York: Simon & Schuster.
Popkin, S.L. (1970) 'Pacification: Politics in the Village', *Asian Survey,* 10 (8):662–71.
Popkin, S.L. (1979) *The Rational Peasant: The Political Economy of Rural Society in Vietnam,* Berkeley: University of California Press.
Porter, G. (1975) *A Peace Denied: The United States, Vietnam and the Paris Agreement,* Bloomington: Indiana University Press.
Porter, G. (1979) *Vietnam: The Definitive Documentation of Human Decisions,* 2 vols, London: Heyden.
Powers, T. (1984) *Vietnam: The War at Home. Vietnam and the American People 1964–68,* Boston, Massachusetts: G.K.Hall.
Public Papers of the Presidents of the United States, *Lyndon B.Johnson 1968–1969,* 2 vols, Washington D.C.: US Government Printing Office.
Race, J. (1972) *War Comes to Long An. Revolutionary Conflict in a Vietnamese Province,* Berkeley, California: University of California Press.

Roper, B.W. (1977) 'What Opinion Polls Said' in P.Braestrup *Big Story: How the American Press and Television Reported and Interpreted the Crisis of Tet 1968 in Vietnam and Washington, vol. I,* Boulder, Colorado: Westview Press.

Rust, W.J. (1985) *Kennedy in Vietnam,* New York: Da Capo Press.

Sansom, R.L. (1970) *The Economics of Insurgency in the Mekong Delta of Vietnam,* Cambridge, Massachusetts: MIT Press.

Schandler, H.Y. (1977) *The Unmaking of a President: Lyndon Johnson and Vietnam,* Princeton, New Jersey: Princeton University Press.

Schell, J. (1967) *The Village of Ben Sue,* New York: Knopf.

Schell, J. (1989) *The Real War,* London: Corgi.

Schlesinger, Jr., A.M. (1965) *A Thousand Days,* London: Andre Deutsch.

Schlesinger, Jr., A.M. (1967) *The Bitter Heritage. Vietnam and American Democracy 1941–1960,* London: Andre Deutsch.

Schlesinger, Jr., A.M. (1974) *The Imperial Presidency,* New York: Popular Library.

Shaplen, R. (1965) *The Lost Revolution: Vietnam 1945–1965,* London: Andre Deutsch.

Shawcross, W. (1979) *Sideshow: Kissinger, Nixon and the Destruction of Cambodia,* New York: Simon & Schuster.

Small, M. (1988) *Johnson, Nixon, and the Doves,* New Brunswick: Rutgers University Press.

Smith, R.B. (1983) *An International History of the Vietnam War—Vol I: Revolution versus Containment, 1955–1961,* Houndmills: Macmillan.

Smith, R.B. (1985) *An International History of the Vietnam War—Vol II: The Struggle For South-East Asia, 1961–65,* Houndmills: Macmillan.

Smyser, W.R. (1980) *The Independent Vietnamese: Vietnamese Communism Between Russia and China, 1956–1969,* Athens, Ohio: Ohio University, Center for International Studies.

Snepp, F. (1980) *Decent Interval: The American Debacle in Vietnam and the Fall of Saigon,* London: Allen Lane.

Sorensen, T.C. (1965) *Kennedy,* London: Hodder & Stoughton.

Starry, D.A. (1981) *Armoured Combat in Vietnam,* Poole: Blandford Press.

Steinberg, D.J. (ed.) (1971) *In Search of South East Asia: A Modern History,* New York: Praeger.

Strong, R.J. (1986) *Bureaucracy and Statesmanship: Henry Kissinger and the Making of American Foreign Policy,* New York: University Press of America.

Summers, H.G. Jr (1982) *On Strategy: A Critical Analysis of the Vietnam War,* Novato, California: Presidio.

Szulc, T. (spring 1974) 'Behind the Vietnam Ceasefire Agreement', *Foreign Policy:* 21–69.

Szulc, T. (1978) *The Illusion of Peace: Foreign Policy in the Nixon Years,* New York: Viking Press.

Tanham, G.K. (1966) *War Without Guns: American Civilians in Rural Vietnam,* New York: Praeger.

Tanham, G.K. (1967) *Communist Revolutionary Warfare: From the Vietminh to the Viet Cong,* revised ed., New York: Praeger.

Tanham, G.K.C and Duncanson, D.J. (1969) 'Some Dilemmas of Counterinsurgency', *Foreign Affairs,* 48 (1):113–22.

Taylor, J. (1976) *China and South East Asia: Peking's Relations with Revolutionary Movements,* 2nd ed., New York: Praeger.

Taylor, K.W. (1983) *The Birth of Vietnam,* Berkeley: University of California Press.

Taylor, M.D. (1972) *Swords and Plowshares,* New York: W.W.Norton.
Taylor, W.J. Jr and Petraeus, D.H. (1987) 'The Legacy of Vietnam for the US Military', in G.K.Osborn *et al.* (eds) *Democracy, Strategy, and Vietnam: Implications for American Policy Making,* Lexington, Massachusetts: D.C.Heath.
Thayer, C.A. (1975) 'Southern Vietnamese Revolutionary Organizations and the Vietnam Workers' Party: Continuity and Change, 1954–1974', in J.J.Zasloff and M.Brown (eds) *Communism in Indochina: New Perspectives,* Lexington Massachusetts: D.C.Heath.
Thayer, T.C. (1985) *War Without Fronts: The American Experience in Vietnam,* Boulder, Colorado: Westview Press.
Thies, W.J. (1980) *When Governments Collide: Coercion and Diplomacy in the Vietnam Conflict, 1964–1968,* Berkeley: University of California Press.
Thompson, J.C. (1980) *Rolling Thunder: Understanding Policy and Program Failure,* Chapel Hill: University of North Carolina Press.
Thompson, R. (1969) *No Exit From Vietnam,* London: Chatto & Windus.
Thorne, C. (1976) Indochina and Anglo-American Relations, 1942–1945', *Pacific Historical Review,* 45 (1):73–96.
Thrift, N. and Forbes, D. (1986) *The Price of War: Urbanization in Vietnam 1954– 1985,* London: Allen & Unwin.
Tilford, E.H. Jr (1987) *'Air Power in Vietnam: The Hubris of Power'* in L.E. Grinter and P.M.Dunn (eds) *The American War in Vietnam: Lessons, Legacies and Implications for Future Conflicts,* New York: Greenwood.
Todaro, M.P. (1989) *Economic Development in the Third World,* 4th ed., London: Longman.
Tran Van Don (1978) *Our Endless War: Inside Vietnam,* San Rafael, California: Presidio.
Trullinger, J.W. Jr (1980) *Village at War: An Account of Revolution in Vietnam,* New York: Longman.
Truong Buu Lam (1967) *Patterns of Vietnamese Response to Foreign Intervention (1858–1900),* New Haven: Yale University Press.
Truong Chinh (1963) *Primer for Revolt: The Communist Takeover in Viet-Nam,* New York: Praeger.
Truong Nhu Tang (1986) *Journal of a Vietcong,* London: Jonathan Cape.
Turley, W.S. (1975) 'The Political Role and Development of the People's Army of Vietnam' in J.J.Zasloff and M.Brown (eds) *Communism in Indochina: New Perspectives,* Lexington, Massachusetts: D.C.Heath.
Turner, K.J. (1985) *Lyndon Johnson's Dual War: Vietnam and the Press,* Chicago: University of Chicago Press.
Ulam A.B. (1968) *Expansion and Co-existence: The History of Soviet Foreign Policy, 1917–1967,* London: Seeker & Warburg.
Unger, I. (1974) *The Movement: A History of the American New Left 1959–1972,* New York: Harper & Row.
United States-Vietnam Relations 1945–1967, (1971) 12 books, US Congress, House of Representatives, Armed Services Committee.
Van Dyke, J.M. (1972) *North Vietnam's Strategy for Survival,* Palo Alto, California: Pacific Books.
Van Tien Dung (1977) *Our Great Spring Victory,* New York: Monthly Review Press.
Vogelsang, S. (1974) *The Long Dark Night of the Soul: The American Intellectual Left and the Vietnamese War,* New York: Harper & Row.

Vo Nguyen Giap (1962) *People's War, People's Army,* New York: Praeger.
Vo Nguyen Giap (1970) *The Military Art of People's War,* New York: Monthly Review Press.
Vo Nguyen Giap (1971) *National Liberation War in Viet Nam: General Line Strategy—Tactics,* Hanoi: Foreign Languages Publishing House.
Waghelstein, J.D. (1987) 'Counterinsurgency Doctrine and Low-Intensity Conflict in the Post-Vietnam Era', in L.E.Grinter and P.M.Dunn (eds) *TheAmerican War in Vietnam: Lessons, Legacies and Implications for Future Conflicts,* New York: Greenwood.
Walker, W.E. (1987) 'Domesticating Foreign Policy: Congress and the Vietnam War', in G.K.Osborn *et al.* (eds) *Democracy, Strategy, and Vietnam: Implications for American Policy Making,* Lexington, Massachusetts: D.C. Heath.
Westing, A.H. (1983) 'The Environmental Aftermath of Warfare in Vietnam', *Natural Resources Journal,* 23:365–89.
Westmoreland, W.C. (1980) *A Soldier Reports,* New York: Dell.
White, C. (1983) 'Recent Debates in Vietnamese Development Policy', in G. White, R.Murray and C.White (eds) *Revolutionary Socialist Development in the Third World,* Brighton: Wheatsheaf.
Wiegersma, N.A. (1988) *Vietnam: Peasant Land, Peasant Revolution—Patriarchy and Collectivity in the Rural Economy,* Houndmills: Macmillan.
Wiesner, L.A. (1988) *Victims and Survivors: Displaced Persons and Other War Victims in Viet-Nam, 1945–1975,* New York: Greenwood Press.
Wilson, H. (1971) *The Labour Government 1964–1970,* London: Weidenfeld & Nicolson.
Wolfe, Jr., C. (1967) 'Insurgency and Counter Insurgency: New Myths and Old Realities,' Yale Review, LVI (2):225–41.
Woodside, A.B. (1971) *Vietnam and the Chinese Model: A Comparative Study of Vietnamese and Chinese Government in the First Half of the Nineteenth Century,* Cambridge, Massachusetts: Harvard University Press.
Woodside, A.B. (1976) *Community and Revolution in Modern Vietnam,* Boston: Houghton Mifflin.
Zagoria, D.S. (1967) *Vietnam Triangle: Moscow, Peking, Hanoi,* New York: Pegasus.
Zasloff, J.J. and Brown, M. (eds) (1975) *Communism in Indochina: New Perspectives,* Lexington, Massachusetts: D.C.Heath.
Zelikow, P.D. (1987) 'The United States and the Use of Force: A Historical Summary', in G.K.Osborn *et al.* (eds) *Democracy, Strategy, and Vietnam: Implications for American Policy Making,* Lexington, Massachusetts: D.C. Heath.

Index

Abrams, General Creighton 87
Accelerated Pacification Campaign 233
advisers, US military 46, 185–6
Afghanistan, Soviet invasion of 273
Agency for International Development 225
Agent Orange 197–8
Agrovilles 44, 216
alcohol 14
Alliance of National Democratic and Peace Forces 172, 173
ambushes 161
ancestors, cult of 133–4
animism 133
anti-war movement 118–30, 258; in armed forces 193; and Congressional hearings 111; and elite opinion 117, 125, 127; and Johnson 66, 69, 73–4, 118, 120, 122, 124–9 *passim;* media coverage of 121–2, 124, 125; and Nixon 86, 87, 89, 92, 118, 124–9 *passim;* (bombing of Cambodia 90–1)
assassinations 164, 170, 233–4
assimilation and association, policies of 10
Association of South East Asian Nations (ASEAN) 271
August Revolution (1945) 29–31, 157, 158
AWOL (absent without leave) 193

B-52 bomber 176, 207, 208

Ball, George 64
Ban Me Thuot 261
Bao Dai 29–30, 35–6, 38, 40–1, 42
Ben Tre 191
Bien Hoa 58
binh van 166
Binh Xuyen 42
black Americans: in armed forces 193; *see also* Civil Rights Movement
'boat people' 270–2
body count *see* deaths
bombing: of Cambodia 88–91, 94; of Vietnam see *Rolling Thunder*
Brezhnev, Leonid 96, 250
Buddhism 47–8, 133, 146, 220
Bundy, McGeorge 58

cadres: revolutionary 178, 181, 220; South Vietnamese 215–16
Cam Ne 113, 115
Cam Ranh Bay 266
Cambodia: bombing of 88–91, 94; French colonial rule of 10–11;and Geneva Accords 40; invasion of 91–2, 93–5, 102, 110, 128; (post-1975 268–70);revolutionary bases in 89–90, 160
Can Lao 45, 220
Can Vuong 18
Cao Dai 20, 136
Caravelle group 43
Carter, Jimmy 273
casualties *see* deaths

Catholic(s) 133, 146, 149, 215, 220; collaborators 12; missionaries 8–9
Cedar Falls operation 190, 222
Central America 273–4, 275
Central Intelligence Agency (CIA) 49, 64, 218, 225, 233
Central Office for South Vietnam (COSVN) 171–2
chi bo 165
Chiang Kai-shek 27, 244, 246
Chicago, 1968 Democratic Party Convention in 121
Chieu Hoi programme 230–1
China: colonization of Vietnam 1–2, 132; Cultural Revolution 85, 250; and Democratic Republic of Vietnam 38, 40, 143, 144, 170–1, 173, 240–54 *passim*, 258–9; 'loss' of 104, 108; and post-war Vietnam 268–70; revolutionary warfare in 155–8, 162, 246, 248, 251, 252; and Soviet Union 240–1, 244–54, 270; and United States 27, 28, 87, 243, 244, 245–6, 249–50; (detente 84, 93, 95–6, 100, 105, 252–3); and Viet Minh 26, 32, 241–2
Christmas Bombing (1972) 98–102, 111, 114, 205, 208
Churchill, Winston S. 27
Civic Action campaign 215–16, 221
Civil Operations and Revolutionary Development Support (CORDS) 226–7, 232, 234
Civil Rights movement (US) 119, 122
Civilian Irregular Defense Group 218
Clifford, Clark 70–1, 72
Cluster Bomb Units 198
coal mining 13
Cold War 24, 36–7, 104, 105, 108, 114
collaborators: with Americans 263–4; with French 12, 13, 17, 137
collectivization: in North Vietnam 137–8, 141, 143–4, 145;in post-war Vietnam 266;in South Vietnam 141
Combined Action Platoons 217–18

Comintern 20, 21, 22
Commercial Import Program 150–1
Communist Denunciation Campaign 216
Conein, Lucian 49
Confucianism 2, 7, 8, 131–2, 133;under French colonial rule 18, 135–6
Congress, US 108–12, 274;and Johnson 52, 55–6, 109, 110–11; and Nixon 92, 93, 96, 110, 111–12; after Paris Agreement 110, 258, 262, 272
Cooper-Church Amendment (US) 92, 93, 111
cotton 25
Council for Mutual Economic Assistance (CMEA) 269
Council of Notables 3–5
counterculture, US 120–1
counterinsurgency doctrine, US 184–5, 212, 213, 274–5
court martial 200
'*credibility gap*': of Johnson 66, 67, 69, 113, 122;of pacification propaganda 231
CS gas 198
Cuban Missile Crisis (1961) 50, 107
cults and rituals 14, 132, 133–4
Czechoslovakia 250

Dak Son 163
dan van 166
Danang 59, 261, 266
deaths: American 67, 86, 87, 195–6, 201, 274;'cross-over point' 187–8; Vietnamese 187–8, 191–2, 198, 199, 259;(civilian 199–200, 213); *see also* assassinations
'Deer Team' 26
Defense Department, US 84–5, 225, 258
defoliation 197–8, 215, 275
democracy: in South Vietnam 227–9
Democratic Republic of Vietnam (DRV) (North Vietnam) 40, 141–8, 170–5;and China 38, 40, 143, 144, 170–1, 173, 240–54 *passim*, 258–

9; and Khmer Rouge 94;land reforms of 137–40, 141; and negotiations 73–4, 76–82, 87–8, 96–7, 99–100, 102;after Paris Agreement 254, 255, 257, 260–2, 264; in post-war Vietnam 173, 246, 265;sends troops to South 56, 63, 173–4, 245;and Soviet Union 143, 144, 170–1, 173, 240–54*passim*, 258–9; *see also* Easter Offensive; National Liberation Front;People's Army of Vietnam;Tet Offensive
demonstrations, US anti-war 92, 119–20, 121–2, 126–7
desertion: of Americans 193; of South Vietnamese 202
detente 84, 93, 95–6, 100, 105, 128, 252–3; *see also* peaceful coexistence
dich van 166
Diem regime *see* Ngo Dinh Diem
Dien Bien Phu 39–40, 168–9, 242
dioxin 197–8
Doan Van Toai 272
Dominican Republic crisis (1965) 111
domino theory 37, 58, 71, 272
draft, US 123–4, 199–200, 201
drug abuse 192
'Duck Hook' plan 89, 127
Dulles, John Foster 37, 40

Easter Offensive (1972) 95–7, 181–2, 252–3
Eisenhower, Dwight D. 36–41, 42–3, 104
Elysée Agreement (1949) 36
emperor *see* monarchy
Enhance and *Enhance Plus* operations 98, 99, 102, 255
Erlichman, John 92
Ewell, Lieutenant General Julian 191
expenditure, US 204, 212–13, 232, 252, 274; and Congress 110, 111–12; under Johnson 65–6, 122; under Nixon 87, 98, 99, 102

Fatherland Front 265

Ferry, Jules 9
First Indochina War 34–41, 158, 245
First World War 19
Flaming Dart operation 57
flexible response, doctrine of 184, 185
Four Points 76–7, 82
'fragging' 192, 193
fragmentation bombs 198
Free World Military Assistance Forces 203
French colonial rule 4–5, 10–17, 31–4, 134–5; arrival of 8–10; collaboration with 12, 13, 17, 137; Japanese interruption of 24–5, 28; resistance to 17–23, 24, 34–41, 167–70
French Communist Party 33, 241
Fulbright, Senator William 110–11
functional liberation associations 166

Geneva Conference (1954) 38–41, 42–3, 46, 76, 170, 243, 245
genocide, imputation of 198–9
Giap, General *see* Vo Nguyen Giap
Goldwater, Barry 56, 57, 126
Gorbachev, Mikhail 270
Gracy, General 31–2
Great Britain 27–8, 30, 31–2, 38; and boat people 271; and Geneva Conference 243; Opium War 9; in Siam 11
'Great Society' legislation (US) 52, 53, 57–61 *passim*, 65, 105, 109; expectations of 122; failure of 73, 74
Grenada 274
guerrilla warfare, principles of 155–8, 160, 161, 162–3, 188
Gulf of Tonkin Resolution (US) (1964) 55–6, 74, 109, 111
GVN *see* Republic of Vietnam (South Vietnam)

Haiphong: Christmas bombing of 98–102, 111, 114, 205, 208; mining of harbour 96, 252–3
Halberstam, David 113
Haldeman, H.R. 92

'Hamburger Hill' 190
Hamlet Evaluation Systems 227, 235
Hannah, Norman 209
Hanoi: August Revolution in 29–30, 157, 158; Christmas bombing of 98–102, 111, 114, 205, 208
Harkins, General 48
Harriman, Averell 74
herbicides 197–8, 215, 275
hippies 120–1, 128
Ho Chi Minh 20, 22–3, 25, 167, 241; funeral of 251; and peasantry 156–7; popularity of 42; reverence for 244
Ho Chi Minh City 269
Ho Chi Minh Trail 93, 175–6, 207, 209, 230, 257
Hoa Hao 20, 136
Hong Kong, boat people in 271
Hue massacre 163, 263
Humphrey, Hubert 83, 126

incendiary weapons 198
Indochinese Communist Party (ICP) 20–2, 26, 29, 43, 137, 167, 241
Indochinese Union, French 10–11
Indonesia 46
industrialization: in North Vietnam 142–3, 145, 206–7; in South Vietnam 149, 151, 152–3
International Control Commission 40, 77
Iran hostage crisis 273
Irangate scandal 274

Japan 19, 32; wartime control of Vietnam 24–6, 28, 29
Johnson, Lyndon B. 49–50, 52–75, 104–5, 276; and anti-war movement 66, 69, 73–4, 118, 120, 122, 124–9 *passim;* and bureaucracy 64–5, 105–6, 107, 206; and Congress 52, 55–6, 109, 110–11; and Diem 44;and 1964 election 55, 56–7; and 1968 election 67, 73, 126; 'Great Society' legislation 52, 53, 57–61 *passim,* 65, 105, 109; (expectations for 122; failure of 73, 74); justification for war 58–9; and media 66, 67, 71, 112–13, 117; and negotiations 73–4, 76–82; and Tet Offensive 67–75, 78–9, 82, 117
Joint Chiefs of Staff (US) 30–1, 187–8; and Johnson 58, 61, 64, 65, 70, 71, 79; and Kennedy 184; and Nixon 85
jute 25

Kampuchea, invasion of 268–70
Kennedy, John F. 52–3, 106–7, 109, 122; counterinsurgency doctrine 184–5; and Diem regime 43, 46–51, 238, 240; and media 112, 113
Kennedy, Robert 73
Kent State University Ohio (US) 92, 121–2
Khe Sanh, siege of 117, 205
Khmer Rouge 94, 268–70
Kissinger, Henry 83–102 *passim,* 237, 240, 253, 254, 258
Komer, Robert 226
Korea, North 70
Korea, South 203
Korean war 38, 104, 150, 250
Kosygin, Alexei 78, 247, 252
Krushchev, Nikita 184, 244, 245, 247
Ky, General 50, 54

Laird, Melvin 85, 87, 90
Lam Son 719 operation 93, 252
Land Development Centers 218
land reform: under French colonial rule 12, 13, 15–16, 17; in North Vietnam 137–41; in South Vietnam 140–1, 224–5, 234–5, 255; of Viet Minh 137, 168, 169, 242
Lang Son 269
Lansdale, General Edward 215
Lao Dong Party 167, 171–2, 247
Laos 11, 40, 46, 209; *see also* Ho Chi Minh Trail
Laos Accords (1962) 209
Le Duc Tho 88, 97–8, 99
Le May, General Curtis 206

Lewandowski, Janusz 77–8
Liberation and Resistance Committees 165
Lien Viet 167
Lin Piao 248
Linebacker I operation 96, 252–3
Linebacker II operation 98–102
linkage 83
Lomperis, Timothy 209–10
Lon Nol, General 91, 93–5, 207, 268
Long An 224

McCarthy, Eugene 66–7, 73
McGovern, George 126
McNamara, Robert 53, 54, 60, 64, 65, 107
Maddox, USS 55
Malaysia 46, 271
mandarins 2, 4, 5, 8, 11, 13
Manila Declaration (1965) 78
Mao Tse-tung 155–8, 162, 249, 250, 251, 252
March Agreement (1946) 33
'March on the Pentagon' (1967) 126
'March to the South' 6
Marigold plan 77–8
Marines, US: counterinsurgency programme 217–18
Marxist Study Groups 167
media, US: and anti-war movement 121–2, 124, 125; and armed forces 201, 275; and Johnson 66, 67, 71, 112–13, 117; and Kennedy 112, 113; and Nixon 113–14; and propaganda 229
Mekong Delta and River 6, 132, 140–1; French control of 9, 10, 17, 19–20, 35; post-war collectivization in 266; 'rice war' in 255–6
Menu bombing programme 88–91, 94
Michigan, University of 121
Military Assistance Advisory Group 183
Military Assistance Command Vietnam (MACV) 183, 203, 218, 226
missionaries 8–9
Mobile Action Teams 217

monarchy 132, 134–5; and French 9–13 *passim*, 18, 29, 134–5; pre-colonial 2, 3, 5–6, 13
Montagnard tribes 218, 265, 267
Moratorium (1969) 127
Mountbatten, Lord Louis 27
Mouvement Republicain Populaire (France) 33–4
mutiny 192–3
My Lai massacre 91, 200

Nam Ky rebellion 26, 29
napalm 198, 215
Napoleon III, Emperor (of France) 9
National Council of Reconciliation and Concord 98, 99
National Liberation Front (NLF) 157, 171–3, 174–5, 179–80, 234–5; and Diem regime 43–4, 47, 50–1, 140–1; and Easter Offensive 96–7, 181–2; intelligence network of 188; and land reform 137, 140–1, 235; local support for 157, 165–6, 186–7; and military juntas 53, 54; and negotiations 76–82, 87–8, 96–7; and pacification 221, 234; after Paris Agreement 255, 257, 260–2, 264; post-war Vietnam 173, 265; refugees from 213; and Tet Offensive 67–9, 88, 163, 180–1, 232; violence of 163, 164–5
National Revolutionary Movement 220
Navarre, General Henri 38, 39
Nazi-Soviet Pact (1939) 21
New Economic Zones 266
New Frontiersmen 106–7
New Left (US) 118, 119–20, 121
'New Life Hamlets' 217
New York Times 90, 113–14
Nghe-Tinh Soviets 20–1
Ngo Dinh Diem 41–51, 136, 148–9, 170; land reforms of 140–1, 224–5; overthrow and murder of 48–50, 51, 53, 173; pacificationprogrammes of 215–17, 219–21; and United States 41–51, 238, 240
Ngo Dinh Nhu 44, 45, 48, 49, 220

Nguyen (dynasty) 6, 7–8
Nguyen Anh 7
Nguyen Thi Dinh, General 147
Nguyen Van Linh 267
Nguyen Van Thieu 50, 54, 93, 227; downfall of 154, 255–6, 260–3; land reforms of 141, 234–5, 255; and pacification 232–3; and peace negotiations 88, 97; (obstruction of 98, 99, 100–2, 237, 240); and US aid 151, 152–3; and 1968 US election 82–3
Nhu *see* Ngo Dinh Nhu
Nhu, Madame 45, 48
Nixon, Richard M.: and anti-war movement 86, 87, 89–92 *passim*, 118, 124–9 *passim;* and Congress 92, 93, 96, 110, 111–12; and 1972 election 93, 96, 97, 99, 100–1, 126; foreign policy of 83–5, 105; and media 113–14; and Vietnam War 82–3, 85–102, 105, 254, 258, 273; (bombing of Cambodia 88–91, 94; Christmas bombing 98–102, 111, 114, 205, 208)
Nolting, Frederick 48
North Vietnam *see* Democratic Republic of Vietnam

Office of Strategic Services (US) 26, 183
'Open Arms' programme 230–1
Opium War 9

pacification programmes 212–36, 239
Palmer, Bruce, Jr 209
Paris Peace Agreement (1973) 99, 102, 182, 253, 258; draft of 98, 99–102, 237, 240; origins of 97; war following 254, 255–64
patriarchy 131, 147
peaceful coexistence policy (USSR) 244, 245, 246, 247
Pentagon Papers 114
People's Army of Vietnam (PAVN) 168–70, 175–7, 181; arrival in South of 56, 63, 173–4, 245; Cambodian sanctuaries of 89–90, 91, 160; and Easter Offensive 95, 96–7, 181–2; and local people 163–4; after Paris Agreement 255, 257, 261, 264
People's Front Against Corruption 260
People's Liberation Armed Forces (PLAF) 172, 175, 177–8, 235; Cambodian sanctuaries of 89–90, 91, 160; defectors from 230; Easter Offensive of 95–7, 181–2, 252–3; and local people 163–4; after Paris Agreement 255, 257; and Tet Offensive 181, 210, 232
People's Revolutionary Party (PRP) 171–3, 174, 265
People's Self-Defense Force 233
Personalism 45, 136, 220
Pham Van Dong 76
Phase A–Phase B formula 78
Phnom Penh 95
Phoenix operation 233–4
Piaster Subsidy 150–1
plantations: under French colonial rule, 13, 15–16
Pleiku 57, 58, 261
Pol Pot 268–70
population regroupment 215–17; post-war 266–7
Presidential elections, US: 1964 55, 56–7; 1968 67, 73, 82–3, 126; 1972 93, 96, 97, 99, 100–1, 126
press: American *see* media; Vietnamese 19, 45
propaganda 229–32
protestors *see* anti-war movement
Provisional Executive Committee 30, 31
Provisional Revolutionary Government (PRG) 99, 172–3, 265
psychological warfare 230
Pueblo, USS 70

quagmire theory of US involvement 103–4
Quang Tri 95

Reagan, Ronald 273, 274, 275
Red River, flooding of 2–3

refugees 213–15, 236, 256; from postwar Vietnam 270–2
Regional Force and Popular Force 226
Regular Force Strategy 175
religion 133, 135–6, 146, 220, 228; see also Buddhism; Catholic(s)
Republic of Vietnam (provisional) 29–30, 32–3; see also Democratic Republic of Vietnam
Republic of Vietnam (South Vietnam): armed forces 201–4, 221; (back-up role of 190, 203; Cambodian operations by 91–2; defections from 166; and Diem regime 44–5, 48–9; and Easter Offensive 95; junta rule by 50, 53–4, 174; after Paris Agreement 255, 257, 259–60, 261–3, 265; salaries of 152; and Tet Offensive 68; US advisers to 46, 185–6; and Victimization 86, 87, 89, 93); democracy in 227–9; final collapse of 255–64, 272–3; land reforms in 140–1, 224–5; military juntas in 50, 53–4, 174; and United States 237–40; (aid 148–54, 202, 234, 236, 239, 258–9, 273; and pacification programmes 212–36, 239); women's role in 147–8; see also Ngo Dinh Diem; Nguyen Van Thieu
reserves, US military 61, 70, 71
Resistance 167–70
'Revolutionary Development' programme 215–16
revolutionary movement 155–66; and war against French 167–70; and war in South Vietnam 170–82; see also individual armies and organizations
Revolutionary Workers' Party *(Can Lao)* 45, 220
rice production 132, 148, 153, 225, 255–6; under French colonial rule 13, 15; under Japanese wartime control 25, 29
Riot Control Agents 198
rituals and cults 14, 132, 133–4

Rogers, William 85, 90
Rolling Thunder bombing campaign 57–8, 59, 62, 64, 79–80, 205–8; halts in 72, 73–4, 79, 205; and negotiations 77, 78, 79–80
Roosevelt, Franklin D. 27, 28, 30
Rostow, Walt 46, 64
Royalist Movement 18
rubber 13, 16
Rusk, Dean 31, 72, 73, 106
Russian Revolution (1917) 19, 169

Saigon: Chinese businesses in 269; fall of 209, 210, 262; media based in 116; refugees in 149; during Tet Offensive 67–8, 69, 116; US embassy in 68, 69, 116
salt 14
San Antonio Formula 78
Schell, Jonathan 222, 273
SEAC (South East Asia Command) 27–8
'search and destroy' strategy 186, 189–90, 205
SEATO (South East Asian Treaty Organization) 42, 55
Second World War 22, 24–9, 80, 106; veterans of 275
Senate Committees (US) 110–11
Shawcross, William 95
Shelepin, Alexander 252
Siam, British influence in 11
Sihanouk, Prince Norodom 40, 89–90, 91, 94, 270
Sihanoukville 207
sixteenth parallel 28–9, 40
Socialist Republic of Vietnam 265–72
South Vietnam *see* Republic of Vietnam
Soviet Union: and China 240–1, 244–54, 270; and Democratic Republic of Vietnam 143, 144, 170–1, 173, 240–54 *passim*, 258–9; and postwar Vietnam 266, 269; and United States 83, 86, 87, 88–9; (detente 84, 93, 95–6, 100, 252–3)
Special Forces, US 184, 218, 275
Spock, Dr Benjamin 124

294 *Index*

stalemate theory of US involvement 104–5
Stalin, Joseph 21, 27, 241
State Department, US 31, 37, 84–5, 106, 225
Stennis, Senator John 110–11
Strategic Hamlet concept 44, 216–17, 220
students: and anti-war movement 92, 118–20, 125, 128; and draft 123
Students for a Democratic Society (SDS) (US) 118, 119, 128
substitution, concept of 156
Summers, General Harry 209
Sunshine Park operation 91

Tan Son Nhut airbase 68
Tay Son rebellion 6–7
Taylor, Maxwell D. 46
tea 13
teach-in movement (US) 121
television coverage 114–15, 116, 117, 121–2: *see also* media
Tet Offensive 67–75, 78–9, 82, 88, 108, 180–1, 264; and anti-war movement 69, 126, 127; and China 248; Hue massacre 163, 263; media coverage of 113, 115–17; and pacification 228, 232; and US strategy 187, 191, 210
Thailand: and Cambodian war 93, 95; and post-war Vietnam 268, 271
Thant, U 76
Thich Quang Duc 48
Thieu regime *see* Nguyen Van Thieu
Thompson, Sir Robert 204–5, 216
Tonle Sap lake 208
tour of duty 195–6
trade unions 19
traps 161–2
Trinh dynasty 6, 7, 8
Truman, Harry 28, 30–1, 37, 104, 108
Trung sisters 132
Truong Chinh 140
Truong Nhu Tang 172–3, 176
trusteeship concept 27, 28, 30
Tu Duc, Emperor 9–10
Tuesday Lunch Group 65

tunnel warfare 176–7, 198
Turner Joy, USS 55

United National Front 30
United States 183–201, 204–11, 272–6; armed forces 183–201, 204–11, 274–5; (availability forcombat 189; coordination 80–1, 106, 206; discipline and morale 192–6, 199–201, 221; draft 123–4, 199–200, 201; initial deployment 55–6, 59–60, 62, 74, 174, 186; interservice rivalry 208; pacification programmes 217–18; post-war strategy 273–4; and refugees 213, 214–15; reserves 61, 70, 71; and South Vietnamese Army 190, 203–4; and South Vietnamese economy 149, 150, 153, 214, 259; and Tet Offensive 70–1, 187, 191; veterans 275); and Asian nationalism 27, 28, 30–1; and China 27, 28, 87, 243, 244, 245–6, 249–50; (*detente* 84, 93, 95–6, 100, 105, 252–3); decision-making machinery of 84–5, 103–8; and Diem regime 41–51, 238, 240; and First Indochina War 36–41; and post-war Vietnam 266, 271; and Second World War 26, 27–9; and South Vietnam 237–40; (aid 148–54, 202, 234, 236, 239, 258–9, 273; and land reform 225; pacification programme 212–36 *passim*, 239; after Paris Agreement 256, 257–8); *see also* Eisenhower;Johnson; Kennedy, John F.; Nixon
United States Intelligence Agency (USIA) 225, 229
universities and colleges, US: anti-war movement in 92, 119, 121–2, 125; *see also* students

Van Tien Dung, General 264
veterans 275
'Viet Cong' 170, 233
Viet Minh 22–3, 25–6, 157, 167–8; and China 26, 32, 241–2; and Diem regime 43, 170; and First

Indochina War 34–40; land reforms of 137, 168, 169, 242; and local people 163–4; and North Vietnam 160–1; *see also* Democratic Republic of Vietnam; Republic of Vietnam (provisional)
Vietnamese Communist Party 265, 267
Vietnamese Nationalist Party (VNQDD) 20
Vietnamese Workers' Party (Lao Dong Party) 167, 171–2, 247
Vietnamization policy 87, 88, 89, 93, 204, 240; and domestic opinion 87, 105, 110, 124, 127; Sino-Soviet view of 250, 252
Vo Nguyen Giap, General 155–6, 157, 175, 181
Vulture operation 39

war crimes 196–201
War Powers Act (1973) (US) 111
Washington Post 114
Watergate scandal 85, 102, 112, 128, 258, 274
Weathermen 128
Westmoreland, General W.C. 68, 70, 71, 186–7, 200, 239
Wheeler, General Earle 70
white phosphorous 198
Wilson, Harold 78, 252
'Wise Men' 72
women: in Vietnamese society 131–2, 147–8

xa (village communes) 2–5, 6, 13

Yen Bay garrison 20
Yugoslavia 254

For Product Safety Concerns and Information please contact our EU representative GPSR@taylorandfrancis.com
Taylor & Francis Verlag GmbH, Kaufingerstraße 24, 80331 München, Germany

www.ingramcontent.com/pod-product-compliance
Lightning Source LLC
Chambersburg PA
CBHW071158300426
44113CB00009B/1239